DISRAELIAN CONSERVATISM AND SOCIAL REFORM

STUDIES IN POLITICAL HISTORY

Editor: Michael Hurst
Fellow of St John's College, Oxford

CHIEF WHIP: The Political Life and Times of Aretas Akers-Douglas 1st Viscount Chilston by Eric Alexander 3rd Viscount Chilston.

GUIZOT: Aspects of French History 1787–1874 by Douglas Johnson.

MARGINAL PRYNNE, 1660–9 by William M. Lamont.

LAND AND POWER: British and Allied Policy on Germany's Frontiers 1916–19 by H. I. Nelson.

THE LANGUAGE OF POLITICS in the Age of Wilkes and Burke by James T. Boulton.

THE ENGLISH FACE OF MACHIAVELLI A Changing Interpretation 1500–1700 by Felix Raab.

BEFORE THE SOCIALISTS Studies in Labour and Politics 1861–81 by Royden Harrison.

THE LAWS OF WAR IN THE LATE MIDDLE AGES by M. H. Keen.

GOVERNMENT AND THE RAILWAYS IN NINETEENTH-CENTURY BRITAIN by Henry Parris.

THE ENGLISH MILITIA IN THE EIGHTEENTH CENTURY The Story of a Political Issue, 1660–1802 by J. R. Western.

SALISBURY AND THE MEDITERRANEAN 1886–96 by C. J. Lowe.

VISCOUNT BOLINGBROKE, Tory Humanist by Jeffrey Hart.

W. H. SMITH by Viscount Chilston.

THE McMAHON LINE: A Study in the Relations between India, China and Tibet, 1904–14; in two volumes by Alastair Lamb.

THE THIRD REICH AND THE ARAB EAST by Lukasz Hirszowicz.

THE ELIZABETHAN MILITIA 1558–1638 by Lindsay Boynton.

JOSEPH CHAMBERLAIN AND LIBERAL REUNION The Round Table Conference of 1887 by Michael Hurst.

SOCIALISTS, LIBERALS AND LABOUR The Struggle for London 1885–1914 by Paul Thompson.

POLAND AND THE WESTERN POWERS 1938–9 by Anna M. Cienciala.

DISRAELIAN CONSERVATISM AND SOCIAL REFORM by Paul Smith.

DISRAELIAN CONSERVATISM
and Social Reform

by

PAUL SMITH

Lecturer in History, University of London
King's College

LONDON: Routledge & Kegan Paul
TORONTO: University of Toronto Press
1967

First published 1967
in Great Britain by
Routledge & Kegan Paul Ltd
and in Canada by
University of Toronto Press

Printed in Great Britain
by Bookprint Limited
Crawley, Sussex

Reprinted in 2018

ISBN 978-1-4875-7228-0 (paper)

CONTENTS

PLATES

(Plates I and VII are reproduced by courtesy of the Trustees of the British Museum, plates II–VI and VIII by courtesy of the Radio Times Hulton Picture Library.)

PREFACE

MANY people have helped me in the writing of this book, which stems from my Oxford doctoral thesis. I cannot mention all of them here, but I hope that those who are omitted will not suppose me the less grateful.

I owe large debts to the Warden and Fellows of St Antony's College, Oxford, who elected me to the Senior Scholarship during my tenure of which much of the work for this book was done; to Professor Michael Roberts and my former colleagues in the Department of Modern History in the Queen's University of Belfast, who generously assisted me to have the maximum time available for writing during my year with them; and to Professor A. G. Dickens and my colleagues in the Department of History at King's College (especially Dr Peter Marshall), who have likewise aided me in carrying my work to a conclusion.

For permission to make use of their family papers, and for much kindness in responding to my importunities, I am greatly indebted to the Earl Cairns, the Earl of Carnarvon, the Earl of Cranbrook, Viscount Cross, the Earl of Harrowby, the Duke of Marlborough, the Duke of Richmond and Gordon, the Marquis of Salisbury, and the Hon. David Smith. I am obliged also to the Controller of Her Majesty's Stationery Office, for permission to use Crown-copyright material in the Public Record Office; to the National Trust, for allowing me to use the Disraeli Papers; to the National Union of Conservative and Unionist Associations, for permission to use their early records; and to Mr F. J. Dwyer, who allowed me to use his unpublished thesis on R. A. Cross.

Numerous libraries and record offices have given me their ready assistance. I owe special thanks to the authorities and staffs of the Bodleian Library, the British Museum, the library of Christ Church, Oxford, the library of the Conservative Research Department, the India Office Library, the Ipswich and East Suffolk Record Office, the London Library, the National Register of Archives, and the West Sussex County Record Office.

Of those who have enabled me to benefit from their comments on my work, I must thank above all, for much shrewd advice and friendly encouragement, Pat Thompson, kindest of supervisors, and Michael Hurst, a very patient editor.

My greatest obligations are recognised in the dedication.

PAUL SMITH

King's College, London
May 1966.

NOTE

THIS book was completed and delivered to the publisher several months before the appearance of Mr Robert Blake's biography of Disraeli and Dr F. B. Smith's study of the second Reform Bill, and before I had the opportunity of seeing Mr Maurice Cowling's analysis of the Reform crisis of 1866–7. It does not, therefore, take account of these works (except in so far as I have adjusted one or two points of detail following Dr Smith), but happily their general findings seem congruent with my own. Mr Blake, in particular, adopts an interpretation of Disraeli and the development of the Conservative party very similar to that presented here, and on the social reforms of Disraeli's second ministry, especially, the reader will note that the identity of our views is remarkable.

P.S.

January 1967

LIST OF ABBREVIATIONS USED IN REFERENCES

Add. MS.	Additional Manuscript, in the British Museum
Brit. Mus.	British Museum
D.N.B.	*Dictionary of National Biography*
Ed.	Ministry of Education Papers, in the P.R.O.
G.C. (in relation to the Salisbury Papers)	General Correspondence
3 Hansard	*Hansard's Parliamentary Debates*, 3rd series
H.O.	Home Office Papers, in the P.R.O.
M. & B.	W. F. Monypenny and G. E. Buckle, *The Life of Benjamin Disraeli, Earl of Beaconsfield*
M.H.	Ministry of Health Papers, in the P.R.O.
M.T.	Ministry of Transport Papers, in the P.R.O.
O.S. (in relation to the Home Office Papers)	Old Series
P.P.	*Parliamentary Papers*
P.R.O.	Public Record Office
S.C. (in relation to the Salisbury Papers)	Special Correspondence

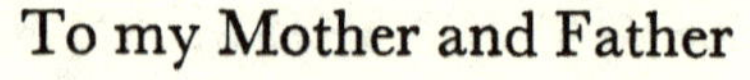
To my Mother and Father

INTRODUCTION

IT was in 1948 that the late Professor Richard Pares described the nineteenth century as 'the great *terra incognita* of British history',[1] but there is still much truth in his phrase. Nowhere is this better illustrated than in the political history of the latter half of the century, which continues to lack the works of fundamental analysis that are needed to explain its course. One of the most striking deficiencies is the absence of any substantial modern history of either of the two great political parties, and of any major attempt to relate the attitudes and fortunes of the parties to those economic and social movements by which, ultimately, the nature and progress of politics are determined. The aim of the present study is to make a contribution to party history and to the exploration of the relationship between politics and society in the later nineteenth century by examining a critical phase in the evolution of the Conservative party and its adaptation to the consequences of economic and social change.

Throughout Europe, the old forces of the right, rooted in the possession and exploitation of land, and centring upon crown and church, were subjected to an increasingly powerful challenge in the decades which followed the defeat of Napoleon. The upsurge of population, the advance of industrialism and urbanisation, the growing strength and self-assertiveness of the urban bourgeoisie and the urban proletariat, the doctrines and practice of liberalism, socialism, and democracy, fundamentally altered the character of society. For conservatives, concerned to resist or moderate change, it was not easy to make the effort of comprehension and adjustment necessary in order to avoid being overwhelmed by the new tides. Some, indeed, failed, and were engulfed; but others succeeded and survived, and nowhere more conspicuously than in Britain. The Tory or Conservative party furnishes a classic case of successful adaptation to a

[1] *Bulletin of the Institute of Historical Research*, xxi (1946–8), 122.

changing environment. The modern party may bear little external resemblance to the party of Lord Liverpool, but between the two the line of continuity stretches unbroken over a hundred and fifty years of economic and social transformation. The process of adaptation was slow, and punctuated by setbacks, the most severe of which, the schism of 1846, came near to ruining the party. But the lengthy tenures of power by Conservative governments since 1874 witness strikingly to its ultimate success.

The essential feature of this process was the reorientation of the party in response to the increase in the socio-political power of the urban bourgeoisie and working classes. Not unnaturally, in the age of universal suffrage, it is the development of the party's relationship with the working classes which has excited most interest. The ability that the party has shown, since the Reform Act of 1867, to capture a significant proportion of the working-class vote has been a vital element in its electoral success, and has done much to give colour to its favourite claim of being a national party, representative of all sections of the community. Nothing seems more crucial in the shaping of the modern Conservative party than its coming to terms with the need to admit the working man to the franchise and promote the consideration of his interests to the forefront of politics, and no period in its history, therefore, seems more decisive than the years between 1867 and 1880, when the fortunes of British Conservatism were ostensibly guided by Benjamin Disraeli.

It is easy to see why Disraeli should so often be regarded as the prophet and founder of modern Conservatism, and the chief agent in the adaptation of the party to the realities of a new era. At the beginning of his political career, he focused attention on social movements and their political implications, threw into sharp relief the dangers inherent in the division between the 'two nations' of rich and poor, and insisted that the task of the Conservative or 'national' party was to seek the reconciliation of classes and the stability of the social order through a timely consideration of popular welfare. In 1867, in what looked to many like conscious pursuit of his ideas of popular and national Toryism, he 'educated' his followers into granting a largely increased share of electoral power to the working classes, turning the face of his party firmly towards the future; and in the following years he lent his approval to the development of the mass organisation needed to secure the party's advance under the new franchise. In 1872, putting before the party the three great objects which were long to form the basis of its creed, he coupled with the defence of the constitution and the maintenance of the empire the elevation of the condition of the people; and in his ministry of 1874–80, suiting actions to words, he presided over the most notable instalment of social reform undertaken by any single government of the century. It is no wonder that it should be argued that it was Disraeli who secured the future of the Conservative party, by inducing it to accept and exploit the political implications of economic and social change, and in particular by reconciling it, between 1867 and 1880, to the conditions resulting from the political emergence of the working classes. For many modern Conservatives Disraeli stands as the originator of the concept of 'Tory Democracy' by which they profess still to be inspired.[1]

The development of 'Disraelian' Conservatism between 1867 and 1880 thus appears as a vital factor in the making of the modern party. So, no doubt, it was. But the most cursory examination shows that the history of the Conservative party in the 'seventies and after cannot be written in terms of its adaptation to 'Disraelian' ideas of popular appeal and social amelioration. As it emerged from the Disraelian era, the party bore only faintly the impress of Disraelian inspiration, and, despite Lord Randolph Churchill, the master's most potent contribution to its persona turned out to be imperialism, rather than the Tory Democracy with which his name is most commonly associated. The party of Salisbury and Balfour can hardly be described as Disraelian, still less the party of Bonar Law, Baldwin, and Neville Chamberlain. The basic theme in the evolution of modern Conservatism, it may be argued, is not *rapprochement* with the masses in the spirit of the Disraelian ideal, but the assimilation of the bourgeoisie, in whose image the modern party is so obviously cast—a process more in accordance with the policy of Peel than with the 'democratic' Toryism attributed to Disraeli. Modern historians have not failed to notice that 'though the myth of conservatism has been more often Disraelian, its practice has been almost uniformly Peelite',[2] and that what emerged from the 'seventies and 'eighties was a 'Peelite' rather than a 'Disraelian' type of party.[3]

It is sometimes held that 1886 was 'the turning-point in the history of modern Conservatism', when Lord Randolph Churchill fell, and

[1] Sir Edward Boyle has written that 'the founder of Tory Democracy' established 'a tradition of Conservatism that is still the inspiration of our own day' (essay on Disraeli in *Great Conservatives*, Conservative Political Centre, 1953, p. 29). Mr Iain Macleod told a summer school in 1954: 'Disraeli started the idea of the Tory Democracy and Lord Randolph [Churchill] proclaimed it; Lord Randolph's son today is the head of a team of ministers that is trying to put it into practice' ('Sanitas Sanitatum—The Condition of the People', in *Tradition and Change*, Conservative Political Centre, 1954, p. 65).

[2] N. Gash, *Mr. Secretary Peel*, p. 14. 'With that', Professor Gash adds, 'Peel would have been content; he preferred facts to phrases.'

[3] E.g., R. E. Riggs, 'Peel and Disraeli: Architects of a New Conservative Party', *Western Humanities Review*, xi (1957), 183–7.

the Liberal split over Home Rule set in motion that influx into the Conservative party of 'injured or apprehensive propertied interests in flight from the radicalism of the "old man in a hurry" ' which was to make it 'the great bulwark of "vested interests" '.[1] Certainly 1886 has considerable importance, but the movement towards Conservatism of 'injured or apprehensive propertied interests' and of the defensively-minded sections of the bourgeoisie was already appreciable in the 'seventies; and the achievement by the party of the alliance of landed with industrial and commercial property which Peel's policy had been directed to securing was in sight before Home Rule became a major political issue. There is reason to maintain that the very period which saw the efflorescence of 'Disraelian' Conservatism was that which witnessed the fruiting of a line of policy closely comparable to the outlook and approach of Peel. It was precisely at the moment when Disraeli was inducing it to coquet with the working classes that the party was tending to consummate its relations with the urban bourgeoisie. The political practice of Disraeli himself seems on close examination to be largely 'Peelite' in spirit.

The question of what was happening to the Conservative party between 1867 and 1880 requires more intensive study than it has hitherto received.[2] It is necessary to ask how far the party's thought and practice were influenced by 'Disraelian' ideas and orientated in a 'Disraelian' direction, and how far, on the other hand, they took a course which might be more properly described as 'neo-Peelite'. The analysis of this problem should throw light on the nature of the process of adaptation to changing social conditions which Conservatism was undergoing, and thus assist in a clearer understanding of the evolution of the modern party.

A central feature of 'Disraelian' Conservatism was social reform. Attention to the material needs of the masses was one of the basic means by which the Conservative party was to bring about class harmony, guarantee social stability, and secure popular support. Disraeli's stress on 'the elevation of the condition of the people' is commonly regarded as one of his most important contributions to the development of his party, vital in enabling it to come to terms with the rising social and political power of the working classes and to sustain its appeal to the post-1867 electorate. The tradition of Conservative social reform which Disraeli did more than anyone to

[1] R. J. White (ed.), *The Conservative Tradition*, 2nd ed., pp 21–2.

[2] There is no substantial study of the Conservative party in the Disraelian era. E. J. Feuchtwanger's article, 'The Conservative Party Under the Impact of the Second Reform Act', *Victorian Studies*, ii (1958–9), 289–304, has some points of interest, but the only aspect of the party's history in this period which has been extensively examined in print is the growth of its organisation (by Dr Feuchtwanger and Professors Hanham and McKenzie).

establish has been markedly useful to the modern party in its efforts to represent itself as the friend of the working man. Yet there is no detailed study of the rôle which social reform played in the thought and action of the Conservative party in the Disraelian era. The subject is worth investigation, not merely as being interesting in itself and in relation to the development of social policy and social legislation, but because it is important for the analysis of the real character of the Conservative metamorphosis in the late 'sixties and the 'seventies. By examining the place of social reform in the strategy of the parliamentary Conservative party, and scrutinising the attitudes which the party in practice adopted towards those social questions which primarily affected the condition of the working classes,[1] in the years which separate the beginning of Lord Derby's third ministry in 1866 from the defeat of the Beaconsfield government in the general election of 1880, it should be possible to gauge more accurately how far Conservatism was moving in a 'Disraelian' direction, and how far it was being shaped in other moulds, and thus to gain insight into the nature of its accommodation to social change. Such is the object of this work.

1866 saw the Conservative party facing a crucial stage in its efforts to meet the problem of adjustment to social change. To make clear the position in which it stood, it is necessary to look briefly at its relation to the problem over the preceding decades.

A great deal of the history of the Conservative party in the nineteenth century is the history of a party based on land gradually coming to terms with the new urban and industrial Britain and its inhabitants. It was increasingly apparent, in the generation after Waterloo, that old-fashioned Church-and-King Toryism must find a *modus vivendi* with the forces of the industrial age, from a head-on collision with which it could reap only disaster. It was not through a blind and uncompromising resistance to the pressures created by the advance of the manufacturing and commercial bourgeoisie and the urban proletariat that Tories could best preserve the essentials of the society they were organised to defend. The pressures were too strong, especially when elements of the urban middle and working classes combined in the 'politics of popular radicalism'[2] to mount a common assault on the positions held by the old privileged classes of aristocracy, gentry, and clergy. The enormous bias of the representative system, even after

[1] That is, for the purposes of this study, labour questions, elementary education, public health (including working-class housing), the drink traffic, and poor relief. Since the present work is not primarily concerned with social problems as such, they will not be treated in greater detail than is necessary to render comprehensible their rôle in politics and legislation.

[2] The phrase is from G. Kitson Clark, *The Making of Victorian England*, pp. 123–5.

1832, in favour of the agricultural counties and small, bucolic boroughs, as opposed to manufacturing counties and large towns, might go far to muffle the impact of the urban classes at parliamentary level, and to guarantee the continuing political predominance of the landed interest, from which Toryism drew most of its strength. But the Tory party could not afford to ignore the new urban forces, and if sometimes it found itself opposed to them in the politics of 'interests', it could hope to profit, in periods of economic dislocation and high social tension especially, from the divisions among them created by the emergence of class conflict.

When the force of popular Radicalism was strong enough to alarm numbers of the propertied middle classes, and the 'politics of class conflict', rooted primarily in division of economic interest and social alienation between employers and employed, set sections of the urban bourgeoisie and proletariat at loggerheads,[1] the Tory party could attempt to draw the more apprehensive and defensively-minded elements of the bourgeoisie into alliance with the landed interest for the preservation of property and order. It could also, conceivably, display popular sympathies, and suggest to the working man that the landed classes were his natural allies against dissenting Whig and Radical exponents of the new industrialism, the betrayers of 1832 and the villains of the struggle for factory reform. The two lines were obviously difficult to pursue together, and it was inevitable that the party should gravitate towards the former. The noblemen, squires, and clergy who formed its backbone could hardly go far in associating themselves with working-class interests and demands, especially when Chartism revealed the urban proletariat in militant and even revolutionary mood; the conservative alliance with the 'satisfied' bourgeoisie was ultimately their natural course. Yet they could not disregard the urban working men, whose condition, grievances, and aspirations, if only as a seed-bed of dangerous social unrest, had to be considered by politicians, and whose electoral influence in the boroughs was not, even under the 1832 franchise, negligible.[2]

Already under Lord Liverpool, through the efforts of men like Canning, Huskisson, Robinson, and Peel, the Tory party had begun to develop the kind of 'liberal' policy which could recommend it to the urban middle classes. The trend was severely checked under Wellington, whose disastrous declaration against Reform allowed the

[1] See *ibid.*, pp. 130–1.

[2] The £10 householder franchise took in a substantial element of the working classes; and working-class non-electors could exercise considerable influence in the larger boroughs, principally through the weapon of economic boycott. See N. Gash, *Politics in the Age of Peel*, pp. 98–100; J. R. Vincent, *The Formation of the Liberal Party 1857–1868*, pp. 100–3.

Whigs to appropriate the cause of moderate progress and revise the franchise, but in the 'thirties and 'forties it reached its height with Peel. Peel's new 'Conservatism', whose foundation deed was the Tamworth manifesto, aimed to absorb the industrial and commercial middle classes from which Peel himself sprang, into the great national party which alone, in his eyes, could guarantee the safety of the constitution and of the social order. Combining with resistance to revolution a readiness for cautious improvement, it offered an increasingly attractive shelter from the threats of Radicalism and Chartism, and by the early 'forties it seemed likely that Peel would succeed in re-establishing the fortunes of his party on the basis of a defensive alliance between landed and commercial property.[1]

To the working classes as such Peel's Conservatism made little attempt to appeal. The 'condition of the people' question, which achieved political prominence in the 'forties, was not one that it took up with special vigour. Peel and his disciples were far from indifferent to the social problem, but their notions of political economy and their desire to reach an accommodation with middle-class interests restricted their approach to it: they had little enthusiasm for direct governmental and legislative intervention in the economy for the benefit of working people, and relied for social improvement rather upon the fostering of general prosperity through economic liberalisation—in the long run, perhaps, the soundest policy, but not one calculated to win immediate mass acclaim.[2]

There was, however, a vein of Toryism in the 'thirties and 'forties that concerned itself more urgently with the working classes and their social state. It had diverse foundations. There was sympathy with the poor, care for their moral and material welfare, and desire for a Christian social order. There was the fear that unless they were energetically tackled the discontents of the urban masses would culminate in revolutionary upheaval. There was the impulse felt by some elements of the landed interest to strike a counter-blow at the advance of the new industrial civilisation and its middle-class acolytes, and to disrupt the attack on the corn laws, by exploiting urban social conflicts in order to draw the working classes into an alliance against the bourgeoisie. There was the realisation of Tories hungry for office in the late 'thirties that social questions could be manipulated against the Whigs. The confluence of these currents produced a brand of Toryism marked by awareness of the social problem and popular, or even Radical, sympathies. It was virulently critical of industrial

[1] See especially on Peel's Conservative party, N. Gash, *Reaction and Reconstruction in English Politics 1832–1852*, c.v.

[2] For a discussion of why Peel did not adopt a 'popular' policy, see G. Kitson Clark, *Peel and the Conservative Party*, pp. 380–7.

capitalism, to whose deification of self-interest and denial of social responsibility the evils of the towns were ascribed, and it saw the duty and profit of the Tory party not in adaptation to the interests and ideology of the bourgeoisie but in the proclamation of a paternalist concept of society, in the name of which the social wants of the people might be met by positive action.

The main practical expression of this type of Toryism was in the manufacturing districts of Yorkshire and Lancashire, where Oastler, Sadler, Stephens, Bull, Wood, and Ferrand led the factory movement and the opposition to the new poor law, and demonstrated how Tories and operatives might come together against the industrial bourgeoisie.[1] In the press, Southey, Alison, Lockhart, and Giffard tried to recall Toryism to a sense of the importance of the social question and the necessity of reform,[2] and in the House of Commons Lord Ashley (later seventh Earl of Shaftesbury) found expression for his animus against the bourgeoisie in the parliamentary leadership of the factory movement, so embarking on the career which was to establish him as the greatest of nineteenth-century social reformers.[3] And with Peel in power, the handful of young Tory members of Parliament known as 'Young England' rose to challenge his Conservatism in the cause of a popular and socially responsible Toryism, appealing to the masses through paternalistic reform. Young England, preaching a kind of revivified and spiritualised feudalism, centred on Crown and Church, in which the upper classes would solve the social question by lavishing on the lower such benefits as public baths, public games, and public walks, contained a strong element of the ludicrous, as its mentor, Disraeli, recognised, gently satirising it in the very novels, *Coningsby* and *Sybil*, in which he gave its ideas their most notable expression. Its leading adherents apart from Disraeli—Lord John Manners, George Smythe, and Alexander Baillie-Cochrane—were men of little weight,[4] and the practical assistance that it gave

[1] The first Conservative working men's organisations appeared in the north at this period, inspired principally by Oastler's ideas: see R. L. Hill, *Toryism and the People 1832–1846*, pp. 47–57.

[2] Their views are usefully summarised in R. B. McDowell, *British Conservatism, 1832–1914*, pp. 30–4.

[3] Ashley's latest biographer emphasises that he took up the factory question largely out of dislike of the millowners. G. F. A. Best, *Shaftesbury*, pp. 81–7.

[4] Baillie-Cochrane was a nonentity, and Smythe (later 7th Viscount Strangford) a man-about-town who eventually took office from Peel, and who once said: 'in politics I have only had one idea—what opinion is likely to turn up trumps' (E. B. de Fonblanque, *Lives of the Lords Strangford*, p. 235). Manners (on whom see principally C. Whibley, *Lord John Manners and His Friends*) was a genuine idealist, and, despite his fifth-rate versifying and tendency to lapse into romantic nonsense, he was not as foolish as he sometimes made himself look: he did something to focus parliamentary attention on social questions

to social improvement was small, though (Smythe excepted) its members backed Ashley in the ten-hours struggle, But it was Young England that most strikingly presented to the Conservative party an alternative to the outlook of Peel.[1]

The disparate activities of Young England, Ashley, and Oastler and the northerners had, however, only a slight impact on their party. The Toryism of popular sympathies and social reform was not without its potential advantages, given the increasing political importance of social questions, which helped to win for the Conservative party the general election of 1841.[2] But there was no real chance that the party as a whole would take it up. Many Conservative members of Parliament tended to regard its exponents as deluded or disreputable. Conservatives were not generally remarkable for sympathy with the people and interest in social questions, and were usually more concerned to control than to ally with the working classes—especially in face of the menace of Chartism, beneath which the factory movement and the popular Toryism of the north were largely submerged. Even when the representatives of the landed interest were organising for self-defence against the corn-law repealers, they showed little inclination to seek working-class support.[3] For Peel and his disciples social paternalism was ruled out both by their political strategy and by their economic principles.

Consequently, the parliamentary party of the 'thirties and 'forties made no attempt to appeal to the working classes with a positive social programme. Ashley's crusading, Young England, the Tory Radicalism of the north, and the fact that Peel's government did pass a Mines Act in 1842 and a Factory Act in 1844, and but for religious difficulties would have made an important advance in the provision of education for pauper and factory children with its Factory Bill of 1843, were all cited subsequently as evidence that the Conservative

[1] To Peel and his disciples, of course, Young England was pernicious nonsense: see W. E. Gladstone to Manners, 30 Jan. 1845, in J. Morley, *The Life of William Ewart Gladstone*, i. 304–5.

[2] The hope that the Conservatives would deal more effectively with the 'condition of the people' question than the Whigs brought them votes even from Radicals and Chartists. The new poor law, especially, was an election issue. See B. Kemp, 'The General Election of 1841', *History*, n.s., xxxvii (1952), 152–7; J. T. Ward, *The Factory Movement 1830–1855*, pp. 224–6.

[3] See Hill, pp. 251–2, 255, 256–7; G. L. Mosse, 'The Anti-League: 1844–1846', *Economic History Review*, xvii (1947), 134–42. W. B. Ferrand did suggest a bid for organised labour by means of revision of the poor law and support for the ten-hours bill.

---

in the 'forties, and Disraeli found him a hard-working student of bluebooks. But he never had much political significance.

party was strongly attached to the cause of social reform and the welfare of the people, which it forced upon recalcitrant Whigs and Radicals. This view came to be accepted even by Liberals in later years.[1] But it is not easy to sustain. The party as a whole was hardly distinguished for its pursuit of popular welfare and social improvement: it overwhelmingly supported (and later renewed) the new poor law, which the country gentlemen welcomed because of its tendency to save the rates, though they were assiduous in using it to blacken the Whigs at election time; it resisted state intervention in education (Disraeli himself being found here among the opponents of paternal government and centralisation); and while a section of it certainly gave substantial support to factory reform, its leaders, in office in 1841–6, secured the rejection of the ten-hours bill and passed a measure which, though an honest effort, paralleled their Mines Act in falling far short of what Ashley and the working men were demanding.[2] Ashley, indeed, if he found his most virulent opponents in Whigs, and in Radicals like Bright, Hume, and Roebuck, reserved some of his bitterest reproaches for the Conservative ministry of Peel.[3] The con-

[1] At least in relation to factory legislation. A. J. Mundella said in 1874: 'it has always been recorded to the honour of the party opposite that they were the promoters of factory legislation when the party with whom I sit were its opponents, and for this the working classes feel to this day that they owe a debt of gratitude to the party now in power' (*3 Hansard*, ccxviii. 1744).

[2] See especially D. Roberts, 'Tory Paternalism and Social Reform in Early Victorian England', *American Historical Review*, lxiii (1958), 325–30, and the same author's *Victorian Origins of the British Welfare State*, pp. 59–66. Professor W. O. Aydelotte's study of Commons' votes leads him to reject the simple propositions that leadership in the social legislation of the 'forties came from the Conservatives rather than the 'Liberals', and that such legislation was supported by the landed and opposed by the manufacturing interest, or supported by protectionists and opposed by free traders ('Voting Patterns in the British House of Commons in the 1840s', *Comparative Studies in Society and History*, v (1962–3), 158–60). On the Conservatives and factory reform, see also Ward, *passim*, but especially cc. x–xiii and pp. 415–17. Ward rates more highly than Roberts the strength of Tory support for factory reform, and emphasises that Peel secured a majority against ten hours in 1844 only by threatening resignation.

[3] See, for instance, E. Hodder, *The Life and Work of the Seventh Earl of Shaftesbury, K.G.*, i. 408, ii. 35, and elsewhere. Ashley's disgust almost caused him to leave his party at one point (see N. Gash, 'Ashley and the Conservative Party in 1842', *English Historical Review*, liii (1938), 679–81), and in 1845 he summed up his relations with it thus: 'Eight years of open support and of suppressed antipathy from the Conservatives *while* in Opposition; three years of coldness, and one of decided resistance from the same *when in Government*' (Hodder, ii. 82; but for a more favourable comment see Shaftesbury to the Earl of Derby, 29 June 1866, *ibid.*, iii. 211–12). Ashley's asperity, however, probably owed something to Peel's failure to give him the major office he had expected, and his attitude to the government was not altogether reasonable (see Best, pp. 93ff.).

tribution of the government of 1841–6 to the betterment of the condition of the people lay primarily in the direction of stimulating the economy and lowering the cost of living through greater freedom of trade, ultimately, no doubt, a more fruitful policy than paternalist legislation, but less immediately effective in winning the artisans over to the Conservative party.

By 1845, when Young England broke up, the Toryism of popular sympathies and social reform had already lost much of its impetus, and the adaptation of the Conservative party to social change seemed likely to be achieved through Peel's policy of alliance with the satisfied and self-defensive elements of the bourgeoisie. But Peel's course had long been viewed with distaste by many of the country gentlemen behind him, and when he came to the logical step of the abandonment of the corn laws Disraeli's malign brilliance gave their discontent an expression and a shape which brought about his downfall. Forced to an issue, the crisis of adjustment to social change which the Conservative party faced was resolved negatively: the bulk of the party turned their backs on the future and refused to move. The schism of 1846 brought almost to a halt the evolutionary movement of the party which had been going on since the 'twenties. By driving out Peel and his adherents, the Conservatives deprived themselves of their most able and forward-looking elements; they gave to the future Liberal party the men, like Gladstone and Cardwell, who should have led them after Peel; and they surrendered into the hands of their opponents the cause of the moderate, constitutional progress which the nation wanted. They turned themselves into the backward and unpopular party, the party of bucolic obstruction and inertia, largely cut off from the new urban and industrial Britain, and lacking any point of *rapport* with its advancing social forces. A generation of almost permanent opposition was the price they paid.

Perhaps the only beneficiary of the disaster of 1846 was Disraeli. His destruction of Peel and the secession of the Peelites put him in the front rank of his party, and after Lord George Bentinck's death the lack of alternative talent gave the Conservatives no choice but to accept as Lord Stanley's second-in-command and their leader in the Commons the outstanding exponent of the Toryism of popular sympathies and social reform.

Disraeli's concept of Toryism was almost fully formed by 1846, and in essentials it never changed. The ideas which he propounded in 1835 in the *Vindication of the English Constitution in a Letter to a Noble and Learned Lord*, summarised in 1836 in *The Spirit of Whiggism*, and developed in 1844–5 in the novels *Coningsby* and *Sybil*, formed the basis of his expressed political outlook for the remainder of his career, and reappeared virtually unaltered in the famous speeches of 1867 and 1872.[1] Upon them much of his fame rests.

Whether, or in what sense, he believed them has always been a matter of controversy. His best friends were never sure.[2] It is a convention in England to regard politics as a matter of principle and conviction. Disraeli saw them primarily as the arena for the display of his remarkable talents. 'We come here', he told Bright once at Westminster, 'for fame!'[3] His political ideas were not the motive force of his performance, but rather the costume which he wore in deference to the susceptibilities of his audience. A Jew, a quasi-intellectual, and a *littérateur*, standing by background and temperament outside the customary frame of British political life, he set himself not to assert a principle or attain an ideal, but to play the rôle of the romantic hero on the most unlikely of all stages, the floor of the House of Commons; and by wit, courage, and extraordinary force of will he succeeded. In order to take part in the game, he had to bow to its rules and adapt himself to the context in which he operated.

> He conceives it right [Bright noted][4] to strive for a great career with such principles as are in vogue in his age and country – says the politics and principles to suit England must be of the 'English type' . . .

But the traditional tenets and allegiances of English politics could have only limited meaning for him, and it is a question how far he took them seriously.

He was a detached and deeply sceptical man, who did not believe in much. His own ideas came less from the logical processes of the intellect than from the imagination; their status was not so much that of rational propositions, which might be true or untrue, as that of mental images, loosely related to reality, and designed for inspiration and for use, not for resistance to criticism.[5] The power of human

[1] The works mentioned, together with his speeches and journalism, form the main sources for Disraeli's thought. The political essays and the journalistic pieces are usefully collected in *Whigs and Whiggism*, ed. W. Hutcheon (where, however, Disraeli is wrongly credited with the authorship of the 'Letters of Manilius'). For the speeches, see *Selected Speeches of the Late Right Honourable the Earl of Beaconsfield*, ed. T. E. Kebbel. Disraeli's mature commentary on his ideas as he expressed them in the 'thirties and 'forties is to be found in the 'General Preface to the Novels', which appeared in the first volume of the collected edition of 1870.

[2] See, e.g. Manners's comment in his journal in 1843, quoted in Whibley, i. 149; and cf. Sir William Gregory, *An Autobiography*, ed. Lady Gregory, pp. 91, 100.

[3] *The Diaries of John Bright*, ed. R. A. J. Walling, p. 297.

[4] *Ibid.*, p. 130.

[5] When, as Viscount Cranborne, he was Disraeli's colleague in the mid-'sixties, the third Marquis of Salisbury found that 'Those of his opinions which

reason was, for Disraeli, severely limited, 'Man', declared his *alter ego*, Sidonia, in *Coningsby*,[1] 'is only truly great when he acts from the passions; never irresistible but when he appeals to the imagination'; moreover, he is 'made to adore and to obey', and needs not so much arguments for his understanding as images for his worship. Given their essentially non-rational character, it is not surprising that Disraeli's ideas should have been formulated with small regard for precision, coherence, and literal truth. Original and bizarre, brilliant and meretricious, fanciful and vulgar, mingling the true coin with the false, like the man himself, their value lies in insights, not in conclusions. They are a personal extravaganza, not an intellectual system. Their author 'believed' in them as an artist in the artifact, not as a mathematician in the theorem. But they form a part of his public personality and of his political significance, and cannot be ignored.

Embarking on his political career in 1832–4, when Radicalism seemed to be on the upgrade, and social questions were coming into prominence, Disraeli had professed Radical and popular views, including a strong concern for the condition of the people.[2] When the search for a seat in Parliament carried him into the Tory camp, he at once produced a version of Toryism which not merely accommodated these views but drew its distinctive character from them. The basis of his creed was his interpretation of English history since 1688 as essentially the story of the efforts of the Whig magnates to rivet a 'Venetian' oligarchy upon an unwilling nation. The Reform Act of 1832 was represented as the latest step in this process, a Whig *coup*

[1] Bk. IV, c. xiii.

[2] See W. F. Monypenny and G. E. Buckle, *The Life of Benjamin Disraeli, Earl of Beaconsfield* (hereafter cited as 'M. & B.'), i. 215, 217, 225. In *What is He?*, in 1833, Disraeli announced that the aristocratic principle of government was dead, advocated an advance to 'the democratic principle', urged Radicals and Tories to coalesce in 'a National Party', and spoke pointedly of 'spirits whose proud destiny it may still be at the same time to maintain the glory of the Empire, and to secure the happiness of the People' (*What is He?* is reprinted in *Whigs and Whiggism*, pp. 16–22). His idea of a Tory-Radical alliance, and his anti-Whig view of history, may perhaps, as R. Blake suggests ('The Rise of Disraeli', in *Essays in British History presented to Sir Keith Feiling*, ed. H. R. Trevor-Roper, p. 228) be explained by the fact that as a Radical candidate for High Wycombe he was opposed by Whigs but not Tories.

could claim the permanent quality of principles had their origin in his imagination and not in his reason. He saw visions; he did not draw conclusions. . . . He had none of the aversion which men of more logical temper feel for incoherence even in minor matters' (Lady G. Cecil, *Life of Robert Marquis of Salisbury*, i. 216). One is tempted to apply to Disraeli Pursewarden's remarks in Mr Lawrence Durrell's *Balthazar*: 'Poets are not really serious about ideas or people. They regard them much as a Pasha regards the members of an extensive *harim*. They are pretty, yes. They are for use. But there is no question of them being true or false, or having souls.'

d'état, designed to facilitate the establishment of a centralising tyranny by enfranchising a class hostile to Crown, Lords, Church, and the landed interest, the institutions which alone could protect the national rights and liberties against Whig aggression. The undermining of the national institutions in the name of 'liberalism' deprived the mass of the people of their main bulwarks against exploitation and oppression, and together with the growth of industrial and commercial wealth divorced from a sense of social obligation was largely responsible for the existence of the social problem, which threatened to rip apart the existing fabric of society. Disraeli was deeply impressed with the dangers inherent in the abandonment of the working classes to the vicissitudes of an industrial society governed by the tenets of individualism and political economy, and struck by the gulf between the 'two nations' of rich and poor which he portrayed in *Sybil*,[1] and the restoration of social cohesion was from the first among his major political themes.

The function of resisting Whig designs and reconciling the two nations was assigned in Disraeli's scheme of things to the landed aristocracy and gentry, the mainstay of England's 'territorial constitution', and the obvious guarantors, together with Crown and Church, of the liberties and privileges of the people, whose 'natural leaders' they supplied. It was in them that the masses must trust, not in their own movements.[2] Theirs was the task of upholding 'popular principles' against the selfish and irresponsible doctrines of Liberalism.[3] It was the reaffirmation of the tenets of the society for which, in Disraeli's eyes, they stood, a hierarchical, paternalistic society, permeated by a sense of social responsibility, and held together by a universal nexus of rights and duties, that would secure the content-

[1] The main passage on the two nations is in bk. II, c. v. The originality and depth of Disraeli's discussion of the social question in *Sybil* are sometimes overrated. The social novel was a common literary *genre* in the 'thirties and 'forties, and the idea of the gulf between classes was not new. Disraeli's treatment of working-class life, trade unionism, and Chartism is often clumsy and shallow, and there is no attempt at a fundamental analysis of the social problem. The novel was not the work of a serious social thinker, but the production of a fashionable *littérateur* and politician with one eye on notoriety and sales.

[2] 'The people are not strong,' says the hero of *Sybil* (bk. IV, c. xv), 'the people never can be strong. Their attempts at self-vindication will end only in their suffering and confusion.' Disraeli gives an unfavourable picture in *Sybil* of trade unionism and of the working-class socialist Morley.

[3] In a speech of June 1847 Disraeli characterised Liberal opinions as 'the opinions of those who would be free from certain constraints and regulations, from a certain dependence and duty which are deemed necessary for the general or popular welfare. Liberal opinions are very convenient opinions for the rich and powerful. They ensure enjoyment and are opposed to self-sacrifice' (*Selected Speeches*, i. 178).

ment and docility of the labouring classes. Disraeli did not really suppose that a return could be made to the medieval social order which Young England idealised, but he did advocate a revival of its imagined spirit.

> The feudal system may have worn out [he wrote in maturity][1], but its main principle, that the tenure of property should be the fulfilment of duty, is the essence of good government.

It was for the Tory party, the political organ of the landed interest, to serve as the instrument of the nation's salvation. 'The Tory party in this country', Disraeli insisted as soon as he had joined it, 'is the national party; it is the really democratic party of England'.[2] It was necessary to recall it to its historic rôle of representing the nation and the people against the assaults of oligarchy, and to ensure

> 1st. That the real character and nature of Toryism should be generally and clearly comprehended: 2ndly. That Toryism should be divested of all those qualities which are adventitious and not essential, and which having been produced by that course of circumstances which are constantly changing, become in time obsolete, inconvenient, and by the dexterous misrepresentation of our opponents even odious: 3rdly. That the efficient organization of the party should be secured and maintained.[3]

There, Disraeli liked to think, was the programme of his life's work.[4]

Disraeli's 'national' Toryism envisaged a mutually advantageous alliance between the party and the people, in which social paternalism would be traded for support of the established order. He agreed, he told the popular politician Charles Attwood, in 1840, that 'an union between the Conservative party and the Radical masses offers the only means by which we can preserve the Empire. Their interests are identical; united they form the nation . . .'[5] Recoiling from the idea that the corn law struggle would result in the transfer of power to the manufacturing class, he declared to the Commons, in February 1846, that instead of falling under 'the thraldom of capital',

1 'General Preface to the Novels', in the collected edition of 1870, vol. i, p.ix.

2 *Vindication of the English Constitution in a Letter to a Noble and Learned Lord*, pp. 182–3. Cf. the speech quoted in M. & B., i. 285.

3 *Vindication*, p. 192.

4 In 1874, on the eve of power, he wrote: 'I have, for forty years, been labouring to replace the Tory party in their natural and historical position in this country' (M. & B., i. 222). It was in 1835, not in 1867, that Disraeli's effort to 'educate' his party began.

5 Disraeli to Attwood, 7 June 1840 (*ibid.*, ii. 88). In the next month he told the Commons: 'the aristocracy are the natural leaders of the people, for the aristocracy and the labouring population form the nation' (*ibid.*).

> if we must find a new force to maintain the ancient throne and immemorial monarchy of England, I, for one, hope that we may find that novel power in the invigorating energies of an educated and enfranchised people.[1]

The cement of the union between party and people was to be social reform, and in *Sybil*[2] Disraeli offered the vision of the Toryism of Bolingbroke and Wyndham rising from the tomb 'to bring back strength to the Crown, liberty to the subject, and to announce that power has only one duty—to secure the social welfare of the PEOPLE'. Against the doctrines of political economists and 'brutilitarians' he pitted the concept of the organic society, deriving its cohesion from the observance of mutual obligation, and ready to employ the force of government to promote the well-being of the masses.

The Disraelian version of Toryism was a strange mixture of insight and *opéra bouffe*. Its contact with reality was precarious: this was especially true of its analysis of the social situation and the possibilities it offered for a junction between the Tory party and the people.[3] Its author never seriously attempted the task of rendering its romantic ideals into the concrete detail of policies and bills; such was not his forte.[4] His advocacy of social reform was accompanied by no programme of measures; his criticism of the evil of allowing the dictates of individualist economics to override considerations of social welfare was not supplemented by the formulation of an alternative economic system upon which a social policy could be based.[5]

[1] *Selected Speeches*, i. 143.

[2] Bk. IV, c. xiv.

[3] Disraeli was probably led to exaggerate the opportunities which the social problem provided for Tory exploitation by excessive reliance for his view of the new urban and industrial England on Manchester, often regarded in the 'forties as the key to the 'condition of England' question. Manchester exhibited the kind of cleavage between bourgeoisie and proletariat which seemed to offer prospects of success for a Tory paternalist appeal to the masses; and the association there of the Tories with the struggle for factory reform and the opposition to the new poor law had given their cause a popular flavour. But Manchester was not, in fact, typical of the great towns. See A. Briggs, *Victorian Cities*, c. iii.

[4] Disraeli's whole career revealed a weakness in translating general ideas into practical action. Though at one period a strong advocate of the study of bluebooks (M. & B., iii. 219, 234; Whibley, ii. 20), he never acquired a mastery of detail. Viscount Cranborne found in the mid-'sixties that 'The suggestions for action which he would bring before his colleagues, though brilliantly original and often largely conceived, were discursive, inconsequent, constantly varying, at times self-contradictory' (Cecil, i. 216).

[5] Protection furnished an economic system which in many ways consorted naturally with Disraeli's political outlook, but he was not strongly wedded to it; indeed what he contended for in the 'forties was not protection pure and simple but 'reciprocity', which, he argued, carried out 'the real principles of free trade', as enunciated by Pitt (see, e.g. *Selected Speeches*, i. 42, 45, 130–1, 182ff.). He abandoned protection readily when it had become a hopeless cause,

His practical contribution towards raising the condition of the people was not very extensive or assiduous: he voted for the repeal of the new poor law, spoke with some sympathy on Chartism, opposing excessive penalties for its leaders,[1] and supported the ten-hours cause, but he did little more. Sharing the prejudices of his party against administrative centralisation, he joined in their hostility to important measures of social improvement which involved its growth, opposing, for instance, the Education Order of 1839 and the Public Health Act of 1848.[2] Disraeli's popular Toryism, in short, was an idea, an attitude, not a policy, and what its progenitor was calling for was a regeneration, not a reconstruction, of society. Moreover, it had no sooner been fully formulated than circumstances compelled the muting of its expression.

It had provided a useful platform against Peel, but after 1846 it was no longer needed for this purpose and was becoming more of a liability than an asset. Transmuted from a back-bench *frondeur* into leader of the Conservative party in the Commons, Disraeli had to adjust himself to his new position. His hold on the party was, and for nearly twenty-five years was to remain, precarious, and he could not afford to risk it by stressing ideas which had no appeal for his chief, Stanley, and to which most of his followers were at best indifferent, at worst deeply hostile. Nor could he fail to realise, as the unrest of the 'forties gave way to the relative calm of the 'fifties, and social tensions relaxed, that the conditions on which the success of his brand of Toryism must depend were becoming rarer. There was little sacrifice involved in thrusting his popular doctrines into the background of his public persona. His attachment to his own ideas was shallow enough, as his conduct over the Mines Bill of 1850 neatly demonstrated. If Disraeli's professions of social concern were heartfelt, he should have supported this measure, vital to the welfare of the miners in providing for mines inspection. In fact, he opposed it at the request of one of the most tyrannical and inhumane coal-owners of the day, his friend Lord Londonderry, although, as he gaily told Lady Londonderry, 'I know nothing about it!'[3] That he was

[1] See M. & B., ii. c. iii.

[2] Roberts, 'Tory Paternalism', pp. 327–8, 331–2.

[3] Disraeli to Lady Londonderry, 2 Aug. 1850, in *Letters from Benjamin Disraeli to Frances Anne Marchioness of Londonderry, 1837–1861*, ed. the Marchioness of Londonderry, pp. 91–3. See five letters from Lord Londonderry to Disraeli on the bill, 27 July–2 Sept. 1850 (Disraeli Papers, B/XX/V/44–8); M. & B., iii. 254–5. Disraeli's opposition was unsuccessful. For Londonderry

though according to Montagu Corry he always said England would return to it (M. & B., iii. 26). In general, while deploring the consequences of its rigid application, Disraeli tended to follow the orthodox political economy of the day.

simultaneously renewing his support of the ten-hours cause does not remove the impression that five years after *Sybil* his practical zeal for 'the social welfare of the PEOPLE' was not strong. From the Disraeli of the 'fifties no call to the junction of party and people and the pursuit of social reform could come.

There was, indeed, virtually no chance in the years after 1846 that the party would pursue the Toryism of popular sympathies and social concern. The protectionists might, perhaps, have tried to draw the urban working classes towards them by associating their economic tenets with a policy of social reform. Manners insisted 'that the operatives can be, and ought to be, the firmest allies of a Tory and Protectionist Government; and that without their support in these times no Conservative party can be really strong'; he wanted to woo them with 'a cautious expression of legislative sympathy'.[1] But the cause of protection had to be abandoned as politically hopeless in 1852, and with the lessening of urban social tensions and class cleavage in the 'fifties the prospect of a combination between the landed interest and the working men against the bourgeoisie became ever more remote. The great majority of the party, in any case, had no taste for appeals to the mainly voteless masses or interest in the exploitation of social reform. In the twenty years between 1846 and 1866 very little effort was made to use social questions as a means to cultivate working-class support.

Social problems in the 'fifties and early 'sixties were far less central to politics than they had been in the 'forties, and there was small need or incentive for the Conservative party to take them up. The party's leader, the fourteenth Earl of Derby (as Stanley became in 1851) had spoken up for the distressed and unemployed in the 'twenties, but now concerned himself no further with social questions than to aid Shaftesbury over the lunacy laws and the problem of the displacement of the London poor through railway construction.[2]

[1] Manners to his father, 19 Dec. 1851, in Whibley, ii. 44–5. Manners was interested in Oastler's plans to agitate the working classes against free trade, and Oastler looked to him in the 'fifties as the heroic leader who would initiate the era of Tory social reconstruction (*ibid.*, ii. 26–7; C. Driver, *Tory Radical: the Life of Richard Oastler*, pp. 509–12). There was some working-class sentiment to which a combination of protection and social reform could have appealed: see, e.g. F. E. Gillespie, *Labor and Politics in England 1850–1867*, pp. 38ff.

[2] See W. D. Jones, *Lord Derby and Victorian Conservatism*, pp. 13, 15, 171; and below, p. 70.

---

as an employer, see A. J. Taylor, 'The Third Marquis of Londonderry and the North-Eastern Coal Trade', *Durham University Journal*, xlviii (1955–6), 21–7; S. and B. Webb, *History of Trade Unionism*, 2nd ed., p. 166.

Under him, Conservatism gave little aid to the improvement of the condition of the people. Factory legislation, where the interests which the party principally represented were not at stake, continued to receive substantial Conservative support—it was the protectionists who finally saw the ten-hours bill through in 1847, and Disraeli and Manners again upheld the ten-hours cause in the 'fifties, when the latter assumed the parliamentary leadership of the factory movement[1]—and the short-lived Derby ministries of 1852 and 1858–9 showed some disposition to appease the demands of labour, looking benevolently on bills which gave the co-operative societies legal status and effectively legalised peaceful picketing.[2] But in other spheres, the attachment of the Conservatives to local independence and the rights of property, and their concomitant suspicion of central intervention as a threat to both freedom and the rates, severely limited their capacity to support measures of social improvement. This came out very clearly in regard to public health: Disraeli, though, like Manners, a founder-member of the committee of the Health of Towns Association, opposed the Public Health Act of 1848 and the General Board of Health Bill of 1854; the government of 1852, with Manners as President of the Board of Health, disgusted Shaftesbury and Chadwick by its feebleness on sanitary reform;[3] and that of 1858–9, with the incompetent Charles Adderley in charge of health, seriously disrupted sanitary administration, abolishing the General Board of Health in a deliberate effort to weaken central control over the localities.[4]

[1] See W. O. Aydelotte, 'The House of Commons in the 1840s', *History*, n.s. xxxix (1954), 260; Ward, c. xv; M. & B., iii. 254. No doubt protectionist support for ten hours owed something to spite against free trade manufacturers.

[2] The former bill, passed in 1852, was promoted by the Christian Socialists. Charles Kingsley, for whom 'the real battle of the time' was 'the Church, the gentleman, and the workman, against the shopkeepers and the Manchester School', thought it a good move to 'carry out true Conservatism, and to reconcile the workmen with the real aristocracy . . .' (*Charles Kingsley: His Letters and Memories of His Life*, ed. Mrs Kingsley, ii. 56, 57). On the second measure, promoted by the National Association of Organized (or United) Trades, and eventually passed in 1859, see Gillespie, pp. 48–9, and S. and B. Webb, *History of Trade Unionism*, 2nd ed., p. 277, n. 1.

[3] See S. E. Finer, *The Life and Times of Sir Edwin Chadwick*, pp. 422–6; R. A. Lewis, *Edwin Chadwick and the Public Health Movement 1832–1854*, pp. 290, 322–4, 326–9; R. Lambert, *Sir John Simon 1816–1904 and English Social Administration*, pp. 177–8. The government made an especially bad job of the London water supply question, surrendering to the vested interests of the water companies.

[4] See Lambert, *Simon*, pp. 269–76, and the same author's 'Central and Local Relations in Mid-Victorian England: the Local Government Act Office, 1858–71', *Victorian Studies*, vi (1962–3), 122–5. Fortunately, the decentralising effect of Adderley's 1858 legislation was limited in practice. The government had to

Conservative support for social reform was very much a matter, between 1846 and 1866, of the sporadic efforts of individuals. These were not negligible: Shaftesbury and Manners were not the only men in the party's ranks, even in its higher ranks, who displayed a serious and practical concern with social questions. Derby's heir and Disraeli's political pupil, Lord Stanley, to whom some looked by 1866 as a future leader, had a remarkable range of interests in factories and mines, education, sanitary reform, co-operative societies, mechanics' institutes, and the provision of libraries and parks.[1] Sir John Pakington, Secretary for War and Colonies in 1852 and First Lord of the Admiralty in 1858–9, 'a prosperous Baronet enjoying all the "Desiderata" including the succession & undisputed possession of *three* wives,[2] had carried measures on beer-houses and juvenile offenders in the 'forties, and in 1853 introduced the bill which made vaccination compulsory in England and Wales; but his great enthusiasm was elementary education, on which he was very much in the vanguard of reform. He was closely associated with the progressive Manchester educationists, and his support for elected education boards and a permissive education rate, embodied in his bills of 1855 and 1857, caused division in his party.[3] It was he who, in 1858, secured the appointment of the celebrated Newcastle Commission on popular education.

The Staffordshire country gentleman Charles Adderley, a specialist in colonial affairs, derived from his deep sense of Christian duty a strong concern for social questions, and if he lacked administrative competence and performed disastrously as President of the Board of

[1] For these, see *Speeches and Addresses of Edward Henry XVth Earl of Derby, K.G.*, ed. Sir T. H. Sanderson and E. S. Roscoe, with a prefatory memoir by W. E. H. Lecky; also Stanley's *D.N.B.* entry. Stanley was really a moderate Liberal, kept in the Conservative party by filial loyalty.

[2] Malmesbury to Disraeli, 15 Oct. 1857; Disraeli Papers, B/XX/Hs/59. George Smythe dubbed Pakington 'Sir Roger de Coverley'.

[3] Stanley and Charles Adderley backed him, and Disraeli and Stafford Northcote sympathised (though the former clearly found his activities a nuisance), but most Conservative opinion, including that of men like Shaftesbury, Manners, and Lord Robert Cecil, was hostile, largely on the ground that a rating system would destroy the existing voluntary and denominational system. See *3 Hansard*, cxxxvii. 640–78, 684–6, 693–7 (1855); Shaftesbury's diary, 3 May 1855, in Hodder, ii. 522; Pakington to Disraeli, 7 Jan. 1855 and 23 Jan. 1857 (Disraeli Papers, B/XX/P/18, 29); Northcote to Pakington, 'Christmas' 1856 (copy; Brit. Mus., Add. MS. 50022 (Iddesleigh Papers), ff. 248–9); M. & B., iv. 63–4.

---

be dissuaded by the Prince Consort in 1859 from letting John Simon's central medical officership lapse and even from relinquishing the responsibility for health retained by the state in the Public Health Act 1858; and in opposition the Conservatives opposed the act making the medical officership and the health functions of the 1858 act permanent.

Health in 1858, he did extensive work for education and penal reform.[1] His main interest was the treatment of juvenile offenders: he was active in promoting reformatory schools, introducing a bill on the subject in 1852, and was responsible for the Youthful Offenders Act of 1854. In education, he introduced the Manchester and Salford Education Bill in 1854 (providing for permissive rating), and after his experience as Vice-President of the Committee of Council on Education in 1858–9, suggested compulsory rating for the provision of schools in areas which had none;[2] he also introduced in 1860 a bill which would have made a degree of education a condition of the full-time employment of children under twelve. He was one of the founders in 1857 of the National Association for the Promotion of Social Science, destined to be a powerful engine of social investigation and reform.[3] Another worker in the reformatory school movement was the Devonshire baronet Sir Stafford Northcote, once Gladstone's private secretary and now a protégé of Disraeli, who carried a Reformatory and Industrial Schools Bill in 1856, and produced the Industrial Schools Bill which Adderley carried in 1857.[4] Northcote was a supporter, also, of factory reform in the 'fifties, and so was Lord Robert Cecil, the future third Marquis of Salisbury. Both were fast-rising stars in the party firmament; another was Gathorne Hardy, Under-Secretary at the Home Office in 1858–9, who at the start of his political career, facing the largely working-class electorate of Bradford in 1847, had voiced notably progressive opinions on social questions,[5] though the enthusiasm seems soon to have waned.

All these men helped to keep alive the flame of Conservative social consciousness. But they were not much interested in using social

[1] See his biography, W. S. Childe-Pemberton, *Life of Lord Norton, passim.* His pamphlet *Punishment is Not Education* (1856) sets out his penological views; for his educational ideas, see his *A Few Thoughts on National Education and Punishments* (1874).

[2] See his address to the Social Science Congress, Oct. 1859, in *Transactions of the National Association for the Promotion of Social Science*, 1859, p. 83.

[3] For the N.A.P.S.S., see B. Rodgers, 'The Social Science Association 1857–1886', *The Manchester School of Economic and Social Studies*, xx (1952), 283–310. At the Association's first meeting, the Education and Public Health departments were presided over respectively by Pakington and Stanley.

[4] On Northcote's reformatory school work, see his correspondence for 1854 and onwards, in Add. MSS. 50034 ff., and A. Lang, *Life, Letters, and Diaries of Sir Stafford Northcote First Earl of Iddesleigh*, i. c. v (where, however, Lang seems to be in some confusion about the bills of 1856–7).

[5] He called for increased education, sanitary improvement, and the mitigation of the severities of the new poor law, giving government a very positive rôle in the social sphere. Broadsheet of speech to the Bradford electors, 23 July 1847, and undated folios containing what appear to be the rough notes for this speech, or another at the same election: Cranbrook Papers, T501/72, T501/104.

questions as a means of cultivating support among the working classes. Like the rest of the party, it was to the bourgeoisie that they looked for the accretion of strength that would rescue Conservatism from the wilderness. When, in 1853, strikes among the cotton operatives in Lancashire produced the kind of urban social conflict from which the Conservatives could hope to profit, Stanley's sympathy with the strikers—who were ready to appeal to the landed interest—did not prevent his seeing the situation largely in terms of the possibilities it offered for gaining their 'frightened, therefore Conservative' employers.

> I hope [he wrote to Disraeli][1] none of our agricultural friends will take up the labour question in a spirit of hostility to capitalists. In the Lancashire manufacturers I see material for Conservative principles to work upon: though the idiot squires treat them as levellers, democrats, etc. A little personal management, added to the fright they have got, will soften the most extreme.

The party was, in fact, tending increasingly in the 'fifties and early 'sixties to resume the course indicated by Peel and cultivate urban middle-class support. Electorally, it had no choice. Derby tried hard to broaden its base by bringing Gladstone and his fellow Peelites back, an effort which might have led eventually to a party reconstructed on Peelite principles with Gladstone at its head, and which perhaps only Gladstone's detestation of Disraeli prevented from succeeding. He did much, with Disraeli, to draw his followers away from the sterility of mere reaction and lead them back towards the mildly progressive Conservatism for which Peel had stood. At the beginning of his second ministry, in 1858, he recognised the necessity of meeting the demands of society by 'judicious changes',[2] and the 1858–9 government was sufficiently liberal in spirit (it even produced a Reform Bill) to cause mutterings among its supporters.

Whatever his popular predilections of the 'forties, Disraeli fully concurred in the renewal of the effort to draw in the satisfied and defensive middle classes. No doubt his political thought, with its

[1] 28 Nov. 1853: Disraeli Papers, B/XX/S/601. The episode illustrates how little the Conservative party could in practice contemplate exploiting urban social cleavage for working-class favour. Derby's attitude, governed by the tenets of orthodox political economy, was very unfriendly to the action of the operatives, which he thought necessarily futile. 'In the end,' he told Disraeli (letter of 14 Nov. 1853: *ibid.*, B/XX/S/122), 'Capital will always be too strong for labour; and after much of suffering to themselves, and loss to their employers, the workmen will always have to give in; and indeed if it were not so, we should soon find a large portion of our manufacturing Capital transferred to other Countries.'

[2] *3 Hansard*, cxlix. 41.

stress on the common interest and sympathies of Crown, aristocracy, and people, had tended to leave the bourgeoisie outside the pale, and even to represent it as a parcel of low Whigs and dissenters, whose spirit was inimical to that of the 'nation'. No doubt as a literary intellectual and a leader of the landed aristocracy and gentry he looked down on bourgeois manners and pursuits. But he was too intelligent not to recognise (as in the portraits of the entrepreneurs Millbank and Trafford, in *Coningsby* and *Sybil*, and in the remark that 'rightly understood, Manchester is as great a human exploit as Athens'[1]) the capacities and achievements of the industrial and commercial middle classes, and as a party leader avid for power he could not ignore the possibilities of incorporating them into a conservative alliance with land, in the manner of Peel.

Though Disraeli had made his fortune as Peel's executioner, it is doubtful how deep his hostility to Peel's general policy had been. Certainly there was a great difference in temper between his Toryism and Peelite Conservatism, with its lack of imagination and popular sympathies; but the philippics of 1844–6 owed as much to spleen at having been refused office by Peel in 1841, and to sheer ambition, as to divergence of political outlook.[2] Disraeli's criticisms of Peel's Conservatism were rather nebulous, boiling down to the vague charge that it failed to assert genuine Tory principles, and it is noteworthy that in the very book, *Coningsby*, in which he gave them their most pungent expression, he approved, as consonant with the Pittite tradition, the kind of adaptive, 'liberal' approach which Liverpool's cabinet had pursued in the 'twenties, and for which Peel stood.[3] He realised, like Peel, that substantial sections of the bourgeoisie had essentially conservative interests and could be induced to co-operate with the old aristocratic and landed classes in defending the established order,[4] and if he laughed at the type of Peel's new Conservative Association, 'with a banker for its chairman, and a brewer for its vice-president',[5] he was far from despising the uses of bankers and brewers as auxiliaries of the aristocracy and gentry.

[1] *Coningsby*, bk. IV, c. i.

[2] Cf. Blake, pp. 234–5.

[3] *Coningsby*, bk. II, c. i. His only complaint against the 'ameliorating career' of Liverpool's ministry was the same as his complaint against Peel—that there was no attempt to promote Tory principles.

[4] As early as 1836, he noted that 'the manufacturing interest', having gained an enlargement of its political power, was beginning to 'lack in movement', and declared that 'the industrious ten-pounder, who has struggled into the privileged order of the Commons, proud of having obtained the first step of aristocracy, will be the last man to assist in destroying the other gradations of the scale which he or his posterity may yet ascend . . .' *The Spirit of Whiggism*, in *Whigs and Whiggism*, pp. 348, 349.

[5] *Coningsby*, bk. IV, c. v.

Disraeli saw clearly in the 'fifties and early 'sixties that if the Conservative party was to get out of minority and into power, it must resume the Peelite policy which he had wrecked in 1846 and render itself more palatable to urban middle-class taste.[1] Protection had no sooner been jettisoned than he was embarking on his curious flirtation with Bright,[2] discussing with his colleagues how to get at the urban vote,[3] and stressing the identity of interest between town and country and the stake of the bourgeoisie in the maintenance of the national institutions[4]. The second Derby ministry found him seeking anxiously to give the party a more 'liberal' aspect and broaden its base.[5] If he still sometimes recurred to the Toryism of 'popular principles', upholding 'the rights of the multitude',[6] it was towards supplying the mildly progressive Peelite Conservatism which answered to the middle-class mood that his main practical effort was directed.

Bringing in the urban middle-class vote was uphill work. In a period of prosperity and low social tension, with the working classes quiescent and the Radical challenge unimpressive, there was little to drive the bourgeoisie into the Conservative party. The party's post-1846 image, despite the efforts of Derby and Disraeli, was too obscurantist, obstructive, and sectional to attract an electorate which, though conservative in temper, was concerned to have moderate progress. With the appeal exerted from the late 'fifties onwards by Palmerston, to many the soundest conservative in the country, it proved almost impossible to compete. There were, it is true, some signs by the 'sixties that the prospects for the Conservative party among the urban bourgeoisie were improving. Important elements of the middle classes, economically and socially satisfied, were taking up a defensive posture against the more radical tendencies of Liberalism, and against the advance of 'democracy'. Stanley told Disraeli in 1860 that the towns were full of 'Conservative opinion, disguised as Moderate Liberalism',[7] and it was only a matter of time before the disguise was thrown off. The Conservative party was beginning to

[1] See, on this point, C. J. Lewis, 'Theory and Expediency in the Policy of Disraeli', *Victorian Studies*, iv (1960–1), 248–50. Lewis thinks that Disraeli was appealing steadily to the middle classes between 1848 and 1867.

[2] See *The Diaries of John Bright*, pp. 128–30 (December 1852).

[3] See Malmesbury to Disraeli, 3 Feb. 1853, in M. & B., iii. 483, where Malmesbury says: 'I agree entirely with you that our party is repugnant to the urban taste, and that we should try something to recover the towns' interest, but no operation can be compared in difficulty to it.'

[4] *Selected Speeches*, i. 442–3 (House of Commons, May 1853).

[5] See his remarks to Derby and Stanley in Aug. and Oct. 1858, in M. & B., iv. 183, 176.

[6] E.g., in speeches of Aug. 1862 and June 1863, quoted *ibid.*, iv. 379, 380.

[7] Letter of 13 Oct. 1860, quoted *ibid.*, iv. 274, n. 2.

show an appreciable representation of the industrial, commercial, and professional bourgeoisie in its ranks, with men like R. A. Cross, the barrister and country banker, who held Preston in 1857–62, the shipbuilder Laird, who represented his fief of Birkenhead from 1861, the Feildens and Hornbys, who led the party in Blackburn, each family providing a member for the borough in 1865, or Hugh Birley, W. R. Callender, junior, and J. W. Maclure, Conservative leaders in Manchester.[1] There was reason to hope that this representation would eventually be reinforced by the accession of Palmerstonians such as the bookstall king, W. H. Smith, who in April 1865 was looking forward to the junction of Palmerston's and Derby's moderate adherents in a Liberal-Conservative party.[2] But the fact remains that by 1865 the Conservatives had achieved only limited inroads among the urban middle-class voters, and their position in the towns was weak, sustained in too many cases by little more than 'family tradition, social prestige, beer, corruption, and the Church'.[3]

The situation of the Conservative party in the mid-'sixties was, indeed, critical. It had failed to come to terms with urban and industrial Britain and its expanding social forces. It remained overwhelmingly the party of the landed and agricultural interest, deriving the great bulk of its parliamentary strength from the agricultural counties and small rural boroughs, and based primarily on southern and south-eastern England.[4] Unable to attract the urban middle or working classes in large numbers, it could win few seats in the major centres of industry and population,[5] and compared with its opponents could muster only a small representation of industrial and commercial

[1] For the three latter, see H. J. Hanham, *Elections and Party Management: Politics in the Time of Disraeli and Gladstone*, pp. 314–16, 318–19; and on the growing conservatism of Manchester middle-class opinion in the 'fifties and 'sixties, D. Read, *The English Provinces c. 1760–1960: a Study in Influence*, pp. 151–6.

[2] Smith to Taylor (the Conservative whip), 26 April 1865, in Sir H. Maxwell, *Life and Times of the Right Honourable William Henry Smith, M.P.*, i. 122, n. 1.

[3] Vincent, p. 97, referring to Rochdale—where, however, there was a substantial middle-class Conservative vote in the 'fifties, including a majority of the large employers.

[4] To some degree, of course, this reflected the bias of the representative system as a whole. After the 1865 general election, according to the figures given in *Essays on Reform*, p. 330, the Conservatives had 149 out of 256 county seats (50.7% of their strength), 139 out of 396 borough seats (47.3% of their strength), and all six university seats.

[5] In 1865, of 100 seats in the United Kingdom in towns with a population (in 1871) of over 50,000, the Conservatives won only 22 (Hanham, p. 92, n. 2). As in 1859, they won no seats in London. As well as being weak in large boroughs, they were weaker in industrial than in agricultural county divisions (C. Seymour, *Electoral Reform in England and Wales*, pp. 302, 303).

interests on its benches.[1] Though it was, of course, very far from monopolising the landed or excluding the manufacturing and commercial interest, which were in any case closely intertwined,[2] the Liberal M.P. Hayter was not guilty of outrageous caricature, at least as regards the Conservatives, when in 1867 he spoke of the two great parties, 'the one of which represented the agricultural, the other the manufacturing and commercial interests of our vast community'.[3]

The land was the only great interest from which the Conservative party drew real strength; and the relative economic and social weight of the land was slowly declining. The party was founded on a shrinking base; it stood for no emergent trend; there was no demand of the hour which it alone could fulfil. Its principles were implemented by its chief opponent: Derby was reduced to a tame support of Palmerston's régime, and it became hard to discern what the difference between Conservative and Liberal policy was. The only hope for the resurrection of the party's fortunes seemed to lie in the eventual disintegration of the opposing force. As Derby wrote despondently to Disraeli, after the Conservative setback in the general election of 1865,

> a purely Conservative Government is all but hopeless, until, upon Palmerston's death (for he will never resign), Gladstone tries his hand with a Radical Government and alarms the middle classes. Then there *may* come a reaction: but it will probably be too late for *my* time . . .[4]

It was, in fact, Palmerston's death in October 1865 which gave the Conservatives a prospect of revival. The political situation was suddenly fluid. Russell and Gladstone were now free to pursue a policy of movement, and in particular to take up in earnest the question of parliamentary reform. A large extension of the franchise among the urban working class and a redistribution of seats in favour of the grossly under-represented manufacturing areas of the north and midlands became serious possibilities; these were the aims of the resurgent alliance between middle-class Radicalism and the working

[1] See, for the economic interests represented in the parties after the general election of 1865, J. A. Thomas *The House of Commons, 1832–1901: A Study of its Economic and Functional Character*, pp. 4–6.

[2] It is an elementary point that landowners frequently had extensive interests in industry, commerce, transport, and urban development. To take some Conservative examples, the Stanleys and the Cecils profited greatly from the growth of Liverpool, and Charles Adderley, in many ways the archetypal country gentleman, got most of his money from collieries and property in the suburbs of Birmingham. But, as F. M. L. Thompson points out (*English Landed Society in the Nineteenth Century*, p. 268), a spread of economic interests did not necessarily create 'any identification with industrialists or sympathy with middle-class objectives'.

[3] *3 Hansard*, clxxxvi. 1281.

[4] Derby to Disraeli, 4 Aug. 1865, quoted in W. D. Jones, p. 281.

classes which Bright symbolised and inspired, and their imminent achievement threatened both the Conservative party and the world which it existed to preserve. Parliamentary reform, to the middle-class Radicals, was primarily a means of introducing into the fortress of the constitution a select contingent of working-class allies, and shifting the balance of representation towards urban and industrial Britain, in order that they might finally break down the grip of aristocracy, land, and Church and re-form the country in their own image, doing what they had failed to do in 1832 and 1846. If they were allowed to carry it out in their own way, Conservatism risked being overwhelmed. But at the same time, the advance of Radicalism and 'democracy' and the energy of Gladstone and Bright promised to reinvigorate the Conservative party by driving into its arms the Whigs and more moderate Liberals and the middle-class Palmerstonians. The Conservatives could hope to achieve at last a monopoly of conservatism, and to construct what Disraeli had called in August 1865 'an anti-revolutionary party on a broad basis',[1] fusing the defensive elements of the bourgeoisie with the landed interest in the great alliance of property which the Radical menace had enabled Peel to initiate a quarter of a century earlier.

Gladstone's introduction of a Reform Bill in 1866 thus opened a crucial phase for the Conservative party in its efforts to extend the socio-economic foundations of its support and extricate itself from a twenty-year minority. The party's leaders were not committed against Reform in principle: they had always been careful to maintain their freedom of manœuvre on the question, and had introduced a very restricted measure themselves in 1859. Disraeli, grasping that, since power followed the distribution of property, a wide franchise was perfectly compatible with government by a limited class,[2] had little innate fear of an enlarged suffrage, and his strong warnings in 1859 and 1865 against the evils of democracy and the reduction of the £10 borough qualification[3] were partly aimed at pleasing conservative middle-class sentiment. But, in the circumstances of 1866, it was inevitable that he and Derby should oppose Gladstone's bill. Their stand conformed to the feeling of the party, which certainly disliked and feared the idea of a substantially-widened franchise, and inclined to follow Viscount Cranborne (the future third Marquis of Salisbury) in seeing the Reform struggle as 'a battle not of parties, but of classes' and 'a portion of the great political struggle of our

[1] Letter to Derby, quoted in M. Cowling, 'Disraeli, Derby and Fusion, October 1865 to July 1866', *Historical Journal*, viii (1965), 37.

[2] See *The Spirit of Whiggism*, in *Whigs and Whiggism*, p. 346.

[3] See M. & B., iv. 208–9, 409–11. The latter brought him congratulations from the steadfastly anti-democratic Shaftesbury.

century—the struggle between property, be its amount small or great, and mere numbers'.[1] It was, however, more a matter of tactics than of principle. Derby and Disraeli could not allow their opponents to alter the representative system on their own terms and to their own advantage, enfranchising just that class of workmen who might be expected to vote for Gladstone and Bright, but leaving a margin for further reductions whenever they should need an issue adapted to place the Conservative party in an obstructive and unpopular position;[2] nor could they let slip the providential opportunity which Reform offered of breaking up the Liberals and winning over the satisfied and apprehensive middle classes.

Their policy quickly paid dividends. The Liberals were, indeed, disrupted. The air was full of projects of combination between the Conservatives and some of the Whigs in the first months of 1866, and in June the revolt of the Adullamites brought Russell's ministry down. The Queen summoned Derby to take office for the third time with a minority in the House of Commons.[3] The moment seemed ripe for a Conservative-Whig fusion, but it failed to materialise, perhaps because Derby and Disraeli feared for their personal positions in a coalition,[4] perhaps also because they wanted to avoid committing themselves too decidedly against Reform.[5] Nonetheless, there was a good prospect that the new government would attract Whig support, and would be able to base itself solidly on the favour of the Palmerstonian middle classes. Derby made it clear in his ministerial statement on 9 July that he looked forward to a speedy political re-alignment in which the Conservative party would consolidate all the conservative forces in the nation in opposition to Radicalism and democracy:

> I do not [he said] conceal my hope—because I look to the real, and not the arbitrary distinctions of party—I do not conceal my earnest hope that the time is not far distant when there may be such a new arrangement

[1] *Quarterly Review*, cxix (1866), 552. Cf. *ibid.*, cxx (1866), 273.

[2] 'We looked upon the measure of last year', Disraeli told the Merchant Taylors in June 1867, 'as one which, if carried, would have seriously injured, if not destroyed, the Conservative party . . .' *The Times*, 12 June 1867.

[3] According to their chief whip's list, in March 1866 the Conservatives numbered 288 (in a House of 658). Northcote's diary, 23 March 1866 (typescript copy): Add. MS. 50063A, f. 88.

[4] See Cowling, pp. 65–71, who thinks they were not really anxious for fusion. Certainly neither could have led a coalition: Stanley was the only Conservative candidate for that job.

[5] Disraeli objected to having the Adullamite Robert Lowe in the cabinet because this 'would be rather too much of a challenge to the Reform party, and would look like the decided adoption of an anti-Reform policy, "while after all, perhaps, we may be the men to settle the question" '. Northcote's diary, 29 June 1866 (typescript copy): Add. MS. 50063A, f. 93, printed in Lang, i. 261.

of parties as to place on the one side those who are in favour of dangerous innovations and violations of the Constitution, and on the other side all those who, while they will not resist safe legislative progress, are determined to adhere to this Constitution and to those institutions under which this country has so long been loyal, prosperous, and happy.[1]

It seemed in July 1866 that the Conservative party stood on the threshold of achieving the goal which Peel had failed to reach twenty years before, and refounding its fortunes on an alliance of landed and commercial property for the defence of the constitution and the social order. It was Peel's Liberal-Conservatism, drawing in the bourgeoisie, not Disraeli's faded popular Toryism, looking to the masses, that was to be the basis of its adaptation to social change.

The masses could not, however, be left out of Conservative calculations. No party which aspired to govern could, in the mid-'sixties, altogether ignore the growing social and political force of urban labour, to which the demand for Reform had begun to give focus and direction. If the Conservatives were to re-establish their fortunes on a stable and permanent foundation, it was essential that they should find means of cultivating support among the urban working men.

The gulf between the Conservative party and the urban working classes in 1866 was a wide one. As the party of land and agriculture, with little strength in the great towns and manufacturing regions, the Conservatives were largely out of touch with urban and industrial Britain and its inhabitants, and little attuned to its problems and needs. They had very slight appeal for the politically-conscious working men, who were generally found in close association with bourgeois Liberalism and Radicalism.[2] Perhaps the only area in which they could claim substantial working-class support was Lancashire, and Lancashire working-class Conservatism was a special case, owing a good deal to Protestant and anti-Irish feeling, and to the association of Toryism in the 'thirties and 'forties with the operatives' struggle for factory reform and against the new poor law.[3]

Nonetheless, it was not inconceivable that the Conservatives should extend their working-class support. It was here that social questions

[1] *3 Hansard*, clxxxiv, 743.

[2] It should, however, be noted, without attaching too much significance to the fact, that the eight boroughs in which working men had an electoral majority returned in 1865 nine Conservatives to five Liberals. B. Cracroft, 'The Analysis of the House of Commons, or Indirect Representation', in *Essays on Reform*, pp. 176–7.

[3] Another factor was the strength of the Stanley influence, enhanced by the leading part played by Derby in relief work during the cotton famine.

were likely to become of increasing importance in the party's strategy. Social improvement was almost the only card with which it could attempt to conciliate working-class opinion. Less closely identified than its opponents with the interests of the entrepreneurial class, and boasting some tradition of social concern, it might hope to show to advantage in compromising with the working men's economic and social demands and bettering their material condition. Even apart from their possible political uses, social questions were bound to impinge increasingly on its attention. They were becoming again, as they had been in the 'forties, part of the staple of politics, and neither party could any longer afford to neglect them. Much would depend in the future on Conservative ability to grapple effectively with social problems and safeguard the welfare of those whom they most directly touched.

The party's interest in, and grasp of, social problems was extremely limited. It had no shadow of a social policy: the conditions of mid-Victorian politics did not require it—or its opponents—to produce one. For nearly twenty years social questions had been in the background of politics; Conservatives had not been compelled to interest themselves in them, and in the mere twenty-six months of office which they had enjoyed since 1846 they had acquired little experience of them from the governmental viewpoint. They numbered in their ranks very few middle-class professional people of the type who were in the nineteenth century the driving force of social investigation and the formulation of social policy. They did not, except for a few individuals like Pakington or Adderley, spend much time thinking about social problems, and had small knowledge of them in their most acute manifestations in the great towns. As was natural with a party based on land and agriculture, what they did know and think about such problems derived largely from their practical experience of them in the countryside. The system of amateur administration by the local gentry, which still governed the countryside, and the social obligations attaching to land, compelled a degree of acquaintance with social questions, and helped often to nurture some sense of social responsibility. It was as magistrates, poor law guardians, and voluntary school managers and subscribers that many Conservatives formed their acquaintance with and views on social issues. The training was doubtless valuable, but the outlook it developed was seldom broad.

It is impossible to say that towards social problems in general and the question of the proper rôle of government and legislation in dealing with them there was any coherent or distinctive Conservative attitude. The antithesis occasionally drawn between a Liberal party wedded to *laisser-faire* capitalism and a Conservative party championing the paternal use of the authority of the state is a crude over-simplification.[1] There was, indeed, an element of social paternalism in the outlook of the Conservative party, but with it mingled doubts about the state's power for good, misgivings as to the increase of centralisation and taxation, and reservations learned from the teachings of political economy, which seriously curtailed its force.

The paternal, reformist Toryism of the 'thirties and 'forties, still remembered to the party's credit by the working men of the north, furnished a tradition of which Conservatism could make good propaganda use, but little of it was left by 1866, except, perhaps, in and around Manchester, where its spirit lived on in the hands of men like Birley, Callender, and Maclure.[2] Oastler was dead, and of his leading colleagues only Ferrand remained politically active.[3] Young England had become a historical curiosity, though in Manners, if not Disraeli, some of its ingenuous idealism survived. Shaftesbury still laboured prodigiously, but he stood largely outside party, and had small influence with his fellow Conservatives. The paternalist approach to social questions continued, however, to be discernible in the party. Its basis was generally a sense of duty towards the poor deriving from religion. With this mingled ordinary humanitarianism, and the consciousness of social obligation which Conservatives liked to think characterised the hierarchical rural world where most of them still had their roots. Such feelings might often issue in no more than private and local philanthropy. But coupled with fear of social upheaval if reform was not pursued, and sometimes with a tendency to welcome outlets for the venting of spite against the encroachments of industrial civilisation and its acolytes, they might generate support for the paternal intervention of the state on a national scale, to protect the social interests of its weaker members. While accepting that social improvement must depend ultimately on the elevation of the individual, a number of Conservatives felt that the minimum conditions for advance should be—perhaps could only be—secured by governmental action; and though attached to liberty, they understood that its enjoyment by the mass of the population might depend as much upon the presence as upon the absence of state interference in economic and social life, and that laws and regulations could be used, as Shaftesbury said, not to abridge 'but to *enlarge* man's freedom;

[1] For a not uncommon view of the Conservatives as the party of paternalism against *laisser-faire*, see White, 2nd ed., c. vi. A similar line of thought is followed in Viscount Hailsham, *The Conservative Case*, pp. 58–9.

[2] See Hanham, pp. 313ff.

[3] He was involved in 1866 with the new working men's Conservative associations in the north. One or two of the old protectionist supporters of the ten-hours cause remained on the Conservative back benches, notably the rabid anti-papist C. N. Newdegate; and, if little involved in party politics, J. R. Stephens was still working for factory reform and other objects.

not to limit his rights, but to multiply his opportunities for enjoying them . . .'[1]

There was, however, much in the outlook of Conservatives to discourage social paternalism. The influence of religion by no means always favoured it: social evils might receive a kind of sanction from the idea of divine ordination,[2] and the power of the state to achieve social amelioration might be discounted by those to whom the doctrine of original sin suggested that it was upon grace, not social reform, that the betterment of mankind must depend. The positive dangers of governmental interference in the social sphere, too, were very present in Conservative thinking. Viewing society as an organism, Conservatives were chary of disturbing what might be supposed to be its natural processes of growth. Social progress, they tended to feel, should come rather by internal evolution than by the artificial action of government, which was as likely to bring damage as benefit. There was very strong Conservative prejudice against the increase of centralised administration which commonly accompanied state intervention in social questions. Local self-government and independence appeared as an essential bulwark of civil liberty and a vital stimulant of those corporate virtues which formed the basis of the national character. Conservatives were determined to resist its erosion, especially in the countryside, where the landed classes had no intention of brooking any serious central challenge to the power which they had exercised since the Restoration. This localism, mingled with engrained respect for the rights of property, and coupled with the particularism of all kinds of special groups and interests, produced a Tory brand of *laisser-faire*, repulsing the interference of government in social matters, and seeking the motive force of social progress, if at all, in individual, corporate, and local initiative.[3]

Nor was the mind of Conservatism unaffected by those objections to governmental social action deriving from political economy which are often listed among the stage properties of classical Liberalism. Conservatives in general looked at social problems in the 'sixties in the light of economic presuppositions identical with those of their opponents. They drew their basic economic ideas, as did Liberals,

[1] Quoted in J. W. Bready, *Lord Shaftesbury and Social-Industrial Progress*, p. 40.

[2] Anglican clergy often held that social evils were divinely ordained and should be suffered patiently by the poor (J. Hart, 'Nineteenth-Century Social Reform: a Tory Interpretation of History', *Past and Present*, no. 31 (1965), 56). The Anglican Church as a whole was hardly a powerful force for social reform in the later nineteenth century: see D. O. Wagner, *The Church of England and Social Reform since 1854*, and K. S. Inglis, *Churches and the Working Classes in Victorian England*, pp. 271–87.

[3] See Roberts, 'Tory Paternalism', pp. 333–5.

from the orthodox political economy of the day, built on the principles of individualism and free trade: there was, indeed, no other source available, for the tide of mid-Victorian prosperity seemed so convincing a proof of the validity of free trade economics as to give them a virtual monopoly of intellectual respectability.[1] Orthodox political economy—or rather that simplified, vulgarised, and slightly outdated version of it with which practical men usually worked—was by no means rigorously *laisser-faire*, but its conclusion was commonly understood to be that the free pursuit of individual interest tended to result in the maximum of public wealth and welfare, and that consequently the interference of the state in economic and social life, while often necessary and inevitable, was generally best kept to a minimum.[2] Conservatives, like Liberals, mostly accepted that governmental social action required jealous scrutiny lest it damage the economic foundations of national prosperity, and agreed that the ineluctable operation of economic laws made its usefulness in many areas highly doubtful.

In a society actuated by individualism, it was primarily from the striving of the individual that social improvement must come, and the overwhelming majority of Conservatives adhered staunchly to that natural corollary of orthodox political economy, the secular religion of self-help. The doctrine of self-help fitted in neatly with the stress on the overriding moral responsibility of the individual derived from religious sources, and the two together persuaded most Conservatives that the 'condition of the people' question must be solved largely by the people themselves. Continence, sobriety, industry, and thrift, coupled with that grasp of the operation of economic laws which was often expected to be a by-product of the increase of elementary education, would enable the working classes to raise themselves, with only minimal external assistance. Where assistance was required, reliance was placed first on the action of voluntaryism, carefully controlled so as to reinforce the existing social system and

[1] By the 'sixties, very few Conservatives any longer believed in protection, which might have provided an alternative economic system and a base for social paternalism.

[2] It may be that, as Asa Briggs contends (*The Age of Improvement*, p. 439), political economy was becoming more flexible and empirical in the 'fifties and 'sixties. But its fundamental ideas were undergoing little development, and the popular notion of its teachings did not change much (see S. G. Checkland, 'Economic Opinion in England as Jevons Found It', *The Manchester School of Economic and Social Studies*, xix (1951), 143–69). It is doubtful how many of his fellow Conservatives would have endorsed J. G. Hubbard's statement, in March 1867, that 'Political economy in its true sense, and properly understood, could not discourage any object from being carried out concerning the welfare of the people' (*3 Hansard*, clxxxvi. 694).

avoid interference with its competitive mechanics.[1] Only secondarily might the state be called upon, to supplement and aid—but never, except in extreme cases, supplant—individual and voluntary efforts.

The Conservative party of 1866 was, in fact, predisposed against rather than towards the extension of governmental intervention in social questions. It would be hard to say that its general ideas on the subject differed much from those of its opponents: certainly there was no obvious division between individualism and political economy on the one side and paternalism on the other.[2] Conservatives were somewhat less dogmatic than many Liberals in their suspicion of state action—they had few Henry Fawcetts and Robert Lowes—and were sometimes quicker to understand that without such action the shibboleths of 'free trade' and 'freedom of contract' might produce a mockery of justice.[3] Their approach was perhaps more empirical, their readiness to employ the force of government in cases where the need for it could be convincingly demonstrated was perhaps more pronounced. That is all that can be said.

Though constantly debated in general terms, the problem of the proper rôle of government and legislation in economic and social affairs was, of course, in the end, one of particular cases, and Conservative attitudes were shaped less by general ideas than by the relation of given problems to the interests which the party represented, the experience it embodied, and the prejudices it harboured. The party of the mid-'sixties inevitably looked at social questions primarily in the context of the rural and agricultural world with which it was so intimately linked. The Conservative reaction towards proposals of social reform was determined very largely by their prospective impact in the countryside. Sometimes this enlarged the party's capacity to support social reform: in particular it could relatively easily back measures for the regulation of urban labour, by which rural interests were scarcely affected. But more often the effect was cramping. In the fields of education, public health, and poor relief especially the party's

[1] See especially on this W. L. Burn, *The Age of Equipoise*, pp. 113–29.

[2] For some remarks on Liberal attitudes to social questions, see Vincent pp. 241–6.

[3] An example is Northcote's approach to the Sunday trading question in 1855 (see Lang, i. 117–19). While a convinced free trader, Northcote rejected the contention that whether the poorer classes were to work on Sunday was 'a matter of private bargain', pointing out: 'Where there is a bargain there must be some kind of equality between those who bargain, and in this case there is not . . . Labourers and persons in the employ of others have no real freedom in these matters.' Mill, he noted, allowed that in these instances the interference of law was required, 'not to overrule the judgment of individuals respecting their own interest, but to give effect to that judgment, they being unable to give effect to it except by concert, which cannot be effectual unless it receives validity and sanction from law.'

bucolic preoccupations severely restricted its approach. Projects of improvement in all these spheres were frequently associated with the advance of centralisation and the increase of rates which the landed interest detested; in education, too, the position of squire and parson and the supply of juvenile agricultural labour were very much at stake.

The rating issue was so important as to deserve special mention, for it probably did as much to shape Conservative attitudes towards social improvement as any other factor. By 1866 the local taxation question was the major grievance of the landed interest, and the creation in that year of the Central Chamber of Agriculture gave its discontent a new focus of organisation.[1] The agriculturalists resented not merely the level of the rates but their allegedly unfair incidence (they fell on real property alone) and the fact that they went largely to meet expenditure imposed by the central government for not strictly local objects. They differed as to what should be done—the establishment of representative county boards to control expenditure, government grants in aid, and the rating of personal property were the main proposals—but pending reform they were united in hostility to all measures threatening to increase rate burdens. Most of their parliamentary advocates were Conservatives. Disraeli had deliberately, in 1849–50, directed the party's attention to the local taxation question, in order to divert the landed interest from the hopeless cause of protection, and by 1866 his followers' preoccupation with it was so strong as seriously to constrict their outlook when social questions involving the rates were discussed.

It is clear from a brief survey of its main characteristics that the general attitude of the Conservative party towards social problems was not such as to encourage (or even permit) the cultivation of working-class sympathies by an extensive programme of social reforms. But there was no reason why, under the stimulus of political necessity, the party should not do something in the field of social improvement to recommend itself to working-class opinion. The question was how far cautious social measures would be adequate to advance the party's position with the working classes. The more independent and intelligent working men were pursuing not merely material betterment but higher social status, symbolised in 1866 by the franchise, which was desired partly as a means to securing material ends, but very largely as a token of acceptance into the national political community. The Conservatives would have to do something

[1] On the issue in general, see Hanham, pp. 36–8, and for the Central Chamber of Agriculture and local taxation, A. H. H. Matthews, *Fifty Years of Agricultural Politics, being the History of the Central Chamber of Agriculture, 1865–1915*, cc. iii–iv.

to satisfy this demand if they were to make serious inroads on working-class favour.

Some of them did grasp the importance of the working-class desire for status. In 1853, writing to Disraeli about the Lancashire strikes, Stanley had noted that what the operatives wanted was 'social emancipation—a higher position—not merely increased pay'.[1] Shaftesbury said during the Reform debates of 1867:

> It has occurred to me for a long time, and I am certain it is true, that we have in a great measure outgrown our institutions. There is an expansive force among the people. The advance of wealth, the increase of education, the capacity, or at least the ambition, that every man now feels to occupy a higher station than that in which he has been placed by Providence—all these things tend to make men dissatisfied with the institutions of the country, because they fancy themselves cribbed, cabined, and confined by the restrictions which these institutions impose.[2]

But it was very doubtful how far the Conservative party could come to terms with the 'expansive force among the people'. To too many of its members the 'masses' were still a separate, inferior, and dangerous species, to be kept at bay. Working-class aspirations were regarded less with sympathy than with apprehension. This was especially true of the demand for the extension of the franchise. Many Conservatives interpreted the knocking at the gates of the constitution not as a request for admission but as the prelude to a sack, and Shaftesbury and the acid Cranborne were agreed in feeling that the coming of 'Democracy' would mean the end of liberty and the spoliation of property by indigence. In such a climate of fear and mistrust a real *rapprochement* between the Conservative party and the masses was bound to be difficult of achievement. The palliatives of social reform alone would not be enough. But such as they were, the party could not afford to neglect them in the effort to escape from its twenty-year minority and refound its power on a wide and lasting basis.

[1] Stanley to Disraeli, 28 Nov. 1853, cited above, p. 22, n. 1.

[2] *3 Hansard*, clxxxviii. 1926.

I

'SAFE LEGISLATIVE PROGRESS'

1866-7

THE need to cultivate working-class support was not absent from the minds of the Conservative leaders as Lord Derby embarked upon his third administration. Despite their preoccupation with the prospect of consolidating the conservatism of the country and rebuilding the fortunes of the party on an alliance with the Palmerstonian middle class, they recognised that if the Reform agitation was to be resisted, and even more if some measure of Reform was to be carried, it would be prudent to take steps to conciliate those who would be dangerously frustrated in the first case or invested with a significant share of electoral power in the second. The working men could not be ignored, least of all by a minority government which needed friends wherever they could be found. For their present stability and future profit, Derby and his colleagues had to show themselves careful of the interests of the working classes. The pursuit of social improvement provided them with their readiest means.

The new cabinet might have contained the foremost name of all in the sphere of social reform. The attempt to persuade Shaftesbury to take office illustrates both the anxiety of the Conservative leaders to appeal to the Palmerstonian bourgeoisie and their sense of the need to commend the new government to the working classes. Disraeli suggested Shaftesbury for the ministry as 'a representative of Palmerstonian sympathies and influences; powerful with the religious middle class, etc., etc.', and as one who might bring with him the Whig Lansdowne.[1] But it was not only these considerations which induced Derby to offer the sixty-five-year-old reformer the Duchy of Lancaster and a cabinet seat.

> I pressed upon him [he wrote] that his adhesion to the Government would be the best answer to the allegation that the Conservative Party was indifferent to the case of the 'Working Man'.[2]

[1] Disraeli to Derby, 27 June 1866, in M. & B., iv. 442.

[2] Derby to General Grey, 29 June 1866, in *The Letters of Queen Victoria*, 2nd series, ed. G. E. Buckle, i. 349.

Shaftesbury, however, while agreeing with Derby 'in the necessity of opposing an obstacle to the unchecked progress of the democratic principle',[1] declined to act as surety for the ministry's good intentions towards the working classes. Office, he believed, would seriously interrupt his labours on behalf of the people, and neither the suggestion that he need not perform cabinet duties, nor the bait of the Home Office (where he would have had charge of that extension of factory legislation which was his major current concern), or the Presidency of the Council (which would have given him the oversight of education), could move him from this position.[2] He did his best, in the government's first months, to put it right with the working classes,[3] but preferred to pursue his life's work of social amelioration from outside its ranks.

Shaftesbury would certainly have added much to the new ministry's fund of acquaintance with the problems of the urban masses. The cabinet which Derby formed was not remarkable for its grasp of conditions and needs in the great centres of industry and population. Its composition in some ways reflected the slenderness of the party's contact with those centres, and the extent of its dependence on the shires and small boroughs of the rural and agricultural south and east. Among its fifteen members, perhaps only Derby himself and his heir, Stanley, as territorial and political magnates in Lancashire, could claim, in 1866, intimate current connection with the manufacturing regions of the north and midlands.[4] Few of the cabinet had ever contested seats in the great industrial areas, and only two, Derby, who had sat for Preston in 1826–30, and Northcote, who had represented Dudley in 1855–7, had actually held such a seat. Of the twenty-eight constituencies for which the members of the cabinet were sitting or had once sat, two were Irish, and the rest, all English, comprised, besides Preston and Dudley, one large provincial town (Norwich), two universities, four counties or divisions of counties,

[1] *Ibid.*

[2] *Ibid.*; Hodder, iii. 211–12; Shaftesbury to Baxter, 2 July 1866 (Disraeli Papers, B/XXI/B/183a).

[3] See his diary entry, 9 Aug. 1866, in Hodder, iii. 214. One proposal he urged on ministers after the Reform riots of 23–25 July was the provision of halls for public assembly and discussion in London, which he thought would furnish safety-valves for the expression of popular feeling and check talk about '"Conservative" dislike etc., etc. of popular gatherings, and free speech'. Derby and Disraeli both favoured the idea. *3 Hansard*, clxxxiv. 1588–92; Shaftesbury to Disraeli, 22 Oct. and 23 Nov. 1866, 12 and 19 Jan. 1867 (Disraeli Papers, B/XXI/S/127, 129–30, 133, and see also 127a and 131); Disraeli to Queen Victoria, 27 July 1866, in M. & B., iv. 450.

[4] The Yorkshireman Gathorne Hardy and the Lancastrian General Peel (brother of Sir Robert Peel) retained only limited contact with their counties of origin.

and seventeen small boroughs and middling provincial towns of the type of Stamford or Shrewsbury.[1] Moreover, of the twenty-six English constituencies in this list, seventeen lay south and east of a line drawn from Gloucester to Boston; that is, lay in southern England, East Anglia, and the southern extremities of the midlands.[2] For most of the new cabinet, the England they knew and cared for best was rural and southern England; the problems and needs of the urban north and midlands lay largely outside their habitual experience and interest, and the Manchester or Birmingham artisan seemed almost a figure from another world. Nor had their previous ministerial endeavours done much to deepen their acquaintance with the social questions which that other world displayed at their most intense. Though fourteen had held office before, their experience had almost all been gained in the brief administrations of 1852 and 1858–9—a mere twenty-six months in the last twenty years—and only three had filled posts which involved direct contact with the social problems most vital to the condition of the people.[3]

Yet at least seven of Derby's cabinet colleagues could be credited with having shown an active interest in questions touching the welfare of the labouring classes. Most prominent, of course, was the ministry's second-in-command and leader in the House of Commons, Disraeli; and if, by 1866, his early professions of social concern seemed submerged beneath other considerations, Lord Shaftesbury still found him 'as I always found him in House of Commons, decided and true to the cause'.[4] With Disraeli were his friend of Young England days, Manners, his erstwhile political pupil, Stanley, and his protégé, Northcote—all men who had supported social improvement. There was Pakington, too, the champion of educational advance; Viscount Cranborne, heir to the marquisate of Salisbury, resident Cassandra of the *Quarterly Review*, the cleverest and most virulent anti-democrat in the party but a man who had interested himself in the problems of education and poor relief and (as Lord Robert Cecil) had backed factory reform in the 'fifties; and the young Earl of Carnarvon, concerned with education and penal

[1] The ten constituencies for which cabinet members were sitting in July 1866 included Oxford and Cambridge Universities, three county divisions (Bucks., N. Devon, N. Leics.), and five small boroughs (Cockermouth, Droitwich, Huntingdon, King's Lynn, and Stamford—all but King's Lynn having under 10,000 inhabitants).

[2] Of the ten constituencies represented by cabinet members in July 1866, seven lay south and east of this line.

[3] These were Walpole, Home Secretary in 1852 and 1858–9; Manners, President of the Board of Health in 1852; and Hardy, Under-Secretary at the Home Office in 1858–9.

[4] Shaftesbury's diary, 9 Aug. 1866, in Hodder, iii. 214.

reform,[1] and currently engaged, with Cranborne, in campaigning for the better treatment of London's sick paupers.[2] The list, indeed, includes almost every leading Conservative seriously interested in social reform: perhaps the sole omission was Adderley, who does not seem to have been considered of cabinet quality. Even if Manners was a charming lightweight, and Pakington's enthusiasms were apt to annoy his colleagues, the combined force of these men was considerable, and their presence in the cabinet suggested that it would not be unmindful of, or incapable of handling, social questions.

They did not, however, hold the offices which were most directly concerned with social questions. Disraeli, as in 1852 and 1858–9, figured incongruously at the Exchequer. Stanley had the Foreign Office, Cranborne India, Carnarvon the colonies, Pakington the Admiralty, and Manners, for the third time, the Office of Works, where he was able to pursue the ideals of Young England by upholding the Gothic style. Only Northcote was departmentally involved in problems of a social character, at the Board of Trade, where the safety and welfare of the merchant seaman were a growing preoccupation. He was an obvious choice for the Board: he had been Gladstone's private secretary during the latter's years there under Peel, had worked there as a legal assistant, publishing a review of the navigation laws in 1849, and had sat on the Commission which reported on the reorganisation of the Board in 1853.

The cabinet posts involving the greatest responsibility for social matters went to men with no special record of interest and activity in these fields, a fact which suggests that Derby, while aware of the importance of social questions, was not minded to attack them with particular vigour. The Presidency of the Council, which carried the oversight of education and public health, was given to Disraeli's old friend the Duke of Buckingham and Chandos. The Home Office, which dealt with the vital subject of labour legislation, and also, through its Local Government Act Office, had certain public health responsibilities, seems to have been intended first for Gathorne Hardy[3] and then for the seventy-three-year-old doyen of the country gentlemen, Henley, but was finally assigned, as in Derby's previous ministries, to the kindly, colourless lawyer, Spencer Walpole, who immediately incurred severe criticism by his weak handling of the Reform

[1] See Sir A. Hardinge, *The Life of Henry Howard Molyneux Herbert Fourth Earl of Carnarvon 1831–1890*, ed. Elisabeth Countess of Carnarvon, i. c. ix and pp. 371–9; also pp. 102–4, for Carnarvon's interest in the condition of the coal whippers.

[2] For this issue, see below, pp. 58–63.

[3] See Hardy's diary, 3 July 1866, in *Gathorne Hardy First Earl of Cranbrook: a Memoir*, ed. A. E. Gathorne-Hardy, i. 189.

riots of 23–25 July, and never really recovered from the fiasco.[1] Hardy, the Yorkshire barrister turned Kentish country gentleman, whose power of debate and defeat of Gladstone in the Oxford University election of 1865 had marked him for advancement, was given the Poor Law Board, an office which, in view of the current outcry over the treatment of sick paupers and the generally high level of public concern about the burden of poor relief, seemed to Derby 'likely to occupy a more than ordinary share of attention in the coming year',[2] and where he was accordingly anxious to have a capable man. Nearly twenty years before, as a young man fighting Bradford, Hardy had taken a progressive line on social issues,[3] and his first parliamentary speech was on a factory bill. He had tried to legislate for the control of beerhouses in 1856 and 1857,[4] and had encountered social problems from a ministerial desk as Under-Secretary at the Home Office in 1858–9. But by 1866 he could scarcely be classed among those with a strong concern for the condition of the people, or a special interest in social matters.

Outside the cabinet, too, the ministerial posts most concerned with social questions were given to men with no particular interests in this field. The Vice-Presidency of the Committee of Council on Education (whose holder was virtually the education minister) might, indeed, have gone to Adderley, as in 1858–9: it was offered to him and accepted by him, but through a blunder Derby had simultaneously offered it to Henry Corry,[5] and it was Corry who finally took it. Adderley would not have brought great distinction to the office—given the Colonial Under-Secretaryship instead, he soon caused his chief, Carnarvon, to complain of his 'incurable inaccuracy & confusion of mind'[6]—but he did possess a concern for educational matters hardly visible in Corry, the sixty-three-year-old member for Tyrone, whose previous ministerial experience had been at the Admiralty. The Corrys were ubiquitous at this moment: Henry's nephew, the young Earl of Belmore, became Under-Secretary at the Home Office, while his son, Montagu, settled into the post of Disraeli's private secretary. Montagu Corry, in his strategic position, was to

[1] Hardy noted in his diary on 29 July 1866 that Walpole, in cabinet, 'was not decisive & seemed confused but he is overworked in all ways'; and on 24 August that there was talk of his superseding Walpole at the Home Office (as happened the following May). Cranbrook Papers, T501/294.

[2] Derby to Hardy, 2 July 1866, in *Gathorne Hardy*, i. 190.

[3] See above, p. 21.

[4] *Gathorne Hardy*, i. 108–9.

[5] Northcote's diary, 4 July 1866 (typescript copy): Add. MS. 50063A, f. 94.

[6] Carnarvon to Derby, 7 Jan. 1867 (copy, endorsed 'never sent'): Public Record Office, P.R.O. 30/6/139 (Carnarvon Papers), ff. 196–8. Cf. same to same, 22 Feb. 1867: *ibid.*, ff. 224–5.

prove not the least influential member of the Conservative party, and, as befitted the nephew of Lord Shaftesbury, not the most backward in the cause of social improvement.[1] His chance came through the desire of Disraeli's erstwhile secretary, the young, clever and faintly *louche* Ralph Earle, to have office as a reward for his varied services. Earle was given the parliamentary secretaryship to the Poor Law Board, an appointment scarcely welcome to his chief, Hardy, who regarded him contemptuously as Disraeli's 'jackall'.[2] The remaining minor post where social problems were to some degree in question, the Vice-Presidency of the Board of Trade, went to the lawyer Stephen Cave, author of two books on the reformation of criminals,[3] but not an enthusiast for the welfare of the merchant seaman. Henry Corry, Belmore, Earle, and Cave were not men of high calibre, and their appointment emphasises the limitations of the talent at Derby's disposal.

All in all, the composition of the ministry suggested that social reform would be neither ignored nor prosecuted with special vigour and ability. The new government had, of course, no defined plans in the social field: there was no policy or programme to announce and implement. The prime minister, in his ministerial statement on 9 July, said nothing about social questions, except to indicate that the government would deal with the problem of the treatment of the pauper sick, which was currently in the forefront of public attention.[4] What ministers would do in the way of social reform would depend upon the interplay of practical exigencies with their general ideas and prejudices. They would deal with what they found awaiting them on their departmental agenda; with what was too pressing to be safely avoided; with what inquiry and discussion had made ripe for treatment; with what seemed to promise political advantage. For the most part, their action would run along lines laid down in others' minds. None of them (except, perhaps, Pakington) could claim real expertise in social questions; their understanding of the issues was often less

[1] There is no evidence that he encouraged Disraeli in pursuing social reform (unless the notes of July 1875, quoted below, p. 203, are taken to represent his own ideas rather than his transcript of his master's), but he engaged in philanthropic work, and was active in the 'nineties in founding the Rowton Houses, a superior type of working men's hostel (Rowton being the title he took on his elevation to the peerage in 1880). See the *D.N.B.*, whence the chapter on Corry in Sir C. Petrie, *The Powers behind the Prime Ministers*, appears almost wholly to derive.

[2] Hardy's diary, 3 July 1866: Cranbrook Papers, T501/293. For Earle's curious and shady career, see G. B. Henderson, 'Ralph Anstruther Earle', *English Historical Review*, lviii (1943), 172–89.

[3] *Prevention and Reformation: the duty of the state, or of individuals?* (1856); *On the Distinctive Principles of Punishment and Reformation* (1857).

[4] *3 Hansard*, clxxxiv. 741.

than perfect.[1] Inevitably, they would rely largely on the advice of their civil servants: Lord Robert Montagu, who held office in 1867–8, was exaggerating a valid point when he wrote a few years later:

> chief clerks are now the real rulers of England, they have already a power too despotic. The ministers above them when first appointed are always ignorant of their subject, and trust to these chief clerks and so commit themselves, and are subsequently too vain to change.[2]

But this very lack of policy and expertise, this very dependence on specialist advice and outside opinion, if it limited ministers' reforming potential in one sense, increased it in another. Unburdened by too many rigid attitudes and precommitments, they could in most cases approach social problems empirically, basing action on practical needs rather than on preconceived ideas. Open to advice and persuasion, they could readily be induced to sanction the reforms which lay waiting for them in the administrative pipeline, or which the logic of the facts and the pressure of opinion seemed to demand. Much might be done under the title of that 'safe legislative progress' which Derby in his ministerial statement had endorsed.[3] If ministers had no positive intentions in the social sphere when they took office, they quickly began to formulate some. When the cabinet met on 10 August 1866, to consider future measures, a variety of social questions figured in its substantial programme. Walpole planned to deal with the extension of the factory acts and with mines; Buckingham with vaccination and the medical inspection of workhouses; Hardy with vagrancy and workhouses; and Northcote with the 'Commercial navy'.[4] A few days later, Hardy recorded in his diary:[5]

> a Cabinet as to future measures for which if we have time we must be in for some years! Such reformers of departments & general law never met. Who can call us obstructive.

The new government did not intend to give cause for jibes about Tory obscurantism, and it did not intend, in particular, to neglect those measures which could best act as an earnest of its goodwill towards the working classes. The session of 1867 is remembered for

[1] This was common enough in the mid-nineteenth century. The Liberal Clarke Jervoise retailed to the Commons in 1868 a former minister's remark that 'if we only legislated on what we understand there would be no legislation at all'. *3 Hansard*, cxci. 2006.

[2] Paper by Lord R. Montagu, 28 April 1870, on 'Watershed Boards or Conservancy Boards for River Basins': Sanitary Commission of 1869, 2nd report, vol. ii, p. 345 (*P.P.* 1871, xxxv. 539).

[3] Above, p. 29.

[4] 'Secret Mem. of cabinet business agreed on 10. Aug. 1866', drawn up by Carnarvon: P.R.O. 30/6/169, ff. 26–7.

[5] 14 Aug. 1866: Cranbrook Papers, T501/294.

the passage of the second Reform Act; but even while they carried the heavy burden of electoral reform, ministers still contrived to give legislative expression to that social reform on which their chance of winning the votes they were creating seemed in part to depend.

No field offered better opportunities to a government anxious to win working-class confidence than that of labour questions. The advantage of refurbishing the tradition of Tory paternalism established in the 'thirties and 'forties was obvious, and Derby had been hardly a fortnight in office before he was assuring Shaftesbury that the ministry would press on with the extension of the factory acts promised by their predecessors.[1] Walpole, at the end of July, envisaged also a bill on mines,[2] and both subjects figured in the cabinet deliberations of 10 August. A third matter was brought forward by Manners, when he wrote to Disraeli on the political situation in Scotland in October:

> The movement among the working classes in some of the large towns makes me anxious that we should endeavour to improve the law of master & servant in the direction indicated in a memorandum I gave Walpole in the summer.
>
> The Select Committee has since then reported, and recommended a change in the law.
>
> To that, and the extension of the Factories Acts we must look for putting us right with the Working Classes.[3]

No doubt the government could hardly have avoided these topics —inquiry and discussion had led the public to expect action on factories and mines, and the master and servant question was the focus of a considerable working-class agitation—but, as Manners's words indicate, it was motivated as much by policy as by necessity in giving attention to them. They were apt subjects for the kind of cautious reform which, it was hoped, would secure the gratitude of working men and act as an anodyne for the denial of the franchise—if it was to be denied. In the eyes of the organised working-class movement, however, their importance was quickly overshadowed by the crisis in the affairs of the trade unions, the appearance of which at the end of 1866 and the beginning of 1867 provided an acid test of the ministry's capacity and will to come to terms with the advance of labour.

The growing strength of trade unionism, and the threat which this seemed to convey to the established economic and social order, were

[1] *3 Hansard*, clxxxiv. 781–2.

[2] *Ibid.*, clxxxiv. 1762.

[3] Manners to Disraeli, 24 Oct. 1866: Disraeli Papers, B/XX/M/138. For the master and servant question, see below, pp. 47–8.

causing much concern in upper- and middle-class circles by 1866. Fear of the power of organised labour found vent in a hostility to the unions which was rationalised by reference to their transgression of the principles of economic science, and invested with moral content through the reprobation of the 'terrorism' which some of their members were alleged to practise against those who would not join them. This hostility received a considerable impetus and an apparent justification in 1866 as a result of the 'Sheffield outrages'—a well-publicised series of acts of violence and intimidation by unionists against non-unionists, which culminated in October in the blowing up of a workman's house. There were calls for the suppression of trade unions, and strong demands for searching inquiry into their practices, demands supported by the unionists themselves, who were anxious to demonstrate how untypical the Sheffield incidents were. At the end of 1866 the whole position of the unions in the community hung in the balance, and it became even more precarious in the new year, when the decision of the courts in the case of *Hornby v. Close* jeopardised the very existence of unions. The status of the trade union in law was a question of much difficulty.[1] In practice, unions were liable to be regarded as bodies acting in illegal restraint of trade, and even as criminal conspiracies. They had attempted to secure some kind of legal status and protection under the Friendly Societies Act of 1855, but the decision in *Hornby v. Close*, in January 1867, in effect deprived them of their claim to the benefit of this measure, and left them virtually outside the law, without even the means of protecting their property against their own officials and members. Unless their legal position could be regularised, their effective conduct might prove impossible.

The trade unions were the most prominent expression of working-class self-consciousness and the primary organ of working-class strivings towards not merely material betterment but a higher status within the national community. The ministry's willingness to help them secure their position would do more than factory legislation or even a revision of the law of master and servant to influence the attitude of organised urban labour towards it. But there was no mistaking the hostility of the Conservative party to the unions. The rooted assumption that labour must always be subordinate to capital and to the dictates of the middle and upper classes made it virtually impossible for Conservatives to welcome the emergence of powerful organisations dedicated to the assertion of working-class independence and rights. Like many on the other side of politics, they seized avidly upon arguments which demonstrated that trade unions were

[1] See, on the legal position of trade unions before 1871, R. Y. Hedges and A. Winterbottom, *The Legal History of Trade Unionism*, c.v.

inimical to individual liberty and, since they ignored the economic laws which governed the rate of wages, incapable in the long run of benefiting their members. The vitriolic attack on trade unions which the *Quarterly Review* published in October 1867 was actually written by Robert Lowe, but it represents what a good many Conservatives felt:

> We say [Lowe wrote] that they [the unions] injure in the most vital manner the interests of the very working class whom they are meant to aid, that they threaten some branches of manufactures with extinction, and seriously limit the diffusion of others, that they are carried on by means fatal to every right that a free country respects, that they are ruinous to the legitimate ambition of industry and merit, that they can only be conducted by a systematic breach of the law, and that they run through the whole gamut of crime, from a mere conspiracy in restraint of trade, to robbery, arson, mutilation and murder.[1]

Given this kind of antipathy, it is not surprising that the ministry made no effort to help extricate the unions from the position in which they found themselves at the beginning of 1867. Its attitude was sufficiently expressed at the opening of the new session of Parliament by Earl Beauchamp, who felt that the 'baleful operations' of the unions were damaging the nation's industry and commerce and harming the interests of the artisans themselves.[2] What the government did was to meet the demand for an inquiry into trade unionism by setting up a Royal Commission. The members appointed included only one friend of the unions, the Christian Socialist Thomas Hughes, and union leaders pressed strongly for further representation of their interests. The government would not have a unionist on the Commission, but gave a seat to a second middle-class sympathiser, Frederic Harrison, and allowed union representatives to attend hearings.

Once the Commission was in being, it was inevitable that government and Parliament should shelve action on trade union questions until it could report, and the campaign mounted by the unionists on the morrow of *Hornby v. Close* for full legalisation of the unions and protection of their funds drew no response from ministers. It was not much helped by the fact that the political connections of its principal organ, the Conference of Amalgamated Trades, were entirely Liberal; or by the unsavoury revelations which the Royal Commission quickly produced in its investigation of the Sheffield outrages and similar events in Manchester, and which caused a new wave of feeling against

[1] *Quarterly Review*, cxxiii (1867), 378. The article is a classic exposition of the political economy arguments against unionism. Lowe would have made unions illegal, except in so far as they functioned as friendly societies.

[2] *3 Hansard*, clxxxv. 12; and cf. 21–3.

the unions, reflected in Lowe's *Quarterly* article. The government refused to accept a bill promoted by friendly Liberals to provide temporary legal protection for union funds pending the Commission's findings,[1] and gave unionists no reason to hope that it would deal with them in a generous spirit.

To conciliate organised labour by according the trade unions an assured place in British society was impossible for the Conservative party of 1867. A long evolution of opinion had to take place before Cross's labour laws could give Conservative sanction to union activity. Those Conservatives who acknowledged that the claims of the workers must be taken into consideration in industrial society did not want to see them asserted through unions and made the subject of conflict between opposed 'sides' in industry. If there was to be an alternative to straightforward paternalism in industrial relations, they sought it rather in arbitration. The idea of arbitration enjoyed a considerable vogue in the 'sixties, partly owing to the example of French practice. It was much canvassed in Parliament and was applied locally in the hosiery and building trades. In 1867 Lord St Leonards, who had been Lord Chancellor in Derby's first ministry, succeeded in carrying into law a bill backed by the moribund National Association of United Trades for the voluntary establishment of local courts of conciliation between masters and workmen. It had hardly any effect, but in default of action on the trade union question it constituted the only serious attempt made from the Conservative benches in 1867 to tackle the crucial problem of the conduct of industrial relations.[2]

Unwilling to deal with the largest issues, the government had to rely in its efforts to win approval in the field of labour questions on the topics it had been considering in the summer and autumn of 1866—factory acts extension, mines, and the law of master and servant, together with the condition of the merchant service. It defaulted on mines, and left the master and servant question to a private member, but it carried through an important factory measure, and made some attempt to improve the lot of the merchant seaman.

Because it directly affected not simply the material interests but the social status of the working man, the law of master and servant was fundamentally a more significant matter than the regulation of conditions of work in factories, mines, and ships, and it is hard to see

1 *Ibid.*, clxxxvi. 1448.

2 For this measure, see G. Howell, *Labour Legislation, Labour Movements and Labour Leaders*, pp. 154–5, 437–8. Though the Conciliation Act remained virtually a dead letter, the Webbs note (*History of Trade Unionism*, 2nd ed., pp. 337–8) a marked growth of conciliation and arbitration in industry between 1867 and 1875.

why the government did not follow Manners's advice and deal with the problem itself. The objection to the law was that it was really an anachronistic remnant of the old penal labour laws, designed to secure the subjection of the workers. An employee who broke his contract of service with his master was guilty of a criminal offence, and liable to arrest and imprisonment with hard labour; but a master breaking such a contract was liable to much less stringent procedures and penalties, and only with difficulty could an employee hope to secure redress against him. The law could be used by masters to attack trade unionism and break strikes, and was often applied repressively by the magistrates.[1] Since 1863 it had been the target of a powerful working-class agitation; the need for amendment had been quickly admitted, and a Select Committee had been set up. The Committee's report[2] appeared at the end of July 1866, recommending the relaxation of the law. It hardly satisfied the leaders of the agitation, but they were persuaded to compromise by their parliamentary spokesman, the old Peelite and Adullamite Whig Lord Elcho, who had been chairman of the Committee; and it was Elcho who, in 1867, with the government's support, carried a bill removing the penalty of imprisonment for breaches of contract by employees, except in 'aggravated' cases, while retaining the criminal character of the offence.[3]

Elcho had asked the government to legislate before taking the initiative himself,[4] and it is curious that ministers (one of whom, Hardy, had sat on the Select Committee) should have let slip the chance of gaining credit for a measure which Disraeli, addressing the working men of Edinburgh in October, singled out for praise:

> In my opinion a more beneficial law, and one which more sensibly improves the condition of the great body of the people, was never introduced and passed through Parliament . . .[5]

The explanation may lie partly in the feebleness of the responsible minister, Walpole, who by May 1867 was altogether broken down,

[1] For the whole question to 1867, see especially Daphne Simon, 'Master and Servant', in *Democracy and the Labour Movement*, ed. J. Saville, pp. 160–87; S. and B. Webb, *History of Trade Unionism*, 2nd ed., pp. 249–53. The law was freely used: between 1857 and 1867 there were on average 9,900 proceedings per year in master and servant cases in England and Wales.

[2] *P.P.* 1866, xiii, 1.

[3] A Conservative backbencher, A. Egerton, was one of the bill's sponsors.

[4] On 1 March 1867. Walpole replied that he would bring in a measure if possible. *3 Hansard*, clxxxv. 1259–60, 1261–2.

[5] *The Chancellor of the Exchequer in Scotland, being two speeches delivered by him in the city of Edinburgh on 29th and 30th October 1867*, p. 36. Disraeli no doubt exaggerated the act's effect: after 1867 the number of proceedings and convictions in master and servant cases in England and Wales fell only slightly, though, of course, prison sentences fell off sharply (Simon, p. 186).

and was replaced at the Home Office by Hardy,[1] but too late to affect the course of the session's legislation; and partly in the overwhelming demands of the Reform Bill on the government's time and energies. The same factors perhaps account for the failure to deal with mines. A bad run of mine accidents in 1866 had underlined the need for intervention to promote safety and better working conditions, and Walpole had the advantage of the work done by the Royal Commission on metalliferous mines which had reported in 1864, and by Russell's government, which had been preparing a measure. But while intimating that he would consider legislation,[2] the Home Secretary does not seem to have got beyond preliminary work.

What Walpole did do before leaving the Home Office was to introduce an important extension of the factory acts. The Factory Acts Extension Bill and the Hours of Labour Regulation Bill of 1867 represented the ministry's main action in the field of labour questions, but they were far from being its own work. They derived from the recommendations of the Children's Employment Commission, set up in 1862, largely at Shaftesbury's instigation, to inquire into the extension of the factory acts to women and children in trades hitherto unregulated. The Commission's first report had led to the Factory Acts Extension Act of 1864; by June 1866 it had produced four more reports,[3] calling for further extension of the factory acts to a wide range of trades and for the regulation of small establishments not classed as factories. Russell's government was preparing to legislate when it fell.

There was every incentive for the Conservatives to carry on with the measures they found in process of formulation at the Home Office, and take an uncontroversial opportunity of increasing their credit with the working class. The days of virulent combat over factory regulation had gone; its benefits to employers and employed were admitted even by its former opponents, and public opinion favoured its spread.[4] Of the two bills which Walpole brought in in March 1867, the Factory Acts Extension Bill applied the factory acts to a large number of scheduled trades and to any premises where 100 or more persons were employed in any manufacturing process, while the Hours of Labour Regulation Bill dealt with establishments (including private houses) which employed under 100 persons, forbidding the labour of children under eight, regulating the working

[1] Walpole remained in the cabinet for some time, without portfolio.

[2] See above, p. 44, and *3 Hansard*, clxxxvi. 407–8.

[3] For which see *P.P.* 1864, xxii. 1, 319; 1865, xx. 103; 1866, xxiv. 1.

[4] See Children's Employment Commission, 5th report, p. xxiii (*ibid.*, 1866, xxiv. 23); *Quarterly Review*, cxix (1866), 364–93—'The Children's Employment Commission'.

hours of older children and young persons, and providing for them a minimum of ten hours a week school attendance. The two measures, Walpole declared, would affect 1,400,000 women and children.[1]

There was no serious parliamentary opposition to the bills. The Liberal representatives of the manufacturing interest, far from resuming the postures of the 'forties, were, by 1867, ready to acknowledge the good the Conservative party had done them in the past by pressing factory legislation upon them.[2] Both measures were enthusiastically passed. Yet there was one major weakness in the government's work which drew criticism from Shaftesbury and others in Parliament, and from the operatives.[3] The responsibility of enforcing the Hours of Labour Regulation Bill was not entrusted to the factory inspectors but was laid upon local authorities. The senior inspector of factories, Redgrave, had told Walpole at least twice that this would mean an inefficient supervision of the very establishments where evasion of the regulations was most likely, and that it would be far better to accept the expense of providing additional Home Office inspectors.[4] He was right, and the neglect of his advice meant that what came to be known as the Workshops Regulation Act was very imperfectly enforced.[5]

In spite of their shortcomings, however, the measures of 1867 were a great step in the long process of extending the protection of the factory acts to all female and juvenile labour in industry, and they were an especial triumph for Shaftesbury, who had worked so assiduously for this outcome. They were also to prove very useful to the party which had the credit of passing them. It was not for nothing that Disraeli considered them important:[6] by reasserting the old connection between Toryism and factory reform they powerfully

[1] For Walpole's introductory speech, see *3 Hansard*, clxxxv. 1271–9; and on the bills, B. L. Hutchins and A. Harrison, *A History of Factory Legislation*, 3rd ed., pp. 165–72, and A. H. Robson, *The Education of Children Engaged in Industry in England 1833–1876*, pp. 199–202. The dividing line between larger and smaller establishments was lowered from 100 to 50 employees in Committee. Some of the main trades affected by the Factory Acts Extension Bill were metal working, printing, paper, glass, rubber and tobacco. The Hours of Labour Regulation Bill affected chiefly the clothing trades.

[2] See Akroyd's speech, *3 Hansard*, clxxxv. 1072, and *ibid.*, clxxxv. 1067, 1071, 1078.

[3] See *ibid.*, clxxxix. 1433–5, 1595–6, and for the views of both masters and men on the bills, the petitions, memorials, etc. in H.O. 45/O.S. 7886 (which include a letter of support to Walpole from Jesse Collings).

[4] Memoranda by Redgrave, the first undated but probably June–July 1866, the second 16 March 1867 (*ibid.*, nos. 1, 29). He correctly envisaged that the inadequacy of local authority control would in time cause the extension of the factory acts to the smaller establishments.

[5] See Hutchins and Harrison, 3rd ed., pp. 225–30; Robson, pp. 208–9.

[6] See Hardy to Disraeli, 24 July 1867: Disraeli Papers, B/XX/Ha/9.

aided the efforts of Conservatives to represent themselves as the friends of the working classes.

Admittedly, the factories and workshops acts emphasised that it was primarily the urban working classes whom Conservatives were ready to befriend by legislation. In the countryside, where the interests which it incorporated were most directly affected, the party showed less willingness to take legislative action to improve conditions of labour. Its members would no doubt have argued that the paternalism which the landed interest claimed to practise largely removed the need for measures in Parliament; and the position of the agricultural worker was tending to improve at this period, as the shortage of labour which had been growing since the 'fifties strengthened his bargaining power and forced the employing classes to pay more attention to his welfare.[1] Nonetheless, it was difficult to deny that some of the worst examples of bad labour conditions were to be found in the rural areas. Walpole acknowledged the case for some regulation of agricultural labour comparable to that imposed on industry when he said, in February 1867, that he had concluded that some of the principles of the factory acts would have to be extended to agricultural districts (he did not specify in what form).[2] Such a notion, however, was hardly welcome to a party based on land; and since there was no question of giving the rural labourer the vote, there was little incentive to take up the improvement of his condition for political purposes.

Agricultural labour would probably have attracted little parliamentary attention in 1867, had it not been for the sixth report of the Children's Employment Commission,[3] which, having concluded its inquiries into manufactures, had now turned its attention to agriculture, and in particular to agricultural gangs. These gangs, through which a good deal of agricultural labour was supplied, were of two types: public gangs, moving round the countryside and working for whomever cared to hire them, and private gangs, maintained by individual employers. The Commission's report dealt with the employment of women and children in the public gangs, and its revelations of the harsh and degrading conditions which obtained brought a strong public reaction. The *Quarterly* echoed the general feeling in calling for the intervention of the state as 'protector of those who are

[1] E. L. Jones, 'The Agricultural Labour Market in England, 1793–1872', *Economic History Review*, 2nd series, xvii (1964–5), 330ff. Labourers' wages began to rise steeply from the mid-'sixties.

[2] *3 Hansard*, clxxxv. 1085. He was speaking on a motion for the extension of the educational clauses of the factory acts to children employed in agriculture, on which see below, pp. 84–5.

[3] *P.P.* 1867, xvi. 67.

unable to protect themselves',[1] and both Liberal and Conservative members of Parliament demanded legislation. Even C. S. Read, the spokesman on the Conservative benches of the farmers, who employed the gangs, accepted the need for regulation and for the exclusion from the gangs of young children.[2] Walpole wanted to delay action until the Commission had investigated the private gangs,[3] but the government's hand was forced by Shaftesbury's impatient introduction of a bill covering the whole field of the employment of women and children in agriculture, and August 1867 saw the passage of an act compelling gangmasters to be licensed, prohibiting mixed gangs, and forbidding the employment of children under eight.[4] This measure, imposed by public opinion, marked the limit of the ministry's immediate readiness to interfere with agricultural labour. The Commission had indicated that it was not merely gang-work that required regulation: in particular, young children employed in agriculture outside the gangs needed protection.[5] But ministers, in spite of Walpole's words in February, were not minded to attempt to impose any general legislative restrictions upon agricultural employment.

One section of the working class that was neither urban nor rural attracted a good deal of ministerial attention in 1866–7. The merchant seamen in the eighteen-sixties were undoubtedly among the worst-used and most callously exploited members of the labouring population: their work was harder and more dangerous, and their pay, food, and accommodation were less adequate than those of almost any category of shore-based workers. The state of the merchant marine and the condition of the men who manned it were giving rise to growing concern when the government came into office. Russell's ministry had introduced a bill for the amendment of the Merchant Shipping Acts earlier in the year, and though this was now abandoned, the question was kept forward by the motion for a Royal Commission on the supply and quality of merchant seamen moved in July 1866 by the Conservative member for Liverpool, S. R. Graves. The

[1] *Quarterly Review*, cxxiii (1867), 189.

[2] *3 Hansard*, clxxxvi. 1019–21. For other Conservative views in favour of regulation, see *ibid.* clxxxvi. 1017–19, 1022–3, 1025.

[3] One of the Commissioners, Tremenheere, in a memo. of 18 March 1867 (in H.O. 45/O.S. 7950), had questioned whether it would be feasible to legislate for public gangs alone, or for private gangs without further inquiry.

[4] All these points were in the Commission's recommendations, together with limitation of the hours of children and young persons and provision for their education. Robson (pp. 175–6) attributes this act (the Agricultural Gangs Act) to Shaftesbury, confusing it with the latter's Agricultural Employment Bill, which did not pass.

[5] Report, p. xxiv.

establishment of training ships was Graves's remedy for the dearth of good seamen of which he complained, but it was evident to others that a substantial effort to improve the seaman's conditions of labour was the first necessity. Henley, President of the Board of Trade in Derby's previous ministries, having told the Commons roundly that 'no honest man aware of the whole circumstances of the case would send a boy to sea', insisted that 'it was not by training ships that men were to be got, but by giving these men such wages and prospects for their old age as would induce them to learn their business'.[1] Increasingly it was coming to be recognised that both the efficiency of the merchant service and common humanity demanded urgent attention to such matters as the seaman's pay, food, accommodation, and safety.

Effective reforms were not likely to be achieved without the action of government, but there was a strong current of opposition to the state's interference, which did not derive wholly from the self-interest of shipowners. Merchant shipping questions provided a classic case of the continuing confusion as to where the limits of governmental intervention in economic and social affairs should be set. Even those anxious for the improvement of the seaman's condition might, like Henley, oppose legislation on the subject on the ground that it 'would only aggravate the mischief by separating master and man'[2]—a version of the standard argument, heard so frequently in the 'sixties and 'seventies, that government regulation, by relieving the employer of the responsibility which ought properly to rest on him, tended to worsen the evils it was designed to cure. Nowhere were misgivings of this sort more vigorously represented than in the government department which dealt with shipping matters. The Board of Trade at this period was dominated by the forceful personality of its permanent secretary, Thomas Farrer, perhaps the most powerful civil servant of his day. Farrer was a dogmatic free-trader, and deeply distrusted state interference in economic affairs. He specialised in merchant shipping questions, and, abetted by the like-minded secretary of the Board's Marine Department, Gray, was a formidable obstacle to the extension of governmental responsibilities in this sphere.[3]

The new President of the Board of Trade, Northcote, both saw the need for action on behalf of the seaman and shared the doubts as to how far it might legitimately go. Though the cabinet of 10 August

[1] *3 Hansard*, clxxxiv. 960, 961. Graves's seconder, H. G. Liddell, also advocated better provision for merchant seamen in old age (*ibid.*, clxxxiv. 955).

[2] *Ibid.*, clxxxiv. 962. Henley even attacked the government shipping offices, which acted as employment exchanges in the ports, and were designed to protect the seaman from unfair terms of engagement.

[3] For Farrer, see the *D.N.B.* After leaving the Board of Trade in 1886, he took a forceful part in economic controversies, and made his presence felt on the London County Council as the chief enemy of that body's 'collectivism'.

1866 found him proposing to deal with the merchant navy, he was by no means clear at this stage as to what should be done. He was not overborne, as most politicians would have been, by Farrer's influence, for his personal experience of the Board went back even beyond the permanent secretary's, and the latter was, in any case, an old friend—the two had been intimates since Eton and Balliol, and Northcote had married Farrer's sister. At the same time, he was not far from agreeing with Farrer's attitude. He too was a lifelong free-trader,[1] and inclined to place narrow limits on the intervention of government in economic and social affairs. His thought was cast in classical liberal and Peelite moulds: believing implicitly that the conditions of economic life were determined by forces largely outside the reach of legislative control, he regarded attempts at state regulation with some scepticism.

Northcote's preconceptions forced him to place the merchant seaman in a different category from the factory women and children for whom Walpole was preparing to legislate. The latter could be protected by the state without violence to the tenets of political economy, because they were unable to protect themselves; but the seaman, as an adult male, was a free agent, and must look after his interests himself. This outlook emerged very clearly in the debate on Graves's motion in July.

> Nothing [Northcote declared][2] can be more important than that the comfort and the proper treatment of the seamen should in every possible way be provided for, but it would be undesirable to take out of the hands of the men the duty of looking out for themselves. All we ought to do is to give them the means of making their own bargain completely and fairly for themselves—to put them on a fair and equal footing with the shipowners, and then let them make their own bargains, and to adopt means to remove unfair and inconvenient restrictions.

The President was, however, too realistic a man to be unaware of the shortcomings of the attitude which his economic tenets drove him to adopt. It was all very well to provide a fair field and no favour, and to insist that the seaman ought to look after himself. But could he, in practice, look after himself? Was it feasible to place him 'on a fair and equal footing with the shipowners'? Northcote knew that liberty for poor and ignorant men to make their own bargains might mean little more than liberty for them to be cheated and oppressed: he defended an existing instance of governmental interference, the shipping offices, precisely on the ground that 'the contract to be made between master and man is one in which it is often found that the

[1] He had supported the repeal of the Corn Laws even before Peel's conversion. Lang, i. 77.

[2] *3 Hansard*, clxxxiv. 970.

seaman is overreached and defrauded'.[1] The facts forced him to recognise that the improvement of the seaman's condition must depend to some extent on legislative regulation. But he wanted to keep that regulation within strict limits, and he did not abandon his stress on the responsibility of the men themselves. Replying, in December 1866, to a plea from Shaftesbury on behalf of the seamen, he emphasised the difficulties in the way of helping them, one of the greatest, perhaps, being 'the character of the Seaman himself'. It was useless, he said, to make laws and regulations if the seaman would not make efforts to secure their enforcement and look after his own interests. Already the law enabled seamen to have their victuals inspected, and required the provision of suitable crew accommodation.

> There is no doubt that if the Seamen would take pains to insist on their rights in these respects they would be far better lodged and fed than I am afraid they usually are. The question for us now to consider is how far we can and ought to interfere to do for them what they ought to do for themselves. It is not an easy one, but we are considering it as well as we can.[2]

They were, indeed, considering it as well as they could. In the latter half of 1866 and at the beginning of 1867 a clutch of proposals for the benefit of the seaman was under review at the Board of Trade. Some of them made little progress. The scheme of establishing a voluntary pension fund, though supported by Farrer,[3] was not pursued. Training ships failed to materialise, in spite of Northcote's strong backing for them—probably because there seemed to be no way round the objection that it was improper to use public money to help shipowners secure efficient labour.[4] The proposals which survived to become the focus of attention early in 1867, as the government prepared its legislation for the coming session, were concerned with the improvement of health on board ship (through the regulation of food, accommodation, and medicines and anti-scorbutics), and with the payment of the seaman's wages.

[1] *Ibid.*, clxxxiv. 966. Cf. his view on the Sunday trading question in 1855 (above, p. 34, n.3).

[2] Northcote to Shaftesbury, 4 Dec. 1866 (copy): Add. MS. 50046, f. 53.

[3] Minute of 15 Aug. 1866 on proposals submitted by a Captain Toynbee: in M.T. 9/26/M. 3049/66. A pension scheme had been under consideration for some time, and Toynbee asserted that the late President had approved it. The Board had already the machinery for such a scheme, and tables had been calculated.

[4] Northcote wanted to circumvent this argument by connecting the training ships with the strengthening of the navy, but Pakington and the Admiralty were apparently reluctant to give the support he requested. See Northcote to Pakington, 9 Nov. 1866 (copy): Add. MS. 50046, f. 37.

On wages no basis for legislation was found. The two main evils here were the advance note—used to give the sailor an advance on wages when signing on for a ship, and liable, because of the need to exchange it for goods and services, to lead to his being swindled by crimps—and the delay in payment of wages when a ship docked, a problem aggravated by the common disregard of the seaman's legal right to a quarter of his wages immediately upon discharge. In neither case did Farrer see a viable solution,[1] and as it became clear in the session of 1867 that pressure of business required the government's merchant shipping legislation to be curtailed, the wages question was dropped for the time being. It was the seaman's health that was to form the object of the measure of 1867.

'Of doubtful policy' had been Farrer's comment in August 1866 on proposals for the regulation of the seaman's accommodation and food,[2] and his doubts were re-emphasised in a memorandum dealing with these matters and with the provision of medicines and anti-scorbutics which was under discussion in January 1867.[3] The permanent secretary insisted vigorously that the right way to protect the seaman's health was less by 'minute so-called preventive measures, or Government Inspection', than by enforcing the shipowner's responsibility and making him liable for expenses and damages arising from sickness caused by his failure to provide proper food, accommodation, medicines, and anti-scorbutics.[4] He was ready for more stringent regulations for the supply and administration of anti-scorbutics, but he rejected the idea of a legal scale for provisions and water on the ground that 'The labourer's food is a matter of agreement & private choice', and while recommending an inquiry (at once carried out on Northcote's orders) into the provision of crew space, he was chary of trying to increase it by legislation, pointing out that 'The minimum of law has a tendency to become the maximum of practice.'

Even for Northcote this anti-interventionism was a little strong. The President could see the difficulty, in practice, of enforcing the liability of shipowners for sickness due to their default—it would be

[1] Memo. of 16 Feb. 1867: M.T. 9/32/M. 1453/67. In August Farrer had minuted on Toynbee's proposal to enforce the law requiring immediate part payment of wages: 'A matter for the Seaman' (minute cited above, p. 55, n. 3).

[2] *Ibid.*

[3] Memo. on 'Health and Disease on board Ship'; three copies in M.T. 9/31/M. 269/67, including one minuted by Northcote and Farrer. The paper is dated 8 Jan. *1866* (altered to 10 Jan. in one copy), but this seems to be a mistake for 1867. Certainly Northcote's and Farrer's minutes belong to 1867, for some are dated 'Jan.', and Northcote, of course, had not been at the Board in Jan. 1866.

[4] 'If the Shipowner finds', he wrote, 'that the neglect of proper and easy precautions renders him liable to heavy damages, he will find out the way to avoid the evil and take care to follow it.'

very hard for a seaman to prove that his illness had been caused by the owner's neglect—and he wondered whether more preventive action was not desirable. Especially was this so in regard to provisions: he agreed with Farrer that the government should not prescribe a scale, but was inclined to favour more inspection.

> There is [he pointed out] one distinction to be drawn between the Sailor and other labourers, viz.:—that he does not find out the bad quality of the provisions till it is too late to remonstrate. If I agree to allow a carter so much flour or so much cider, he can at any time remonstrate if I supply a bad article, there being plenty more to be got. But it is not so with a Sailor who discovers in mid-ocean that there is no good water on board.[1]

It was Northcote's common sense which ensured that the measure which the Board was forging came to contain a greater degree of governmental regulation than Farrer would apparently have wished.

In the cabinet reconstruction which followed the resignations of Cranborne, Carnarvon, and Peel over Reform, in March 1867, Northcote left the Board of Trade for the India Office, and was succeeded by the agricultural Duke of Richmond, who had been President of the Poor Law Board in 1859. It was thus the latter who carried the government's Merchant Shipping Bill, restricted in scope to health matters, but avowedly a prelude to a more extensive measure.[2] The bill incorporated Farrer's principle of making owners and masters liable for the expense of illness caused by lack of proper food and accommodation, but it also bore the mark of Northcote's readiness for greater direct control. Inspectors of provisions, medicines, and anti-scorbutics were to be appointed; the medical inspection of seamen was provided for; measures were taken to see that crew space was better lighted and ventilated, and free of ships' stores, and to make it subject to inspection; regulations were made to ensure the wholesomeness and proper serving-out of the principal anti-scorbutic, lime juice. At the last minute, Richmond even tried to extend the reach of the bill to the fundamental question of safety, by inserting a clause providing for the survey of ships alleged by seamen to be unseaworthy, but this had to be dropped in order to secure the bill's passage.[3] The measure was a small one, and of limited practical effect, but it was a significant step in the movement towards the pro-

[1] Minute on Farrer's memo.

[2] There are some papers on the bill, including a review of its proposed contents for Richmond's use, in the Goodwood Papers, box 16.

[3] As did a few other clauses, including that providing for inspectors of medicines.

tection of the seaman which was to command so much attention in the years ahead, and it illustrated the willingness of Conservative ministers to give, where need could be shown, a cautious and pragmatic assent to the extension of governmental interference and control for social ends.

The ministry's handling of labour questions in its first year of office demonstrates both the importance which it attached to them and the limitations on its capacity to turn them to profit. By its factories and workshops legislation, and even by its Merchant Shipping Act, it had reaffirmed the tradition of Tory paternalism, and shown its readiness to protect those who could be held to be not fully capable of protecting themselves. By supporting the Master and Servant Act, it had registered willingness to improve the legal and social status of the working man and free him from discriminatory treatment. But its legislative paternalism had seemed to falter before the fences which guarded its own terrain of the land, and it had displayed neither ability nor inclination to make terms with the unions, as emergent expressions of working-class power and aspirations. It remained to be seen whether a limited paternalism could be enough to convince the working man that the Conservatives were his best friends.

The most immediate of the social questions which confronted the ministry on its accession to office was that of the treatment of sick paupers in London's workhouses. The matter was peculiarly important in that it was bound up with the whole problem of the provision of medical care for the mass of the population, who could not pay for it themselves. Most poor people who fell ill were, in practice, dealt with by the medical services of the poor law, which came thus to incur an extensive responsibility for the nation's health. But poor law medical services tended, naturally, to be run more from a poor law than a medical point of view. Though the principle of 'less eligibility' (i.e., that the position of a pauper should always be less eligible than that of an independent labourer) was hardly applied to the sick,[1] they were, nonetheless, commonly crammed together with the other classes of pauper in the workhouse, under the general operation of the system of deterrence which the principles of 1834 had prescribed for the able-bodied; or else they had to depend on an outdoor medical relief which might or might not be adequate. This state of affairs attracted rising criticism in the early 'sixties, and though a Select Committee on poor relief, sitting in 1861–4, failed to recom-

[1] In respect of outdoor medical relief, especially, it had been virtually abandoned by the mid-'sixties. S. and B. Webb, *English Poor Law Policy*, pp. 117–18.

mend significant changes in regard to the sick,[1] public opinion was brought to see the need for action, at least in the capital, by a series of scandals over the treatment of the sick in London workhouses which ran from the end of 1864 to late 1866, and was the subject of an influential inquiry by the *Lancet* in 1865.

The reform agitation which grew up incorporated such elements as Florence Nightingale and the nursing reformers, the National Association for the Promotion of Social Science, a number of the poor law medical officers, and various politicians of both parties, including two leading younger Conservatives, Carnarvon and Cranborne. The latter were active in the foundation, in March 1866, of the Association for the Improvement of the Infirmaries of Workhouses, on whose executive committee they served, and whose members included the Archbishop of York, F. D. Maurice, Thomas Hughes, and Charles Dickens.[2] The main aim of the reformers was to get London's pauper sick out of the workhouses and into special institutions, detached from the cheeseparing control of the guardians, where they could receive proper attention. To this end, they urged the consolidation of the metropolitan workhouse infirmaries under a uniform management linked with the Poor Law Board, and their support by a general metropolitan rate; and by April 1866 their pressure had driven Villiers, Russell's President of the Poor Law Board, to contemplate legislation on these lines.[3] But two months later Villiers was out of office, and it was to the Conservatives that the reformers had now to turn.

The change of government occurred just at the moment when the defects in the treatment of the sick poor were being spotlighted afresh by the reports of two Poor Law Board inspectors, Farnall and Smith (the former a close collaborator of Florence Nightingale), which called for the improvement of accommodation, nursing, and medical care, and (in the case of Farnall's report) for the provision of special hospitals financed by a metropolitan rate.[4] With public opinion

[1] For the report of the Committee, whose members included Walpole and Cranborne (then Lord Robert Cecil), see *P.P.* 1864, ix. 187. It did recommend that more should be done towards separating the different classes of pauper in workhouses.

[2] On the reform movement up to 1866, see J. E. O'Neill, 'Finding a Policy for the Sick Poor', *Victorian Studies*, vii (1963–4), 268 ff.; B. Abel-Smith, *The Hospitals 1800–1948*, pp. 69–73; Sir E. Cook, *The Life of Florence Nightingale*, pt. VI, c. i; Hardinge, i. 217–20. There is some material on the work of the Association for the Improvement of the Infirmaries of Workhouses in the Carnarvon Papers (P.R.O. 30/6/169, ff. 223–46, 257–9).

[3] Cook, ii. 134.

[4] Report of H. B. Farnall to the Poor Law Board on the infirmary wards of the metropolitan workhouses, *P.P.* 1866, lxi. 389; report of Dr Edward Smith to the Poor Law Board on metropolitan workhouse infirmaries and sick wards,

roused, and Carnarvon and Cranborne in his cabinet, Derby did not need the interview with Farnall which Miss Nightingale arranged[1] to make him aware of the urgency of the question. He marked his sense of its importance by placing Gathorne Hardy at the Poor Law Board to deal with it, and by singling it out in his statement of 9 July as a matter for action.[2]

'These London workhouses', wrote Hardy in his diary on 13 July,[3] 'will be a wonderful trouble.' The reformers, their agitation now reinforced by no less a figure than Edwin Chadwick, were disappointed in the new President. Inevitably, he tended to listen first to the permanent officials of the Board, whose inertia the reformers had long attacked, and against whose influence Rogers, the President of the infant Workhouse Medical Officers Association, tried to caution him.[4] One of his first acts was to remove the reformers' main ally inside the Board, Farnall, from his post as poor law inspector for the metropolitan area and banish him to Yorkshire.[5] Hardy hoped initially that the shortcomings of the workhouse infirmaries could be remedied by using the existing powers of the Board to require adequate accommodation, nursing, and medical care, and by securing the co-operation of the guardians;[6] and he contented himself at the outset with issuing recommendations to the guardians and setting on foot further official inquiries, especially into the cubic space needed for pauper sick.[7]

Gradually, however, the study of the facts made Hardy realise that reliance on the Board's existing powers and on the better feeling of the guardians was not likely to be enough, and that legislation would

[1] Cook, ii. 134.

[2] Above, p. 42.

[3] Cranbrook Papers, T501/294.

[4] J. Rogers, *Reminiscences of a Workhouse Medical Officer*, ed. J. E. Thorold Rogers, p. 59.

[5] It was perhaps partly of Farnall that Hardy was thinking when he wrote in his diary on 21 July (Cranbrook Papers, T501/294): 'The pleasures of my office do not improve, as I am sure there are secret hostile agencies at work within it.' The diary makes it clear that he was having trouble with some of the permanent staff. Miss Nightingale apparently maintained covert contacts within the Board even after Farnall's removal (Cook, ii. 136–7).

[6] *3 Hansard*, clxxxiv. 939–41 (17 July).

[7] O'Neill, pp. 281–2; Abel-Smith, p. 76 (where Hardy appears as 'Hardy Gathorne'). Cranborne apparently contributed to the investigation of the space problem with a paper on hospital accommodation: see H. W. Acland to Cranborne, 2 Nov. 1866 (Salisbury Papers, S.C.).

---

ibid. 171. Both reports, together with the findings of an inquiry made into the London workhouses in 1866 by commissioners appointed by the *Lancet*, are summarised in Abel-Smith, pp. 50–64, 74–6. It is possible that Miss Nightingale wrote much of Farnall's report.

have to be forged. He set to work, leaning heavily on one of his poor law inspectors, John Lambert, and by November was able to put an acceptable draft measure before the cabinet—though it was strongly criticised by Carnarvon, who saw in it no adequate security against the repetition of the abuses which had made it necessary.[1] The Metropolitan Poor Bill was considered sufficiently important to be given a leading place in the government's programme for 1867, and was introduced on 8 February, only three days after the opening of the new session of Parliament.

It was a remarkable measure. Hardy's examination of the sick pauper question had led him to diagnose as the root of the trouble the application to the sick of a system intended to deter the able-bodied,[2] and he did not shrink from the logical remedy—the open abandonment, where the sick were concerned, of the deterrent principles of 1834. He had come, too, to understand how much of the problem was due to the incompetence, parsimony, and indifference of the local guardians, and to recognise the need to extend the power of the Poor Law Board at their expense. Sharing the prejudice of the age against the promotion of centralisation and the reduction of local self-government, he nonetheless faced facts:

> when gentlemen have come to me, as some of them have [he told the Commons][3], and expressed themselves in the highest terms of their own capacity, and of the ability with which they have administered the workhouses and infirmaries committed to their charge, and when at that very moment I had lying on my table reports which were directly the reverse, I am obliged to say that the system has failed under their management, and must be improved.

The bill proposed to remove children, lunatics and imbeciles, and fever and smallpox cases from the workhouses to special establishments, while the treatment of the sick remaining in workhouse infirmaries was to be improved under the close supervision of the Poor Law Board, which was given power to combine poor law districts, place nominees on boards of guardians, and appoint proper officers where guardians or managers refused to do so. The Board was further empowered to establish a system of dispensaries for outdoor medical relief. On the rating question, Hardy compromised. Besides the reformers' demand for a general metropolitan rate for the sick, there

[1] There is a copy of the draft bill (printed 6 Nov. 1866), and a list of objections in Carnarvon's hand, in P.R.O. 30/6/169, ff. 236–9, 246. Carnarvon disliked the bill's retention in power of the old incompetent guardians, and its transfer of powers of taxation from the ratepayers to the Poor Law Board. For Lambert's rôle in framing the bill, see *Gathorne Hardy*, i. 195.

[2] See his speech introducing the bill, in *3 Hansard*, clxxxv. 150–75.

[3] *Ibid.*, clxxxv. 772.

was a good deal of opinion which held that for the proper management of London's poor the richer parishes must be made to contribute to the burdens of the poorer through some such device as the equalisation of the metropolitan poor rate.[1] Hardy's parliamentary secretary, Earle, had urged that a new metropolitan rate administered by a new authority would be essential for the settlement of the sick pauper question,[2] though Earle's advocacy was scarcely a recommendation to the President, whose relations with his junior were not close.[3] In the event, while rejecting the equalisation of the metropolitan poor rate, Hardy did take a step towards it by placing part of the cost of the sick poor on a metropolitan common fund.

The state of public feeling on the workhouse question ensured the bill an easy passage. Its centralising tendency was hardly remarked: indeed, though a few Liberals attacked Hardy's proposals as a subversion of local self-government, the main criticisms came from reformist sympathisers (including Carnarvon) who felt that he had not gone far enough, and wanted full equalisation of the poor rate and greater simplicity and unity of management for the sick, with a central board for the whole Metropolis.[4] Still less was there serious opposition to the bill's radical development of public policy towards the sick poor. Grappling empirically with an urgent problem, neither Hardy nor Parliament realised the full meaning and implications of what they were doing. The Metropolitan Poor Act signalled the final freeing of the pauper sick from the last vestiges of the old poor-law principle of less eligibility: in fact, as the Webbs point out,[5] the special

[1] The question had been considered but left open by the Select Committee on Poor Relief of 1861–4, and by the Select Committee on the local government and local taxation of the Metropolis, which reported in 1866 (*P.P.* 1866, xiii. 171, 317).

[2] Earle wanted the whole subject of metropolitan government to be revived with a view to simplification and unification, and induced Disraeli to press the matter on Hardy, but without concrete results. Memo. by Earle for Disraeli, 8 Aug. 1866, and undated note from same to same (Disraeli Papers, B/XX/E/393, 417); M. & B., iv. 479.

[3] Earle addressed his manifold policy suggestions to his old employer, Disraeli, rather than to his departmental chief. His relations with Disraeli, however, rapidly deteriorated, and were the real cause of his resignation (ostensibly over Reform) in March 1867 (M. & B., iv. 527–9). His successor at the Poor Law Board was the Hampshire member, George Sclater-Booth.

[4] For the debates on the bill, see principally *3 Hansard*, clxxxv. 746–80, 1608–23, 1861–6; and for Carnarvon's view (which his resignation over Reform in March 1867 left him free to voice), *ibid.*, clxxxvi. 389. Miss Nightingale found the measure too tentative and permissive (Cook, ii. 138), and the reformers generally disliked the fact that it left many sick paupers still subject to the cheeseparing control of the guardians. Hardy was not averse from the idea of a central board, but preferred to go gradually (*3 Hansard*, clxxxv. 1610–11).

[5] *English Poor Law Policy*, pp. 264–5, and cf. p. 118.

treatment of the sick which it fostered marked the advent of a precisely opposite principle—that of 'Curative Treatment', or 'Greater Eligibility', whereby the position of the pauper in illness became better than that of the lowest class of independent poor. The state recognised the obligation not simply to keep the pauper alive, but to provide him in sickness with a standard of medical care hitherto virtually unattainable by the poorer classes.

Hardy's measure, of course, applied only to London—where the Poor Law Board quickly put it into vigorous operation[1]—but in the years after 1867, despite stubborn resistance from many of the guardians, the pressure of the central authority gradually secured the implementation of its principles in the country at large, until it formed the basis of something like a national policy for the sick poor. As the system of special treatment of the sick developed, and its facilities came to be used by those who scarcely qualified as paupers, so the medical activities of the poor law were transformed into what was, in effect, a working-class health service.[2] The act of 1867 had inaugurated a new era in state provision for health: to the modern historian of the hospitals it stands as 'the first explicit acknowledgement that it was the duty of the state to provide hospitals for the poor' and 'an important step towards the National Health Service Act'.[3] The most important social measure of the government of 1866–8, it exemplified Conservative pragmatism and secured for Hardy—bitterly though he would have resented the rôle—a place among the unconscious architects of the welfare state.

Having done the job for which he had been appointed, Hardy left the Poor Law Board in May 1867 to take over the Home Office. His successor, the Earl of Devon (who held the Presidency without a seat in the cabinet), was unusual in having direct experience of the department's work: after a short period as a poor-law inspector, he had served from 1851 to 1859 as secretary to the Board, albeit with no apparent distinction.[4] It was quickly clear that under Devon as under Hardy practical needs and official pressures would prevail over whatever prejudices Conservative ministers might have against the enlargement of central authority. At the end of the 1867 session a govern-

[1] See Abel-Smith, pp. 80–1. Rogers, however, complains (pp. 61, 83–4) that it was in some cases several years before the Poor Law Board, under pressure, implemented the dispensary clauses of the act.

[2] See S. and B. Webb, *English Poor Law Policy*, pp. 121–3, 211–19; *English Poor Law History*, pt. II, vol. i. 321–9. By 1870, say the Webbs, 'the extent to which the Poor Law had become the public doctor was indeed remarkable'. Cf. O'Neill, pp. 269, 284.

[3] Abel-Smith, p. 82.

[4] See S. and B. Webb, *English Poor Law History*, pt. II, vol. i. 195–6. According to the Webbs, Devon's appointment was a political job.

ment bill at last made the Poor Law Board—hitherto existing only on an annually renewable tenure—a permanent fixture, as the Select Committee of 1861–4 had recommended. It also made a bold attempt to expand the Board's powers, in particular by allowing it to appoint a wide range of poor-law officials previously appointed by the guardians; but in face of sharp opposition from Liberal anti-centralists these clauses had to be dropped.[1]

The same process of the consolidation and extension of central authority was at work in the sphere of public health. By 1866, largely under the influence of the reports and inquiries of the Medical Department of the Privy Council (the main government organ concerned with public health), opinion had become more friendly to central intervention in sanitary matters, and local authorities, so far from entrenching themselves in defence of their independence, were showing an increasing tendency to accept and even demand such intervention—especially the smaller ones which needed free expert advice.[2] A sanitary agitation was emerging, headed by such bodies as the British Medical Association and the National Association for the Promotion of Social Science, and demanding the consolidation of the sanitary laws, the substitution of compulsory for permissive legislation, and the reorganisation of sanitary administration.

Since Adderley's wrongheaded demolition of the General Board of Health in 1858, responsibility for health matters had been dispersed among several government departments. As the sick pauper question and Hardy's Act demonstrated, the Poor Law Board had the largest rôle in the provision of medical facilities for the poorer classes when in illness; but where preventive medicine and the administration of the sanitary acts were concerned, the principal departments were the Privy Council, with its Medical Department, and the Home Office, with its Local Government Act Office, and the Duke of Buckingham and Spencer Walpole were accordingly, in 1866, the ministers most directly involved in health questions. Walpole, as Ralph Earle remarked, 'is not a vigorous minister & with respect to public Health questions, he is known to be reactionary';[3] but Buckingham possessed ability, and was ready to follow the lead of the Privy Council's formidable medical officer, John Simon, the outstanding figure in the development of public health administration in England.[4]

[1] *3 Hansard*, clxxxviii. 1417–21, 1874; clxxxix. 142–6.

[2] See Lambert, *Simon*, pp. 366–8; 'Central and Local Relations', pp. 144–8.

[3] Memo. by Earle for Disraeli, 30 Nov. 1866: Disraeli Papers, B/XX/E/404a. Lambert, 'Central and Local Relations', p. 138, n. 91, notes Walpole's softness while Home Secretary towards anti-sanitary and vested interests.

[4] Lambert, *Simon*, p. 409. For an example of Buckingham's vigour in the

A severe cholera epidemic in London helped to force public health issues on the ministry as soon as it arrived in office. It did not cope very energetically with the cholera. Disraeli, as Chancellor, cut down the funds for a large research programme into the disease projected by Simon with Buckingham's support.[1] Hardy resisted demands for government intervention to supplement the inadequate action of the local health authorities, and refused to take steps to supply the authorities with money, either from the Treasury or through a metropolitan rate, despite feeling on both sides of the Commons that in the poorer districts their failure adequately to discharge their sanitary duties was partly owing to lack of means.[2] Here, of course, the very thorny question of the local government and taxation of London was involved, and with this, whatever Earle's promptings, the ministry was reluctant to deal, a fact which helps to account for Walpole's refusal of the Commission on the sanitary and social condition of the capital for which the Metropolitan Sanitary Association asked him in September.[3] But the cholera did at least make government and Parliament more ready to pass the Public Health Act of 1866, a landmark in English sanitary legislation and in the advance of administrative centralisation.

The Public Health Bill, brought in by Russell's ministry, was in process of passing when the Conservatives took office, and was carried through its final stages at the end of the 1866 session. It dealt primarily with the provision of sewerage, water supply, and nuisance removal, but touched on many other matters, including overcrowding in dwelling-places. While it largely increased the powers of local authorities to execute sewerage and other works necessary to public health, its main importance lay in its attack on the central problem of sanitary improvement—the difficulty of ensuring that the powers provided by legislation were actually used. Dropping the permissive tone which had stultified so many sanitary measures, the bill not only gave health authorities powers but prescribed for them duties, and provided for their coercion where they defaulted. In the original bill, the function of compelling negligent authorities to use their powers was assigned to the magistracy and the police, thus preserving the principle of local autonomy; it was after the change of ministry that the power of central government was suddenly and drastically widened by the

[1] Lambert, *Simon*, p. 379.

[2] *3 Hansard*, clxxxiv. 2034, 2100–6.

[3] See Hon. Sec. of the Metropolitan Sanitary Association to Walpole, 20 Sept. 1866, and attached minutes: H.O. 45/O.S. 7932/33. Walpole was able to plead that a Select Committee was already covering much of the ground.

discharge of his duties, see H. Preston-Thomas, *The Work and Play of a Government Inspector*, p. 46.

transfer of this intervening rôle to the Home Secretary.[1] It is a commentary on Parliament's grasp of social legislation that this abrupt advance of centralisation seems to have been almost accidental and its implications unrealised. Thanks partly to the cholera, there was little opposition to the bill.[2] Simon later wrote that the act of 1866 'represented such a stride of advance as virtually to begin a new era',[3] and it is this measure, rather than the better-known but mainly consolidatory Public Health Act of 1875, that deserves to be remembered as the major sanitary enactment of the later nineteenth century. It was followed in 1867 by a Public Health Act for Scotland, which similarly gave increased force to the central authority.[4]

The Public Health Act had owed little to the newly-installed government, but ministers soon showed readiness to help the work of sanitary and social improvement forward. Vaccination and the medical inspection of workhouses headed Buckingham's agenda at the cabinet of 10 August. Adderley, his interest in sanitary matters unabated, planned to introduce a bill to consolidate public health legislation,[5] a vital reform, since there was no greater obstacle to the implementation of the sanitary laws than their multiplicity and complexity. Walpole's 'reactionary' tendencies did not prevent the Local Government Act Office from embarking on a vigorous use of the coercive powers conferred by the Public Health Act,[6] and the Home Secretary himself seems to have intended to grapple with a major social problem closely related to public health by bringing in a licensing bill.[7]

London's inadequate and impure water supply was another subject which came under notice. The government's attitude was at first complacent,[8] but the case for action was pressed by Shaftesbury, who told Disraeli in August 1866:

> It is essentially a matter affecting the *Working-Classes*. The well to do have some power to protect themselves; the Poor have none at all. Both

[1] Lambert, *Simon*, pp. 387–8.

[2] Even the representatives of bucolic Tory localism acquiesced, though Henley especially was doubtful about many of the powers conferred by the bill (*3 Hansard*, clxxxiv. 1376–82, 1644–52). For Shaftesbury the measure hardly went far enough (*ibid.*, clxxxiv. 2072–3).

[3] Sir John Simon, *English Sanitary Institutions*, 2nd ed., p. 299.

[4] For this measure, see T. Ferguson, *Scottish Social Welfare, 1864–1914*, pp. 155ff.

[5] *3 Hansard*, clxxxiv. 1687.

[6] Lambert, 'Central and Local Relations', pp. 138–44.

[7] See *3 Hansard*, clxxxvi. 164, 1850, 1874–5.

[8] See Corry's answer, 7 Aug. 1866, to a question on the allegedly impure state of the River Lea (the principal source of supply for Bow and Stratford). *Ibid.*, clxxxiv. 2134–5.

in respect of quantity, quality, & time of supply, they are entirely helpless; and no one, but a person who has studied, as it were, the question, can form a notion of the physical, moral, and domestic losses & suffering which the Poor have to endure, by consequence of this denial of one great necessary of Life.

Shaftesbury fixed especially on the fact that the supply was generally intermittent—i.e. it was turned on only at certain times, so that water required for use in the interim periods had to be stored, often in extremely unhygienic conditions—and advocated a constant supply; but above all he wanted a Royal Commission on the whole question, covering sources of supply, causes of pollution, schemes for improved service, and the entire system and conduct of the water companies in whose hands the supply rested.[1] Ministers were at first chary of so searching an investigation: they did set up a Commission on London's water supply in December 1866, but only to consider new schemes for that supply. Later, however, the Commission's instructions were extended to enable it to consider the problem in general, and under the Duke of Richmond's chairmanship it did important work.[2] A Commons Select Committee, in June 1867, declared for the enforcement of constant supply,[3] but the existence of the Commission furnished an excuse for inaction perhaps not unwelcome to the men who had coped so feebly with the water question in 1852.

The most important issue, however, which ministers had under consideration was that of administrative reorganisation. The dispersal of public health functions among several different departments was clearly undesirable. Ralph Earle, in November 1866, put to Disraeli a proposal which foreshadowed the creation of the Local Government Board five years later: he thought that health matters should be entrusted to the Poor Law Board, pointing out that money for sanitary objects came from the poor rates and that local authorities charged with sanitary matters also appointed the poor-law guardians.[4] Buckingham, prompted no doubt by Simon, had other ideas. In

[1] Memo. by Shaftesbury for Disraeli, 14 Aug. 1866: Disraeli Papers, B/XXI/S/123. Shaftesbury concluded his plea by writing: 'It is not necessary to say more to Mr. D'Israeli, who has always, exhibited a real desire to consider, & promote, the welfare, and comfort, of the Working people.' For the whole water question at this period, see 'The Water-supply of London', *Quarterly Review*, cxxvii (1869), 414–77.

[2] For its findings, see below, p. 294.

[3] Report of Select Committee on East London Water Bills and the operation of the Metropolis Water Act 1852, p. xvi (*P.P.* 1867, ix. 16).

[4] Memo. of 30 Nov. 1866, cited above, p. 64, n.3. Earle opposed giving the Council Office control of health on the ground that it was fully occupied with education and its head was in the Lords; the Home Office, too, was already overworked, and was under the 'reactionary' Walpole.

January 1867 he brought before the cabinet an ambitious programme of reorganisation, proposing:

> 1. To place the control and direction under these several Acts [the Sanitary Acts] in some one Department.
> 2. To provide an efficient control over the expenditure in connection with the powers of the Sanitary Act [of 1866] for drainage and water supply, which are, in fact, powers of taxation.
> 3. To assimilate local authorities, and provide in all cases an effective and available one.
> 4. To consolidate the many statutes now relating to sanitary matters.

He wanted to deal with the first two points in the approaching session, and, rejecting the notion of a new department, concluded that it was the Council Office which should assume control of health matters, with the Vice-President becoming Vice-President of the Committee of Council for Health.[1] But nothing came of the plan. The government had enough to do in 1867 without embarking on fundamental administrative changes, and Buckingham's admirable points were not destined to be dealt with until the legislation of 1871–5.

No doubt, also, the change of ministers at the Council Office in March 1867 helped to prevent the pursuit of Buckingham's scheme. In the cabinet reshuffle caused by the Reform resignations, Buckingham took the Colonies and was succeeded as Lord President by the Duke of Marlborough, another longstanding friend of Disraeli, whose opinion of his 'culture, intellectual grasp, and moral energy'[2] was probably his main qualification for the job. Marlborough did not accept Simon's guidance, and took limited interest in health questions,[3] preferring to concentrate on the educational side of his department's business. The Vice-Presidency also fell vacant in March, through Corry's translation to the Admiralty, and here again the

[1] Printed memo. by Buckingham on the sanitary code, endorsed 'Cabinet Jany 28.67': P.R.O. 30/6/166, ff. 166–7. Cf. Lambert, *Simon*, p. 409. It is not clear whether it was intended at this stage that the Council Office should shed its responsibility for education. According to Dr Lambert, Buckingham wanted education to be transferred to a separate ministry. But the idea of an education ministry does not seem to have been prominent in the cabinet's mind until the end of 1867 (below, pp. 107 ff.), and Earle told Disraeli, in an undated note, probably of late 1866 or early 1867 (Disraeli Papers, B/XX/E/417) that Henry Corry was objecting to the plan for putting health under the Council Office on the ground that the work in the Commons would devolve on the Vice-President, who was already fully occupied with education—which suggests that no transfer of education was initially contemplated. Cf. also Earle's memo. of 30 Nov. 1866, cited in the previous note.

[2] Disraeli to Derby, 20 Feb. 1868, in M. & B., iv. 585. Marlborough was the son-in-law of Lady Londonderry—Disraeli's Frances Anne.

[3] Lambert, *Simon*, pp. 410–12. He cared little enough to use a vacant inspectorship of vaccination as an item of patronage.

choice of a successor seems to have owed something to Disraeli's taste for the strawberry leaves. The new minister was Lord Robert Montagu, brother of the Chancellor's old friend the Duke of Manchester, and an eccentric character who repeatedly demonstrated what Disraeli had meant in saying of him: 'If he had only a single ray of common-sense he would be a leading man.'[1] But Montagu, if odd, did have a serious interest in sanitary questions. He had secured and chaired in 1864 a Select Committee on sewage disposal in large towns, and carried the Sewage Utilization Act of 1865, and at the Social Science Congress of October 1866 had put through a resolution in favour of compulsory legislation against the pollution of rivers by town sewage.[2]

It was probably the intention that Montagu should deal largely with public health matters, while Marlborough handled education. In the event, the Vice-President, too, spent much of his time on education, and little was done in the public health field in 1867. The Metropolitan Poor Act was, in its long-term implications, the most significant health measure of the session. Otherwise, apart from the Scottish public health act, the only advance of note came when Montagu, under Simon's influence, carried the Vaccination Bill which had been abandoned after the change of ministry in 1866: this, consolidating and amending all previous legislation on the subject, secured the quality of vaccination and severely tightened its enforcement.[3] There was another important area, however, where some ground was cleared for progress, and where the ministry, while leaving the initiative to a Liberal backbencher, showed itself ready for cautious action. This was working-class housing.

The insanitary and overcrowded conditions in which millions both of the urban and the rural poor were housed constituted perhaps the most fundamental social evil of the nineteenth century. Nothing did more damage to the nation's health; nothing worked more to produce drunkenness, crime, vice, and plain despair. The mid-'sixties saw an increasing public awareness of this problem, stimulated mainly, no doubt, by its unpleasant and obtrusive manifestations, but also by the extensive inquiry into the housing of the urban and rural poor

[1] Recorded in Northcote's diary, 6 Feb. 1866 (typescript copy): Add. MS. 50063A, f. 67 (printed in Lang, i. 235, with the omission of Montagu's name).

[2] See *Transactions of the National Association for the Promotion of Social Science*, 1866, pp. 578–82, 587–8. Montagu was also one of the very few Conservative supporters of trade unions. After backing in 1860 a measure for councils of conciliation to settle labour disputes, he was, says George Howell (p. 370), 'converted to trade unionism by some of us in the early 'sixties'.

[3] See Lambert, *Simon*, pp. 391–4. Strong opposition and government misgivings about some of its provisions, as well as lack of time, had caused the bill's shelving in 1866 (*3 Hansard*, clxxxiv. 1363–4).

carried out in 1864–5 by the Medical Department of the Privy Council, as a result of which Simon called for strong measures against overcrowding and slums.[1] Parliament had hitherto made scarcely any attempt to tackle the question of working-class housing—apart from Shaftesbury's Lodging Houses Acts of 1851, which had enabled local authorities to inspect and even build lodging houses, but had been very little utilised—and it was therefore significant when in 1866 (before Russell's exit) a measure was passed empowering the Public Works Loan Commissioners to lend money for the erection of working-class housing, and provisions against overcrowding were inserted in the Public Health Act. The loans measure helped the private associations and companies specialising in building tenements for the working classes to make some impression on the problem, and enlightened municipal authorities—notably in Liverpool—did more. Nonetheless, the magnitude and urgency of the question convinced many that still further legislative action was needed, despite the deep prejudice against state interference in what was regarded as a sphere pertaining essentially to private enterprise.

The call for action was strongest in relation to London, where the deficiencies of working-class housing were acute, and were constantly being aggravated not only by population increase but by the extensive demolition of existing dwellings to make way for railways, a problem which Shaftesbury and Derby had tried to grapple with as long ago as 1853.[2] In November 1866, metropolitan housing was pressed on the government's attention by the president and fellows of Sion College, who advocated legislation giving facilities for the utilisation of unoccupied and neglected land for housing purposes;[3] and Earle suggested to Disraeli a Commission on 'the improvement of London, dwellings of the Poor, & sites for Gov. offices', writing:

> I think it to our interest to make as much noise as possible about the thing & to excite the greatest possible amount of interest—therefore I am in favour of a *Royal* Commission. The inquiry wd. amuse & interest the public, even if we chose to do nothing about it, after all, & really it is necessary that something should be done, & that in a manner to inaugurate a system for doing more.[4]

[1] Lambert, *Simon*, pp. 346–50.

[2] See H. J. Dyos, 'Railways and Housing in Victorian London', *Journal of Transport History*, ii (1955–6), 11–21, 90–100; 'Some Social Costs of Railway Building in London', *ibid.*, iii (1957), 23–30. Shaftesbury had wanted to make railway bill promoters rehouse those displaced, and Derby had obtained a committee on the subject.

[3] Memorial to Walpole, 27 Nov. 1866: H.O. 45/O.S. 7906.

[4] Earle to Disraeli, 28 Nov. 1866: Disraeli Papers, B/XX/E/403. Disraeli had apparently found the idea absurd, but Earle claimed that Cranborne supported such a Commission.

Earle's concern was not, perhaps, very serious, but Buckingham, too, with Simon behind him, was alive to the importance of the London housing problem, and brought it before the cabinet in February 1867.[1] Buckingham's memorandum, however, suggested no positive course of action, and Marlborough and Montagu, when they took over the Council Office, were not more inventive. Instead of devising a measure of its own, the government gave its backing to the Artizans and Labourers Dwellings Bill which the Liberal member for Finsbury, Torrens, had re-introduced, having failed to pass it in the previous session.

Torrens's bill, aiming to assist slum clearance in the towns, was based on a scheme successfully operating in Liverpool. It enabled local authorities to require necessary work to be done on property condemned by the officer of health, and, in case of default, allowed them, in certain circumstances, to purchase such property and provide for its rebuilding. If only mildly, the bill encroached upon property rights and promoted municipal enterprise, and the ministry's acceptance of it illustrates again the Conservatives' relative freedom from dogmatic prejudices when at grips with practical needs. Opposition came mostly from Torrens's fellow metropolitan Liberals, who, with the metropolitan ratepayers breathing down their necks, were often the most obstructive group in the House of Commons in matters of social improvement. Their contention that the bill transgressed the principles of political economy and faced private builders with unfair competition did not make much impression on the opposite benches. Henley and Powell, it is true, were doubtful about allowing local authorities to build, and the former refused his assent to

> any principle so wide and dangerous as that the public was, under all circumstances, bound to provide dwellings for the labouring classes. If the public was once brought into the matter you would stop the private enterprize which was now to a certain extent at least meeting the difficulty.[2]

But other Conservatives strongly supported the bill. To Graves, of Liverpool, who knew the extent of the problem in the great towns, something of the kind was 'a political necessity'.[3] The Essex member Selwin wanted a larger measure, and suggested that the government should guarantee a minimum return of 4% on capital invested in building for the working classes.[4] Greene, of Bury St Edmunds, who

[1] Printed cabinet memorandum on overcrowding in the Metropolis, unsigned and undated, but endorsed 'D. of Buckingham 22 Feb. 67.': P.R.O. 30/6/166, ff. 184–6.

[2] *3 Hansard*, clxxxvi. 682. For Powell, see *ibid.*, clxxxvi. 692.

[3] *Ibid.*, clxxxvi. 690.

[4] *Ibid.*, clxxxvi. 675–7. Selwin changed his name in 1867, and will hereafter appear as Selwin-Ibbetson.

also drew attention to the lack of housing for agricultural labourers, said thoughtfully that with better dwellings the working men 'would the better be able to labour', and warned:

> If this Bill were rejected, the House would lay itself open to the charge that they cared very little for the interests and welfare of the poor except to make it a matter of claptrap on special occasion. . . . The people ought not to be housed any longer in dwellings which were unfit for a sporting dog, while the House of Commons were wasting their time about matters of much less importance than the improvement of the condition of those classes whom they professed to desire to raise in the social scale. It was in vain to attempt to educate the people and to talk morality to them as long as they dwelt in houses that were not even fit for the accommodation of cattle.[1]

Pressure of business retarded Torrens's bill in 1867, and its passing was delayed until the following year, but it was a portent for the future of state intervention in the housing question.

The most notable omission from the list of topics discussed at the cabinet of 10 August 1866 was, so far as social questions were concerned, education. The new government shared in the complacency about the state of elementary education which was widely evident in political circles, and whilst Pakington prevented it from altogether ignoring the darker side of the picture, it was not anxious to confront the complex problems which any major move in the educational field would bring up. Yet a point of crisis in popular education was rapidly approaching, and few domestic subjects were to occupy so much of the Conservative party's attention in the ensuing decade.

The elementary education of the poorer classes furnished the outstanding example of the principle of voluntaryism in social affairs. Though many children in the 'sixties still depended on the usually wretched ministrations of schools of the dame and private adventure type, the backbone of elementary education in England and Wales (Scotland being a case apart) was provided by the efforts of the religious denominations, applying to the building and running of their schools the voluntary subscriptions of their members and the fees paid by the children attending. Since 1833, the denominational schools had been eligible for assistance from state grants, administered by the Committee of Privy Council on Education set up in 1839, and carrying with them, inevitably, government inspection and a limited degree of government control. The voluntary, denominational system was dominated by the Established Church, which had the largest resources and made the greatest efforts; and the fact that their

[1] *Ibid.*, clxxxvi. 678; clxxxix. 756.

objection to state interference in education caused many nonconformists to refuse the government grants meant that it was overwhelmingly the Anglicans who reaped the benefit of state aid. The grip achieved by the Church on elementary education for the masses, especially strong in the rural areas, had become one of the main bulwarks of and guarantees for its supremacy, and educational issues in the 'sixties were intimately and unfortunately linked with religious and political questions. Education was a battleground in the bitter contest between Church and Dissent and between the social and political forces with which they were associated—a battleground on which the interests of the children were frequently the first casualties.

It was becoming increasingly difficult in the early 'sixties to burke the question of how far the voluntary system was capable of meeting the country's educational needs. A very unsatisfactory condition of affairs was revealed in 1861 in the massive report of the Duke of Newcastle's Commission, set up on Pakington's motion in 1858 'to inquire into the present state of education in England, and to consider and report what measures, if any, are required for the extension of sound and cheap elementary instruction to all classes of the people'.[1] The report made it clear that the elementary education received by the children of the poorer classes was very brief and of very doubtful quality. Accepting, like most contemporaries, that the demands of the labour market required working-class children to be employed at ten or eleven, and that the children's education should be strictly related to their social status and functions, the Commissioners concentrated on the need to secure efficient teaching of the elements, reading, writing, and arithmetic, which were what the poor principally required for their station in life, and could, they thought, be adequately implanted by the age of ten. They recommended searching examination to check on the acquisition of the elements by children in state-aided schools, and their proposal was taken up by the Vice-President of the day, Robert Lowe, who, in response to the demand for value for money in education, made the greater part of the state grant to schools dependent on their pupils' attainments in the three Rs, determined by annual examination in six standards, thus riveting upon English elementary education the pernicious system of 'payment by results', which virtually forced teachers to concentrate on the often mechanical drilling of children in the elements, to the detriment of other subjects and of higher instruction. But while attempting, disastrously, to take security for the efficiency of state-aided education, neither the Newcastle Commission nor Lowe got to grips with the basic problem of how to extend it to the whole of the poorer classes.

[1] For the Commission's conclusions, see vol. i of the report: *P.P.* 1861, xxi, pt. I, 1.

The obvious defect of state-aided voluntaryism was that it depended on the uneven incidence of local effort and resources. In areas where effort and resources were weak there might be no voluntary schools, or those that there were might—as often happened—be incapable of fulfilling the conditions imposed for state grants; yet these areas, notably the poorer parts of the great towns and the smaller rural parishes, were frequently the ones where the need of efficient education was most acute. The existing system, in other words, was far from covering the country: large numbers of working-class children existed outside its reach, receiving either an education unassisted and unsupervised by the state or no education at all. Throughout the 'fifties and early 'sixties there was growing pressure for a truly universal system of elementary education, and extensive debate on how this was to be achieved.

There were two main ways in which government might act to ensure efficient elementary instruction for all the nation's children. It might promote the progressive expansion of the existing system, increasing its own aid and making it easier to obtain, and perhaps supplying the deficiencies of voluntary effort by providing for an education rate for the support of existing schools and the establishment of new ones. Or it might give up subsidising denominationalism and create a new national system of an unsectarian or even secular character, backed by rating and ultimately by compulsory attendance. No course could avert violent controversy. The idea of an unsectarian system was unacceptable to the Church, to whose position such a system—as many of its proponents intended—would deal an enormous blow; while state support for the expansion of an existing system so heavily dominated by the Anglicans was bound to irritate dissenters.

Rating was a highly contentious issue. The Newcastle Commission had favoured rate aid for existing schools, managed through elected boards of education. But not only would an education rate be resented by many in the upper and middle classes as a new burden for the benefit of the poor, its application to the support of the denominational schools would be strenuously resisted by the dissenters, who would find themselves subsidising Anglican education on a large scale. Moreover, many churchmen shied away from rating in the fear that ultimately it must destroy the voluntary system, whose supporters, faced with a rate on top of their voluntary subscriptions, would discontinue the latter; and in the fear also that it would entail an unpalatable degree of control over the schools by locally-elected committees—a prospect especially menacing to the educational and social rôle of the clergy and squirearchy in the countryside.[1]

[1] For the Church's strong opposition to rate-aided education in the 'fifties and 'sixties, see H. J. Burgess, *Enterprise in Education*, pp. 189–92.

Compulsion was just as thorny a problem. Though it was already applied to some extent in the industrial areas under the educational clauses of the factory acts, its general introduction had been dismissed as unattainable and undesirable by the Newcastle Commission, and, in any case, could not come until school accommodation had been greatly increased. To many it was contrary to the spirit of English institutions; it threatened employers with the loss of cheap juvenile labour;[1] and it promised to be expensive, in that it would necessitate paying the school fees of children whose parents could not afford them, and might put on the poor rate parents who needed their children's wages.

These were some of the considerations which made the education question one of peculiar difficulty in 1866. Because of its fundamental social and political significance, the elementary education of the people was probably the social problem with which the Conservative party was most deeply concerned, though the concern was as much negative as positive in character. There still remained in Conservative thinking in the 'sixties a strong vein of suspicion of popular education, a fear that by enlarging the mental horizons of the working classes, laying them open to Radical influences, and stimulating them to entertain ideas above their station, it would prove subversive of the social order. The natural product of this was a marked reluctance to see elementary instruction extended beyond the narrowest limits. But overlaying the basic distrust of education was the recognition that under the right auspices it could be used to reinforce the existing system of class relationships. The limited and functional education, strictly related to social status and prospective employment, and permeated by religion, which the denominational system provided was an invaluable instrument for training the working classes for the performance of their duties in life and indoctrinating them with the virtue of respect for the established scheme of things. What else did Disraeli mean when, in 1862, he numbered among Tory principles the favouring of popular education, 'because it is the best guarantee for public order'?[2]

Moreover, the overwhelming predominance within the denominational system of the Church of England held out the hope of powerful reinforcement to the social and political position of Conservatism. The bonds which united Church and party were being drawn tighter

[1] Though, as B. Simon, *Studies in the History of Education 1780–1870*, pp. 358–60, points out, in some industries by this period the employment of young children was neither necessary nor profitable; and it was coming to be felt in some quarters that the discipline of school was a good training for the discipline of the factory, and that an educated labour force was demanded by the increasing refinement of industrial techniques.

[2] Speech quoted in M. & B., iv. 379.

in the early 'sixties, as Disraeli sought electoral profit under the banner of Church defence, and the more closely allied the two institutions became, the more did the educational activity of the Church appear, at least prospectively, as a vital security not simply for social stability but also for the inculcation of Conservative sympathies. Conservatives at all levels in the party were frequently directly involved in the Church's educational effort, as subscribers to, and managers and trustees of, her schools, and as supporters of the National Society, her main educational agency; and their satisfaction in Christian duty performed was not seldom heightened by the apprehension of possible party advantage. This was especially true in the countryside, where the educational functions of the clergy were an integral part of the social and political system of the landed interest, upon which so much of the Conservative party's strength was based; and it was largely of the countryside that Conservatives thought. Nothing illustrates better than education the party's predominantly rural preoccupations, and its constant tendency to view social questions primarily in terms of their relation to rural society.

The maintenance of the denominational system and of the Anglican preponderance was thus the cardinal point in the Conservative party's attitude to education. Conservatives were very ready, in the controversies of the 'sixties, to convince themselves that the denominational system was adequately meeting the nation's needs, particularly in the rural areas,[1] and very determined, when educational deficiencies were forced upon their notice, that whatever further provision might be required should be achieved through the strengthening and expansion of that system. Most of them thought it would be enough to give a fresh impetus to the voluntary schools by rendering it easier for them to secure state assistance. They were generally strongly opposed to an education rate: they shared the Church's fear that it would ultimately destroy denominationalism, and as representatives of the landed interest they regarded it as a new aggravation of the local taxation grievance. The idea of compulsion was similarly abhorrent, not least because its impact on labour supply would be particularly serious in the countryside.

In short, the bulk of the Conservative party in 1866 was unimpressed by the urgency of the educational problem, and was ready for nothing more than a mild boosting of the existing system. But there were a few educational progressives who saw the extent of the problem and wanted vigorous action. The doyen of these was, of

[1] The Duke of Northumberland was typical of many in holding that while 'some large towns' required special assistance, 'our country parishes are well supplied with Schools'. Northumberland to Disraeli, 21 Feb. 1862: Disraeli Papers, B/XXI/N/184.

course, Pakington, who, convinced of the inadequacy of voluntaryism, had been battling for permissive rating under elected education boards in the 'fifties, opposed by some of those who were now his cabinet colleagues—Cranborne, Manners, and Walpole—but with the cautious sympathy of others—Disraeli, Stanley, and Northcote.[1] A number of Conservatives in the country at large, especially in the great towns, knew the real extent of educational destitution and were anxious for trenchant measures: this was notably true in Manchester, a forcing-house of educational advance in this period, where various Conservatives were active in the educational movement, perhaps the most outstanding being William Romaine Callender, junior, a pillar of the Manchester and Salford Education Aid Society, which came out in 1866 for nothing less than free education with compulsory rating and attendance.[2] The progressives, however, formed a small minority, and at the outset of the new ministry the episode of Pakington's report demonstrated how unpalatable their views were.

If education figured little on the political scene in early 1866, it was partly because the Commons were awaiting the report of a Select Committee appointed in the previous year under Pakington's chairmanship to inquire into the constitution and working of the Committee of Council on Education, and into the best mode of extending government inspection and parliamentary grants to schools as yet unassisted by the state. The misgivings felt by some Conservatives as to the use Pakington might make of the Committee[3] seemed to be justified when, as luck would have it, the formation of the Derby ministry coincided with his production of a draft report which reflected his advanced educational views and threatened seriously to embarrass his party. The draft's proposals for increasing state aid to the smaller schools and relaxing the conditions on which it was granted were innocuous enough; but it called also for the abolition of the Committee of Council and the appointment of a Minister of Public Instruction with a seat in the cabinet; for the establishment of local organs of educational administration, analogous to boards of guardians; for the granting of power to levy an education rate; and for the universal application to state-aided schools of the so-called conscience clause.[4] The idea of an education minister had been

[1] Above, p. 20. Adderley, who had also supported rating in the 'fifties, no longer did so by 1866.

[2] S. E. Maltby, *Manchester and the Movement for National Elementary Education 1800–1870*, p. 100.

[3] E.g. by the Hon F. Lygon, M.P., who told Disraeli that he hoped Pakington would not be allowed to pack the Committee with his friends, 'to the prejudice of genuine Tory principles'. Letter of 9 Feb. 1866: Disraeli Papers, B/XX/Ln/43.

[4] For the draft report, see the report of the Select Committee on Education, 1866, pp. ix-xvii (*P.P.* 1866, vii. 123–31).

endorsed by Disraeli as long ago as 1855,[1] and might have been swallowed, but local boards and rating were another matter, and Pakington's advocacy of a universal conscience clause raised an issue of deep seriousness to many Conservatives.

The conscience clause was simply a provision allowing parents to withhold their children from a school's religious instruction when they objected to it: its main use was to protect the children of dissenters who were obliged by lack of any alternative to attend an Anglican school. It was of crucial importance in the education question in the mid-'sixties. It is clear in retrospect that acceptance of it had become perhaps the only chance for the survival of the denominational system, in the sense that it would ultimately be impossible to go on justifying the large-scale application of public money (and if rating were introduced, the application of rates) to the support of what were mainly Anglican schools, unless the universal enforcement of a conscience clause allowed a secular education to be obtained from them by children of any creed or none. Pakington and those who thought like him saw this, and made the conscience clause an integral part of their schemes for the re-invigoration and expansion of the existing system. But others were less sensible.

The clause gave violent offence to that party in the Church which resented any interference with the absolute freedom of the clergy in their own schools, and the Committee of Council's attempts, since the 'fifties, to require its insertion in the trust deeds of Church schools as a condition of the parliamentary building grant (especially in single-school areas) had alienated also those clergy and school managers who were prepared to operate a conscience clause in practice, but detested its formal imposition. The National Society strongly resisted the enforcement of the clause, and in order to avoid it Churchmen frequently chose to forgo the building grant, so that it acted to some extent as a brake on the provision of schools. Archdeacon G. A. Denison, the leader of the extreme clerical party, had urged Disraeli in 1864 to take up the conscience clause issue 'as *the* aggression upon the Church', and in February 1866 had passed a motion attacking the clause in the Lower House of Convocation.[2] Many Conservatives shared the Church's dislike of the clause, and Pakington's proposal not only that its insertion in trust deeds should be a condition of building grants, but also that its violation in practice should be a ground for suspension of the annual grants, was fiercely controversial. If his draft report were adopted by the Committee, which contained three other members of the new cabinet, Cranborne,

[1] See M. & B., iv. 35ff.

[2] Denison to Disraeli, 18 May 1864 (Disraeli Papers, B/XXI/D/129); G. A. Denison, *Notes of My Life, 1805–1878*, p. 328.

Northcote, and Walpole, and also Adderley, the government would be dangerously compromised.

At first sight of Pakington's proposals, Cranborne had written in alarm to Disraeli:

> . . . he makes stronger propositions in the Conscience Clause direction than *any one* has yet made. Now if he is to be a Cabinet Minister in your incoming Administration, this is a very serious matter. I do not venture to anticipate what your policy in regard to this matter will be. Probably you will wish, under existing circumstances to stir it as little as possible. But you may very possibly have to meet the constituencies next spring. What do you think the effect in some of them will be if a Committee of the House, at the instance of one of your Cabinet has made such recommendations as those which I enclose? My own opinion is that Gladstone's friends will work it to the disadvantage of our side in many country places, & that it will lose you the support of the clergy to a considerable extent.
>
> If Pakington takes office with you he ought to be strongly urged to modify or abandon this Report.[1]

Disraeli at once took the issue up with Pakington, but the latter's first reaction was to stand his ground, and to point out that the principle of the conscience clause was not without support in Church and party:

> there is [he told Disraeli][2] nothing new in the 'Conscience Clause' being supported by members of the Conservative Party. Lord Derby himself advocated the principle in a speech at Liverpool. I, as you well know, have supported it for years. Adderley pressed it officially from the Education Office when V.P. 4-5ths of the Clergy *act* upon the principle, though they do not like it as law. Several of the Bishops now approve of the clause.
>
> It seems to me therefore that it may be fairly considered, as it has in fact long been, an open question. I will take any conciliatory course that I consistently can, but I am sure you would not wish me to do more.

Pakington was slurring over the fact that support for the principle of the clause was not the same as support for the stringent and universal imposition of it which he was proposing, and in the end he had to yield to his colleagues' pressure. It was Northcote who (as so often in the internal difficulties of the party) arranged matters, drawing up a formal and totally non-committal report for the Committee which Pakington agreed to accept in place of his own draft.[3] The new

[1] Cranborne to Disraeli, 29 June 1866: Disraeli Papers, B/XX/Ce/6.

[2] Pakington to Disraeli, 1 July 1866: *ibid.*, B/XX/P/78.

[3] See Northcote to Disraeli, 3 July 1866 (Add. MS. 50015, ff. 146–7); and for the final report, *P.P.* 1866, vii. 117. Having been formally proposed in the

government was saved from embarrassment, and the highly controversial issues raised by the draft report were temporarily evaded.

Yet however great their reluctance to become entangled in the difficulties of the education question, ministers could not ignore its existence, and in one respect Pakington's proposals presented them with a course of action fully consistent with sound Conservative objectives. Increasing state aid to the smaller schools and easing the conditions which they had to fulfil to obtain it were essential steps for the consolidation and expansion of the denominational system, especially in the poorer rural parishes, where very often voluntary effort was too weak to qualify for government assistance. It was largely on this theme that the new Vice-President of the Committee of Council on Education, Henry Corry, pondered in his first months in office, and in December 1866 he put before the cabinet proposals designed both to aid the smaller schools and to tackle the pressing problem resulting from the discouragement offered by Lowe's Revised Code[1] to the employment of pupil-teachers, which was impairing teaching strength and endangering the prospective supply of certificated teachers.

Seeking Disraeli's endorsement of his plan, he wrote:

> As a general rule it may be said that the smaller classes of Schools—nearly all in the agricultural districts—which gives them a peculiar claim on us—receive no assistance from the State. They are practically proscribed by the Code as it now stands, & a feeling of discontent, as well as a sense of injustice, is the general consequence, not to mention the injury done to the education of the rural population—which in so many instances is doomed to bad schools, or to no school at all. You will see that the scheme I propose would give the smaller rural schools what I have ascertained would be considered substantial relief—unaccompanied by any onerous obligation—while in the larger Schools the conditions I require would be productive of great advantage. . . . I am quite satisfied that we could do nothing at once more useful and more popular in the line of the Education of the people than what I propose (or something as well adapted to its object) . . .
>
> The chances are . . . that, if we miss the opportunity of effecting this great good, we shall leave it to our political opponents to get the credit with the Country which is within our reach.[2]

[1] The name applied to the Education Code (i.e. the body of administrative regulations laid down by the Committee of Council) after Lowe's revision of it in 1861–2.

[2] Corry to Disraeli, 24 Dec. [1866]: Disraeli Papers, B/XXI/C/441.

Committee, however, Pakington's draft was printed in its proceedings. Northcote opposed Pakington on the conscience clause: see his diary, 19 Feb. 1866 (typescript copy); Add. MS. 50063A, f. 70.

Corry's scheme was to increase the rate of grant for the first 120 examination passes in any school, but to make this conditional on an increase in the proportion of teachers to scholars, where the latter exceeded a certain number. This would help the smaller schools, and in the larger schools, as well as providing more money, would promote the employment of more pupil-teachers, whom Corry saw as 'the pivot on which the whole system of Education under the Committee of Council may be said to turn'.[1] Corry also proposed to use grants to encourage the flow of male pupil-teachers into training colleges, an idea he got from the secretary of the Committee of Council, Lingen. The cost of the plan would reverse the current trend towards the reduction of educational expenditure by the state, but it was less than that of the similar scheme which Corry's Liberal predecessor, Bruce, had contemplated, and in any case, Corry reminded his colleagues, 'there is no branch of public economy of greater national importance than the education of the poor, and none in respect of which the Government might obtain greater credit with the country'.[2] Corry's proposals, put into effect in 1867, did not do much to help those areas which had difficulty in meeting the conditions for state aid (he explicitly skirted the question of relaxing for their benefit the rule which made the employment of a certificated teacher a condition of government grant), but they were useful as far as they went, and the Vice-President did well to promote them in face of 'the general feeling in the Office that the Revised Code is infallible'.[3] Their tailoring to the needs of the small, rural Church schools, however, emphasised the determination of the Conservative party to look after its own in the educational field.

Apart from Corry's scheme, the government made little attempt to adopt a positive approach to educational issues in its first months. Much time was taken up by the conscience clause question, the opponents of the clause looking for some satisfaction from the Conservatives and pressing ministers to act. Denison had hopes of Carnarvon, with whom he was in close touch on education, but their co-operation did not survive the latter's taking office.[4] The best friend of the clerical zealots turned out to be Manners. After a meeting held at York in October 1866, in connection with the Church Congress, had passed the resolution of a Conservative M.P., J. G. Hubbard, for a deputation to Derby against the Education Department's

[1] *Ibid.*

[2] Confidential printed memorandum by Corry, 1 Dec. 1866, on the estimate for the financial year 1867–8: P.R.O. 30/6/169, ff. 114–18.

[3] Corry to Disraeli, 24 Dec. [1866], cited above, p. 80, n. 2.

[4] See Denison, pp. 330–1; Denison to Carnarvon, 20 Aug. 1866 (P.R.O. 30/6/138, ff. 60–1).

practice of making the conscience clause a condition of building grants,[1] Manners wrote to Disraeli:[2]

> the practical Church question of all others which we can, and, in my opinion, ought to solve without any appeal, necessarily, to Parliament, is the Conscience Clause. Pakington, I know, dissents strongly from what may—after the discussion at York, be called the Church view; but the great majority of the Cabinet and of the party are, I am persuaded favourable to that view as also, much to my surprize, it seems are many of the Welsh Dissenters for whose special benefit the Clause was originally concocted. It is now operating as a check to education and is in direct contradiction to the acknowledged Denominational system of English education.

But if Manners could not see that the conscience clause in some form was essential to render the denominational system defensible, others could. It was impossible to drop the clause: what could be done was to seek some kind of accommodation between the government and the more moderate Churchmen. The Bishop of Oxford worked for a compromise,[3] and in December 1866 the Archbishop of Canterbury looked favourably on a suggestion from Derby that for the existing clause should be substituted a provision allowing parents to withdraw their children from attendance at *any* school lesson—the attraction of this being that it did not discriminate specifically against religion.[4] Nothing, however, was settled, and when Lord Robert Montagu succeeded Corry as Vice-President in March 1867 he at once blunderingly inflamed the sore.

Fresh in office, and under the influence of his civil servants, Montagu declared himself in his re-election speech 'decidedly in favour of secular education being given to all who came for it in schools which received a subsidy from Her Majesty's Government', and suggested that it might prove necessary to compromise between the claims of the dissenters and those of the clergy by making any violation of the conscience clause in practice a ground for withholding the annual grant (as Pakington had proposed), while removing the formal compulsion of which the clergy complained by ceasing to make the

[1] See *The Conscience Clause in 1866. Speeches delivered in the Chapter-House of York Minster, on the 13th of October, 1866, by John Gellibrand Hubbard, M.P., and the Rev. George Trevor, Canon of York.* Hubbard called the conscience clause 'a bond to give a secular education on demand', and, like many Conservatives, argued that working-class dissenters 'entertain generally no dislike to the religious teaching of Church schools'.

[2] 24 Oct. 1866: Disraeli Papers, B/XX/M/138.

[3] Denison, pp. 330–1.

[4] See Canterbury to the Earl of Harrowby, 8 Dec. 1866: Harrowby Papers, vol. xxxvii, ff. 126–8. The Archbishop was anxious for an agreement between the National Society and the government on the issue.

insertion of the clause in trust deeds a condition of building grants.[1] This, of course, meant a conscience clause wherever public money was received, and the speech provoked sharp protest from the clerical militants and their friends. Spurred by a furious letter from Denison,[2] Disraeli took Montagu to task, and seems deliberately to have relegated him to the background for some months in handling educational affairs in the House of Commons.[3] The conscience clause question came no nearer solution.

The fundamental problems of educational expansion were necessarily shelved while the ministry struggled with Reform. Marlborough as Lord President and Montagu as Vice-President, from March 1867, did no more than stolidly uphold the existing system, conscientiously belittling evidence of its deficiencies. Even in the debate in which he admitted the existence of 8,000 parishes with a population under 500 as yet unsupplied with schools, Montagu defended the voluntary system on the ground that it had put Britain foremost among the nations in the field of education.[4] With Pakington silent on educational matters (doubtless to avoid further embarrassment to his colleagues), there was little impetus towards action in the Conservative party. There were, certainly, Conservatives who, stimulated partly by the prospect of working-class enfranchisement, expressed concern about the educational situation. H. G. Liddell spoke of 'a general feeling in the country that the existing educational system had broken down'.[5] F. S. Powell thought popular education was tending to regress, and compared English schools unfavourably with Irish.[6] Henley regretted that the Privy Council did not try to reach the host of neglected children in the great towns: 'They', he said,[7] 'were the most needy, and yet they never had anything.' There was much complaint about the failure of the Privy Council system, also, to reach adequately the poorer rural districts, and some Conservatives would have liked to help the rural schools by ceasing to make the employment of a certificated teacher a condition of the parliamentary

[1] Report in *Cambridge Independent Press*, 30 March 1867; Montagu to Disraeli, 8 April 1867, explaining the speech (Disraeli Papers, B/XXI/M/444).

[2] 5 April 1867: *ibid.*, B/XXI/D/141. Only a few days earlier, Hubbard had reminded Disraeli of clerical hostility to the conscience clause, and warned that ministerial remarks on the subject would be closely watched (letter of 28 March 1867: *ibid.*, B/XXI/H/726).

[3] See Montagu's letter of 8 April, cited above, n.1, showing that Disraeli had remonstrated with him, and Montagu to Disraeli, 9 April and 18 June 1867 (Disraeli Papers, B/XXI/M/445–6), complaining about others' being selected to answer on important educational matters in the House.

[4] *3 Hansard*, clxxxvi. 2007–8. Hardy made a similar claim (*ibid.*, clxxxviii. 1357).

[5] *Ibid.*, clxxxix. 501. [6] *Ibid.*, clxxxv. 1161. [7] *Ibid.*, clxxxvi. 1197.

grant.[1] But for the kind of measures that would be necessary to tackle the education problem with real effect there was little support among Conservatives.

This was illustrated in July 1867 in the debate on a bill introduced by the former Vice-President, Bruce, to allow districts to rate themselves for school building and maintenance (with the necessary corollary of a conscience clause in all rate-assisted schools). This was really the old Manchester and Salford Education Bill which Adderley and Pakington had supported in the 'fifties, and the Conservative member for South Lancashire, Algernon Egerton, who was closely associated with the Manchester educationists, was one of its sponsors. Egerton saw the educational problem mainly in terms of the needs of the manufacturing towns, like Manchester, where the voluntary system had, he felt, utterly failed: he not only wanted rating, accompanied by a conscience clause, but was even ready for compulsory attendance.[2] He was, however, a lonely figure. The more typical Conservative approach was voiced by Henley, who, looking at the bill 'of course, more in reference to the country districts', argued that rating with the conscience clause would destroy the denominational system, as well as putting additional burdens on real property, and that there was in any case plenty of school accommodation, the problem being to get the children to attend.[3] Hardy, for the government, endorsed this attitude.[4]

Still less did Conservatives respond with enthusiasm when Henry Fawcett proposed that the half-time system of education prescribed by the factory acts should be extended to children employed in agriculture, and asked them ironically to confer on 'the industry with which they were more intimately connected' the benefits which, by helping to pass the factory acts, they had already conferred on manufacturing industry.[5] Walpole, it is true, thought that some of the principles of the factory acts would have to be extended to the agricultural districts,[6] but in general, while protesting their anxiety to promote the education of the rural population, Conservatives dismissed Fawcett's scheme as impracticable.[7] Here, too, Henley spoke for the majority in contending that the agricultural labourers 'would be found to be better educated for the fulfilment of their duties than the lower classes of any other country in the world', and in repudiating the charge that landowners had not always done all in their power

[1] *Ibid.*, clxxxvi. 1998–9; clxxxix. 495, 500, 510. The government resisted this suggestion on the ground that the certificated teachers were a security for the quality of the education (*ibid.*, clxxxvi. 2009; clxxxviii. 1055–7).

[2] *Ibid.*, clxxxviii. 1342–4.

[3] *Ibid.*, clxxxviii. 1344–50.

[4] *Ibid.*, clxxxviii. 1356–61.

[5] *Ibid.*, clxxxv. 1071.

[6] See above, p. 51.

[7] For the debate on Fawcett's motion, see *3 Hansard*, clxxxv. 1066–88; clxxxix. 487–518.

'in behalf of those over whom it had pleased God to place them'.[1] The tenant-farmer Read, while asserting that the farmers favoured education (which in many cases was hardly true), made it clear that they expected it to be of the most functional kind:

> He admitted that in order to work the improved agricultural machinery well it was almost necessary to have a thoroughly well-educated labourer; but a superficially educated man, who knew nothing of his business, was the very worst labourer one could have. He had been in workhouses where he had seen children intended for the farm going through a course of geography, when they should properly have been learning the use of the spade. Education, to be useful, should be suited to the future position of the child.[2]

Given the reception accorded to Fawcett's proposal, it is not surprising that the recommendation of the Children's Employment Commission, in its sixth report,[3] that the principles of the factory acts should be adapted to provide for the education of children employed in agricultural gangs, and that a certificate of education should be a condition of a child's employment in such a gang, was ignored. The representatives of the landed interest were not going to disrupt the rural labour supply for the sake of an education towards which few of them were more than lukewarm.

Tepidity, indeed, was almost the keynote of the Conservative approach to education in the new ministry's first year. With some exceptions, the party lacked the genuine enthusiasm for popular instruction which could have reconciled it to the measures—especially rating—on which educational advance more and more seemed to depend. Its attitude was based upon social and political considerations, and conditioned very much by the ostensible interests of the Church (which it thought co-extensive with its own) and of the rural community (which sought protection against the burden of rates on real property and the impact of compulsion on labour supply). These led it into a stubborn defence of the voluntary, denominational system, and into self-induced delusions of that system's adequacy which were plainly at variance with fact. At the end of the 1867 session, the Conservatives seemed to have no ideas in education beyond propping up the existing system, and their capacity and will to cope with the nation's educational problems were seriously in doubt.

[1] *Ibid.*, clxxxix. 506, 508.

[2] *Ibid.*, clxxxix. 509–10. Read thought that the government should aid night schools for farm boys (*ibid.*, clxxxv. 1077–8). Cf. his *The Education and Wages of the Agricultural Labourer, An Address to the Prize Takers of the Tunstead & Happing Labourers' Association at North Walsham* (Nov. 1867); and for the effect on farmers' attitudes to education of the need for skilled men to operate machinery, E. L. Jones, pp. 333–4.

[3] For which, see above, p. 51.

The performance of the Derby government in the social field in its first year of office was far from negligible, especially when the enormous demands made upon its time and energies by the Reform Bill are recalled. But for electoral reform, social reform would have constituted the staple of its programme in the session of 1867. It largely extended the factory acts, began (if unwittingly) a new era in medical provision for the sick poor, took a significant step forward in the protection of the merchant seaman, greatly strengthened the vaccination system, and acted to regulate agricultural gangs. Moreover, it helped Elcho to pass his Master and Servant Act, and supported Torrens's housing bill. This was not a trivial record for one session.

These measures, however, were in no sense the product of a premeditated Conservative policy. They did not stem from a coherent programme aimed at winning the support of the classes whose interests they most directly touched, though the Factory and Workshops Acts and the Master and Servant Act were certainly seen as useful means of conciliating labour. They were not the planned accompaniment of the extension of the franchise, for nearly all of them were on the government's agenda before Derby had decided that Reform would have to be dealt with. The Metropolitan Poor Act was an *ad hoc* response to a public scandal. Hardy did not grasp its long-term implications and would scarcely have willed them had he done so. The Factory and Workshops Acts derived directly from the work of a Royal Commission and simply continued a well-established process of extension. They had been in preparation under Russell's government and would have been passed by any ministry. The Vaccination Act, too, and the Merchant Shipping Act in certain respects, were measures which the Conservatives found in the administrative and legislative pipeline when they took office. The Gangs Act was brought about largely by the pressure of public opinion, following a Royal Commission report.

All these measures were safe, relatively uncontroversial legislation to meet obvious and admitted needs, and did not in the main seriously affect those interests which the Conservative party specially represented. It was easy for the government to pass them: they constituted precisely the kind of piecemeal, pragmatic adjustment of the existing socio-economic order for which most Conservatives were prepared. Where more fundamental change was at issue, the ministry had shown to less advantage. With the most important and difficult problems on the social scene, elementary education and the position of the trade unions, it had done least to cope. In dealing with the education of the people, where the interests it embodied were vitally concerned, the Conservative party was at its most unprogressive, and both here and

PUNCH, OR THE LONDON CHARIVARI.—JULY 7, 1866.

THE FIRST QUESTIÒN.

WORKING-MAN. "WELL, GENTLEMEN, WHAT ARE *YOU* GOING TO DO FOR ME?"
LORD DERBY (*aside to* DIZZY). "AH! IF HE WERE ONLY A RACEHORSE NOW——"
DISRAELI. "OR AN ASIAN MYSTERY——"

Sir John Pakington

in its attitude to trade unionism it emphasised its determination that whatever might be done for the masses in the way of piecemeal reform, their social subordination should be strictly maintained.

But despite its limitations, the work of 1867 illustrated the capacity of Conservative ministers to come to grips empirically with social questions. Prejudices and preconceptions against the extension of governmental interference in economic and social matters and against the growth of central administrative authority were overborne by practical needs. Hardy's handling of the sick poor question and Northcote's of the merchant seaman problem are good examples. This empiricism of the Conservatives enabled them to demonstrate what they knew they had to demonstrate for their political future—that far from being an obstructive and obscurantist party, they were capable of responding to the nation's needs with moderate reforms. They had shown their willingness, through 'safe legislative progress', to revive the echoes of Tory paternalism and look to the betterment of the condition of the people. It was timely, for by the end of the session of 1867 the second Reform Act had been passed, and the wide extension of the franchise among the urban working men had opened, or seemed to open, a new political era.

II
LEAPING AND LANDING, 1867-8

THE relationship between the Conservative party and the working classes, a secondary consideration so long as Derby and Disraeli pursued the policy of conservative concentration aimed at attracting the Palmerstonian bourgeoisie, became with the passing of the second Reform Act crucial for the party's future. Their creation of a working-class majority in the borough electorate made it essential for the Conservatives to cultivate popular appeal, and gave an added importance to social reform, as a vital instrument in the struggle for the new voters. It seemed to some contemporaries, and has seemed to some later commentators, that Derby and Disraeli consciously willed this altered situation. The extraordinary *volte-face* whereby they passed in 1867 a measure so much larger than that which they had resisted in 1866 that it gave even Bright qualms has been taken to represent the deliberate abandonment of the policy of the earlier 'sixties in favour of an attempt to construct a Conservative democracy, and rebuild the fortunes of the party on the basis of an alliance with a working class entrusted with a large share of political power, but restrained in its exercise by traditional social influences, and rendered docile by paternal social legislation. Disraeli, in particular, on whom responsibility for the conduct of the Reform Bill largely rested, has been pictured as seizing the opportunity to realise a lifelong dream by achieving the union of party and people which had formed the cornerstone of his expressed philosophy since his beginnings in politics in the 'thirties and 'forties. Some Conservatives even suspected him at the time of having determined to call in the people to smash the political power of the bourgeoisie. The old Peelite Beresford Hope, member for Stoke, and, after his brother-in-law, Cranborne, the fiercest Conservative critic of the government's action, protested on behalf of 'the enlightened Liberal-Conservatism of the present free-trade generation, cradled in the days of the great Reform Bill':

This generation ought to have learned during the last thirty-five years, the importance of relying on the middle classes. It ought to appreciate the education and competence of that class, and to understand the elements which are needed to create a good, stable, and enlightened Government. This is the Conservatism of the Reform Bill, the Conservatism on which Peel built up his great party. The old Toryism of the ante-reforming days was a great tradition, but it is past and gone never to return. What are we thus to say of those who, in the face of this fact, and for their own self-interest, pretend to raise up a pale and marrowless ghost of that old Toryism of Bolingbroke and his *Patriot King*—and wish to set the middle and upper class against each other to their mutual destruction, until nothing will be left but the Crown on one side and the mob on the other.[1]

In reality, however, it was the tactical situation, not some project of Conservative democracy, which governed Derby's and Disraeli's change of course. Neither wanted Reform as such. Disraeli, if he toyed momentarily, in July 1866, with the idea of passing Gladstone's bill, in order to get rid of the question, subsequently proved even more reluctant than the prime minister to act.[2] What eventually impelled the Conservative leaders to carry Reform in 1867 was what had impelled them to resist it in 1866—political expediency.

A major influence on their calculations was the powerful working-class agitation for Reform which appeared in mid-1866, and was intensified by economic recession and by the trade unionists' realisation, under the impact of *Hornby v. Close* and the Royal Commission, that the franchise was essential to the protection of their interests. Downright resistance to this pressure offered serious risk of an explosion: concession, on the other hand, was encouraged by the nature of the movement, which aimed rather at social advancement than social upheaval, and could be conciliated with some assurance of safety.[3] In any case, if the ministry, lacking a majority in the Commons, tried to evade the Reform issue, its opponents would almost certainly seize the chance to combine behind some reforming resolution and eject it. The Liberals might then do precisely what Derby and Disraeli had striven in 1866 to prevent their doing—carry Reform on their own lines for their own advantage; or the Conservative party might find itself facing a general election in a posture of resistance to the popular cause.

It was only by dealing with Reform themselves that the Conser-

[1] *3 Hansard*, clxxxvi. 1605–6. 'Toryism', Hope later insisted, 'was really the cause of property and intellect by whomsoever held against numbers . . .' (*ibid.*, clxxxvii. 812). Cf. *Quarterly Review*, cxxii (1867), 550–1.

[2] M. & B., iv. 452–63.

[3] See especially R. Harrison, *Before the Socialists: Studies in Labour and Politics 1861–1881*, c. iii.

vative leaders could hope to turn the situation to profit. A judicious settlement of the question would be a brilliant triumph for the adaptive, 'Peelite' Conservatism, answering to the nation's practical needs, which they had for a decade been trying to foster. It would go far to achieve their aim of ridding their party of the taint of obstruction and reaction, and destroying the idea that whenever the country wanted moderate progress it must turn to the Whigs and Liberals; and if skilfully devised to avoid working-class electoral preponderance, it might still enable the government to achieve its initial aim of consolidating moderate middle-class opinion around the Conservative party, in opposition to Radicalism and democracy.[1] At the same time, it might bring the party the unfamiliar but enticing benefits of identification with a popular measure, and in reaching below the ten-pound line of 1832 might produce a constituency more favourable than that at whose hands the Conservatives had suffered twenty years of permanent minority.[2]

Derby and Disraeli took the superficially Radical principle of household suffrage as the basis of their bill because it seemed to offer a popular and permanent resting-point for the borough franchise, and because it was widely (and perhaps correctly) thought that it would be more beneficial to the Conservatives than a £5 or £6 franchise, bringing in just that class of skilled artisans and trade unionists who would be likely to vote for Bright and Gladstone.[3] But so far were they from intending a Radical or 'democratic' measure that they deliberately smothered it with checks and counterpoises. The Reform Bill as introduced by Disraeli on 18 March 1867 made household suffrage dependent on personal payment of rates, thus excluding the

[1] Such was the hope of the *Imperial Review* (organ of a group of younger Conservatives owing their political inspiration to Disraeli) in its article on 'Conservatism and the Middle Classes', 26 Jan. 1867.

[2] This hope no doubt weighed powerfully with Disraeli, who had no cause to love the existing borough electorate. Sir William Gregory had 'heard him a hundred times in private proclaim his preference for the working-man over the sleek, narrow-minded, dissenting rulers of the boroughs' (Gregory, p. 100).

[3] 'As Claughton [Bishop of Rochester] said to me,' noted Hardy in his diary (28 June 1867: Cranbrook Papers, T501/294, printed, inaccurately, in *Gathorne Hardy*, i. 211) 'our security is in going lower than the combining class.' The Earl of Malmesbury (now Lord Privy Seal) had been, in 1853, perhaps the first leading Conservative to argue the advantage to the party of 'universal' suffrage (W. D. Jones, p. 193). Walter Bagehot told Carnarvon in November 1866 that a moderate measure would favour the Liberals and that the Conservatives would have to go very low in suffrage. 'This he said wd. probably give them the command of the boroughs—& large towns. Rank & position & wealth combined wd. make them irresistible: & this wd. make them supreme for the next five or six years' (memorandum of conversation by Carnarvon, 2 Nov. 1866: P.R.O. 30/6/169, ff. 89–90). See also J. H. Park, *The English Reform Bill of 1867*, pp. 236–7.

476,593 householders under the ten-pound line (about two-thirds of the total) who were compounders, paying their rates through their landlords.[1] It also exacted a two-year residence qualification, and heavily counter-balanced household suffrage with the 'fancy franchises', especially the 'dual' vote, whereby a man qualified under both the household and direct taxation franchises could vote twice (though this the government was prepared from the outset to drop if it proved too unpopular).

It was, in fact, a very limited and conservative measure: it would scarcely have created more new voters than Gladstone's 1866 bill (about 400,000), and the dual vote would have increased the power of the wealthier classes.[2] It represented the attempt of the Conservative chiefs to extricate themselves from the Reform imbroglio with a measure large enough in appearance to quieten the popular clamour, but sufficiently restricted in its practical effects to be palatable to the bulk of the middle classes. So far from appealing to the people as against the bourgeoisie, they were trying to satisfy the one without alienating the other. Disraeli stressed that the government recognised 'the extreme expediency of the principle that the influence of the middle classes of the country should not be diminished', and made no bones about the fact that the bill contained checks and counterpoises designed to maintain a balance between classes.[3] They were granting, he insisted, not 'democratic rights' but 'popular privileges'.

> Popular privileges are consistent with a state of society in which there is great inequality of condition. Democratic rights, on the contrary, demand that there should be equality of condition as the fundamental basis of the society which they regulate. . . . We do not, however, live—and I trust it will never be the fate of this country to live—under a democracy.[4]

When he wrote to Beauchamp, in April, of his hope of 'realising the dream of my life and re-establishing Toryism on a national foundation',[5] it was not a 'Tory Democracy' which Disraeli had in mind, but a system in which the party would draw support from both middle-

[1] Compounding householders above the ten-pound line were also excluded. Clause 34 enabled a compounder to acquire the vote by paying his full rates, and Disraeli stated that every facility would be given to compounders to pay their rates personally and so secure the franchise (*3 Hansard*, clxxxvi. 13–14), but he had told the Queen's secretary, Grey, that he thought not 50,000 would ever use these facilities (letter of 15 March 1867, in *Letters of Queen Victoria*, 2nd series, i. 408).

[2] Seymour, pp. 258–61. The smallness and conservatism of the bill's redistribution scheme, also, would have prevented it from having much impact on the balance of political power.

[3] *3 Hansard*, clxxxvi. 16, 25. Cf. Derby, *ibid.*, clxxxv. 715–16.

[4] *Ibid.*, clxxxvi. 6–7.

[5] M. & B., iv. 528.

and working-class elements in a carefully balanced borough electorate.

The deception which Derby and Disraeli were attempting to practice on the reformers was too crude to have a chance of success, and as they had been forced to take up Reform, so they were forced to carry it on a larger scale than they had intended. Strong popular agitation against their bill's restrictiveness, and the pressure of the opposition, left them little choice but to abandon the checks and counterpoises. Without a majority, and unable to rely entirely on the conservative Whigs, they could not control the Commons, and it was obvious that only a genuinely large measure could bring them any popularity in the country. Only a large measure, too, could put the Reform question to rest, and prevent the Liberals from using it as a recurring device to place themselves in a popular and the Conservative party in an obstructive posture.[1] So the dual vote and the other fancy franchises were given up, the residence qualification was halved, the bill's redistribution scheme was extended, a lodger franchise was provided for the boroughs, and Disraeli made household suffrage a reality by accepting the tenor of a Liberal amendment which abolished compounding in the boroughs, and thus added to the potential electorate the half a million compound householders.

The transformation of the bill was certainly unwelcome to Derby: it made the measure, in his famous phrase, 'a leap in the dark'. Disraeli was less reluctant to broaden the bill: determined to bring off a great coup, and obsessed with the mechanics of parliamentary success, he preferred almost any concession to defeat, and if he did not aim at 'Tory Democracy', he was ready to go far to align his party with the popular and progressive trend. But even he was perhaps a little apprehensive at the extent to which the government was driven. His surrender to Hodgkinson's amendment abolishing compounding, when he could probably have mustered a majority against it, has sometimes been cited as proof that he really wanted a 'democratic' measure. The step was, however, essential to pacify the Reform agitation and salvage the ministry's popularity, and it was virtually enforced, too, by the fact that, owing to the very uneven incidence of compounding, the exclusion of compounders would have created indefensible anomalies in the franchise as between different districts, making the bill, as Gladstone said, a lottery as well as an imposture. What it is important to notice is that having made the concession Disraeli tried deviously to limit its effect, introducing provisions which, by allowing compounding to continue at the wish of landlord and tenant, would have preserved the practice in many cases, so that large numbers would still have been excluded from the register, as

[1] For Disraeli on this point, see his speech at Aylesbury, 19 Nov. 1868, reported in the *Standard*, 20 Nov. 1868.

under the original bill.[1] The Chancellor's statement that the government had always wanted to get rid of the obstacles to the admission of the compounder[2] was just one of his frequent attempts to give a veneer of consistency to his course and to persuade the new voters—as he must—that he had willed their creation. Neither he nor Derby had bargained for a measure as large as that which they actually passed: it was a product neither of their principles nor of their stratagems, but of their necessities.

Still less did the Reform Act represent the wishes of their colleagues and followers. Hardly any of the cabinet really wanted Reform, and if only Cranborne, Carnarvon, and Peel resigned, those who remained were deeply disturbed at the removal of the checks on which they had relied to make household suffrage safe. In the party at large, there was certainly widespread realisation of the necessity of a substantial measure, and when Derby and Disraeli sought to avert the cabinet resignations by abandoning household suffrage as the basis of their prospective bill, its reinstatement was due largely to the pressure of a strong section of the party, headed by Graves of Liverpool and Laird of Birkenhead.[3] But the supporters of household suffrage wanted it with safeguards, and the admission of the compounders was unwelcome to most of them. The great bulk of the party had never desired Reform, and resented the way in which Disraeli led them into a measure of such size. Among the country gentlemen, Sir Michael Hicks Beach wrote in old age, 'very many, including myself, felt that there was something like a repetition of Sir R. Peel's betrayal'.[4]

It is possible that only Cranborne's disinclination to organise resistance in the party preserved Disraeli from something like a repetition of Sir R. Peel's fate. Cranborne's misgivings were felt in some degree by many on the Conservative benches. Working-class preponderance in the boroughs was an unnerving prospect. It might wreck the party's strongholds in the smaller boroughs, without bringing compensating gains in the great towns: not a few Conservatives would have endorsed Cranborne's warning to Derby that 'it is on the smaller boroughs we depend. Nothing will ever give us

[1] See *3 Hansard*, clxxxvii. 1135–40, 1142–7, 1176–83; H. Cox, *A History of the Reform Bills of 1866 and 1867*, pp. 206–8. Landlords, too, would have been able to control the enfranchisement of their tenants, by dictating whether or not they should compound. Derby expressed his regret that the Commons would not sanction these arrangements (*3 Hansard*, clxxxviii. 1791).

[2] *Ibid.*, clxxxvii. 723–4, 725.

[3] No doubt men like Graves and Laird (and, indeed, Derby and Disraeli) were influenced by their knowledge of the strength and potential of working-class Conservatism in the north-west, especially Lancashire. See A. Briggs, *Victorian People*, pp. 301–3.

[4] Quoted in Cecil, i. 251, n. 1.

real strength in the large boroughs.'[1] It was mere guesswork whether the new electors would be guided by traditional social influences and prove predominantly Conservative. Shaftesbury, one of the stoutest opponents of Reform, argued that traditional social influences hardly operated on the masses in the great towns, and proclaimed it a delusion to suppose that 'out of this hecatomb of British traditions and British institutions there will arise the great and glorious Phoenix of a Conservative democracy'.[2] No doubt the potential effect of household suffrage on Parliament was limited by the lack of any substantial redistribution, but there was force in Cranborne's and Peel's contention[3] that this check could only be temporary: the distribution of seats must soon be brought into conformity with wealth and population, and the balance of power be tilted away from the rural and agricultural south and east towards the urban and industrial north and midlands, where the new electoral strength of the working men was greatest. Disraeli admitted that it was in the nature of things that the distribution of parliamentary power should be towards the north of England,[4] and many felt with Shaftesbury that the consummation announced by Cobden was approaching—'the towns must govern'.[5] The working men would ultimately dominate the electoral system, and, perhaps under the whip of their trade unions, might vote as a bloc to promote the material interests of their class, turning Parliament into their instrument in what Shaftesbury called 'that great feud instituted between the House of Want and the House of Have',[6] and using it to enforce a drastic remodelling of the economic and social order.[7] The redistribution of property, the penal taxation of the rich, the subordination of capital to labour, and the imposition of trade union tyranny were seen as some of the possible results.

Few Conservatives were entirely unaffected by such fears, and few wanted a measure as large as that which emerged. But for the most part they saw it was inevitable, and convinced themselves that perhaps its consequences would not bear out their misgivings.[8] No doubt there was some safeguard in 'the enormous powers of resistance to democratic levelling in our *social* habits and institutions, ingrain,

[1] Cranborne to Derby, 22 Feb. 1867 (typescript copy): Salisbury Papers, 'Stanley', p. 2.

[2] *3 Hansard*, clxxxviii. 1929–31, 1934.

[3] *Ibid.*, clxxxviii. 839, 1099–1100.

[4] *Ibid.*, clxxxviii. 283.

[5] *Ibid.*, clxxxviii. 1932.

[6] *Ibid.*, clxxxviii. 1933.

[7] Some of their own pronouncements gave colour to this fear. See Park, pp. 82–4, 98–9, 109–10, 112–13, 130–1.

[8] See, on the willingness of Conservatives to believe that the working men would behave with moderation and deference when enfranchised, F. B. Smith, ' "Democracy" in the Second Reform Debates', *Historical Studies, Australia and New Zealand*, xi (1964), 319–21.

deep-rooted, hard-knotted as our country's oaks'.[1] And the urban working men might turn out to have Conservative leanings. Disraeli's friend, Beauchamp, held that some of the largest towns were already becoming Conservative, owing to the spread of education, 'leading the artizan to withdraw his countenance from the demagogue, to abstain from agitation, and to give his sympathies to those who were his true friends';[2] and the *Imperial Review*, organ of a group of younger, 'Disraelian' Conservatives, was confident that the bill of 1867 would give the Tories power as the scheme of 1832 had secured the supremacy of the Whigs, writing: 'In the large boroughs the extension of the franchise will destroy the present Liberal monopoly.'[3] Cranborne's bitter characterisation of the considerations which influenced the party is well-known and contains some truth:

> A vague idea that the poorer men are the more easily they are influenced by the rich; a notion that those whose vocation it was to bargain and battle with the middle class must on that account love the gentry; an impression—for it could be no more—that the ruder class of minds would be more sensitive to traditional emotions; and an indistinct application to English politics of Napoleon's (then) supposed success in taming revolution by universal suffrage; all these arguments, never thought out, but floating loosely in men's minds, and accepted as motives for action at a time when the party battle was too hot to admit of close reflection, went to make up the clear conviction of the mass of the Conservative party, that in a Reform Bill more Radical than that of the Whigs they had discovered the secret of a sure and signal triumph.[4]

The conviction was less clear and less general than Cranborne alleged, but certainly it was possible to hope that the Reform Act would not injure and might help the party. And if hopes were deceived, if social influences failed and working-class Conservatism proved largely mythical, at least the damage would be limited by the lack of any serious redistribution. In any case, the majority of Conservatives had no stomach for a dangerous and probably futile resistance to the Reform agitation: as Henley said, there was no point in opposing advance until they 'almost forced people in the humbler classes to set themselves in antagonism to all other classes'.[5] It was better, and more attractive, to satisfy the popular demand.

[1] Henry Cecil to Cranborne, 7 March 1867: Salisbury Papers, S.C. '*Influence*', Cecil reminded Cranborne, 'is not told by counting votes.'

[2] *3 Hansard*, clxxxviii. 1850. Beauchamp also thought that the counties were gradually passing into the hands of the Liberals, which is perhaps why he favoured a large reduction of the county franchise.

[3] *Imperial Review*, 13 July 1867. Cf. *ibid.*, 4 May 1867—'Conservatism Among the Working Classes'. For the group with which the *Imperial Review* was associated, see below, p. 117.

[4] *Quarterly Review*, cxxvii (1869), 541–2.

[5] *3 Hansard*, clxxxvii. 800–3. Cf. *ibid.*, clxxxix. 571.

There were a few Conservatives who accepted Reform in a more generous spirit, recognising that the political aspirations of the working classes were legitimate and that the national community had much to gain by meeting them. Ward Hunt took issue with Cranborne and Lowe for clinging to the idea that 'Parliament should govern for the people', and objecting to the principle that 'Parliament should govern by and with the people', and suggested that the former should contest a large constituency:

> He would then find that an immense number of those whom he wished to exclude from the franchise had thoughts working in their brains little dreamed of by those who in the pride of their intellect looked down upon the struggling sons of toil.[1]

Powell declared:

> a more direct representation of the working men in that House would lead to a more accurate knowledge of their condition and their capacity; and that circumstance would necessarily be productive of some amount of advantage, enabling Parliament as it would to legislate with more wisdom on matters relating to the most numerous classes of society.[2]

A speech of Disraelian undertones came from that uncharacteristic Conservative, H. A. M. Butler-Johnstone, who saw in the enfranchisement of the working man a condition of that union of England's 'two nations' without which the country's most vital interests must be in jeopardy:

> so long as Reform remained unsettled the unity of the country was destroyed; because a feeling existed in the country among a large class of the community that they were unjustly excluded from a share in the Government of the country.... It was a far greater evil that our mechanics should be careless of the position, and indifferent to the interests, of their country than that they should succeed in getting passed laws with which the present House of Commons disagreed, or that they should run counter to the preconceived ideas of the upper classes, or even somewhat overtax the rich. England, unhappily, was not now so united as she ought to be; but was like those animals which possessed a double organism—two centres and two hearts.... If this country was to be engaged in a life and death struggle with any of the nations of the world—if we had to defend our overland route to India—if we had to maintain our passage through Egypt—how should we fare if the whole country was not united?[3]

[1] *Ibid.*, clxxxvi. 1623–4.

[2] *Ibid.*, clxxxvi. 626. Liddell spoke of 'wholesome pressure' being put upon the upper classes (*ibid.*, clxxxvi. 1632).

[3] *Ibid.*, clxxxvi. 75. Butler-Johnstone was to vote for Gladstone's Irish Church resolutions in 1868, differ with his party over the Eastern question and

The young ex-Palmerstonian Viscount Sandon, too, saw Reform as a means to social harmony. There had arisen among the artisans, he told the Stone Constitutional Association,

> a spirit almost of separation, as if they were another nation and had no friendly relations with the classes above them—and I hold nothing to be more dangerous than that a great class like that should have no exponents of their views in the councils of the nation. (Hear, hear.) Don't let us feel as if we had been forced into admitting that great body of new electors, but let us feel that great numbers of them are men whom we should hail as men whose views ought to influence the House of Commons. (Hear, hear.)

Sandon felt it would be a good thing if some of the great towns returned trade union leaders as representatives of the working classes:

> I venture to say that these classes are wholly unrepresented in Parliament at this moment, and by introducing their representatives into Parliament you would fix the attention of the working classes on questions of the deepest interest to the nation, and by discussion in the presence of the greater minds of the nation many fallacious theories would be exposed and exploded, which hold their ground in the narrower circle in which they are cherished. (Applause.)[1]

But even these views were partly rationalisations of necessity, and they were not very widespread. The overwhelming majority of the Conservative party, like its leaders, did not want large-scale Reform, but reluctantly accepted it as unavoidable, and hoped that it might prove profitable. Derby and Disraeli and their followers, in 1867, did not determine to trust the people, or put their faith in a Conservative democracy. They did what they felt they had to do, to satisfy the popular agitation, reconcile the upper strata of the working classes to the established political system, and 'dish the Whigs'. They did it, in the main, grudgingly, and it was doubtful on the morrow of the Reform Act whether they would be willing and flexible enough to accommodate themselves to the consequences of their own action, and achieve the support among the urban working class on which the party's future must now partly depend—all the more doubtful because if in the short term Reform focused attention on the need to appeal to the masses, its long-term implications offered increased prospects of that junction with the bourgeoisie which the party instinctively preferred.

. . . . .

[1] Report in *Staffordshire Advertiser*, 27 July 1867. Sandon was out of Parliament at this time.

resign his Canterbury seat in 1878, give his friend H. M. Hyndman the copy of *Capital* which converted the latter to Marxism, and join Hyndman in 1881 in founding the Democratic (later Social Democratic) Federation.

The second Reform Act was far from effecting an immediate revolution in British politics, or initiating a working-class take-over of political power. It added perhaps 960,000 voters to an electorate of 1,057,000, and gave the working men a majority in the borough electorate, which it increased by about 138%.[1] But the impact of this apparently sweeping change was softened and diffused by a variety of factors. Their lack of independent political organisation meant that the new working-class voters were in no position to flood Parliament with 'labour' members, or enforce their will on the existing parties; nor did they prove, after 1867, totally unamenable to management by the old methods of corruption and influence. Most important in limiting the act's effect on Parliament, and in preserving, as the Conservatives had wished, the strength of the landed interest, was the absence of any substantial redistribution: the urban and industrial north and midlands, where the new electoral power of the working men was most heavily concentrated, gained a few seats, but remained grossly under-represented, in proportion to wealth and population, compared with the rural and agricultural south and east.[2]

Yet if it caused no sudden upheaval, the Reform Act necessarily altered the conditions of politics. Both parties now had to compete for working-class votes, and working-class interests, aspirations, and needs took on a novel importance, becoming increasingly part of the staple of the political contest, instead of one of its peripheral inconveniences. A principal effect of this change was considerably to enhance the status of social questions in national politics: dealing directly with the most vital concerns of the labouring population, they inevitably attracted growing attention, and came to exercise, as they had not often done in the past, a serious influence on the relative fortunes of Liberal and Conservative. Derby and Disraeli had indeed edged reluctantly into a new political era, and the Conservative party was faced with the necessity of making a major effort to adjust to the coming of the mass electorate by cultivating popular appeal and demonstrating its ability to occupy itself in a sympathetic spirit with the social wants and aspirations of the working classes.

It was, however, problematic from the first how vigorously that

[1] In England and Wales. Reform acts for Scotland and Ireland were passed in 1868. The extension of the borough franchise was in practice a good deal restricted by the operation of the registration system, which kept many qualified persons—especially working men—off the register, and made the lodger franchise virtually a dead letter.

[2] See Seymour, pp. 335–50. As late as 1884, the 111,000 inhabitants of 15 rural boroughs in Cornwall, Devon, and Wilts returned 18 members, while the 2,100,000 inhabitants of Birmingham, Leeds, Liverpool, Manchester, Sheffield, and Wolverhampton returned only 16.

effort would be prosecuted. The bulk of the party was cut off from the urban masses, resentful and fearful of the need to seek their applause, and hardly capable of appealing to them in a wholehearted manner. Moreover, its instincts and its interests alike severely restricted its capacity to bid for the new voters by focusing on their social condition and promising governmental and legislative action to promote their welfare. Most Conservatives had acquiesced in Reform the better to consolidate the existing economic and social system, and the substantial modification of that system in an attempt to buy the votes which Reform had created was almost inconceivable to them. Many of them emerged from the traumatic experience of 1867 more anxious than before to put a brake on the advance of the 'democracy' and on the pace of economic and social change. Liddell had said during the Reform debates:

> When the excitement of present events had gone by, the old duty of the drag-chain would have to be resumed, and the influence of the country party would have to be used to check anything like rash or hasty legislation.[1]

One of Derby's first cares after the passage of Reform was to warn the new working-class voters against supposing that Parliament could now be induced to pass legislation of an exceptional kind for their especial benefit.[2] To some extent, indeed, the Reform Act, while rendering governmental and legislative action on behalf of the working classes more necessary and more inevitable, both from a national and a party point of view, had also made Conservatives more wary of it. Such action appeared in a new light in a political situation which offered the prospect that government and Parliament might ultimately fall under working-class control: principles of state intervention in economic and social affairs admitted now might one day be given very wide application, to the drastic discomfiture of the propertied classes.

The Reform Act, too, if it made working-class support indispenable, tended in the long run to engender a limiting influence on the party's pursuit of that support by hastening the movement towards it of middle-class elements for whom its attraction depended largely on its potential as a focus of resistance to working-class advance. Household suffrage in the boroughs was a disturbing development not only to the most defensively-minded sections of the bourgeoisie, who had opposed Reform in 1866–7, but also to many who had hitherto

[1] *3 Hansard*, clxxxvii. 1158.

[2] Speech at Manchester: *The Times*, 18 Oct. 1867. Derby had in mind particularly the regulation of wages. 'To interfere between labour and capital', he said, 'is beyond the legislation of any Parliament . . .'

worked in alliance with labour and encouraged its aspirations. It increased their nervousness at the growing power of the working-class movement, fed their anxiety to protect their economic and social position against proletarian pressure, and intensified their conservative instincts;[1] and ultimately, by strengthening the Liberal left wing and enlarging the impact upon Liberalism of its affiliations with organised labour, it made it more and more likely that those instincts would find expression in support for the Conservative party. The coup of 1867, as Disraeli perhaps foresaw, opened two avenues to the Conservatives simultaneously: it enabled them to pose as a great popular party, extending the hand of trust to the artisan and bringing him within the pale of the constitution, but also drastically increased the pressures which had for some time been tending to bring them the support of the apprehensive middle class. Superficially a bold appeal to the people, it created in the long term the conditions necessary to the success of the policy of drawing in the conservative bourgeoisie which Derby and Disraeli had been pursuing before 1867, and which their original Reform Bill had been devised to preserve—a policy, however, which was bound to place severe constraints on the party's approach to the working man.

The middle-class reaction towards the Conservative party implicit in the Reform Act could not, of course, get up speed at once. The party's *volte-face* on Reform had temporarily rendered its credentials suspect and intensified dislike and distrust of Disraeli, and there was a good deal of middle-class opinion which, if it was concerned about the Liberals' capacity to resist the pressure of labour, yet wanted a programme of legislative reforms which only the Liberals could be expected to implement. But there was no mistaking, even at the end of 1867, the possibilities which the post-Reform era held for the Conservatives in the way of increased middle-class support. The question was how the pursuit of this was to be reconciled with the necessary appeal to the working man. The two would not necessarily be easy to run in harness: this was pointed out in November by the *Imperial Review*, which saw already a middle-class movement towards Conservatism out of fright at household suffrage, but at the same time found the working class not indisposed to follow 'the gentlemen of England' in revulsion from the bourgeoisie, writing:

> it is of vital importance not to neglect the opportunity, now offered, of conciliating the artizans who, having unfortunately learned to regard the

[1] As early as February 1868, the Reform League's secretary, George Howell, visiting Bradford, noted: 'My private impression is that the manufacturing class are rather afraid of the power the People now have. They are beginning to be shy' (quoted in Harrison, p. 146). Cf. Granville to Gladstone, 7 Sept. 1867, quoted in Vincent, p. 251.

> millowner with suspicion, if not with hatred, are greatly inclined to repose their confidence in the landed gentry, as a class that has no interest even apparently antagonistic to their own, and to which they owe the only boon they have recently won from Parliament—the Ten-hours Bill.[1]

The 'opposite tendency' of the two trends, the *Review* considered, made the course of the Tory leaders 'one of unexampled difficulty'. The Conservative party was faced once more with the old problem of exploiting simultaneously middle-class support which depended largely on its reliability as a bulwark against the masses, and working-class support which in some areas (the *Imperial Review* was obviously thinking primarily of the north-west) rested partly on a supposed common antipathy towards the bourgeoisie. It could no longer afford to follow too exclusively its preference for a coalition with the middle classes in the Peelite alliance of landed and commercial property, for its own enlargement of the franchise had made substantial working-class support vital to its electoral future; but its anxiety to take advantage of the rightward trend of the bourgeoisie necessarily qualified the tone of its approach to the masses.

Thus the appeal which the Conservatives were obliged to make to the new working-class voters could not be couched in anything like Radical or 'democratic' terms. The party could not commit itself strongly to the furtherance of working-class interests as such, or hold out the prospect of major adjustments to the existing economic and social order. It had to address itself to the working men primarily in terms of the interests which they could plausibly be said to have in common with the classes above them. It had to try to convince them that it was precisely the established institutions and arrangements of the country to whose defence it was bound that constituted the best security for their welfare. It had to exploit every emotion of patriotism, loyalty, and deference which might induce in them attachment to those institutions and arrangements, and allegiance to the party which upheld them. It had, in short, to identify itself with the forces and feelings making for national cohesion, and to proclaim the community of class interests in the preservation of the constitution, the maintenance of social stability, and the enlargement of national prestige. Only thus could it draw on all the possible sources of future strength.

Disraeli saw this clearly. The party's chances of popularity and power in the post-Reform era seemed to him dependent on its ability to take on the aspect of the great national party the principle of which he had been propounding for more than thirty years—a party deriving its strength from, and representing the interests of, all classes, combining stalwart constitutionalism and the defence of

[1] *Imperial Review*, 30 Nov. 1867. The 'Ten-hours Bill' is Walpole's factory act.

the economic and social order with popular sympathies and readiness for moderate and necessary change. The progressive Conservatism of Peel fused at last with the romantic Toryism of Young England—such was the formula that was to enable the party to reconcile the assimilation of the apprehensive middle class with the cultivation of the urban working man. At the Mansion House in August 1867 and at Edinburgh in October, Disraeli recurred forcibly to his lifelong insistence that the Tory party was the national party of England:

> It is formed of all classes, from the highest to the most homely, and it upholds a series of institutions that are in theory, and ought to be in practice, an embodiment of the national requirements and the security of the national rights . . . . when the people are led by their natural leaders, and when, by their united influence, the national institutions fulfil their original intention, the Tory party is triumphant: and then, under Providence, will secure the prosperity and the power of the country.[1]

The national party was a 'popular' party, but not a 'democratic' one. The object of Reform had been, and the object of the national party must be, to foster 'popular privileges', not to countenance the assertion of 'democratic rights', to reinforce the social order by conciliating those who formed its base, not to assist in a process of levelling.

> Believe me [Disraeli had assured the Merchant Taylors in June] that the elements of democracy do not exist in England. England is a country of classes, and the change that is impending in this country will only make those classes more united, more complete, and more cordial.[2]

The appeal of the national party to the working man must start from the proposition that 'the due subordination of the various grades of society to those above them is essential to the welfare of the great body of the people';[3] it must rely on convincing him that it was in the context of the existing social system, under the paternal ministrations of his 'natural leaders', that his interests were most secure. Addressing a working-class audience at Edinburgh in October, Disraeli set the pattern for the Conservative party's approach to the people in the age of the mass electorate.

> I have [he said] from my earliest public life been of opinion that this

[1] Speech at Edinburgh, 29 Oct.: *The Chancellor of the Exchequer in Scotland*, p. 29. This speech also contained an important reminder to the party of the inevitability of change. Cf. the extracts from the Mansion House speech in M. & B., iv. 553.

[2] Report in *The Times*, 12 June 1867. Introducing the Reform Bill of 18 March, Disraeli had insisted that 'this country is a country of classes, and a country of classes it will ever remain' (*3 Hansard*, clxxxvi. 25; and cf. above, p. 91).

[3] *Imperial Review*, 26 Oct. 1867.

Sir Henry Selwin-Ibbetson

Richard Assheton Cross

assumed and affected antagonism between the interests of what are called the Conservative classes and the labouring classes is utterly unfounded. . . . I have always looked on the interests of the labouring classes as essentially the most conservative interests of the country. The rights of labour have been to me always as sacred as the rights of property, and I have always thought that those who were most interested in the stability and even in the glory of a State are the great mass of the population, happy to enjoy the privileges of freemen under good laws, and proud at the same time of the country which confers on its inhabitants a name of honour and of glorious reputation in every quarter of the globe. . . . do not listen to those who pretend to you that society is to be revolutionised because the people are trusted. Do not listen to those who tell you that you have been invested with democratic rights, and that, therefore, you must effect great changes in the fortunes and form of one of the most considerable nations and Governments that ever existed. Be proud of the confidence which the constituted authorities of the country have reposed in you, by investing you with popular privileges; prove that you know the value of such privileges; and that you will exercise them to maintain the institutions of your country, and to increase its power, its glory, and its fame.[1]

The Conservative party's appeal to the working-class voter was to depend primarily upon his natural susceptibility to conservative feeling; it was to reflect the belief that the basic principles of Conservatism, 'loyalty to the Throne, reverence for the Church, and the desire to maintain and promote the social and political greatness of the Empire—are such as enlist the support of all sections of society alike'.[2] Patriotism and religion, allegiance to the crown and deference to the quality, would, it was hoped, sustain enough genuine Conservatism among the new voters to ensure the electoral future of the 'national' party, without the necessity of that party's adopting an advanced popular platform.

Such was the approach to the post-Reform electorate that both its natural instincts and its strategic interests impelled the Conservative party to adopt. It was an approach in which social reform could be given only a muted rôle. Yet even that muted rôle was an important one. Working-class Conservatism could not be fostered solely by patronising incantations and injunctions to remember that 'national institutions' were the security of 'popular privileges'. The party had

[1] *The Chancellor of the Exchequer in Scotland*, pp. 35, 36–7, 44. Cf. the well-known message to the London and Westminster Working Men's Constitutional Association, quoted in M. & B., iv. 563: 'None are so interested in maintaining the institutions of the country as the working classes. The rich and the powerful will not find much difficulty under any circumstances in maintaining their rights, but the privileges of the people can only be defended and secured by popular institutions.'

[2] *Imperial Review*, 16 Nov. 1867.

to give the working men concrete assurance of its willingness to look after their material interests, such as the pursuit of social improvement could best provide. If the social reform which it could endorse was limited in character and scope, it was nonetheless an essential element in the appeal to the new borough constituency.

The extension of the franchise certainly helped to make Conservatives more conscious of the interests and needs of the urban working classes, and more convinced of the necessity of paying increased attention to them, for the stability of the country as well as the profit of the party. Viscount Sandon coupled with his welcome to the new voters, in July 1867, an urgent plea for action to tackle the social evils of the great cities in which so many of them lived:

> The future [he declared] is entirely for the great cities. Population is more and more tending towards them, and they should excite the earnest attention of statesmen, who can find no greater and no more important work than to make them more healthy and more decent places for people to live in, to afford them a better supply of good and pure water and air.[1]

The potential usefulness of social reform as a means of winning the working-class vote, and the advisability of fostering and exploiting the party's traditions of social paternalism, were obvious enough. The young Disraelians who ran the *Imperial Review*, if sceptical of the efficacy of social legislation, asserted that the Tories would make more progress with it than the Whigs—'what little legislation can do to effect amelioration will undoubtedly be attempted'—and stressed the contrast between Whig opposition to social reform, based on the self-interest of middle-class employers and on individualistic, *laisser-faire* ideas, and the Tory record of protecting the labouring population by such measures as the factory acts.[2] No one, of course, showed more awareness of the electoral value of social reform than Disraeli himself. Addressing the working men at Edinburgh, in October 1867, he emphasised his support for social improvement over thirty years, and made play with the measures passed in the last session, which, he said, had shown that ministers had not forgotten 'that which is one of the first and principal duties of any Minister, which is to consider whether, by legislation, the condition of the great body of the people can be improved'.[3] It might have been expected that under Disraeli's impulsion the government would make some effort in the

[1] Speech to the Stone Constitutional Association: *Staffordshire Advertiser*, 27 July 1867.

[2] *Imperial Review*, 13 July 1867, 25 Jan. 1868.

[3] *The Chancellor of the Exchequer in Scotland*, pp. 33–4, 35ff.

session of 1867–8 to exploit social reform as a way of acquiring working-class support. When Derby's retirement through ill-health in February 1868 gave Disraeli the positions of power he had striven for throughout his political life, the leadership of the Conservative party and prime ministership of England, he had, in theory, the opportunity to make the cautious pursuit of social improvement a principal feature of the Conservative platform. But he gave no decisive lead, and the government took no striking initiative in the social field.

It was partly that much had already been tackled in the session of 1867; partly that after the government's defeat on Gladstone's Irish Church resolutions in May 1868, and Disraeli's announcement of a dissolution in the autumn, only essential business could be transacted. But there was also the clear realisation of Disraeli and his colleagues that neither the party's interests and prejudices nor the need to take a line which would attract the conservative bourgeoisie permitted too marked a stress on measures designed to benefit primarily the working classes. Social reform must be part of the equipment of the national party; it could not, at least for the present, be one of its major themes. The government did attempt to press forward, in 1867–8, with the work of social improvement, but it could do so only on a limited basis.

Its main concern in the social sphere in the first post-Reform session was education. During the latter half of 1867, ministers became increasingly aware that failure to come to grips with the education question would seriously damage their credit, and might result in the opposition's stepping in. The growing pressure of dissatisfaction (especially in the great towns) with the deficiencies of the existing system, which threatened to place Britain, both socially and economically, irretrievably behind states like Prussia, undoubtedly affected them; but perhaps an even more powerful factor was the widespread feeling that the extension of the franchise made national elementary education essential to ensure that future working-class voters grew up under influences promoting acceptance of the established order.[1] Whether popular education would actually foster Toryism, as the *Imperial Review* thought,[2] was doubtful; but at least it might prevent social upheaval.

At Edinburgh in October, Disraeli paid marked attention to education. If Britain's limited population was to sustain her great imperial position, he declared,

> it is not only our duty, but it is an absolute necessity, that we should study to make every man the most effective being that education can

[1] On this, see B. Simon, pp. 354–8.

[2] 13 July 1867.

> possibly constitute him. In the old wars there used to be a story that one Englishman could beat three members of some other nation; but I think if we want to maintain our power, we ought to make one Englishman equal really in the business of life to three other men that any other nation can furnish.

On how this was to be done Disraeli was vague, and he showed some complacency about the existing state of things, but he announced that there would be a measure in the approaching session.[1] The government had apparently decided to grasp the nettle.

It had, however, no clear plan. Conservative opinion was far from united on the method of tackling the education problem. Some welcomed the announcement of a measure, like Earl Nelson, who told Disraeli: 'our greatest chance for the future is to win the confidence & thanks of the people before we have to appeal to their suffrages.'[2] But many shared the attitude of the *Quarterly*, which, in reviewing the prospect of educational expansion, was obviously irritated by the idea of the higher classes having to pay for the instruction of the lower, and saw in the advent of universal, compulsory education the fatal shattering of the existing system, with its superintendence by gentry and clergy, and 'harmony with the present state of society'.[3] The anxiety of the Conservative party to protect the existing system severely limited the possible scope of the government's measure; yet it was necessary to produce something large and useful enough to satisfy public opinion. Ministers were in a difficult position, and nothing had been settled by the opening of the new session in November. The Queen's Speech referred to education only in the most cautious terms, and Derby said that much more information was required.[4] It seems to have been Earl Russell's initiative from the Liberal benches in giving notice of a series of resolutions calling for educational reforms, including the appointment of an education minister, that galvanised the cabinet into setting Marlborough to work on a bill.

Marlborough had accepted the Presidency of the Council mainly

[1] *The Chancellor of the Exchequer in Scotland*, pp. 25–7. This was the first Edinburgh speech; in his second, to the working men, Disraeli said much the same, but also urged greater attention to technical education, to enable the British artisan to keep up with his foreign competitors (*ibid.*, pp. 39–43).

[2] Nelson to Disraeli, 4 Nov. 1867: Disraeli Papers, B/XXI/N/47, and see also 47a. Nelson had some interesting suggestions: he favoured a conscience clause for all denominational schools in single-school areas, extra payment for the better schools, liberal assistance for art and night schools, and the extension of the university local examinations 'to a lower class of our people', and enclosed a scheme for the adaptation of the half-time system to agricultural labour.

[3] *Quarterly Review*, cxxiii (1867), 274.

[4] *3 Hansard*, cxc. 5, 49.

because it carried the superintendence of education,[1] and had, in fact, assumed the control of educational matters normally exercised by the Vice-President.[2] Hence he opposed from the first the idea of creating a special education minister, who would take education away from the Council Office: such a step was discussed in cabinet on 30 November, but evidently received little support, since Marlborough was able to pour cold water on it when replying to Russell's resolutions two days later.[3] The Lord President's desire to keep hold of education, however, was unaccompanied by any large proposals for its advancement. The scheme which he devised in December 1867 and January 1868 did not apparently go much beyond an educational census, the statutory consolidation of the Privy Council rules, and a compromise on the conscience clause issue, worked out in consultation with the Archbishop of Canterbury, who advised that a clause limited to single-school parishes and allowing parents to withdraw children from *any* lesson (as Derby had suggested in 1866) would be acceptable.[4] The vital issue of rating seems hardly to have come up, though Marlborough had to squash a crackbrained proposal from Montagu, who wanted to empower town councils to levy rates for existing schools (in lieu of subscriptions) and for the building of new ones (on the application of any denomination).[5] This attempt to subsidise denominationalism out of the rates would have roused every dissenter in the country.

By mid-January 1868 Marlborough's measure was ready, but now confusion set in. Disraeli, thinking entirely in terms of political tactics—'All his thought', noted Hardy wryly,[6] 'is what Parliament will take & what will secure the Govt.!'—decided that the country was not ripe for substantial legislation, and suggested deferring a bill to the next session, while recurring to the idea of creating an education minister (no doubt as a device to make it seem that the

1 See Derby to Disraeli, 5 Feb. 1868: Disraeli Papers, B/XX/S/482.

2 Probably Montagu's conscience clause *gaffe* (above, pp. 82–3) contributed to his subordination in educational matters.

3 See Stanley's report of a cabinet on 30 Nov. 1867 (Disraeli Papers B/XX/S/790a); *3 Hansard*, cxc. 504–5. Montagu had raised the question of an education minister on 13 Nov., when sending Disraeli a copy of an extraordinarily confused memorandum proposing to substitute for the Committee of Council a Board or Council of Education under the Lord President. This is in the Disraeli Papers, B/IX/B/1, bearing Montagu's note of 13 Nov.; there is another copy in the P.R.O. (Ed. 24/54). Administrative reorganisation was apparently much under discussion at this moment: see also the 'Memorandum relative to the Business of the Privy Council Office', 18 Nov. 1867 (Ed. 24/55).

4 Canterbury to Marlborough, 31 Dec. 1867: Marlborough Papers, vol. ii, no. 160. Cf. same to same, 18 Jan. 1868: *ibid.*, no. 174.

5 See Montagu to Marlborough, 4, 6, and 7 Jan. 1868: *ibid.*, nos. 162, 165–6.

6 Diary, 10 Jan. 1868: Cranbrook Papers, T501/294.

government was doing something).[1] He was brought round by Derby, even talked to Corry of bringing in the bill himself, and approved Marlborough's scheme;[2] but the way ahead was not yet clear. There was considerable divergence of view in the cabinet as to what the government measure should contain, reflected publicly in speeches by Stanley and Hardy at Bristol, which made it obvious that the former wanted much more extensive legislation than the latter.[3]

Evidently Stanley and others felt that the education question must be tackled on a really large basis, and proposals far outrunning Marlborough's were now brought into discussion—in particular, the application of the conscience clause to the annual grants, and the introduction of rating. Pakington, of course, had long supported both; and though the first remained unpalatable to his colleagues, some of them were by this time ready to accept the second. Northcote was one, though, as always, he was worried by the difficulty of reconciling rating with voluntaryism.[4] Another was Walpole, whose ideas interestingly foreshadowed the main lines of Forster's act of 1870. He rejected merely permissive rating, telling Disraeli:

> . . . I am driven to this conclusion, that the only fair thing, and (as far as I can see) the only wise thing is for the central authority to take upon itself, after due enquiry, the compulsory establishment of rate Schools where no Schools or no sufficient Schools exist; to prescribe the district for which they should be built; to charge that district with a specified portion of the expence [*sic*], and to defray the payment of the other portion out of the Parliamentary Educational grant.
>
> I would make these Schools undenominational unless & until any religious body would undertake to build or to maintain them; and in either of these cases, I would allow them to become denominational Schools with a Conscience Clause.
>
> This would at once meet the difficulty, as to supplying Schools, where either none exist, or where those which do exist are insufficient: and at the same time it would do less to disturb the present system than any plan which has yet been proposed.[5]

These advanced views inevitably divided the cabinet, and ministers found themselves in a quandary between a far-reaching measure

[1] See Disraeli to Stanley, 17 Jan. 1868, in M. & B., iv. 577; Derby to Disraeli, 11 Jan. 1868 (Disraeli Papers, B/XX/S/471). Apparently Disraeli suggested Walpole as the new minister, a nomination Derby did not favour.

[2] Letters cited in the preceding note, and Disraeli to M. Corry, 16 Jan. 1868 (Disraeli Papers, B/XX/D/70).

[3] Report in *The Times*, 23 Jan. 1868.

[4] See Northcote to Disraeli, 25 Jan. 1868: Add. MS. 50016, ff. 3–4. Northcote was one of the small group whom Disraeli consulted on the education question at the end of January, the others being Hardy, Manners, and Pakington: see Hardy's diary, 28 Jan. 1868 (Cranbrook Papers, T501/294).

[5] Walpole to Disraeli, 27 Jan. 1868: Disraeli Papers, B/XXI/W/74.

which would shock much Conservative opinion, and a limited scheme which might fail to satisfy the country at large. Derby (away ill at Knowsley) wanted to go tentatively: he was very reluctant to accept rating, and continued to oppose the creation of an education minister, which was again in the air. His preference was for an effort to put new life into voluntaryism by assisting all schools on the basis of results, without requiring their connection with a religious denomination.

> Setting out upon this basis [he wrote] I think it wd be absolutely necessary that there shd be without loss of time an educational Census, which shd show where, & to what extent, such a scheme fails to meet the public requirement, & it is only upon a proof that in no other mode can the evil be reached, that I shd be willing to consent to a principle of compulsory rating under the superintendence & management of some local authority.[1]

Rating, indeed, was too much for the majority of the cabinet to swallow at this juncture, and the bulk of the party was certainly strongly opposed to it.[2] But the very cautious approach favoured by Derby was hardly adequate to get the government creditably out of its difficulty. The situation was highly delicate, and the cabinet in the end slid rather weakly out of it, as Disraeli explained to Derby on 30 January:

> Any forced decisions, at this moment, on conscience clauses and rating, and boards of managers,[3] would break up the Cabinet.
>
> What the Cabinet decided on, I may say unanimously, was that legislation was necessary; that it should be preliminary, not definitive; that, to be preliminary and not insignificant, the institution of an Education Minister was necessary . . . It was felt that, if our Bill were limited to census and incorporation,[4] the Opposition would successfully start Mr. Bruce's Bill, and the question of the day would be taken out of our hands. It was felt that, if our action was limited to extending aid to the poor schools, a minute to be laid on the table would be sufficient, and that in the present temper of Parliament and the country that would not suffice . . .
>
> If we gain a year, the public mind, now in a state of effervescent inquiry on these matters, will ripen on such subjects as conscience clauses and

[1] Derby to Disraeli, 29 Jan. 1868: *ibid.*, B/XX/S/478.

[2] Even Adderley, who had supported rating in the 'fifties, now regarded it as 'utterly out of the question', because of its impact on the existing system, its partial incidence, and the difficulties involved in its administration. See his undated memorandum for Disraeli on education (*ibid.*, B/XXI/A/89), which was probably produced about this time.

[3] Presumably this means boards of managers for rate-established or aided schools.

[4] I.e. of the Privy Council regulations in a statute.

rating, and especially on the non-interference of the State with the religious element in schools, which might render conscience clauses unnecessary.[1]

The cabinet's divisions, in short, had forced it to adopt a scheme shelving the really important questions, but made to look forceful to the public by the creation of a new ministry. Even this botched job was nearly wrecked when Marlborough, faced with losing education, first threatened to resign and then accepted the creation of an education ministry only on condition that the Lord President should be the minister.[2] Derby and Disraeli saw this was impossible, if only because the Commons would resent an arrangement which in practice put the education minister in the Lords,[3] and Marlborough finally gave way. The government drew up its bill, without enthusiasm:

> so far as I can judge [Disraeli informed Derby on 6 February] the Education flame is more bright than lasting, and in a month's time I am not sure the Lord President may not bring in a strictly preparatory measure in the House of Lords, and keep the great question for the next Parliament. But it must be in the Lords now; at any rate, we want education discussed by Dukes and Bishops. It will have a beneficial effect on all.[4]

The Education Bill was introduced by Marlborough on 24 March 1868. The Lord President made the fundamental admission that

> The administration of public education in this country is not carried on as it ought to be. The great defect of the existing system is that it is not initiative, but merely follows in the wake of voluntary efforts.

But his proposals did nothing to overcome this defect. Denying that the wants to be supplied demanded any extraordinary remedy, he rejected rating as likely to cripple the voluntary system. The main features of his measure were the creation of an education minister, and an attempt to extend the reach of state aid on the lines favoured by Derby, by ceasing to require schools to be connected with a religious denomination in order to qualify for it, and by giving payment for results on secular teaching alone (this, it was expected, would produce a large increase in applications for state grants, especially from nonconformist schools which had hitherto refused public money

[1] Disraeli to Derby, 30 Jan. 1868, in M. & B., iv. 579–80. The passages omitted in M. & B. may be supplied from the draft of the letter in Disraeli Papers, B/XIII/100.

[2] See note passed between Stanley and Disraeli in cabinet, 2 Feb. 1868 (*ibid.*, B/XIII/27); Malmesbury to Disraeli, 2 Feb. 1868 (*ibid.*, B/XX/Hs/138); Northcote to Disraeli, 3 Feb. 1868 (Add. MS. 50016, ff. 8–10); Disraeli to Queen Victoria, 4 Feb. 1868, in M. & B., iv. 580–1.

[3] *Ibid.*; Derby to Disraeli, 5 Feb. 1868 (Disraeli Papers, B/XX/S/482).

[4] Disraeli to Derby, 6 Feb. 1868, in M. & B., iv. 581.

because of their objection to the state's making religious instruction a condition of grant). To help the poorer districts and small rural parishes, where many schools were excluded from aid by their inability to comply with the condition requiring the employment of a certificated teacher, it was provided that schools with under 65 pupils should be able to secure a reduced-rate grant without a certificated teacher. Building grants were to be increased. A conscience clause allowing withdrawal of children from *any* lesson was to be inserted in trust deeds in single-school parishes. The new education minister was empowered to order an educational census in any district.[1]

This attempt to prop and patch the existing system was not in itself objectionable, but it could hardly satisfy a public opinion which suspected that the existing system had already failed. The opposition found the bill hopelessly inadequate in relation to the magnitude of the problem,[2] and pressed strongly for a national system with rating. Their hostility, and the state of parliamentary business, gave the measure no chance of passing, and it was withdrawn in May, before reaching the Commons—a fitting conclusion to a tale of division and uncertainty.

The government's inability to cope with the education question was embarrassingly plain, and for the rest of the session Montagu had a rough passage in the Commons against the Liberal educational spokesmen, Bruce and W. E. Forster, having to take refuge in clumsy attempts to discredit and belittle their evidence of educational deficiency or to show that the evils they exposed were impossible to cure by their nostrums of rating and compulsion.[3] At least his line represented the feeling of the bulk of his party, which continued to recoil from the only measures capable of making a serious impression on the educational problem. The dislike of the landed interest for rates was focused afresh in 1868 by the opening of the Central Chamber of Agriculture's campaign on the local taxation grievance, and the Central Chamber specifically opposed an education rate in March.[4] It also opposed compulsion[5]—this, too, remained unacceptable to most Conservatives, though a few were coming round to it.[6]

[1] For Marlborough's introductory speech, see *3 Hansard*, cxci. 105–29.

[2] See the Lords' debate of 27 April: *ibid.*, cxci. 1305–31. W. E. Forster did, however, say later that almost everything in the government bill was a step in the right direction (*ibid.*, cxcii. 1152).

[3] See his speeches of 4 and 24 June 1868: *ibid.*, cxcii. 1156–60, 1998–2007. Bruce had reintroduced his 1867 bill, strengthened to provide for compulsory rating where educational deficiency was proved.

[4] Matthews, p. 78.

[5] *Ibid.*, pp. 307–8.

[6] Graves told Richmond in a letter of 14 March 1868 (Goodwood Papers, box 15, bundle 3, D No. 212): 'We may have to come to compulsory attendance but any introduction of the principle at present would be premature and im-

The representatives of the shires and country towns often convinced themselves that there was no need for such measures in the countryside: if they had become necessary in the great cities, through the failure of the bourgeoisie to emulate the paternal care of the rural clergy and gentry in the education of the poor, that was no reason to foist them on the agricultural districts.

> Why [asked Greene] could not the manufacturers do as much for their working people as the landowners and employers in the country had done for theirs?... He agreed that the condition of things described as existing in the manufacturing districts was a disgrace to those who had made large fortunes out of their working people; but he would not admit that either a system of rating or compulsory education was required in the country districts, where the landowners had done their duty in regard to education.[1]

It was clearer than ever, at the end of 1868, that the Conservative party had nothing to offer in education beyond the piecemeal adjustment of a blatantly unsatisfactory system. The educational measure which the country's needs called out for could not come from them. The government might, however, have made some progress in the distinct field of Scottish education, had there been time. The Scottish Education Commission, reporting in 1867,[2] had recommended the creation, under a central Board of Education, of a new national system based on rating (long established in Scotland), with elected school committees, into which it was envisaged that the existing parochial and denominational schools would ultimately be absorbed. This scheme went somewhat beyond what ministers could readily accept: it was immoderately assaulted by Montagu and disfavoured by Marlborough.[3] But the Lord Advocate, E. S. Gordon, produced early in 1868 a plan founded on it which would apparently have been brought in as a bill but for the pressure of parliamentary business.[4]

No attempt was made in the session of 1867–8 to appeal t othe

[1] *3 Hansard*, cxcii. 1992. In fact, in many rural areas landowners and farmers gave very scant support to education.

[2] 2nd report: *P.P.* 1867, xxv. 1.

[3] See Montagu's speech, 21 June 1867 (*3 Hansard*, clxxxviii. 321–38); memorandum by Marlborough, 10 Oct. 1867 (Disraeli Papers, B/XX/Ch/6).

[4] See Gordon's statement in *3 Hansard*, ccix. 267. The unsigned and undated 'Memorandum on the subject of Scotch Education' in the Goodwood Papers (box 15, bundle 9), which internal evidence puts not earlier than late February 1868, is clearly his exposition of his scheme, printed for the cabinet.

politic on party grounds.' The committee of the Metropolitan Conservative Working Men's Association favoured making education 'as compulsory as vaccination' (*British Lion*, 23 May 1868).

urban working-class voter by taking up labour questions. The main issue here remained the legal status of the trade unions, and with this the government would not deal until the Royal Commission had finished its work. When the Edinburgh working men drew his attention to the subject, in October 1867, Disraeli merely said cryptically that the workman 'should not only be secured his rights, but called upon to fulfil his duties'.[1] The unions did, however, get some relief in 1868 from the difficulties created by *Hornby v. Close*, through the Larceny and Embezzlement Act carried by the Conservative member for Southampton, Russell Gurney. This, they found, gave their funds a degree of protection by enabling them to prosecute defaulting officials successfully—a fact about which Gurney had to advise them to keep quiet, in case it should wreck the measure.[2] Anti-union feeling in the Conservative party was still strong, but it was perhaps diminishing in virulence, and in September 1868 Carnarvon was able to allow the unions some merits (especially as benefit societies), though he looked forward to their fading away as arbitration and co-operation gained ground in industry.[3]

The government would have extended the legislative protection of the merchant seaman, had it been able. Following on the act of 1867, further legislation to tackle the wages question and promote the safety of shipping was planned at the Board of Trade. The main point about wages was how to secure their speedier payment on a ship's arrival, and the Board came tentatively to favour a system of paying-off through the superintendents of the local mercantile marine offices.[4] In regard to safety, the principal question under review was what could be done to stop the common and all too often fatal practice of overloading. The idea of a load line (marked on a ship's side to indicate the maximum permissible submersion) was mentioned, but the supremacy of the dogma that too-detailed regulations for safety would simply have the disastrous effect of transferring responsibility from owners and masters to the government ensured its rejection.[5] In the end, all Farrer could suggest was the limitation of marine

[1] *The Chancellor of the Exchequer in Scotland*, p. 39.

[2] See Howell, p. 175; Hedges and Winterbottom, p. 57.

[3] Presidential address to the Social Science Congress, 30 Sept. 1868: *Transactions of the National Association for the Promotion of Social Science*, 1868, pp. 15–20.

[4] For the discussions on the wages question, see the papers in M. 9364/67, annexed to M.T. 9/32/M. 1453/67; M.T. 9/37/M. 9117/67; M.T. 9/133/M. 9612/76. Farrer's memorandum in the latter file, described by the attached minute paper as being on the Merchant Shipping Bill of 1869, is clearly of Feb. 1868.

[5] See minutes by Farrer and Richmond, 28 and 31 Jan. 1868, in M.T. 9/39/M. 598/68.

insurance, to make it unprofitable to lose ships through overloading them.[1]

One safety proposal which, together with load line, was put forward by the seamen themselves was the periodical inspection of ships,[2] but this again was thought to carry government supervision too far. 'Inspection of every ship before sailing', wrote the Vice-President, Cave, 'wld either be a farce, or wld stop the trade of the Country'.[3] The Board seems finally to have recurred to the proposal to provide for the survey of ships alleged by seamen to be unseaworthy, which had had to be dropped from the 1867 bill, and it was this, with clauses on wages, that was apparently to form the core of the bill whose details Richmond and Cave discussed with the Law Officers at the end of February 1868.[4] But the state of business rendered legislation in 1868 impossible, and the government lost the credit of what would have been a useful measure.

One thing the government was able to do in 1868 was to continue the advance in the treatment of the sick poor begun in the previous year. It was not only in London that the condition of workhouses and their infirmaries was unsatisfactory, and under mounting pressure of public opinion ministers were driven to conclude that it was necessary to try to do for the country at large what Hardy's act had done for the capital, by giving the central authority greatly increased powers of intervention to deal with bad local administration. The Poor Relief Bill which Devon introduced in March 1868 enabled the Poor Law Board to nominate workhouse officers when guardians failed to do so, to appoint a visitor where the visiting committee of the guardians neglected its duty, and to provide drainage, ventilation, and furniture for workhouses and infirmaries. It also provided for the establishment of asylums for the insane and imbecile poor.

This new manifestation of the ministry's readiness to countenance increased centralisation where local self-government was proving inadequate had a mixed reception. The workhouse reformers (including Carnarvon) wanted even stronger action, and a deputation

[1] See M. 3064/68, annexed to M.T. 9/39/M. 598/68. Heavy insurance made some owners careless of whether their ships sank through overloading—or even anxious that they should sink.

[2] See the memorandum of the newly-formed Seamen's Parliamentary Committee, and the scheme of the United Seamen's Society, submitted to the Board of Trade in Feb. 1868: M.T. 9/40/M. 2495/68, and M.T. 9/39/M. 1692/68.

[3] Minute on the Seamen's Parliamentary Committee memo. Cave thought that for the government to do too much for the sailor would be to make him 'the mere child he is sometimes represented to be, but which we do not wish him to remain'.

[4] See Farrer's memorandum and annexed transcript of notes on the conference with the Law Officers, in M.T. 9/133/M. 9612/76.

asked Devon to take power to lay down a national code of instructions for the treatment of sick paupers, and to establish a system for the medical inspection of county workhouses.[1] On the other hand, the prospect that enlarged central control would mean enforced higher expenditure and a rise in the poor rate alarmed members of Parliament of both parties. F. W. Knight, one of three Conservative county members to oppose the bill's increase of centralisation, remarked:

> When hon. Gentlemen went to the elections he believed they would be asked whether they had voted for or against clauses in Bills largely increasing the rates.[2]

Three Lancashire Conservatives, Graves, Greenall, and Turner, accompanied a deputation from provincial towns which urged on Devon that the government should subsidise the maintenance of the sick poor, since sickness was a national calamity.[3] But the bill went through, reinforcing the new trend in public policy towards the sick poor which Hardy's act had signalised.

There was little activity in the field of public health in 1868. Administrative reorganisation on the lines of Buckingham's scheme was still being considered, and Northcote was advocating a new Committee of Council for sanitary matters in February,[4] but nothing followed. Pushed by the British Medical Association and the Social Science Association, the government did, however, take the important step of setting up a Royal Commission on the sanitary laws in November, the findings of which were to lead to comprehensive legislation in 1871–5.[5]

Torrens's Artizans and Labourers Dwellings Bill was finally passed in 1868, with renewed government support. Torrens later acknowledged 'the unsleeping sympathy, the untiring aid, and the true succour rendered them [the bill's sponsors] from first to last' by Disraeli.[6] The new prime minister had evidently already formed the conviction which was to be evident in 1874–5, that no social reform was more important than the provision of adequate working-class housing, or better calculated to win working-class favour for the party which supported it. But he could not prevent a Select Committee

[1] Minute of interview, apparently 21 March 1868, in M.H. 25/19 (no. 39178/68). Devon said that a code was under consideration. For Carnarvon's views, see Hardinge, i. 220–1.

[2] *3 Hansard*, cxciii. 1424.

[3] Minute of interview, 27 March 1868, in M.H. 25/19 (no. 10820/68).

[4] Northcote to Hardy, 2 Feb. 1868: Cranbrook Papers, T501/271.

[5] Hardy offered the chairmanship of the Commission to the third Marquis of Salisbury (as Cranborne had become in April 1868). Hardy to Salisbury, 25 Aug. 1868: Salisbury Papers, S.C.

[6] *3 Hansard*, ccxviii. 1981 (8 May 1874).

of the Lords from ruining the bill by removing the clauses allowing local authorities to acquire defective property and to provide for its rebuilding. With power to demolish property unfit for habitation, but not to purchase and rebuild, local authorities would not utilise the measure, and it remained virtually inoperative until its amendment in 1879.

If it had not been able to achieve much, the government had shown, in the first post-Reform session, its consciousness of the need to carry forward the work of social improvement, both for the benefit of the country and as a means of commending itself to the new working-class voters. It had passed a useful Poor Relief Act, and assisted Torrens's Act; it had made a serious, if confused, effort to grapple with the education problem in England and Wales; and had time permitted, it would have introduced measures for Scottish education and for the further protection of the merchant seaman. With the measures of the 1867 session to its credit, it could claim to have demonstrated its care for working-class interests as it approached the moment of confrontation with the reformed constituency in the general election of 1868.

> The working men now hold in their hand the destinies of the country. They are still malleable, and may be attached to our side if approached in the right way, I think. I question if they have as yet realised their power, for things seem to be running in their old grooves, but sure as water finds its level they will realise it, in time—and we must be ready for them.

So wrote J. H. Kennaway to Viscount Sandon, in August 1868.[1] The general election brought the Conservatives face to face with the problem of mobilising support among the urban workers. It was a problem which they had already begun to tackle in one aspect, by starting to create the mass organisation which Reform had made essential. In the latter half of 1866 there had been an attempt to build up working men's Conservative or 'constitutional' associations (largely in the north, where the Conservative operative societies of the 'thirties and 'forties had flourished), as a counter to the influence of the Reform agitation. With the passing of Reform, this organisational effort became still more vital, not least because the sheer size of the new electorate in the larger boroughs made efficient local associations on a broad base indispensable to cope with the tasks of registration and canvassing, to secure a full turn-out on polling day, and to

[1] Letter of 6 Aug.: Harrowby Papers, vol. liii, ff. 89–92. Kennaway was to become Conservative member for East Devon in 1870.

achieve the most effective distribution of the vote where the Reform Act's minority clause operated.

Throughout 1867 the development of the Conservative working men's associations continued. While sometimes set going by the working men themselves, they were generally under strong upper- and middle-class influence, tending to institutionalise the deferential relationship between the Conservative artisan and his social superiors, rather than serve as agencies for the promotion of working-class independence and initiative in politics, and having stated objects that were severely Conservative in tone and placed little emphasis on specifically working-class interests.[1] The task was soon undertaken of linking them in a national body. Though supervised by the chief party manager, Viscount Nevill, and the whip, Colonel T. E. Taylor, the work was done mainly by a group of young men, mostly barristers, who had been strongly influenced by Disraeli's ideas, and took seriously the mission of bringing together the party and the people. They included the member for Cambridge, J. E. Gorst, and four future members of Parliament—H. C. Raikes, prominent in running the *Imperial Review* and in producing, in an effort to provide the new associations with a cheap paper, the penny-weekly *British Lion*; W. T. Charley; Edward Clarke; and A. G. Marten.[2] The result of their labours was the foundation, in November 1867, of the National Union of Conservative and Constitutional Associations.

The Conservative hierarchy had qualms about the development of a mass organisation outside Parliament. As a party organiser, Major the Hon. C. J. Keith-Falconer, put it:

> It is quite wonderful the way these working men devote their time & energy to politics. I trust however that we shall not be like Frankenstein,

[1] The objects of the London and Westminster Working Men's Constitutional Association, for instance, were: 'to unite the friends of constitutional principle in resisting any attempt to subvert the Protestant faith or the Constitution of the Country; to protect the prerogative of the Crown; and to defend the rights and privileges of the People' (quoted in Hanham, p. 107). Cf. the aims of the Liverpool Working Men's Conservative Association, quoted in the Liverpool *Daily Courier*, 10 Jan. 1872. The Metropolitan Conservative Working Men's Association included among its objects promoting the education of its working-class members and securing for them better accommodation in churches, but these points were later expunged (*British Lion*, 23 May 1868).

[2] See Sir E. Clarke, *The Story of My Life*, pp. 42–3, 95–8; H. St. John Raikes, *The Life and Letters of Henry Cecil Raikes, late Her Majesty's Postmaster-General*, pp. 55ff.; E. J. Feuchtwanger, 'J. E. Gorst and the Central Organisation of the Conservative Party, 1870–1882', *Bulletin of the Institute of Historical Research*, xxxii (1959), 195. Clarke had been inspired to become a politician by *Coningsby* and *Sybil*; Raikes was especially influenced by Disraeli's exposition of 'national' and 'popular' Toryism in his speech of 26 June 1863 (for which see M. & B., iv. 379–80).

> & have raised a spirit that we cannot control!—it is a dangerous power to give them, but they are so determined to have it, that all we can do is to keep them on the right road.[1]

The party leadership, fearing embarrassment from the activities of the National Union, at first refrained from associating themselves with it closely, and Disraeli stopped the issue of its circular because its terms committed them too strongly.[2] But there was little to worry about. The National Union's managers were anxious to obey the party chiefs,[3] and the working men delegates to the foundation meeting proved almost comically eager to accept party control and the leadership of their social superiors.[4] There was no question of the new body's taking an independent line, or serving as an organ for the expression of working-class opinion and the exertion of working-class influence on party policy.

The potential of the National Union as a means of building up the party's working-class support was limited from the beginning. Many Conservatives were too nervous about the encouragement of organised working-class participation in politics to give it enthusiastic backing. Its rôle, and that of its affiliated associations, was to harness the Conservative artisans to the work of propaganda and electioneering, not to make them an integral and significant part of the party. Such a system could not readily attract the more independent-minded working men, who wanted genuine political influence and an enhanced social status not derived from upper-class patronage. But the National Union did provide a useful medium of contact with the new working-class voters, and it made a decided propaganda effort in 1868 to convince them that the Conservative party was a popular party with their interests at heart.

One of its pamphlets, after stressing the plebeian origins of such Tory premiers as Perceval, Canning, and Peel, and describing Disraeli as 'entirely a man of the people' (perhaps the least plausible of that protean character's many rôles), declared:

> The policy of the Tories is to fraternise with the people to diminish and mitigate social differences, not by lowering themselves, but by elevating

[1] Keith-Falconer to Nevill, 1 Sept. 1867: Disraeli Papers, B/XX/T/96.

[2] See Nevill to M. Spofforth, 6 Nov. 1867 (with M. Corry's endorsements); G. J. Noel to Spofforth, 6 Nov. 1867; and Noel to Corry, 7 Nov. 1867: *ibid.*, B/IX/D/32d, 32b, 32c (correspondence referred to in Hanham, p. 108, n. 2).

[3] See L. Sedgwick (hon. secretary of the National Union) to M. Corry, 25 Nov. [1867], and H. C. Raikes to Corry, 11 Dec. 1867: Disraeli Papers, B/IX/D/32g, 32j.

[4] See the MS. minutes of the inaugural meeting, 12 Nov. 1867, at the Conservative and Unionist Central Office; R. T. McKenzie, *British Political Parties*, 2nd ed., pp. 150–4.

> their humbler fellow-countrymen, and on all occasions to afford free scope and facility for the advance of merit to the highest positions.[1]

Two pamphlets by W. T. Charley outlined Conservative measures for the benefit of the working classes on mines, factories, and truck, lashing the record of opponents such as Bright, whose policy was based on 'selfishness and middle-class interest'.[2] National Union speakers also carried the message into the constituencies: Edward Clarke, for instance, addressed a special meeting at Cardiff on 'Questions for Working Men'.[3] However, the popular tone of this propaganda and its emphasis on social questions outran what the bulk of the party could countenance, and did not set the pattern of the Conservative approach at the general election.

Despite the influx of working-class voters,[4] the election did not turn out to be a competition in popular appeal, and social questions did not, on the national level, play a large part in it. It was fought on traditional lines, without much special reference to the particular interests of the new voters, who showed, as yet, little political self-assertiveness. Gladstone had determined the main issue—the disestablishment of the Irish Church. This conveniently symbolised the real question before the electorate, which was whether the Liberals were to be given a mandate to carry out the programme of reforms which the era of Palmerstonian calm had frustrated.

Both parties were glad to fight on an issue that cut across class lines.[5] They were anxious to avert the emergence of the politics of class conflict, which so many dreaded as a result of the Reform Act, and which would threaten the social and political dominance of the classes they embodied and represented. Neither made a special appeal at national level to the working men as such, or gave social questions much prominence, though education, the position of the trade unions,

[1] *Practical Suggestions to the Loyal Working Men of Great Britain on Points of Policy and Duty at the Present Crisis*, by 'E. A.' (Publications of the National Union, no. V, March 1868), pp. 5, 6.

[2] *Conservative Legislation for the Working Classes*, No. I *Mines and Factories*; No. II *The Truck Acts* (Publications of the National Union, nos. VI, X). Cf. the broadsheet *To the Workers in Mines & Factories*, by G. C. Colleton Rennie, a member of the National Union's Council (copy in Disraeli Papers, B/IX/D/38), which asserts that 'the whole Factory and Mining Acts are due to the Conservative party'.

[3] Clarke, p. 101.

[4] Which, however, did not represent the full extent of the Reform Act's addition to the borough electorate: this was attained only after the adjustment of the rating conditions of the franchise in 1869.

[5] This seems to be the implication of some words of Disraeli to the Queen on 23 March 1868: *Letters of Queen Victoria*, 2nd series, i. 518.

and the Permissive Bill,[1] were widely discussed in the constituencies. The Liberals already had the general support of the organised labour movement, and the Reform League worked hand-in-glove with their whips. This was, in fact, 'the real beginning of the Lib-Lab era in working-class politics',[2] though the alliance had its strains from the first, not least because of the Liberal unwillingness to assist working-class candidatures, with which Conservatives made some play.[3]

The Conservatives, as a whole, had no enthusiasm for appealing to the working men or taking up social questions, and their 'national party' strategy precluded any pronounced stress on working-class interests. In any case, as with the Liberals, a high proportion of their candidates were not facing large working-class electorates, but were standing for counties and very small rural boroughs, where local taxation, cattle disease, and the malt tax were, after the Irish Church, the matters of moment, and social improvement tended to connote primarily the screwing-up of the rates. A good deal of the Conservative campaign was directed to bringing in the apprehensive middle-class voter, by exploiting the disquiet already perceptible at the forward march of labour and the advanced tendencies of post-Reform Liberalism under Gladstone's leadership.[4] The patriotic Liberal was exhorted to join 'the party which has become identified with the cause of national salvation', in order to resist 'the too rapid progress of Democracy in England',[5] and the bigger the apparent potential of this kind of appeal, the less inclined were the Conservatives to bid for the working men.

All the same, Disraeli could have made a greater effort to cultivate the working-class vote. The trouble was that, like most politicians, he had not adjusted himself mentally to the new electoral conditions in the boroughs. Nor was the archpriest of popular Toryism temperamentally fitted to appeal to the people. A brilliant parliamentarian, he had no capacity or, indeed, desire to emulate Gladstone in rousing the enthusiasm of the masses, and he did no campaigning. His Bucks election address—the leader's address being the nearest thing to an official manifesto in an age innocent of the party 'programme'—

[1] A bill to give localities power to prohibit, by majority vote, the sale of intoxicating liquors.

[2] Harrison, p. 209.

[3] E.g., Lord Sandon at Liverpool, reported in *Daily Courier*, 22 Oct. 1868; *Morning Herald*, 2 Nov. 1868. Both Sandon and the *Herald* approved the idea of having some working men in the House of Commons.

[4] 'The recruiting agents of the Conservative party have been Messrs. BRIGHT and GLADSTONE', noted the *Standard* (12 Nov. 1868), discussing the vigour of the Conservative challenge in the metropolitan constituencies, which it ascribed rather to this than to 'the growth of positive Conservatism'.

[5] Lord Lindsay, *Conservatism: its Principle, Policy, and Practice. A Reply to Mr. Gladstone's Speech at Wigan, 23rd October, 1868*, pp. 4, 34–5.

was negative in tone, and offered nothing specific to the new voters. Social questions were not discussed, though at Hardy's prompting a reference was inserted to 'those legal and social improvements which are so much required, and to the necessity of which we had proved we were not insensible'.[1] Only when the polls were largely over did the prime minister, in his re-election speech, touch on social matters: he came out for permissive rating and a separate ministry for education (while opposing compulsory rating and attendance), and in discussing the level of government expenditure warned that cheap government could be secured only 'by endangering the country—by depriving the great body of the people of an expenditure which is really incurred in order to elevate them and to improve their condition'.[2] His leading colleagues made no greater attempt to appeal to the working men or to exploit social issues. A question as vital to the working classes as the legal position of trade unions was so far from central to their preoccupations that Northcote could write to Hardy in September 1868:

> Can you tell me anything about Trades Unions? The Trades-unionists in Exeter are (I hear) pledging themselves not to vote for anyone who will not promise to 'legalise' unions. I don't quite know what they are driving at. Is there anything that one ought,—or ought not,—to say on the subject?[3]

The Conservative leadership seems to have relied for its share of the working-class vote on engrained Conservative instincts and influences among the working men, on gratitude for the Reform Act, and on Protestant and anti-Irish feeling—Disraeli clearly thought that the Irish Church issue gave the Conservative party a heaven-sent opportunity of uniting members of all classes behind it in an access of Protestant and nationalistic passion. But Conservative instincts and influences were not strong enough; gratitude for Reform tended to be directed to its longstanding Radical and Liberal champions rather than to its new Conservative converts; and Protestant zeal did not prove overpowering—except, perhaps, in Lancashire, on whose example it may be that Disraeli was once again building too

[1] The address is printed in *The Times*, 3 Oct. 1868. See also Hardy to Disraeli, 24 Sept. 1868 (commenting on the draft of the address), in *Gathorne Hardy*, i. 282.

[2] Speech at Aylesbury, 19 Nov. 1868: report in *Standard*, 20 Nov. The government's expenditure was under heavy Liberal criticism at the elections.

[3] Northcote to Hardy, 8 Sept. 1868: Cranbrook Papers, T501/271. Hardy referred Northcote to Lowe's *Quarterly* article of Oct. 1867, and wrote: 'Friendly Societies & Trades Unions ought to be apart, but some illegality in the Society should not allow robbery of its funds' (letter of 10 Sept. 1868: Add. MS. 50037, ff. 153–4).

much. To gain real strength among the working classes the party needed to adopt a more positive approach to them. It needed to show some sympathy for their social aspirations—'the real struggle of the day', a correspondent had told Lord Sandon in July, 'is whether the working classes shall or shall not have any admitted social status'[1]—and it needed to offer them prospects of material improvement. The National Union had already made efforts along these lines, and might have served as the medium of a campaign for working-class votes. At national level, however, no such campaign was, or could have been, mounted.[2]

It was at ground level in the larger borough constituencies, where Conservative candidates came face to face with working-class electors in substantial numbers, that serious efforts were made to appeal directly to the working men, and social questions assumed a position of importance. The Conservatives had a hard struggle in the larger boroughs, where organised and politically conscious labour was frequently closely associated with the Liberal party, and the influence of the major employers (a vital factor in middling industrial towns) was generally on the Liberal side—though there were some important exceptions to this latter rule, especially in the north-west.[3] They could rarely hope to make much headway with the old methods of corruption which still served well in the smaller boroughs, though these were by no means abandoned,[4] and could hardly rely simply on natural working-class Conservatism. They had to make some attempt

[1] Mr Williams to Sandon, 19 July 1868: Harrowby Papers, vol. xlviii, ff. 185–8.

[2] For a criticism of the party's failure to put its case across to the working men, see *Imperial Review*, 19 Dec. 1868—'The Press and The Platform'.

[3] Among the exceptions were Liverpool, where the shipping and mercantile interest was largely Conservative; Birkenhead, dominated by its Conservative member, Laird; Blackburn, where the Feildens and Hornbys provided the Conservative members, and strong pressure was exerted on the workpeople; Carlisle, where the London and North-Western Railway influence was used on the Conservative side; and Preston, where the proprietor of the great cotton firm of Horrocks, Edward Hermon, stood as a Conservative (Hanham, pp. 69–70, 72, 73, 83, 87–9, 284–5; Harrison, pp. 156–7). Their number was probably increasing at this period. A writer in the *Fortnightly* in Oct. 1868 saw a movement of Liberal capitalists to the Conservative side, based on the desire of self-made men to advance themselves socially. 'Their foremost wish', he wrote, 'is to be isolated from the class out of which they came, and political renegadism has the apparent effect of consummating that isolation. It places them *en rapport* with the territorial gentry' (W. A. Abram, 'Social Condition and Political Prospects of the Lancashire Workmen', *Fortnightly Review*, iv, new series (1868), 439–40).

[4] In Westminster, the Working Men's Conservative Association assisted in corrupting the electorate. The same thing happened in some smaller places, like Beverley and Bewdley. C. O'Leary, *The Elimination of Corrupt Practices in British Elections 1868–1911*, pp. 49–50, 50–1, 51–2.

to give their platform popular appeal and to satisfy the working men on the questions which touched their special interests.

The social questions most prominent in the larger boroughs were the position of trade unions, education, and the Permissive Bill. Conservatives were almost invariably against the Permissive Bill, and they could offer little for the promotion of education, beyond the development of the existing system (few were ready to support compulsory rating and attendance). On the trade union issue, which was perhaps the most important to the working men, attitudes were divided. The bookseller W. H. Smith, whose campaign in the great popular constituency of Westminster leaned heavily on money,[1] was one of those who would not go far to meet the unionists: he declared that legislation was less needful than 'the correction of economic fallacies' and the removal of distrust between employers and employed, whose interests were identical.[2] But there was by this time a body of opinion in the party prepared to offer the unions a degree of legal recognition and protection for their funds,[3] and a number of candidates, anxious to seize electoral advantage, were more forthcoming than Smith. Nor were they discouraged from being so by the party leadership, to judge from the example of E. P. Price, Q.C., who was invited to contest Sheffield by a Protestant Defence League got up by some working men, on condition that he promised legalisation of trade union funds. Montagu Corry (evidently acting with the party's managers) told him '*certainly* not to stick at that', and he promised legalisation of unions with a will in his campaign, throwing in compulsory education as well.[4] In Birmingham, where the Conservatives 'went out of their way to appeal to the local artisans in economic terms', their candidates put full legal recognition of unions in the forefront of their addresses.[5] But neither in Sheffield nor in Birmingham, with their close alliance between politically conscious

[1] He spent nearly £9,000. See Viscount Chilston, *W. H. Smith*, pp. 60–1.

[2] See his election address, Aug. 1868 (copy in the Hambleden Papers, PS 1/21); speech reported in *Standard*, 23 Oct. 1868. He advocated boards of conciliation or arbitration in industry, and, better still, profit-sharing.

[3] See, for instance, J. H. Kennaway to Sandon, 6 Aug. [1868], cited above, p. 116, n. 1. Kennaway remarked: 'There will no doubt be legislation on the subject, and I do not feel inclined to let the Liberals have the whole credit.'

[4] See Corry to Disraeli, 23 Sept. 1868 (Disraeli Papers, B/XX/Co/46), and reports of Price's election address and speeches in *The Times*, 2 and 3 Oct. 1868, and *Sheffield Daily Telegraph*, 11 Nov. 1868. Corry told Disraeli: 'We have considered this very carefully today & yesterday, as not only in itself, but as an example to the working men of the country, it is of great importance.' Price was crushingly defeated at the polls.

[5] They also called for legislation to improve working-class housing. C. Gill and A. Briggs, *History of Birmingham*, ii. 191–2; Briggs, *Age of Improvement*, p. 519.

labour and the Liberal and Radical bourgeoisie, did the Conservatives stand a chance. It was in the very different social and political climate of Lancashire, in Manchester and the neighbouring cotton towns and in Liverpool, that the Conservative appeal to the working men was both vigorous and successful.[1]

In the south-east Lancashire boroughs the Conservatives started with the advantage of an established vein of working-class support. The Irish Church issue, with its effects on a Protestant and anti-Irish feeling already inflamed by Fenianism and the Orange lecturer Murphy, was calculated to consolidate this, and the growing alienation of the operatives from the middle-class Liberal leaders was tending to enlarge it. The Conservatives had, too, a number of local leaders like Birley, Callender, and Maclure in Manchester, whose paternalist brand of Toryism was well-adapted for the winning of working-class votes. The Conservative campaign in Manchester and the surrounding area was carefully attuned to working-class feeling, and was based on the twin pillars of Protestantism and social improvement. Nearly all the candidates supported the legalisation of trade unions, and the Conservative party's record in social reform was stressed.[2] In Liverpool, where again there was a working-class Conservative tradition and Protestant and anti-Irish fervour ran high, the campaign of Graves and Viscount Sandon was likewise aimed largely at the working men.

Sandon, contesting Liverpool for the first time, was, like his friend, W. H. Smith, an example of the new Liberal-Conservatism of Palmerston's old following. His father, the Earl of Harrowby, who had once represented Liverpool, was a Whig-turned-Peelite who had sat in Palmerston's cabinet; he himself had represented Lichfield as a Palmerstonian in 1856–9. He came, perhaps, closer than anyone in the Conservative party to embodying the Disraelian ideal of a socially-conscious aristocracy giving leadership to the people. He had

[1] Conservative prospects among the working men were very much correlated with differences in urban economic and social structure: they tended to be better in 'cities of social cleavage', like Manchester, with large-scale industry and a marked social gulf between employers and hands, than in 'cities of social union', like Birmingham and Sheffield, with small-scale industry and masters and men in close social relations (for the cleavage–union distinction, see Read, pp. 35–7). J. E. Gorst recognised this fact when, as chief party organiser, he wrote: 'Where the artizans practice small trades ministering to the wants of the rich as in Birmingham London & so many of the minor boroughs, it is easy to see the influences which make them dissenters & radicals. It is among the employés of large staple trades like the cotton trade or ship-building trade that we must look in the first instance for conservative workmen' (Gorst to Noel, 22 Sept. 1870: Disraeli Papers, B/XXI/N/120a).

[2] For the general election in the south-east Lancashire boroughs, see Hanham, pp. 302–21.

welcomed Reform as a means to bring the working classes together with the rest of the nation,[1] and had little fear of its results. He thought that the new electors would introduce 'some of that vigour of organisation, some of that love of country, some of that supervision of those whom they have chosen as their representatives, some of that devotion to great principles which I have seen carried out among themselves', and he wanted to have some working men in Parliament—it would be better, he felt, to send even Bradlaugh, Hartwell, and Odger to the Commons than some of the Liberals.[2] But he believed firmly in the duty of rank and wealth to guide the masses. Men of title, he declared, in his first speech as candidate for Liverpool, were 'bound to rush to the front' and 'associate themselves with the great populations, to learn from them, and, if they will allow them, to take some share in being their leaders'.[3] From his beginnings in politics, Sandon had stressed the importance of social questions, taking special interest in education and in the relations of capital and labour—he even spoke of the aristocracy's rôle as a mediating force between employers and employed[4]—and though in his Liverpool campaign the religious issue greatly preponderated, the social condition of the working classes was also prominent. He was no great friend of trade unions (preferring arbitration to collective bargaining) and would do no more than support protection for their funds; and while eager to expand education he was, as a devoted Anglican, too attached to the denominational system to assent to rating and compulsion; but, 'considering the object of all Government to be the greatest welfare of the greatest number', he wanted Parliament to attack the social problems of the great towns, with which his experience in the poorer parts of London had familiarised him, and called for regulation of the liquor trade and for more decisive action on working-class housing, public health, and the adulteration of food.[5]

[1] Above, p. 97.

[2] Speeches at Liverpool reported in *Daily Courier*, 9 July and 22 Oct. 1868. Bradlaugh, Hartwell, and Odger were attempting to put up as working men's candidates at the general election.

[3] *Ibid.*, 9 July 1868.

[4] *Ibid.*; *Staffordshire Advertiser*, 27 July 1867. For some of his early pronouncements on social questions, see his election addresses of 1856 and 1857 at Lichfield and of 1860 at Stafford (copies in Harrowby Papers, vol. xlviii, ff. 70–2), and his Stafford nomination speech reported in *Staffordshire Advertiser*, 4 Aug. 1860.

[5] Liverpool election address (proof in Harrowby Papers, vol. 1, f. 51); speeches reported in *Daily Courier*, 9 July, 16 and 22 Oct. 1868. For Sandon's own commentary on the Liverpool election, at which he and Graves addressed seventeen great meetings of working men, see his letters to his wife, Oct.–Nov. 1868, and a letter to his brother Henry Ryder, 15 Nov. 1868, in Harrowby Papers, vol. xlv, ff. 26–48, vol. lxv, ff. 145–51.

The highly successful Conservative appeal in Liverpool and the Manchester region could not, however, make up for the failure of the party to attract the new voters in other areas. The result of the general election was a severe defeat for the Conservatives, who won only 274 seats in the new House of Commons to the Liberals' 384.[1] They were badly beaten in the boroughs, and especially in the great centres of industry and population where the working-class vote was most heavily concentrated: of 114 seats in towns in the United Kingdom with a population of over 50,000, they could secure only 25.[2] Despite W. H. Smith's victory in Westminster, and successes in Coventry, Hartlepool, Norwich, Nottingham, Portsmouth, Southampton, and Stockport, their showing in the larger boroughs would have been abysmal but for Lancashire, where the Conservative working man gave proof of his existence. Hugh Birley topped the poll in Manchester, outstripping the Liberals in both middle- and working-class wards,[3] Sandon and Graves were returned for Liverpool, W. T. Charley, one of those active in the foundation of the National Union, was one of two Conservatives returned in Salford,[4] and other Conservatives were elected in Ashton, Blackburn, Bolton, Preston, and Stalybridge. It was largely these Lancashire victories that enabled Disraeli to tell the Queen that his party's 'moral influence appeared to be increased from the remarkably popular elements of which the Conservative party was now formed under the influence of the new Reform Act', and that emboldened the *Morning Herald* to claim that it was ' "the people" in the largest sense of the word' who had rallied to the Conservative cause.[5] But there was no disguising the fact that over the country as a whole the new working-class voters had proved predominantly Liberal.

The effect of its thrashing in the larger boroughs was to throw the Conservative party back on its traditional sources of support in the counties and the smaller boroughs. It was even more dependent on the counties after Reform than it had been before: they provided nearly 60% of its seats in 1868, against nearly 51% in 1865.[6] English

[1] Figures from Hanham, p. 217. They are only approximate, because of the difficulty of classifying some members.

[2] *Ibid.*, p. 92, n. 2 (population according to the 1871 census). In the English, Welsh, and Scottish boroughs as a whole, according to tables in the *Standard*, 5 Dec. 1868, 91 Conservatives were returned, representing a population of 2.01 million, and 235 Liberals, representing a population of 8.02 million.

[3] See Hanham, p. 320, table XVI.

[4] Another National Union figure, H. C. Raikes, won Chester, but J. E. Gorst lost his Cambridge seat.

[5] Disraeli to Queen Victoria, 23 Nov. 1868, in M. & B., v. 98; *Morning Herald*, 28 Nov. 1868.

[6] Percentages based on figures in *Pall Mall Gazette*, 21 Feb. 1874 (for 1868), and *Essays on Reform*, p. 330 (for 1865). The Conservatives took 124 of 170

and Welsh counties and English boroughs of up to 20,000 inhabitants furnished altogether 66% of Conservative seats, and Scottish and Irish counties another 12%.[1] As much as ever, the party's strength rested on the support of the landed and agricultural interest, and this was reflected in its members of Parliament, among whom there was a much smaller proportionate representation of industrial, commercial, and financial interests than among the Liberals.[2] There were, however, some signs of a growth of Conservatism among the middle classes. Distrust of Disraeli and desire for reforms which only the Liberals could be relied on to implement prevented this from going far, but here and there it had a significant impact—for example in Middlesex, where the expanding suburban population of professional men, tradespeople, and clerks helped to return the young guardee Lord George Hamilton.[3] New representatives of the industrial and commercial bourgeoisie appeared in the parliamentary party, such as W. H. Smith, the garment manufacturer Birley, the colliery owner and manufacturer George Elliot, and the cotton manufacturers Fielden and Hermon. The conservative alliance between the landed interest and the middle classes at which Derby's and Disraeli's policy had aimed might still be realised, under the stimulus of Gladstonian energy, and certainly it seemed, in the light of the polls, a more feasible objective for the future than the capture of the urban working man.

[1] Based on figures in *Pall Mall Gazette*, 21 Feb. 1874, and Hanham, p. 39, n. 2.

[2] See Thomas, pp. 14–16.

[3] See Lord George Hamilton, *Parliamentary Reminiscences and Reflections 1868 to 1885*, p. 11.

---

seats in English counties (excluding Monmouthshire) in 1868 (Hanham, p. 25 n. 1).

III
'THE UTMOST RESERVE AND QUIETNESS'
1869-71

THE defeat of 1868 inevitably seemed at first to mark the failure of the effort to refound the Conservative party's strength on an enlarged basis. Following on, and apparently from, the turnabout of 1867, it did much to discredit Disraeli and the forward-looking, adaptive Conservatism which he had sought to foster. There was a serious danger in the years after 1868 that the party would slide back into its old ways of obstruction and inertia, and resign the attempt to come to terms with the conditions which the second Reform Act had created. Many were ready to join with the third Marquis of Salisbury (as Cranborne had become in April 1868) in denouncing the policy which had led to the 'leap' of 1867, and in maintaining that the duty of Conservatives was now to resume the function of dogged resistance to the tides of political and social change.[1]

A disheartened, ageing, and continually ill Disraeli could do little but acquiesce in his party's withdrawal into its shell. This was not the moment for the assertion of his concept of national and popular Toryism, or for any fresh endeavour to broaden the party's appeal to the new electors. There was nothing for it but to stand firm on traditional Conservative principles, and wait for the moment when the energy of the more advanced Liberals should begin to disturb moderate opinion. They must observe, Disraeli told Stanley, 'the utmost reserve and quietness'.[2]

There could be little serious attempt in this situation to build up the party's position among the working classes. Something, it is true, was achieved in the organisational field, by the efforts of J. E. Gorst, whom Disraeli placed in charge of the central party organisation in 1870. Gorst did his best to nurture Conservative strength among the

[1] See Salisbury's article, 'The Past and the Future of Conservative Policy', *Quarterly Review*, cxxvii (1869), 538–61.

[2] M. & B., v. 103. Cf. Hardy's diary, 28 May 1870, in *Gathorne Hardy*, i. 296.

large urban populations which, he felt, held the key to electoral success, and received steady encouragement from Disraeli.[1] But he was severely hampered by the indifference of the mass of the party, symbolised by the failure to support and develop the National Union, which was allowed to become almost moribund in 1869–71.[2] In any case, organisation by itself could secure only limited results.

The Conservative party almost completely neglected, in 1869–71, the opportunities for the cultivation of working-class support which social questions offered. These were not insignificant. The Liberal party as it emerged from the general election of 1868, owing much in personnel and outlook to the industrial and commercial bourgeoisie,[3] was in some aspects ill-equipped to sympathise with working-class aspirations and interests. Apart from the Education Act of 1870, the Gladstone government did comparatively little in its first three years for the improvement of the condition of the people, and on the trade union question it actually alienated working-class sympathies. The Conservatives might profitably have exploited its shortcomings by taking up the cause of social improvement and representing themselves as the real friends of the masses. But there was no concerted effort in this direction.

Such attempt as were made by Conservatives to stress their concern for working-class interests and to use social questions against the Liberals were usually the sporadic forays of uninfluential backbenchers. The most active was the old protectionist C. N. Newdegate, who would have liked to see his leader do more to identify the party with working-class interests.

> While the head of the Government and the Leader of the Opposition [he complained in 1870] agreed in so wonderful a manner upon general policy, there was a feeling growing up among the operatives that they were not represented in that House.[4]

[1] Disraeli's interest is attested by H. E. Gorst, *The Earl of Beaconsfield*, pp. 125, 128, 130, where the views and memories of the author's father, J. E. Gorst, are reflected. The picture of the reorganisation of the party after 1868 according to the principles of 'Tory Democracy', given by J. E. Gorst himself in his well-known letter in *The Times*, 6 Feb. 1907, represents what Gorst would have liked, not what actually occurred.

[2] See the MS. minutes of its annual conferences, 1869–71. The 1869 conference was conscious of the party's lack of enthusiasm for the Union, and W. T. Charley declared: 'it was necessary to shew the Conservative Party Leaders that they must rely upon the Conservative Democracy which had been enfranchised by Mr. Disraeli.' Steps were taken at this period to bring the Union more closely under party control, and in 1871 it was virtually merged with the Central Office, set up under Gorst in the previous year.

[3] See, on this point, D. Southgate, *The Passing of the Whigs 1832–1886*, pp. 336 ff.

[4] *3 Hansard*, cxcix. 107.

Newdegate strongly criticised in 1871 what he alleged to be the reluctance of the Commons to discuss subjects connected with the welfare of the working classes, asserting that it was 'Members who profess peculiarly the popular creed on the other side of the House' who were most to blame.[1]

It was Newdegate and a few others who made in 1870 the only significant attempt of these years to tie the can of 'political economy' to the Liberal tail and to represent their opponents as men wedded to a system of economic theory and practice which was inherently hostile to working-class interests. The occasion was furnished by the discussion in March and June of some temporary and local distress resulting from unemployment, which the government steadily refused to try to alleviate by state action. Conservatives were quick to ascribe the distress to the working of Liberal economic principles, and to criticise the governmental passivity which those principles were made to justify. Newdegate painted the Liberals as the adherents of an economic system characterised by periodic depression, and questioned what he described as a cardinal point of political economy, the maxim that the state should do nothing in support of the labouring classes.[2] The cotton manufacturer Hornby, purporting to speak for the working men of his Blackburn constituency, said:

> They by no means approved that Radical political economy which cast all principle to the winds whenever it pleased Gentlemen opposite, but which allowed them to starve.[3]

It was one thing, however, to pillory the economic and social outlook of Liberalism, and quite another to offer a more attractive alternative. Conservatives might snipe at 'Radical political economy', but most of them shared its basic presuppositions, and those who did not had nothing viable to put in its place (there was no chance in 1870 for Newdegate's protectionism). They might attack the Liberal failure to grapple with distress, but they had little idea of what to do about it themselves: they tended in the debates of March and June 1870 to support the widely-favoured nostrum of state- or rate-assisted emigration, which, if a logical corollary of the wage-fund theory, was in a sense less a policy for dealing with the problem of economic and social dislocation than a means of evading it by exporting its victims.[4] There was no sign of the emergence of that coherent Con-

[1] *Ibid.*, ccv. 1543–4. [2] *Ibid.*, ccii. 446. [3] *Ibid.*, ccii. 442.

[4] Its supporters saw it largely as the readiest means of saving the rates and getting rid of men whose discontent might prove dangerous. A Conservative member, F. S. Corrance, had in 1869 suggested employment on public works as a way of relieving distress (there was, of course, a precedent for this in the Public Works Act 1863, passed to alleviate the effects of the Lancashire cotton famine), but had found no favour, Sir Michael Hicks Beach, especially, denouncing the idea (*ibid.*, cxcvi. 488, 529).

servative approach to economic and social questions on the basis of which alone Liberal deficiencies in the social sphere could have been exploited to the full.

The Conservative attitude to social problems in general, and to the rôle of government and legislation in dealing with them, remained too ill-defined to provide a foundation for positive policy. There were, it is true, indications that among some members of the party it was undergoing development. Northcote delivered a very interesting presidential address to the Social Science Congress in September 1869, in which, while cautioning against over-reliance on the state in social matters, and declaring 'to many of us, I hope to the majority of us, individual freedom and fair competition are the very breath of our nostrils', he acknowledged 'the immense power for good which resides in the State, and which can only be exercised by the State'. He said:

> any candid person, who takes a comprehensive view of our position, must admit that in some respects the intervention of the Government is much more necessary now than it used to be in former times; and that social questions are assuming such large dimensions that they cannot be adequately dealt with except by the employment of the central administrative machinery. This arises partly from the magnitude of the operations which have to be effected, and partly from the complication of the interests which they affect, and from the increased power of classes which in former times exercised comparatively little influence over our social arrangements . . . It may still be true that an enlightened sense of self-interest is a powerful agent for effecting public good, but the difficulty is to bring men up to the necessary pitch of enlightenment.

Government should not take over 'exclusive responsibility for any class of work which it can get fairly well done by well-regulated and well-aided voluntary agency', but the state, Northcote felt, was not doing anything like enough for the advancement of important social objects.[1]

Northcote saw the practical necessity of the enlargement of the government's rôle in social affairs. So did the author of an article in the *Quarterly*, which delivered a swingeing attack on the national predilection for local and amateur administration, and suggested that the time had come to trust central government and expand its functions—an expansion which Conservatives could support 'because their principle has always been to increase the strength and authority of Government'.[2] Upon such views a programme of measures of

[1] *Transactions of the National Association for the Promotion of Social Science*, 1869, pp. 4 ff. Northcote said in this address that he thought there must soon be a Ministry of Health and a Ministry of Education.

[2] 'Scientific versus Amateur Administration', *Quarterly Review*, cxxvii (1869), 41–68.

social improvement might have been built. But they were not typical of feeling in the party as a whole. Most Conservatives continued to be very chary of enlarging the sphere of action of a government which, under the new franchise, was subject actually to working-class pressure and potentially to working-class control. If they rarely went as far as Thomas Collins, who 'objected on all occasions to increasing the power of the Executive, his maxim being rather to cripple it',[1] they had every reluctance to countenance proposals of social legislation which would substantially increase the power of central over local administration and of state over individual and voluntary action. In this atmosphere, a positive Conservative approach to social problems could not easily evolve.

The bulk of the party had no interest in trying to capture the initiative in social questions and offer the working-class voters a Conservative alternative to the tardy ministrations of official Liberalism. Such a course might have attractions for the small number of Conservatives who depended heavily on working-class support, but it held little appeal for the representatives of the shires and bucolic boroughs, whose minds, in the ordinary course of day-to-day politics, still focused less on the social problems of the masses than on such topics as the cattle plague, the malt tax, and the inequity of local taxation.[2] The last of these matters, local taxation, was exercising an increasingly restrictive influence on Conservative attitudes to social reform at the beginning of the 'seventies. With the establishment in 1869 of the Central Chamber of Agriculture's Local Taxation Committee, the campaign of the landed interest on the rating issue had been intensified. As its parliamentary leader, the Conservative member for South Devon, Sir Massey Lopes, made clear, until satisfaction was obtained, the spokesmen of the land would resist all further impositions on the rates for whatever object,[3] and social measures entailing an increase in rate burdens were thus subject to the undiscriminating hostility of a large section of the Conservative party. Conservative 'local taxation men' like Sir Lawrence Palk might pay lip service to the idea that 'the great strength of England would consist in social reform', but the fact was that their especial grievance had become, as another of them, F. S. Corrance, put it, 'an obstacle to every social improvement'.[4]

. . . . .

[1] *3 Hansard,* cciii. 657.

[2] For some remarks on the Conservatives as the party of the agricultural interest at this period, see Hanham, pp. 32–8.

[3] See Lopes's speech in *3 Hansard,* cxcix. 652–3; and for the Central Chamber of Agriculture's local taxation agitation in 1869–71, Matthews, pp. 80–9.

[4] *3 Hansard,* cciv. 133; ccii. 1657.

Social questions figured prominently in the opening years of the first Parliament elected under the 1867 franchise, largely because of their magnitude and urgency, but partly as a result of the politicians' growing awareness that henceforward the problems most directly touching the condition of the masses would be a major political theme. The educational issue reached a climax, the increase of pauperism and vagrancy stimulated intensive discussion of poor law matters, the position of the trade unions was at last, if very unsatisfactorily, defined, Plimsoll opened his great campaign on behalf of the merchant seaman, and licensing first revealed its possibilities as a political question. Only the first two of these subjects, however, education and poor relief, both of which closely concerned the interests of the landed classes, engaged the serious attention of the majority of Conservative members.

Education was probably the social question which bulked largest when the new Parliament assembled in 1869. In the course of the year, the main parties in the education battle organised their forces. The Radicals and militant nonconformists formed the National Education League, to campaign for free, rate-supported, compulsory, and unsectarian (or even secular) instruction. Faced with this challenge, those who wanted to maintain the voluntary and denominational system established in November the National Education Union, based on Manchester, and numbering among its original supporters such local Conservative figures as Birley, Callender, and Algernon Egerton, M.P. The Union wanted to proceed by 'judiciously supplementing' the existing system: while rejecting rating (except for the education of pauper and vagrant children), it accepted the conscience clause and a degree of compulsion.[1]

The Conservative party was coming to realise that the education problem must be effectively tackled, and greater flexibility was apparent in its approach in 1869. But it remained determined that whatever was needful should be done through the expansion of the existing system, and it continued resolutely opposed (all the more so now that the local taxation agitation was in full swing) to the proposal which seemed to many a precondition of real progress—an education rate. Rating would be a new aggravation of the landed interest's burdens, and bitterly resented as such,[2] and it might well

[1] It supported the half-time system, and would have required a certificate of school attendance from children under thirteen seeking work. For the Union, see J. W. Adamson, *English Education 1789–1902*, pp. 351–3; Maltby, pp. 113–15.

[2] Salisbury declared: 'if in addition to the other burdens which land has now to bear you assume that it should also bear the expenses of national education, you will create a spirit of resistance which will secure for your system an amount of unpopularity which no improvement you may make in education will be able to counterbalance.' *3 Hansard*, cxciv. 819. Cf. Lowther, *ibid.*, cxcviii. 1498.

dry up voluntary subscriptions and shatter the denominational system. It might, Adderley and Liddell thought, be introduced permissively in large towns, where educational deficiency was most acute,[1] but for its general application there was very little Conservative support (Pakington, as usual, being the principal exception). It was largely the rating issue which accounted for the action of the Conservative majority in the Lords in throwing out the Parochial Schools (Scotland) Bill, introduced by the government in 1869 to give Scotland a national educational system into which the existing voluntary schools should be absorbed. The objection to the bill was not merely that it aimed to destroy denominationalism in Scotland, but that the rate on real property for which it provided might be treated as a precedent when English education was dealt with.[2]

Given the virulent campaigning of the Education League, whose programme had strong working-class support,[3] and the strength of the militant nonconformists in the Liberal party, the Conservatives had reason to fear that when the government tackled education it would show little sympathy for the voluntary and denominational system. But in fact it was a moderate compromise which appeared in the Elementary Education Bill brought in by the Vice-President of the Committee of Council on Education, W. E. Forster, in February 1870. Forster announced that the government's object was to complete, not destroy, the existing system.[4] Only in districts where inquiry showed education to be deficient would the state intervene to compel the provision of schools by school boards with power to levy a rate, and even then a year's grace would be allowed to give voluntary effort a chance of filling the gap instead. The boards (they were to be appointed in the original bill, but an amendment was later carried providing for their election by ratepayers) might assist existing schools out of the rate, make bye-laws for compulsory attendance, establish free schools, and pay school fees for poor parents. They themselves were to determine the religious teaching to be given in the schools they established. The conscience clause was henceforth to be applied in every elementary school receiving state assistance.

In many ways, this was a better bargain than the Conservative party and the Established Church had had reason to expect, and both recognised the fact. Forster's introductory speech was well received by the opposition: Montagu's attempt to show that the bill was un-

[1] *Ibid.*, cxciv. 1225; cxcviii. 177. Liddell acknowledged that the problem in the great towns had got beyond the reach of voluntary effort.

[2] See the speeches of Lowther, Collins, Hope, and Sclater-Booth, *ibid.*, cxcviii. 1388, 1442–4.

[3] See B. Simon, pp. 362–4.

[4] *3 Hansard*, cxcix. 443–4.

necessary hardly represented the feeling of his party, and was rebuked by Sandon, who, with Pakington, welcomed the measure.[1] Hardy, staunchest of Anglicans, wrote contentedly: 'The Union triumphs over the League'.[2] The Church acknowledged the bill's spirit of fairness, and even the National Society was now prepared in private to swallow the conscience clause, though still protesting against it in public.[3]

The reason for this complaisance is obvious. The bill not only left the existing system substantially intact but even held out hope of its reinforcement. The 'year of grace', to be given before school boards were introduced in educationally deficient areas, furnished a great opportunity for voluntary effort to go to work and make boards and rates unnecessary. Where school boards were established, they might, if Anglican-dominated, support Anglican religious teaching out of the rates, both by prescribing it in their new, rate-provided schools, and by giving rate assistance to existing Anglican schools. Conscience clause, rating, and permissive compulsion might well be tolerated when the two latter were to operate only where voluntary effort had manifestly failed, and could themselves be applied to bolster denominationalism.

But what pleased Conservatives infuriated many nonconformists, and a vociferous section of the Liberal party fell tooth and nail on a measure which they regarded as framed wholly in the interest of the existing system and the Anglican Church. Their determination to prevent the use of rates to subsidise denominationalism set going a running fight over the 'religious difficulty', and created an open breach between them and the government, which was to have electoral repercussions. Ministers had to depend on the Conservatives for support against their own backbench militants. This was readily given: there was no real Conservative opposition to the bill's second reading, and the course of action in Committee which Montagu suggested to Disraeli involved no challenge to its principles.[4]

The situation was, however, altered when, in June, the government bent before the nonconformist pressure and made important changes in the bill. Cowper-Temple's amendment providing that in rate-founded schools no catechism or formulary distinctive of any par-

[1] *Ibid.*, cxcix. 466–75, 480–2, 483–8.

[2] Diary, 18 Feb. 1870: Cranbrook Papers, T501/294.

[3] See Wagner, pp. 92–3; Burgess, pp. 194–6.

[4] See Montagu to Disraeli, 9 June 1870 (Disraeli Papers, B/XXI/M/451), where amendments to be supported or opposed are listed. Montagu's main aims were to extend the year of grace, resist attempts to exclude religious teaching from rate-established schools, and provide additional safeguards for the denominational schools. Lord Robert was reaching the end of his term as the party's Commons spokesman on education: he was about to go over to Rome.

ticular denomination should be taught was adopted,[1] and the school boards were no longer to be allowed to assist voluntary schools from the rates, though in compensation the existing state grant to elementary schools was to be increased by up to 50%. Building grants to voluntary schools were to cease, and the 'year of grace' was cut to six months. This was virtually a new measure, and one much less agreeable to the Church and her representatives. No longer, in theory, could Anglican doctrines be taught in board schools or subsidised from the rates, and the provision of new Anglican schools had received a severe blow. The increased grant hardly seemed adequate recompense.

The Church's dismay was heightened by the attitude of the militant nonconformists, who refused to be appeased by the government's concessions, assailed the increased grant, and, in some cases, demanded a totally secular system.[2] Their mounting offensive against the edifice of Anglican supremacy had already helped to bring down the Irish Church, and was threatening to destroy university tests: they were determined that the Anglican predominance in elementary education should be the next pillar to crumble. The Church looked to the Conservative party for its defence.

The task was one which the party had no idea of shirking. It saw the Anglican position in education as a fundamental bulwark of the social order and of its own power. But its leaders do not seem to have felt that the threat to that position was especially grave, even after the remodelling of Forster's bill and the opening of the main nonconformist offensive in the Commons. The extreme party on the Liberal backbenches was remarkable more for lungpower than strength, and the revised bill was still no bad bargain[3]. To oppose it would be to risk closing the breach in the Liberal ranks, and might ultimately result in the production of a much worse measure. Moreover, it would put the Conservatives in the position of seeming to obstruct a reform on the necessity for which the bulk of the country was now agreed. The Conservative leaders, therefore, resigned themselves to the bill's passage, and concentrated their combative energies

[1] Gladstone ascribed the dropping of the original proposal (which, like Forster, he preferred) to the lack of active support for it from the Church, the National Society, and the opposition, and to the fact that several bishops, many of the clergy, and the Education Union abandoned the catechism. Morley, ii. 306.

[2] Secularism was the only answer for those nonconformists who feared that the unsectarian instruction permitted by the Cowper-Temple clause would in many areas be a cloak for Anglicanism, and that the conscience clause would not suffice as a protection.

[3] It is, however, difficult to see why Hardy should have thought the government's new provisions favourable to the existing schools at first sight (diary, 19 June 1870: Cranbrook Papers, T501/295).

upon Irish land.[1] The party at no point resisted the bill as a whole, but strove during the interminable debates to protect by amendment in detail the interests which it represented.

For a number of Conservatives, anxious for educational reform, the measure was not difficult to accept. Pakington, whom Forster recognised to have been 'always in advance of most of us on both sides of the House',[2] saw in it the achievement of much for which he had long struggled. Some younger men like Sandon, W. H. Smith, and R. A. Cross, who were in touch with the urban and industrial areas where educational needs were most glaring and the existing system most patently inadequate, gave it substantial support.[3] But the bulk of the party, looking at it overwhelmingly from the point of view of Anglican and rural interests, found cause for deep concern in its provisions for religious instruction, rating, and compulsion.

The bill's exclusion of distinctive religious teaching from school board schools was fairly quietly accepted, though Northcote and Manners made a half-hearted challenge to it in Committee, supported by Disraeli, who pointed out that in turning the schoolmasters into 'a new sacerdotal class' the revised scheme would cause as much trouble as its predecessor.[4] Still, it was felt by most Conservatives to be a serious blemish on the bill. So was the fact that the measure left it open to school boards to exclude religious instruction altogether from their schools; and Pakington and others tried unsuccessfully to ensure the daily use of the Bible.[5]

Rating seemed likely to many Conservatives to deal a death-blow to the denominational system. In the contest (for so they thought of it) about to begin between the board and voluntary schools, the scales were, they felt, heavily weighted in favour of the former, backed by the funds the levy of which would kill off the subscriptions which financed the latter. There was considerable fear that hard-pressed supporters of denominationalism would deliberately abandon their

[1] Their papers show the relative importance of the two subjects in 1870: there is much on the Irish Land Bill, very little on education.

[2] *3 Hansard*, cxcix. 448. Forster's bill owed much to Pakington's bills of 1855 and 1857.

[3] Sandon, Smith, and Cross operated as a group at this period. On their attitude to the Education Bill, see Maxwell, i. 177–82. Smith worked closely with Forster and became his personal friend in these months.

[4] See *3 Hansard*, ccii. 1236–63. Northcote's amendment received only 95 votes, and evidently did not represent a serious attempt by the party to erase the Cowper-Temple clause. Hardy's diary for 2 July 1870 (Cranbrook Papers, T501/295) suggests that he had been lukewarm about dividing on the issue, and that the whips had opposed it. Sandon, Smith and Cross backed the government's line; Pakington, however, was not altogether happy about it (see *3 Hansard*, ccii. 570).

[5] See *ibid.*, ccii. 1265–9; cciii. 501–6.

efforts and allow board and rate to take over, a danger rendered more acute when Forster made provision for boards to be formed on the demand of the ratepayers or where managers of an existing school could or would maintain it no longer. Conservatives were very worried about the effect of these clauses in the countryside, where clergymen struggling to support schools with inadequate aid from landowners and farmers might choose to throw them on the rates,[1] and some of the ratepayers might combine to introduce boards and rating as a means of sapping the position of squire and parson.[2]

The fresh burden imposed by rating on real property provoked a sharp reaction from the local taxation enthusiasts. The Central Chamber of Agriculture protested, Massey Lopes got 88 votes for an amendment limiting the education rate to a penny, and Albert Pell made a forlorn attempt to obtain relief for agricultural occupiers.[3] Northcote tried to insert a provision that where a school board's needs exceeded the return of a threepenny rate, the state should furnish half the excess.[4] Proposals tending to increase the charge on the rates, such as free education, were stoutly resisted.[5]

Compulsion was a prospect no less unwelcome than rating. A few Conservatives, like Pakington and Gordon, supported it, and Colonel Brise favoured compulsory powers for voluntary school managers as well as school boards.[6] But in general the party was hostile, damning compulsion as repugnant to the feeling of the country, and using the issue to present itself as the friend of the working man. Lowther, referring to a strong impression that this was 'a species of class legislation, specially directed against the working classes', secured 119 votes for the erasure of the bill's compulsory provisions.[7] Montagu and Shaftesbury stressed that compulsion would deprive poor families of the children's earnings on which many of them depended, and the latter had some success in the Lords in limiting the scope of the compulsory clause.[8] The Conservative attitude, of

[1] Forster had this type of case specifically in mind (*ibid.*, ccii. 1015), and Northcote was in no doubt that many country clergymen wanted to put their schools on the rates (*ibid.*, ccii. 1239).

[2] See speeches by Read, Selwin-Ibbetson, and Barttelot, *ibid.*, ccii. 1226–7, 1231–3; Read to Salisbury, 28 July 1870 (Salisbury Papers, S.C.).

[3] Matthews, pp. 84–5, 308; *3 Hansard*, ccii. 1667–8.

[4] *Ibid.*, cciii. 92.

[5] In the Lords, Richmond attacked the clause allowing school boards to pay fees for poor children (*ibid.*, cciii. 857), and the clause permitting the establishment of free schools was deleted (the Commons later re-inserted it).

[6] *Ibid.*, cxcix. 487; ccii. 827; cciii. 59.

[7] *Ibid.*, ccii. 1739; cciii. 41ff. W. H. Smith also opposed compulsion partly on the ground that the working men did not want it (*ibid.*, ccii. 904–6).

[8] *Ibid.*, cxcix. 473–4; cciii. 846–8, 1187–90. Shaftesbury favoured the half-time system, and evening schools.

course, was closely connected with the potential impact of compulsion on the rural labour market, as Welby and Salisbury made clear.[1]

The efforts of the Conservative party to render the bill more favourable to the interests of Church and land were almost all abortive. The final measure was accepted without enthusiasm. Conservatives and Anglicans felt that they had made large concessions over formularies, the conscience clause, and the principles of rating and compulsion, and saw no adequate recompense.[2] Many shared Shaftesbury's fear that the affirmation of the state's right and duty to see that a child was educated would gradually destroy the whole voluntary system.[3] But they realised that they might easily have fared worse, and that the new order was far from disastrous either to the position of the Church or to the interests of rural Conservatism. Denominationalism might still be consolidated and even extended; many country districts might hope to escape boards, rating, and compulsion. Concessions were inevitable if Parliament was to deal seriously with a problem which Disraeli described as more difficult than the Irish Land Bill or the Reform Bill.[4] The Elementary Education Act was a tolerable compromise. But neither the Conservatives nor their fiercest opponents, the militant nonconformists, were satisfied by it, and it offered limitless ground for future combats.

Temporarily, however, it produced a lull in educational politics at national level. Salisbury apparently remonstrated when the general secretary of the Education Union, Stanyer, in June 1871, urged the necessity of removing the Cowper-Temple clause: he had evidently no desire to see the whole education question reopened.[5] The arena of battle shifted from the centre to the localities, where the voluntaryists answered the challenge of the Education Act with a burst of school building,[6] and Churchmen and Conservatives fought to secure representation on the new school boards,[7] the elections to which were virulently contested. The greatest of the boards was the School Board for London, and Sandon and W. H. Smith were

[1] *Ibid.*, cciii. 53–6, 1267.

[2] Hardy and Raikes complained that the concessions had been altogether on one side (*ibid.*, ccii. 532; cciii. 750). Not only Gladstone and Cowper-Temple but also the League's spokesman, Dixon, recognised how much the Church and the opposition had yielded (*ibid.*, ccii. 790, 929–49; cciii. 740).

[3] *Ibid.*, cciii. 849.

[4] *Ibid.*, cciii. 309.

[5] See Rev. W. Stanyer to Salisbury, 8 June 1871, and E. Akroyd to Salisbury, 13 June 1871: Salisbury Papers, G.C., 'Political 2'.

[6] Between 1870 and 1876, the churches provided about one million school places. F. Smith, *A History of English Elementary Education, 1760–1902*, p. 291. Cf. Thompson, pp. 208–9.

[7] Their purpose was sometimes to frustrate the board system: see M. Cruickshank, *Church and State in English Education: 1870 to the Present Day*, p. 41.

returned among its first members.[1] They took a large part in achieving a solution of the major question which agitated all school boards, that of religious instruction, inducing the London School Board to decree the use of the Bible in all its schools, an example which was widely followed.[2]

The other social question which had serious importance for the mass of Conservative members in 1869–71 was poor relief. Accentuated by economic difficulties, the level of pauperism and vagrancy was rising at the beginning of the 'seventies, and the growing burden of the poor rate was keenly felt, not least by a landed and agricultural interest already in arms on the local taxation issue. Considerable time was therefore devoted by 'the ratepayers' Parliament'[3] to poor law matters, and both Liberals and Conservatives sought anxiously for means to keep poor relief within acceptable limits. The welfare of the poor was very much a subordinate consideration to the interests of the propertied classes. For the protection of the ratepayer it seemed essential to ensure that the consequences of pauperism were made unpleasant and the administration of the poor law rigidly economical. The assumption that poverty was generally a sign of fecklessness or vice provided a convenient moral justification for the policy of deterrence and the maintenance, at least towards the able-bodied, of the law's semi-penal character. Few followed Corrance in asking whether society was entirely blameless for the improvidence with which it was common to reproach the working classes, or another Conservative, Fielden, in denouncing the cruelties of the existing poor law system.[4]

Their concern at the increasing burden of pauperism led some Conservatives to ask whether the principle of poor relief in itself was not partly to blame. W. H. Smith told the Commons in 1871 that the right of relief existing in England 'was opposed to the practice of all other countries in the civilized world', and seemed a little reluctant in his acknowledgement that there was nonetheless no prospect of getting rid of it.[5] The foremost of those Conservatives who suspected that all poor relief was basically undesirable was the member for

[1] They had been instrumental in persuading Forster to create a single authority for the whole Metropolis. See Maxwell, i. 180–1.

[2] See *ibid.*, i. 187–8; Smith, pp. 294–6; Cruickshank, pp. 43–5; T. A. Spalding, *The Work of the London School Board*, pp. 96–9.

[3] As Corrance was in the habit of calling the legislature (e.g. *3 Hansard*, ccii. 1214).

[4] *Ibid.*, cxcvi. 485, 533–7; cxcix. 826–30; ccv. 1539–40.

[5] *Ibid.*, ccvi. 272–3. Hicks Beach, however, pointed out that the right to relief was 'a great social safeguard', and had much to do with England's freedom from social upheaval (*ibid.*, ccvi. 306–7).

South Leicestershire, Albert Pell, first chairman of the Central Chamber of Agriculture, and, with C. S. Read, the representative of the farmers on the Conservative benches. Convinced that improvidence was being wantonly encouraged by the indiscriminate giving of relief, Pell, both as an M.P. and as a guardian, conducted a campaign to abolish out-relief altogether.[1] Few were ready to follow him so far, but there was strong feeling that outdoor relief in particular encouraged pauperism and should be cut to the minimum. Moving for a Royal Commission on the policy and administration of the poor law in the Metropolis, in May 1871, Smith showed special anxiety to secure stringent control over out-relief; and Sir Michael Hicks Beach, who specialised in poor law questions, and had been briefly Parliamentary Secretary to the Poor Law Board in 1868, thought out-relief might even be prohibited in London, except in time of unusual distress.[2] Conservatives fully supported the campaign for the limitation of outdoor relief which the central authority waged from 1871 onwards.

There was much concern among Conservatives to improve and tighten poor law administration. The most comprehensive critique of the subject came from F. S. Corrance, member for East Suffolk, moving, in May 1869, for a Select Committee on pauperism and vagrancy and the principles of poor law administration.[3] Corrance fastened on the disastrous failure of the system to distinguish adequately between the different classes of poor—the permanent paupers, the aged, the sick, the children, the professional vagrants, the temporarily out of work. His suggestions for its better working were representative of much thought on both sides of the House, except for his idea of aiding superannuation schemes from the rates, which the President of the Poor Law Board, Goschen, denounced as 'the beginning of Communism'.[4] He took it for granted that the poor must continue to 'feel the degradation of relief'. Relief to the able-bodied should be cut as much as humanity permitted and made deliberately unattractive. Vagrants should be supervised by the police. For the treatment of the aged and sick, of course, a different régime was

[1] See *The Reminiscences of Albert Pell Sometime M.P. for South Leicestershire*, ed. T. Mackay, especially pp. 236–49. Pell's epitaph for his own tomb reads: 'Of long experience as a guardian of the poor in London and in the country, he condemned Poor Law relief as inconsistent with real beneficence and adverse to the best interests of the poor' (*ibid.*, p. xli).

[2] *3 Hansard*, ccvi. 272–84, 306. Hicks Beach had worked among the London poor, and in 1869 went to America largely to study poor law administration there (Lady Victoria Hicks Beach, *Life of Sir Michael Hicks Beach* (*Earl St. Aldwyn*), i. 22, 27ff.).

[3] For his speech, see *3 Hansard*, cxcvi. 471–91. It is quoted by Burn, p. 124.

[4] *3 Hansard*, cxcvi. 528. Hicks Beach agreed with Goschen (*ibid.*, cxcvi. 529).

required: for the latter Corrance advocated the dispensary system. He wanted government aid for poor law expenditure, and (in this respect diverging from many of his colleagues) was apparently ready to sacrifice local control to obtain it, attacking

> the faulty and vicious principle of local administration, extending into departments more properly the function of the State—to medical cases, to education, to emigration. For those things you have no right to come upon the local rate, more especially if levied upon the occupier class. Depend upon it you will have no district schools, no infirmaries, no emigration, no prospective permanent measures of improvement so long as this is the case. Their interests do not extend to the extinction of the pauper class at a period more or less remote, and yet this should be the aim of any law throughout.

With a great deal of this Corrance's fellow Conservatives agreed. Hicks Beach echoed his call for sharp treatment of the able-bodied;[1] Bromley-Davenport and Read joined him in 1870 in supporting a Liberal motion for putting vagrants under police control;[2] Kennaway, rightly stressing the rôle of sickness in creating paupers, wanted a trial of the dispensary system;[3] Jenkinson and other local taxation men demanded aid to the rates from imperial funds.[4] Stringent administration, rigid economy, relief for the ratepayer rather than the pauper, these were the keynotes of the Conservative approach to poor law problems.

The same is true of the Liberals. There was no discernible difference between the parties on poor law matters, and the government's policy in this sphere met little Conservative criticism. Pell saw much to approve in Gladstone's Presidents of the Poor Law Board, Goschen and Stansfeld, with whom, he later wrote, 'the principles of the Poor Law were safe from official trifling, such as was to follow in a few years at the hands of the Conservatives'.[5] The government measures of 1869–70 for London, which were essentially developments of Hardy's 1867 act and continued the trend to greater centralisation, found their fiercest challengers in the metropolitan Liberals, though Lopes and W. H. Smith had something to say about the highness of the rates and the diminution of local control.[6] The bill of 1871, implementing the recommendation of the Sanitary Commission[7] by creating a

[1] *Ibid.*, cxcvi. 533. He was against making the workhouse too comfortable even for the sick.

[2] *Ibid.*, cci. 632–70.

[3] *Ibid.*, ccvi. 310–12.

[4] *Ibid.*, cxcvii. 446. But they were sometimes less ready than Corrance to admit that increased central aid must mean increased central control.

[5] *Reminiscences*, pp. 248–9.

[6] *3 Hansard*, cxcvi. 1361–3, 1365–7; cc. 1777–9.

[7] For the Commission's 1871 report, see below, p. 163.

single authority—the Local Government Board—to supervise poor relief and public health, had an easy passage, despite some Conservative, as well as Liberal, murmurings against increasing centralisation.[1] The 1871 Pauper Inmates Discharge and Regulation Bill, which abandoned the attempt to distinguish among vagrants between the professional tramp and the genuine wayfarer, and applied the principle of indiscriminate relief under deterrent conditions in the casual ward, was the only one which provoked any kind of attack from the Conservative side, and this came merely from Fielden and Newdegate, still upholding the Tory paternalism of the 'forties, who denounced the idea of treating the honest work-seeker on a level with the habitual vagrant and criminal and subjecting him to penal treatment.[2] Their colleagues were little worried by this prospect, and supported the bill: their main concern was for the burden which the provision of casual wards would place on the rates.[3] The episode may stand as symbolic of the scale of values which governed the Conservative approach to the problem of poor relief, as to other questions, at the beginning of the 'seventies.

Little interest was shown by Conservatives in labour questions during these years. For many working men the problem of the hour was the position of the trade unions. The final report of the Royal Commission set up by Derby's ministry appeared in March 1869, recommending the legalisation and registration of the unions, and incorporating a minority report by Frederic Harrison, Thomas Hughes, and Lord Lichfield which advocated the removal of all special legal provisions against workmen and their combinations.[4] The Commission's investigations had done much to convince public opinion of the respectability of the majority of the unions, and it was a good deal easier in 1869 than it had been in 1867 for Conservatives to acquiesce in giving them legal recognition. Charley even supported Hughes's bill giving effect to the minority report.[5] But feelings of hostility towards the unions were still harboured in the party, and when the government introduced a measure to give protection to union funds, Lord Cairns, Disraeli's Lord Chancellor in 1868 and now Conservative leader in the Upper House, objected 'to giving

[1] Especially from Knight and Newdegate. *3 Hansard*, ccviii. 80–1.

[2] *Ibid.*, ccv. 1538, 1544–7. The bill gave guardians powers of detention. Newdegate warned that breaking down poor men's honest pride would tend to produce a class like the 'Communists' of Paris.

[3] See the speeches of Salisbury, Carnarvon, Lopes, and others; *ibid.*, cciv. 1159–60; ccv. 1543; ccviii. 1740–1, 1745–6.

[4] Eleventh Report of the Royal Commission on Trades Unions: *P.P.* 1868–9, xxxi. 235.

[5] *3 Hansard*, cxcvii. 1364.

trades unions, illegal in their object, the protection of the law'.[1]

The sort of settlement Conservatives in general were prepared to endorse was fairly well represented by the Trade Union Act and Criminal Law Amendment Act which Gladstone's government passed in 1871. These measures gave the unions legal status and offered them registration, but severely penalised intimidation, molestation, and picketing, and offered no protection against the threat posed by the law of conspiracy. They were deeply unsatisfactory to the working men and caused immediate friction between the Liberal Party and organised labour, but there could be no question of the Conservatives' supporting a more generous approach. Cairns, indeed, strengthened the penal provisions which the working men most detested by carrying in the Lords an amendment rendering the clauses against molestation and picketing still more stringent; and the change was confirmed by the Commons despite the government's opposition, the Conservatives voting solidly for it, with considerable Liberal support[2]. The party might be ready, by 1871, to admit the propriety and usefulness of unions,[3] but it was anxious to file their teeth.

No effort was made to reap credit with working-class voters by pursuing the legislative protection of labour, despite Conservative traditions in this sphere. Individual Conservatives did, however, take up the interests of particular groups of the working population. Charley, Manners, and others championed the cause of women and children in print works, Shaftesbury that of children employed in brickfields;[4] and Pell, Wheelhouse, Fielden, and F. C. Smith introduced a bill to deal with truck in the hosiery trade, whose centres they represented. There was, too, some Conservative interest in a question which was exciting growing attention in the early 'seventies—the further regulation of merchant shipping.

Carrying on the work of the Derby-Disraeli ministry, the government brought in measures for the protection of the seaman in both 1870 and 1871, their object being to make it a misdemeanour to send an unseaworthy vessel to sea, to allow seamen to secure a survey of vessels which they alleged to be unseaworthy, to restrict the system of advance notes, and to promote quicker payment of wages. But what

[1] *Ibid.*, cxcviii. 993.

[2] See *ibid.*, ccvi. 779–80; ccvii. 282–8; Howell, p. 194. The working-class paper the *Bee-Hive* published (15 July 1871) the Commons division list on the Lords' amendments—a significant indication of labour's growing determination to use its political influence.

[3] See *3 Hansard*, cciv. 2033 (Cave), 2039 (Adderley).

[4] *Ibid.*, cxciv. 1535–42; ccvii. 1401–11. Sandon in 1871 put his name on A. J. Mundella's bill for the regulation of female and juvenile labour in brick and tile yards.

really set the merchant shipping question on the boil was the remarkable agitation over the safety of the seaman got up by the Liberal member for Derby, Samuel Plimsoll. Plimsoll alleged that ships were deliberately over-insured, and overloaded to make them sink, and he introduced bills aimed at curing the evils of overloading and unseaworthiness by the enforcement of compulsory survey and a maximum load line.

The strong objection of the shipping interest to increased state intervention was voiced in the Commons mainly by such Liberals as Gourley, Norwood, Rathbone, and T. E. Smith. But on the Conservative side, Graves, of Liverpool, himself a shipowner, and Cave, the former Vice-President of the Board of Trade, were conspicuous for their adhesion to the doctrine that minute governmental regulation, relieving shipowners of their proper responsibility, depressed standards of management and tended to increase the ills it was designed to cure;[1] and Henley went so far as to declare:

> No one could look back for the last 30 years without connecting the constant increase in the number of wrecks with the continual interference of the Government in maritime affairs.[2]

These men, while prepared to support the limited remedial measures embodied in the government's bills,[3] had little time for Plimsoll's proposals. There were Conservatives, however, who saw that only an attempt such as Plimsoll's to take preventive rather than retributive action against men who sent ill-found and overloaded vessels to sea could satisfactorily solve the safety question. Most prominent was Pakington: in May 1870, calling for a Commission on loss of life and property at sea, he urged measures against overloading and over-insurance, and he supported Plimsoll's 1871 bill.[4] W. St. J. Wheelhouse, member for Leeds, put his name on both Plimsoll's bills.

The year 1871 saw the beginnings of the political prominence of the drink question. Many people in the 'seventies regarded drink as the major cause of social evils: this was an especially convenient idea for those who were opposed to serious structural interference with the existing arrangements of society, since it suggested that the only essential social reform was the closing of public houses.[5] But the

[1] See *ibid.*, cxcix. 307; cci. 1119, 1121.

[2] *Ibid.*, cciv. 681.

[3] On certain aspects of seamen's welfare Graves was ready to go further than the government, canvassing *inter alia* the suppression of advance notes and the establishment of a compulsory benefit fund. *Ibid.*, cci. 2006–7.

[4] *Ibid.*, cci. 1094–1106; cciv. 662–91.

[5] Cf. on this point, P. Mathias, 'The Brewing Industry, Temperance and Politics', *Historical Journal*, i (1958), 107–9.

regulation of the liquor traffic posed peculiarly difficult problems. The licensed trade constituted an enormous vested interest whose influence was felt throughout the country, and to tamper with it was an operation of high political danger. The brewers and publicans had money, organisation, and electoral power. They were well represented in Parliament, and would have little difficulty in rousing their customers against any attempt to curtail their business. No government, noted the Home Secretary, H. A. Bruce, in May 1869, had yet felt itself strong enough to bring in an effective measure against drunkenness.[1]

The drink interest was represented in and exerted its influence on both political parties at the beginning of the 'seventies. Though in many places the publicans had long had traditional connections with Toryism, it is doubtful whether the liquor trade as a whole had favoured one party much more than the other.[2] Seven brewers and distillers sat on each side of the House of Commons after the election of 1868.[3] The Liberal party, however, did contain nearly all the militant assailants of the drink interest, and the great temperance movement, the United Kingdom Alliance, was becoming increasingly linked with it.[4] Those hardy annuals the Permissive Bill (to allow prohibition in any given district by majority vote of the ratepayers) and the Sunday Closing Bill (to shut public houses altogether on Sundays) were both sponsored and supported primarily by Liberals, and the pressure of temperance feeling, particularly strong among its nonconformist adherents, was pushing the party inexorably towards dealing with the drink question.

There were few strong temperance men among the Conservatives. The Permissive Bill bore the names of the Irish Tories Dalway and Lord Claud Hamilton, and was supported by Birley, one of the rare Conservative members of the United Kingdom Alliance;[5] and the Sunday Closing Bill had Birley among its sponsors.[6] But the party in general disliked both measures, objecting to the prohibitive principle which they embodied as a gross interference with individual

[1] *3 Hansard*, cxcvi. 674.

[2] See Vincent, pp. 99–100.

[3] Thomas, pp. 14–16. The Liberals had, in particular, M. A. and M. T. Bass, and it was not until August 1871 that the Conservative benches balanced this weight of beer by acquiring a Watney.

[4] Hanham, p. 122.

[5] Another was Birley's Manchester colleague Callender, son-in-law of the Alliance's honorary secretary.

[6] It should be noted that the Sunday Closing Bill had been sympathetically received by some Conservatives when debated in 1868, Hardy (then, of course, Home Secretary) declaring that in regulating the liquor traffic 'he should regard the interests of the public and not those of the licensed victuallers' (*3 Hansard*, cxc. 1831–71).

liberty.[1] Conservatives were, however, fully conscious of the problem created by excessive facilities for drinking, and while rejecting the draconian approach of the temperance militants they freely admitted the need for greater regulation of the liquor traffic. A step towards it was taken in 1869 by their leading authority on licensing questions, the Essex baronet Sir Henry Selwin-Ibbetson, who carried a Beerhouses Bill, transferring the licensing of beerhouses from the revenue officers to the magistrates, and providing for increased police supervision and the better enforcement of the law.[2] Selwin-Ibbetson and R. A. Cross urged on the Liberal government when, in 1871, it finally tried to grasp the licensing nettle.[3]

Bruce's licensing bill of April 1871 was anything but timid: as well as curtailing hours of opening, it aimed at a substantial reduction in the number of licences by means of a scheme whose effect was that after ten years all licences would lapse, with the possibility that large numbers of them would not be renewed.[4] When Bruce explained his proposals to the Commons, three of the four Conservatives who spoke were friendly, only Colonel Beresford showing hostility and attacking the ten-years plan (in which he was joined by two Liberals).[5] The drink interest, however, mounted a violent campaign against the bill, representing the ten-years scheme as a virtual confiscation of property, and its anger began to broaden into a general opposition to the government.[6] The pressure generated in the country was felt in Parliament, and the attitude of the Conservative party towards Bruce's bill hardened. It is perhaps from this moment that the significance of the licensing question for the fortunes of the parties should be dated.

Yet the Conservatives were far from aligning themselves outright with the drink interest or taking up an attitude of opposition to licensing reform. They would not accept Bruce's ten-years scheme,

[1] See, e.g., speeches by Selwin-Ibbetson, Sandon, Fielden, and Henley: *ibid.*, ccvi. 936, 944; ccvii. 362, 374. Fielden and Wheelhouse denounced prohibition as class legislation, discriminating against the working people by closing their public houses while leaving the rich free to drink in their clubs (*ibid.*, cciii. 181–2; ccvi. 928; ccvii. 362, 380). Conservatives were also very conscious of its effects on the interests of the trade (*ibid.*, cciii. 184–5; ccvi. 937, 944).

[2] Hitherto the increase of beerhouse licences had been virtually unrestricted. Selwin-Ibbetson seems to have been very attentive to the representations made to him by the trade: see a letter from the agents of a committee of country brewers to Salisbury, 9 June 1869 (Salisbury Papers, G.C., 'Political 1').

[3] *3 Hansard*, cciv. 131–2, 136.

[4] After ten years, the licensing authority was to decide (within limits) the number of licences to be issued for the next ten years, and these were to be sold to the highest bidder, the process being repeated decennially.

[5] *3 Hansard*, ccv. 1097–8, 1100, 1101–2, 1104–5, 1106–8.

[6] See the principal trade organ, the *Morning Advertiser*, for May 1871.

seeing it as an unjust and intolerable attack on a great property interest,[1] but much else in his bill they were prepared to support. When the government, in face of the licensed trade's clamour, dropped the measure, a number of Conservatives regretted that its more moderate proposals had not been persevered with. As Sandon said,

> Many on that [the Conservative] side were willing to assist the Government in passing a good sound measure, and with that object had resisted great pressure from influential quarters; but that unlucky 10 years' clause made it hopeless to try to carry the Bill.[2]

Selwin-Ibbetson wanted to see the government take 'a strong line without attempting to meet the views of either of the extreme parties to the controversy', and suggested raising the rateable value requirement for public houses, restricting the discretion of the magistrates to grant licences, and curtailing opening hours.[3] Palk thought that the number of houses might be reduced by allowing the licensed victuallers to buy up existing interests from a fund created by themselves, and also favoured a mild form of the Permissive Bill.[4] Most Conservatives, in fact, like most Liberals, wanted moderate reform. While opposed to any wholesale onslaught on the liquor traffic, threatening the loss of a substantial proportion of the capital invested, they by no means regarded the interests of the licensed trade as sacrosanct, and for a limitation of hours and a gradual reduction of licences they were perfectly prepared to vote. The drink interest at the end of 1871 might see the Liberals as its enemies; it was not entitled to regard the Conservatives as its champions.

The Conservative party's failure, in 1869–71, to exploit the opportunities which the government's dilatoriness in social reform offered it was part of a more general failure to provide a positive alternative to Liberalism. Disraeli was content to leave the ministry to multiply its enemies and disenchant its friends, without attempting to offer the electorate a Conservative programme. There were signs by 1871 that his strategy was working. The reforming energy of ministers had disturbed entrenched interests and worried moderate opinion without satisfying their more exigent supporters. On the fringes of Liberalism, the vocal opponents of Crown, Lords, and Church were helping to drive into the arms of the Conservatives a substantial section of the middle class which felt that change was proceeding too fast, and whose nervousness was considerably heightened by the advent of the

[1] See the speeches of Palk and Hill, *3 Hansard*, ccvii. 185–7, 190.
[2] *Ibid.*, ccvi. 944. Cf. Fowler, *ibid.*, ccvii. 194.
[3] *Ibid.*, ccvii. 189. Cf. *ibid.*, ccvi. 938, 939.
[4] *Ibid.*, ccvii. 185–7.

Commune in Paris and the activities of the First International in London itself. The by-election results of 1871 showed satisfying Conservative progress.[1] Disraeli's great anxiety was that the process should continue: the last thing he wanted was for the rapidly weakening ministry to collapse too soon, before its credit had reached bottom, and before the Conservative party was sufficiently restored in morale and cohesion to replace it.[2]

For a party aiming to provide a haven for all those whom the forward tendencies of Liberalism repelled, the absence of a programme was in some ways an asset. But the Conservatives could hardly appeal to the electorate in purely negative terms, and some of Disraeli's followers were beginning to find their lack of a definable policy a serious embarrassment. Their leader's inertia forced them to look to others for the positive direction which the party clearly needed. Asking Salisbury to a banquet in March 1871, Lord George Hamilton told him that his constituents were anxious for 'some indication, if not of the policy, at least of the objects of the Conservative party';[3] and Henry Drummond Wolff wanted Salisbury to come forward with a new 'Radical Conservative' policy, to take the wind out of Gladstone's sails and rally moderates.[4] The party could not much longer support a situation in which the best definition its apologists could give of the programme for which it stood was that of the *Globe*—'the substitution of plain straightforward business for legislation for effect'.[5]

One facet of the desire to give Conservatism a more positive appearance was a feeling that the party should explore the possibility of doing something to recommend itself to the new working-class voters. It is no doubt largely this that accounts for the interest displayed by a number of leading Conservatives in the curious enterprise known as the New Social Movement. Much about the New Social Movement is still obscure, but its outlines can be traced with

[1] The government lost six seats and made no gains. It had had a net loss of two in 1869 and one in 1870 (Hanham, p. 218, n. 1). But cf. J. P. D. Dunbabin, 'Parliamentary Elections in Great Britain, 1868–1900: a Psephological Note', *English Historical Review*, lxxxi (1966), 85, showing a marked swing of votes *to* the Liberals in 1871 in by-elections in the special selection of constituencies reviewed.

[2] See Whibley, ii. 151; Disraeli to Northcote, 10 March 1871, in M. & B. v. 138–9. Hardy evidently agreed that the Conservatives were not yet fit to take over: he noted in his diary for 1 May 1871 that the government were still the only possible government (*Gathorne Hardy*, i. 299).

[3] Hamilton to Salisbury, 25 March 1871: Salisbury Papers, S.C.

[4] See Lord Eustace Cecil to Salisbury, 9 Aug. [1871]: *ibid.* Wolff and others (including, apparently, the whip, Noel) seem to have been thinking of the possibility of a coalition ministry.

[5] 'Have Conservatives a Programme': *Globe*, 8 Sept. 1871.

confidence.[1] Its originator was the marine engineer and builder of the *Great Eastern*, Scott Russell, who professed to be inspired by the example of the Prince Consort. Scott Russell was deeply concerned about the dangers of class cleavage, and was one of a group who, around October 1870, discussed the purchase of the *Sun* newspaper, with a view to using it as a means of promoting a *rapprochement* between the upper and working classes.[2] But he turned from this scheme to a plan of his own, the first step in which was the formation under his presidency of a representative Council of Working Men. The members were far from being nonentities: they included Applegarth, Guile, and Howell, of the 'Junta' (the latter becoming in 1871 secretary of the Trades Union Congress Parliamentary Committee); Potter, editor of the working-class paper the *Bee-Hive*, and in 1871 president of the Trades Union Congress and chairman of the Parliamentary Committee; Latham and Lloyd Jones, first president and secretary respectively of the Labour Representation League; and Henry Broadhurst.[3] The Council endorsed, at the beginning of 1871, a seven-point programme of working-class demands, which was subsequently publicised in a book entitled *The Workman's Wrongs and the Workman's Rights*, written by Scott Russell's coadjutor, P. Barry.[4] This programme called for the rescue of the working classes from the urban slums and their rehousing 'out in the clear'; for an organisation

[1] The accounts given in G. J. Holyoake, *Sixty Years of an Agitator's Life*, 3rd ed., c. xciv, and W. H. G. Armytage, *A. J. Mundella 1825–1897; the Liberal Background to the Labour Movement*, pp. 98–100, are inaccurate. What follows is based largely on statements and documents given to the press when the affair became public, and especially on (i) Scott Russell's report to the Council of skilled workmen, 10 Aug. 1871 (*The Times*, 23 Oct. 1871); (ii) the statement of the peers and M.P.s concerned, including the text of their memorandum of 1 Aug. 1871 (*ibid.*, 25 Oct. 1871); (iii) the statement of the working men concerned (*ibid.*, 26 Oct. 1871); (iv) Scott Russell's letter to the parties involved (*ibid.*, 14 Nov. 1871). See also Applegarth's account, in A. W. Humphrey, *Robert Applegarth: Trade Unionist, Educationist, Reformer*, pp. 76–9.

[2] See T. de Meschin to Disraeli, 23 Oct. 1871 (Disraeli Papers, B/XXI/M/339); and an article under the heading 'Our Social Reform Expedition', in the *Morning Advertiser*, 12 Aug. 1873, which was almost certainly written by Blanchard Jerrold (see below, p. 185, n. 2).

[3] The other members were A. Barker, J. Deighton, T. W. Hughes, J. Leicester (another member of the Parliamentary Committee and a future M.P.), J. Squires, W. Swindlehurst, and F. Whetstone.

[4] It is tempting to speculate as to whether Barry was connected with Maltman Barry, the paid Conservative agent and correspondent of the *Standard*, who in the 'seventies and later intrigued for an alliance between the labour movement and the Conservative party. H. Collins and C. Abramsky suggest (*Karl Marx and the British Labour Movement: Years of the First International*, p. 299) that Maltman Barry's manoeuvres on the English Federal Council of the International in 1871 may have been linked with the Scott Russell affair, but this seems unlikely.

for the self-government of counties, towns, and villages, with power to acquire and dispose of land for the common good; for an eight-hour day; for the establishment of schools for technical education; for the provision of places for public recreation, knowledge, and 'refinement'; for the setting-up of public markets to sell first-quality goods at wholesale prices; and for the extension and reorganisation of 'the public service'[1] on the model of the Post Office.

Scott Russell sought to get this programme sympathetically considered by peers and members of Parliament, and after failing to make headway in primarily Liberal circles he turned to the Conservatives. He persuaded Pakington to organise a 'Council of Legislation', consisting of members of both Houses, whose purpose was to see whether anything could be done to meet the workmen's points. Several front-rank Conservatives were drawn in, and one Liberal, Lord Lichfield. They seem to have met once, on 1 August 1871. Hardy records the occasion:

> . . . I attended a meeting summoned by Pakington of a quasi Committee formed at the request of Mr Scott Russell to receive proposals from an organisation of skilled workmen & see if we can in any way support them. A paper wh. was put in our hands gives me little if any hope of co-operation and I very reluctantly even wait formal communications. However Carnarvon John Manners & Sandon were there and on the whole agreed to a guarded paper reserving perfect freedom of action. I do not know but from what I hear distrust Scott Russell & certainly the names of Howell Applegarth & Potter do not inspire confidence in my mind. I got a headache with thinking of it all but did not like actually to withdraw when others well qualified to judge think it possible good may be done. Salisbury & Northcote the other members who have seen what we did concur. Ld Lichfield the eighth is away.[2]

The names mentioned by Hardy made up the whole of the 'Council of Legislation'.[3] It seems remarkable that six former cabinet ministers, plus Sandon, should have been induced to participate in a scheme which, as Hardy's words show, had from the start little chance of success, and even more remarkable that when faced with the seven points they should nonetheless have been prepared to continue negotiations. Sandon was later concerned to stress that they had acted from public spirit, not from party motives,[4] but it is hard to suppose that the possibility of dishing the Liberals and increasing

[1] Some versions have 'the railways'.

[2] Hardy's diary, 2 Aug. 1871: Cranbrook Papers, T501/295.

[3] Derby (the former Lord Stanley, who had succeeded as fifteenth earl in 1869) had also been invited to join, but would evidently have nothing to do with the affair. See Pakington to Salisbury, 28 July 1871: Salisbury Papers, S.C.

[4] Sandon to Pakington, 18 Oct. 1871 (copy): Harrowby Papers, vol. xxxix, ff. 272–5.

Conservative credit with the working men had not entered their minds. Disraeli probably knew what was afoot, and may have encouraged the scheme.[1] Organised labour was in a mood of disillusion with the Liberals at this period—the Labour Representation League even discussed the creation of an independent party to secure legislation in working-class interests[2]—and might conceivably have shown some interest in co-operation with the Conservatives for specific ends. But the Conservative leaders were very cautious: in their 'guarded paper' of 1 August they promised merely to consider whether they could co-operate with the Council of Working Men in measures for the benefit of the working class, and recognised 'the national necessity of a hearty good feeling between the different classes of society'.[3] And, in fact, this was as far as the business was to go. No further negotiations appear to have taken place. Before anything of substance could be done, the affair became public.

Pakington half-revealed it in his presidential address to the Social Science Association on 4 October 1871, when he urged governments and parliaments to devote more time to social questions, referred to the seven points, and pressed for legislative action on technical education, working-class housing, and the provision of good, cheap food (these doubtless being the most acceptable of the seven points to him and his colleagues).[4] A few days later the whole matter was in the newspapers, though in garbled form.[5] There was some entertaining fluttering in political and trade union dovecotes. Astonished Liberals treated the Conservative attempt on the virtue of the working man as a breach of their proprietary rights or as simple farce.[6] The Council

[1] Pakington's letters to Disraeli of 16 and 24 Oct. 1871 (Disraeli Papers, B/XX/P/111, 112) suggest that 'the Chief' had known of the movement and was friendly to it. There is no evidence that he played any active part, though Scott Russell used his name with the working men.

[2] *Bee-Hive*, 9 Sept. 1871.

[3] The paper was published in *The Times*, 25 Oct. 1871.

[4] *Ibid.*, 5 Oct. 1871.

[5] In particular, it was asserted (as Scott Russell had encouraged the working men to believe) that the Council of Legislation had accepted the seven points and the responsibility of putting measures through Parliament. Also, Sandon's name was omitted from the Council, and Lord Henry Lennox and the Marquis of Lorne were wrongly included. It was Applegarth who leaked the affair to the press.

[6] A. J. Mundella was at first incredulous: 'I am quite sure from my conversations with Pakington', he wrote, 'that there is no danger of his side going in for reduced hours, but they are willing to take up social questions and ride them' (Armytage, pp. 99–100). 'This Manifesto, Internationale & something more', said Gladstone, 'ought to make some sport for us. Is it Dizzy? The brain that produced the India Bill of 59 might well have produced even this' (Gladstone to Granville, 17 Oct. 1871, in *The Political Correspondence of Mr. Gladstone and Lord Granville 1868–1876*, ed. A. Ramm, ii. 275).

of Working Men, which had been perfectly serious in the affair,[1] stood by the seven points and was apparently ready to continue its work,[2] but the bulk of organised labour was inclined to regard it as the dupe of a Tory plot. As for the Conservatives, their first reaction was embarrassment, but they had, after all, done nothing discreditable, and their press put a good face on the matter. The *Standard*, officially inspired,[3] welcomed the idea of diverting legislation from 'factious contests and artificial attempts at needless political and constitutional change to greatly-needed social reform', in which direction, it held, 'it is the natural function of Conservatives to take the lead'. It added:

> Once let the leaders of the wage-receiving portion of the community acknowledge without any ambiguity the inherent and inalienable right of property, they will find every man who deserves the name of Conservative ready to condemn as loudly as themselves the *laissez-aller* system which is the eldest child of Whiggism, and which has been adopted by the majority of Radical politicians.[4]

The *Globe*, too, which had lately been suggesting that it was the Conservatives who had working-class interests most at heart, initially favoured the new movement.[5]

Yet while the New Social Movement fitted conveniently into the argument, often heard at this time, that the working classes were sick of the failure of Liberalism to attend to their wants, and had more to hope for from the Conservatives, the party was perturbed by this flirtation with men like Potter and notions like those of the seven points. Pakington would have liked to go on with the movement, and Sandon also expected the work of the Councils to continue, but their colleagues were unenthusiastic, and Disraeli apparently counselled quiet.[6] The affair passed into oblivion. It had, however, two interesting echoes in January 1872. First the old Radical J. A. Roebuck, who had been offered the *Bee-Hive* and the services of Potter,

[1] A start seems even to have been made in setting up branch organisations: at least there was a committee at work in Manchester. *Manchester Guardian*, 12 Oct. 1871.

[2] See its statement in *The Times*, 26 Oct. 1871, and the *Bee-Hive* for Oct.–Dec. 1871. The *Bee-Hive* published explanatory statements by Lloyd Jones (21 Oct. and 18 Nov.), Howell (4 Nov.), and Guile (25 Nov.).

[3] Its editor, Hamber, wrote to both Disraeli and Salisbury on 11 Oct. 1871, asking whether they wanted the movement supported (letters in Disraeli Papers, B/XX/A/128; Salisbury Papers, G.C., 'Political 2').

[4] *Standard*, 14 and 16 Oct. 1871.

[5] *Globe*, 13 and 18 Oct. 1871. Cf. the leading articles of 5 Sept. and 12 Oct.

[6] See Sandon to Pakington, 18 Oct. 1871 (cited above, p. 151, n. 4); Carnarvon to Sandon, 20 Oct. 1871 (Harrowby Papers, vol. lii, ff. 104–5). Carnarvon, Salisbury, and Hardy were inclined to blame Pakington for mismanagement.

approached Disraeli, evidently with the idea that the Conservative party might use the paper as a means of reaching the working class.[1] Secondly, Northcote, unhappy about the party's position in the late transactions, suggested to Hardy that it might be wise to pursue social reform:

> . . . I own I think it desirable [he wrote] that we should try to take some line of our own upon the questions which have been raised, and if possible to initiate some measure of practical legislation or at the least of inquiry. I should like, as I told Pakington the other day, to take up the question of dwelling houses, and to try our hand at some measure on the subject.[2]

Neither of these schemes appears to have had a sequel, though the Conservatives might have exploited the housing question, in which some of them had recently been showing interest.[3] The New Social Movement remained without practical issue, but it had served to show both the dissatisfaction of labour with the government and the willingness of the Conservative leaders to give cautious consideration to the promotion of the welfare of the people.

One of the actors in the New Social Movement, Sandon, was concerned simultaneously in an effort by some of the Lancashire Conservatives to give their party a more positive approach, with an element of working-class appeal. His principal associates in this were R. A. Cross, member for South-West Lancashire, and his Liverpool colleague, Graves. Sandon and Cross, with W. H. Smith, had for some time formed a ginger group on the Conservative side, supplying (with Disraeli's connivance) that vigour in harrying the government which the front bench was apparently unwilling or unable to display, and acquiring in the interchange of the smoking-room a broader outlook than was common in their party.[4] By the summer of 1871 the Lancashire Conservatives were convinced that the time had come for a forward movement, and a great Conservative demonstration in the county palatine was mooted.[5] But, Cross pointed out to Sandon, it

[1] See Roebuck to Disraeli, 1 Jan. 1872: Disraeli Papers, B/XXI/R/109. Roebuck said £5,000 was needed. 'For myself,' he wrote, 'I dread the working man in his ignorance & in his power . . .' A second letter of 30 Jan. (*ibid.*, B/XXI/R/110) indicates that the Conservative party would not touch the scheme.

[2] Northcote to Hardy, 13 Jan. 1872: Cranbrook Papers, T501/271.

[3] In June 1871 Derby, who was a member of several societies for the provision of working-class dwellings, had focused on the necessity of decent housing in a speech at Liverpool, though insisting in the following January that it was not the business of the state to supply it (*Speeches and Addresses*, i. 129–35, 170–1); and W. H. Smith had agreed in late 1871 to co-operate in a plan of George Howell's for improving the dwellings of the very poor in London, or so Howell said in the *Bee-Hive*, 4 Nov. 1871.

[4] Maxwell, i. 172–4.

[5] See Graves to Sandon, 23 Aug. [1871]: Harrowby Papers, vol. 1, ff. 132–5.

was no good having demonstrations without a positive platform: the Conservatives must show that they were not merely seeking office but had 'some thoroughly sound views of their own which they really were determined for the sake of the Country to carry out'. The thing would be for the late government to come down with a definite policy 'not of dram drinking but of sober earnest work which has been left alone and laid aside only too long. I will take your own words willingly "Social administrative & economical reform". I would add colonial matters so as to unite our Empire.' If the party leaders would not commit themselves, Cross continued, why should the Lancashire members not seize the initiative?[1]

Sandon was doubtful whether the positive, reforming Conservatism he and Cross wanted could be got from the existing party leadership: he opposed the idea of a visit from the late cabinet, of whose capacity he had a low opinion.[2] But in one member of the late cabinet a number of Conservatives saw the man who could revivify the party and give it the respectable yet progressive face which it seemed to require: this was the fifteenth Earl of Derby, as Lord Stanley had become on his father's death in October 1869. The Lancashire Conservatives persuaded their great magnate to take the chair at the annual meeting of the Liverpool Working Men's Conservative Association in January 1872, and Graves, at least, seems to have hoped that he would emerge as a challenger for the leadership of the party.[3] In fact, Derby made no challenge and gave no lead in his speech at Liverpool.[4] Yet support for him was considerable. Dissatisfaction at Disraeli's inertia was by now acute: a chief who spent the relative leisure of opposition in writing *Lothair*, instead of pressing home attacks on the government, seemed of little use, and Derby, with his attraction for the moderate middle classes, promised better things. The highest ranks of the party were ready to consider a palace revolution. At the end of January 1872 an impressive body of Conservative leaders, including Hardy, Northcote, Cairns, Manners, Pakington, Ward Hunt, Marlborough, and Noel, the whip, met at Lord Exeter's house, Burghley, and discussed the possibility of Derby's taking over the leadership.[5] Only Manners and Northcote,

[1] Cross to Sandon, 28 Aug. 1871: *ibid.*, vol. lii, ff. 246–9.

[2] Sandon to Graves, 1 Sept. 1871 (copy): *ibid.*, vol. 1, ff. 306–7.

[3] Graves to Sandon, 27 Nov. and 25 Dec. 1871: *ibid.*, vol. xxxix, ff. 83–8.

[4] For which see *The Times*, 10 Jan. 1872.

[5] See Hardy's diary, 31 Jan. and 1 and 3 Feb. 1872 (Cranbrook Papers, T501/295; partly printed in *Gathorne Hardy*, i. 304–6); *The Journals of Lady Knightley of Fawsley*, ed. Julia Cartwright, p. 226. Also at Burghley were Graves, Corry (presumably Henry), Lord Eustace Cecil, Annesley, Chaplin, and Hay. Cf. M. & B., v. 173.

apparently, held to Disraeli,[1] but for whatever reason no action followed from the conclave.

It is not certain that Disraeli knew of the Burghley discussion. But he could not be unaware of the discontent at his failure to lead. The moment had come when he must give his party a more positive platform on which to base its appeal to the nation, and in particular, perhaps, to the newly-enfranchised working classes. 'My hope in them hourly increases!' he had written of the working men in October 1870.[2] It was time to do something to assist that hope towards fulfilment.

[1] Northcote's diary, 12 July 1880 (typescript copy): Add. MS. 50063A, f. 366. Northcote wondered in 1880 whether Disraeli had ever heard of the Burghley meeting.

[2] Letter to Manners, 30 Oct. 1870, in M. & B., v. 130.

IV

ACHILLES FROM HIS TENT, 1872-4

THE range of possibilities open to Disraeli, as he faced the necessity of giving his party a more definite direction, was very limited. The principal attraction of Conservatism must continue to lie in its defensive and moderating aspects: there were few positive lines that it could pursue without the risk of alienating part of its actual or potential support. Yet some positive content it would have to acquire, especially if it was to make an effective appeal to the working men. It was in this context that Disraeli saw the advantage of returning to the themes of his youth and taking up social reform.

The choice was no accident. To begin with, social questions were highly topical in the first months of 1872. There was in political circles a growing realisation that the social wants of the people must receive greater attention than they had done in the past three years. The government, though its main measure was the ballot, promised to devote much of the 1872 session to social questions—licensing, sanitary reform, mines, and Scottish education. The Home Secretary, Bruce, declared in February:

> For the last five years . . . Parliament had been engaged, under two different Administrations, on great political subjects; it was to be hoped that they were now entering upon a cycle of questions of social importance of a narrower but of very great interest.[1]

Charley, from the Conservative benches, remarked in March that public opinion, 'tired of party politics, demanded that a large portion of the present Session should be devoted to the consideration of social and sanitary reform'.[2]

The emergence of social questions into prominence was thoroughly welcome to Disraeli, who had for some time been convinced that they would bring party advantage. In the middle of 1871 he had revealed

[1] *3 Hansard*, ccix. 233. [2] *Ibid.*, ccix. 1489.

his mind to Lord Lytton, whose version of his conversation was reported to Salisbury by G. M. W. Sandford:

> D. in his heart wishes the Lords to pass the ballot, as he thinks it is the only question which keeps the Liberal party together; & that then social questions would come on, upon which the Liberal party would be divided.[1]

Disraeli saw, too, that on social issues, the Conservatives, by supporting cautious reforms, could make a strong appeal to the material interests of the working class, without alienating the bourgeoisie. It did not need the New Social Movement or the feeling of Sandon, Cross, and Northcote (though both may have made their impression on his receptive mind) to show him the value of social reform in the platform which the party must now construct. As social questions took the centre of the stage in the early months of 1872, he determined that the ministry should not monopolise the cause of improvement. At the outset of the session, he asserted his party's interest in social reform by regretting that the government's Mines Regulation Bill and sanitary measures seemed destined to be delayed by its ballot bill, while in the Lords, Derby, who had devoted much of his Liverpool speech in January to social matters, assured the government of cordial support from the Conservatives for equitable reforms.[2] But these were merely preliminaries to the consecration of social reform as one of the abiding objects of the party which Disraeli performed in his great speeches at Manchester and the Crystal Palace in April and June.

At Easter 1872 Disraeli responded at last to the invitation which his northern friends had been pressing on him for nearly two years, and visited Lancashire.[3] There could have been no more fitting arena for the vindication of his leadership and the initiation of the Conservative renaissance than the county palatine, where the Conservative working man had proved his reality, and the movement towards Conservatism of the bourgeoisie was showing signs of increase.[4] Encouraged by the massive demonstration of enthusiasm which the Lancashire operatives provided for him, Disraeli resumed at Man-

[1] Sandford to Salisbury, 15 July [1871]: Salisbury Papers, S.C. Sandford added: 'Lrd L as owner of Knebworth is not so anxious to [?pave] the way for the agitation of these social questions.' Cf. Disraeli to Hardy, 23 Dec. 1871, in M. & B., v. 147.

[2] *3 Hansard*, ccix. 34, 57 (6 Feb. 1872).

[3] On the Lancashire visit, see Feuchtwanger, 'J. E. Gorst', pp. 197–9: M. & B., v. 183–93.

[4] On S.E. Lancs., for instance, Gorst remarked, in the notes which he supplied for Disraeli's visit: 'The employers of labour are generally Radical with an increasing number of exceptions. The sons usually inclining to Conservatism'. Feuchtwanger, 'J. E. Gorst', p. 198.

chester on 3 April 1872 the remodelling of his party's outlook which had been halted by the defeat of 1868.

Though the Manchester speech was avowedly an answer to the taunt that the Conservatives had no programme, much of it was devoted merely to the standard Tory defence of Crown, Lords, and Church. Its positive content lay in its stress on the need for social improvement. 'Increased means and increased leisure are the two civilisers of man', Disraeli declared, and he recognised that the working classes were entitled to both. Their elevation, of course, must depend largely on themselves, but there was, Disraeli acknowledged, an area in which the state might properly aid them. Disraeli fastened primarily upon sanitary reform, a question very much in the public eye because of the introduction a few weeks previously of the government's Public Health Bill, based on the report of the Sanitary Commission. He had had himself briefed on the subject by Adderley, a member of the Sanitary Commission, who had a public health measure of his own before the Commons at this moment.[1] Public attention, Disraeli said, should be concentrated on sanitary legislation:

> That is a wide subject, and, if properly treated, comprises almost every consideration which has a just claim upon legislative interference. Pure air, pure water, the inspection of unhealthy habitations, the adulteration of food, these and many kindred matters may be legitimately dealt with by the Legislature . . .

There followed the execrable pun 'sanitas sanitatum, omnia sanitas', and the declaration that 'the first consideration of a minister should be the health of the people'.[2]

Sanitary reform might seem a safe and uncontroversial subject for Disraeli to take up, but the current Public Health Bill was causing some discontent among his backbenchers,[3] and his endorsement of the sanitary cause indicated a firm resolve to commit his party to the support of social progress. This resolve was made clearer, and its scope broadened, when on 24 June he addressed the National Union at the Crystal Palace, and laid down the principles which for long formed the basis of his party's creed.[4] It was in the Crystal Palace speech that Disraeli recurred most decisively to the themes of October 1867, and reasserted his conception of national and popular Conservatism. He represented British politics as the struggle between the

[1] See Adderley to Disraeli, 24 and 26 March [1872] (Disraeli Papers, B/XXI/A/100, 127); Childe-Pemberton, p. 213.

[2] The text of the speech is in *Selected Speeches*, ii. 490–522. The celebrated phrase 'sanitas sanitatum' had been used before by Disraeli, in 1864 (M. & B., v. 190, n. 1).

[3] See below, pp. 164–6.

[4] Text of speech in *Selected Speeches*, ii. 523–35.

Tory or national party, defending 'national principles', and the Liberal advocates of 'cosmopolitan ideas', attacking the country's institutions in the name of reform and the manners and customs of its people in the name of progress. The body of the people, he contended, were on the 'national' side, and the working class, 'English to the core', was anxious to uphold the country's greatness and maintain its empire and institutions. But he was not content to appeal simply to the patriotism of the working class: he wanted also to engage its material interests on his side. Thus in defining the three great objects of the Conservative party he set beside the maintenance of the country's institutions and the upholding of the empire 'the elevation of the condition of the people'.

By this he now meant more than simply sanitary reform. He again focused attention on health, pointing out that what Liberals derided as 'the policy of sewage' was a matter of life and death to the working population, but he widened the definition of the question to include the regulation of labour. Very likely the nine-hours agitation in Lancashire and the growing force and militancy of the trade unions had hastened his realisation that something more direct than better sewerage was needed to commend his party to the working man, and only six days previously he had given an interview to that old stalwart of factory reform, Philip Grant.[1] Hours of labour, he said, had to be reduced and toil humanised. He made a genuflection to the dismal science: the problem was 'to be able to achieve such results without violating those principles of economic truth upon which the prosperity of all States depends'. But he indicated that the problem might be solved, as it had been, under Tory impulsion, in the past. Freedom and political rights, Disraeli asserted, the people possessed; they knew that the time had now arrived for the pursuit of social improvement.

The speeches at Manchester and the Crystal Palace, and the triumph he had enjoyed in Lancashire, re-established Disraeli's leadership. True, he had not provided his party with a policy or programme, but he had given it a sense of direction and an electorally viable image. To the negative defence of existing institutions and interests which was its traditional *raison d'être* he had added two positive objects—imperialism and social reform. Though he had not the economic imagination to integrate them as others would after him,[2] the combination was powerful.[3] Imperialism, offering the kind

[1] See M. Corry to Grant, 17 June 1872: Balme Collection, Bradford City Reference Library (cited in Ward, p. 421). The subject of the interview is not indicated, but it is unlikely to have been other than factory legislation.

[2] He did, however, advocate at the Crystal Palace an imperial tariff.

[3] It had, of course, been foreshadowed by Cross's words to Sandon in August 1871 (above, p. 155). Whether Disraeli had heard Cross's ideas and been influenced by them we do not know.

of romantic image whose influence on men's minds Disraeli so well understood, appealed forcefully to a bourgeoisie beginning to tire of change at home but ready to assert the nation's greatness overseas, and to large elements of the working class whose essential chauvinism it gratified. Social reform reinforced the appeal to the working man's patriotism with the promise of care for his material well-being. The concept of the national party, identifying itself with the country's greatness, appealing to the masses first as Britons, but attending to their vital needs at the same time as it nourished their patriotic pride, was a brilliant comment on the mentality of the British working man, and it was to serve the Conservative party well for more than eighty years.

The 1872 speeches are sometimes regarded as laying the foundation of modern Conservatism, and it is true that to some extent Disraeli had reorientated his party. As in 1867, he had recognised the impossibility of its resurgence as long as it remained identified in the public mind with all in politics that was unpopular and unprogressive; as in 1867, he had turned it towards courses that were neither. But his propagation of imperialism was to sink deeper into his followers' consciousness than his advocacy of social reform. Whatever clarion notes might be borne on the wind from Manchester and the Crystal Palace, the party remained unenthusiastic to take up the social needs of the people. There were, of course, exceptions. The genuine Conservative social reformers were delighted to be able to say with Charley that their leaders 'had declared that it was the peculiar function of that party to promote measures of social reform'.[1] In general, however, the 'peculiar function' was not vigorously performed. The fault was partly Disraeli's own: always good at conceiving a line of action, always bad at its detailed implementation, he made no effort to translate his zeal for social reform into concrete measures.

When it came to concrete measures, indeed, the party continued to be constrained in its outlook by an increasing dislike of state intervention, which it would take more than a couple of rhetorical excursions to remove. Even a man so keenly conscious of social questions as Derby felt obliged to insist:

> for those social improvements which we all desire and which are in everybody's mouth, we must look to the community acting for itself in the first instance, and to Governments and legislators only in rare and exceptional cases.[2]

[1] *3 Hansard*, ccxv. 470. The Seduction Laws Amendment Bill, whose second reading Charley was moving, was not, however, the sort of social reform Disraeli had had most in mind.

[2] Speech at Liverpool: *The Times*, 10 Jan. 1872.

Many Conservatives were becoming deeply concerned about the trend of legislation in the social sphere. They saw state intervention and control, despite established dogmas, spreading almost by their own laws of growth, and reacted sharply. J. H. Scourfield represented a significant body of feeling when, in June 1872, he attacked what he called the tendency to subject everyone to penal legislation, and said:

> If anybody were called on to portray the advancing civilization of England, it might be fitly conveyed by the representation of a large prison.[1]

Men in this mood were not likely to endorse with alacrity the extension of governmental and legislative action for social ends.

Not the least consideration in their minds was the impact of much social legislation on the rates, and here Disraeli had adopted, in March 1872, a position altogether incompatible with his subsequent professions at Manchester and the Crystal Palace. If social reform were to receive his party's backing, it was essential that he should curb the inclination of the local taxation men to resist any measure, irrespective of merit, which threatened to increase the rates. In fact, pandering to the susceptibilities of his rural backbenchers, he encouraged it.

> I think [he said] the time has come when it ought to be made clearly apparent to any Government that may exist in this country that no increase of the rates can be tolerated so long as the area of taxation from which these rates are drawn is limited, as it is at present . . . I am convinced it is the wisest policy of the ratepayers of the country to resist any increase of the rates, however slight, or however plausible the pretext may be, until the Government make up their minds to encounter that difficulty . . .[2]

Within a fortnight of his Manchester speech, he was supporting Lopes, when the latter carried his annual motion for the relief of local taxation against the government's opposition. Declaring that the country's mind was now concentrated on education and health, Disraeli tried to resolve the conflict between the cause of social reform and the pocket of the ratepayer by suggesting that the cost of the former should not fall wholly on the latter.[3] But he had himself to blame when in the following months he had to intervene to stop the local taxation men obstructing the sanitary legislation which the Manchester speech had glorified.[4]

The local taxation enthusiasts were at their most rampant after the

[1] *3 Hansard*, ccxi. 2013. Cf. Greene, *ibid.*, ccxii. 180.

[2] *Ibid.*, ccix. 1999–2000 (14 March 1872).

[3] *Ibid.*, ccx. 1397.

[4] Below, p. 165.

passage of Lopes's motion, calling for national contributions to the cost of lunatics, justice, and police. The government's refusal to give them satisfaction led them to offer vigorous resistance to almost all measures increasing rate burdens. It was difficult for the Conservatives to emerge as the party of social reform when throughout 1872 and 1873 a powerful body of them were busily obstructing social legislation and complaining about expenditure on health, education, and poor relief simply on the ground of the ratepayer's crushing and inequitable load.

It is the history of the public health question in 1872 which best illustrates the factors retarding the Conservative party's response to Disraeli's summons to the furtherance of social improvement. Public health matters had come into prominence in the previous year with the final report of the Sanitary Commission appointed by Disraeli's ministry in November 1868. The Commission had a strong Conservative element: Adderley was its chairman, and it included four more Conservative M.P.s: Cave, Gurney, Montagu, and Powell. Its report[1] was a devastating critique of the maladministration and non-enforcement of the sanitary laws, noting among the causes of the trouble the operation of the permissive principle in sanitary legislation, the confusion of laws and authorities, and the lack of motive power in the central authority. While clinging to the principle of local self-government, it insisted that local administration must be 'simplified, strengthened, and set in motion', and recommended that the law should be consolidated in one general statute, compulsory in application, that every area should have a single elected public health authority, with an officer of health and inspector of nuisances, and that public health and poor relief should be placed under one central department, with powers of inspection and control over the local authorities. To the last proposal the government at once gave effect in 1871 by setting up the Local Government Board, which assumed the functions of the Poor Law Board and the powers relating to health and local government formerly exercised by the Privy Council, the Home Office, and the Local Government Act Office. The implementation of the rest of the report, however, promised to bring strong criticism from the champions of the ratepayers, who saw foremost in its recommendations the prospect of largely increased expenditure enforced from above.

On the Conservative side, Adderley, with his fellow commissioners, was determined to see the report carried out, and as a demonstration

[1] *P.P.* 1871, xxxv. 1.

he introduced a bill to give effect to it in July 1871. At the beginning of the 1872 session, he welcomed the government's introduction of a Public Health Bill providing for the constitution of local sanitary authorities according to the Commission's proposals, and giving substantial powers to the Local Government Board. But he found the bill inadequate in not attempting the consolidation of the sanitary laws which the Commission had urged, and which he regarded as vital. Accordingly, he introduced his own consolidating measure backed by Cave, Gurney, Montagu, Powell, and several Liberals. It was clear that both bills would meet trouble from the opponents of increased central control and local expenditure. Responding to Disraeli's request for a memorandum on the measures at the end of March, Adderley outlined the critical feeling which was developing in the party, and urged his chief to support the government measure.[1] Disraeli, as we have seen, co-operated by taking up sanitary reform in his Manchester speech of 3 April, and endorsing the Public Health Bill, while noting that it shrank from the consolidation which was one of the merits of Adderley's measure.[2]

Disraeli's influence, however, could not make the majority of his followers enthusiastic for sanitary reform. Hardly any of them bothered to attend the Public Health Bill's second reading, only two days after the Manchester speech,[3] and while Hardy and Adderley were giving the bill the party's general support, elements behind them were planning its mutilation. A number of Conservatives were up in arms against the implications of the measure for local independence and the level of the rates. They were concerned primarily with the rural districts, where they feared that the boards of guardians who were to constitute the new sanitary authorities would be too weak to resist the advance of central direction, and would end up as mere tools in the hands of a Local Government Board full of expensive schemes of sanitary improvement. One of the bill's sharpest critics, Corrance, a spokesman of the joint committee of the Social Science Association and the British Medical Association,[4] believed that the local authorities had deliberately been made ineffective, so that governmental control could be extended.[5] Palk declared:

[1] Adderley to Disraeli, 24 and 26 March [1872], cited above, p. 159 n.1.

[2] *Selected Speeches*, ii. 511.

[3] For remarks on the low attendance, see *3 Hansard*, ccx. 850, 853, 861, 867, 878.

[4] Lambert, *Simon*, p. 516, n. 41.

[5] *3 Hansard*, ccx. 868; Corrance to Salisbury, 4 Aug. [1872] (Salisbury Papers, G.C., 'Political 3'). Cf. Fielden, *3 Hansard*, ccx. 850–1. Lambert notes ('Central and Local Relations', p. 125) that some M.P.s were evidently unaware in 1872 of the public health powers which the state still possessed after the act of 1858.

> He was convinced that before many years had passed the Board in London would put their hands deeply into the pockets of the ratepayers in rural districts, and compel them to carry out fancy regulations quite unsuitable to the circumstances of the labouring classes.[1]

To avert these evils, Corrance, Ward Hunt, and Goldney, among others, wanted to secure as rural sanitary authorities the county boards which many of the local taxation men had long called for, and which, it was thought, would be strong enough to resist the pressure of the centre. Another safeguard was to insist that if the government forced greater expenditure on the localities, it should contribute to it itself. This was the line taken by Lopes, who, after the passing of his local taxation motion, was in a strong position to demand state aid for sanitary purposes. At one point he contemplated trying to stop the Public Health Bill unless the government gave satisfaction over the whole field of local taxation, and Adderley appealed again to Disraeli, stressing how unpopular such obstruction would be in the country.[2] It was Disraeli's own fault if the local taxation men were following the spirit of his March speech on rating rather than that of his Manchester address, but he did his best to restrain them: 'the influence of Mr D Israeli upon Sir M. Lopes & his following', complained Corrance, 'made effective resistance impossible in our House.'[3] The Conservative leader was a good deal assisted by the government's consenting to make cheap loans to sanitary authorities and pay half the expenses of medical officers of health and nuisance inspectors. These concessions, based on Lopes's own proposals, went far to mollify him and his friends, and enabled Disraeli to urge his party to pass the bill now that satisfaction had been obtained on local taxation.[4]

But Conservative resistance to the Public Health Bill did not end here. Even when the government dropped a good deal of the measure, Corrance and others maintained their hostility. A section of Conservative county members battled hard for the interests of the rural ratepayer in Committee,[5] and even tried to throw the bill out. Of its clauses, said the old Worcestershire member, F. W. Knight, '18 might be classed under the head of "tyranny", and 23 under the head of "taxation" '.[6] Corrance declared that the bill involved 'almost unparalleled sacrifices' for the ratepayers, while Newdegate thought it bade fair to become 'the commencement of a social revolution in this country', and complained, with the attitude of his leader in mind, that the House was 'compromised by an official coalition'.[7] The Tory

1 *3 Hansard*, ccxii. 1260.

2 Adderley to Disraeli, 2 July [1872]: Disraeli Papers, B/XXI/A/101.

3 Corrance to Salisbury, 4 Aug. [1872], cited above, p. 164, n. 5.

4 See *3 Hansard*, ccxii. 1068–75, 1244–51, 1269–70.

5 See *ibid.*, ccxii. 1373–1403. 6 *Ibid.*, ccxiii. 252. 7 *Ibid.*, ccxiii. 257–8, 259.

malcontents, however, could do little against Disraeli's influence, and in the thin end-of-session House they made a poor showing. Goldney's attempt to secure county boards was beaten down by 84 votes to 7, Knight's to stop the bill by 168 to 16. Corrance made a final effort to impede the measure by trying to get Salisbury to intervene in the Lords,[1] but without result. Adderley and the sanitary reformers, with Disraeli behind them, had won, and the Conservative party had avoided too strong an appearance of hostility towards the reforms which its leader had just summoned it to support. But Corrance and his friends had demonstrated how thin Conservative social concern could wear when the price of philanthropy seemed likely to fall on the pocket of the rural ratepayer.

In 1873, indeed, the malcontents secured a minor revenge, when Adderley, with Cave, Montagu, Powell, and two Liberals, introduced a bill to carry out the amendments of the sanitary laws suggested by the Sanitary Commission, the principal effect being to enlarge powers against nuisances.[2] Corrance gave notice of opposition before the bill had even been printed, and Adderley yet again appealed to Disraeli.[3] But this time Disraeli had no incentive to baulk his rural right, and in face of determined opposition from a phalanx of country gentleman, including Corrance, Pell, Knight, Hicks Beach, Henley, and Lowther,[4] Adderley gave up the struggle. His isolation probably helps to account for the 'growing want of sympathy with my party, and wish to retire from Parliament' which he noted in this year.[5] The progress of the public health question had revealed how far the Conservative party was from the enthusiastic commitment to social reform towards which Disraeli's 1872 speeches had pointed.

The prospect that 1872 would see the government make another attempt to solve the licensing question posed problems for the Conservatives. They were naturally conscious, after the agitation of 1871 and the vigour of the drink trade in a series of by-elections, that there was political capital to be made out of the issue, and many of them were inclined to feel with Greene that the drink interest 'should be

[1] Corrance to Salisbury, 4 Aug. [1872], cited above, p. 164, n. 5. Derby was also approached by the bill's opponents: see H. W. Rumsey to Corrance, 24 July 1872 (Salisbury Papers, G.C., 'Political 3').

[2] Adderley and Powell were still pressing also for consolidation of the sanitary laws, but the government would do no more in the public health field. *3 Hansard*, ccxiv. 169–70, 171–2, 198.

[3] Adderley to Disraeli, 'Thursday 24' [April 1873] and 'Tuesday' [probably 8 July 1873]: Disraeli Papers, B/XXI/A/125, 126.

[4] *3 Hansard*, ccxvii. 90–5. It was argued that the bill would increase centralisation and the ratepayers' burdens, and that it was too late in the session (8 July) for it to receive proper consideration.

[5] Childe-Pemberton, p. 214.

protected and cared for like any other interest'.[1] Yet they saw the necessity of some reform, and could hardly ally themselves with the licensed victuallers against the government. Their attitude was therefore that of Derby at Liverpool in January 1872, when he rejected all 'sour and morose fanaticism', like that of the United Kingdom Alliance, and cast doubt on the value of legislation, but proclaimed himself ready to assist reasonable measures.[2] Disraeli, apparently, was glad to see Bruce move in the direction of moderation, so diminishing the threat of another head-on clash between the ministry and the licensed trade, which would have presented the Conservatives with an embarrassing choice of sides.[3]

Selwin-Ibbetson was anxious that the party should not merely exploit the government's difficulties but take a constructive initiative of its own, and he brought in a bill at the beginning of the 1872 session, supported by W. H. Smith, Goldney, and the Liberal Headlam. It was designed largely to codify and simplify the licensing laws, and to protect vested interests, while putting a gentle brake on the increase of licences by forbidding the grant of new ones where there was already one house per three hundred inhabitants. This was thoroughly acceptable to the Conservative benches, and Hardy, Graves, and the brewers Greene and Watney all supported it.[4] But the Liberal licensing reformers, while sharing the general respect for Selwin-Ibbetson's knowledge and energy, felt that his bill held out no prospect of reducing the number of houses and gave far too much security to existing interests. It was essentially, Trevelyan alleged, a trade measure, corresponding closely to a paper agreed on by a trade congress in the previous November.[5]

The main effect of Selwin-Ibbetson's initiative was to force the hand of the government, which introduced its own proposals in April 1872. Bruce's second licensing bill was a much milder measure than his first: its leading provisions were for a substantial reduction

[1] *3 Hansard*, ccx. 1450 (April 1872).

[2] *The Times*, 10 Jan. 1872.

[3] This seems the best interpretation of his words to Corry in a letter of 29 Jan. 1872 (Disraeli Papers, B/XX/D/166): 'Bruce by his last speech has evidently truckled down to the Publicans: so the breakers ahead are much diminished, tho' the increasing deconsideration of the government perhaps [? injured].'

[4] For the second reading debate, see *3 Hansard*, ccx. 1409–59. Watney, returned for East Surrey at a by-election in August 1871, was one of the leading spokesmen for the licensed trade on the Conservative side, and an advocate of cautious reform.

[5] *Ibid.*, ccx. 1440. Whatever the truth of this statement, Selwin-Ibbetson's bill was severely criticised by one of the leading trade organs, the *Licensed Victuallers' Guardian* (2 and 9 March 1872), which changed its tone only after the introduction of the government measure had presented it with an even less acceptable alternative.

of opening hours and more stringent penalties for breaches of the law. Even the trade had to acknowledge its moderation, though preferring Selwin-Ibbetson's bill.[1] The Conservative attitude was from the outset fairly favourable, despite a good many reservations on specific points, and there was no opposition to the second reading in either House. For a few Conservatives, indeed, the measure was excessively lenient. One of these was Bishop Magee of Peterborough, whose celebrated remark in debate that 'it would be much better that England should be free than that England should be sober' was a comment on the alternatives posed by the Permissive Bill, not, as it is commonly represented to be,[2] an attack on Bruce's proposals.[3] Magee, in fact, was a strong supporter of temperance, and regretted that Bruce's bill was less stringent than that of 1871.[4] Selwin-Ibbetson, too, would have liked greater strictness in some directions.[5]

Only in Committee in the Lords (where the bill had been introduced) did Conservatives make any major effort to water Bruce's proposals down in the interest of the trade. Conspicuous here was Salisbury, who strongly disliked attempts to make people moral by legislation, as he put it, and whose services were much in requisition by the licensed victuallers in the 'seventies.[6] Salisbury attacked the bill as 'a piece of Puritanical legislation which he was sure would not work, for it was utterly opposed to the habits and feelings of the people . . .'[7] By way of allowing free play to the habits and feelings of the people, he joined Richmond (who had succeeded Cairns as Conservative leader in the Lords at the beginning of 1870) in a series of amendments which sought to ease the penalties prescribed for repeated offences against the law, to extend opening hours, to delete the clauses intended to restrict the granting of new licences, to remove the provision for special public-house inspectors (this was successful), and to regulate retail sales of wines and spirits by grocers (a great demand of the publicans, who disliked the competition).[8] Even Salisbury and

[1] *Morning Advertiser*, 17 April 1872; *Licensed Victuallers' Guardian*, 20 April 1872.

[2] E.g., in R.C.K. Ensor, *England 1870–1914*, p. 21.

[3] Magee's words are here quoted from *The Times*, 3 May 1872. *3 Hansard*, ccxi. 86 gives: 'it would be better that England should be free than that England should be compulsorily sober'. While rejecting the Permissive Bill, Magee agreed that the ratepayers should have some voice in the control of the liquor traffic. Cf. J. C. MacDonnell, *The Life and Correspondence of William Connor Magee, Archbishop of York, Bishop of Peterborough*, ii. 43–6.

[4] *3 Hansard*, ccxi. 84–5.

[5] *Ibid.*, ccxii. 969–74.

[6] On the appearance of the government bill, the *Morning Advertiser* (17 April 1872) had expressed the hope that it would be much improved with the aid of men like Lords Salisbury and Beauchamp.

[7] *3 Hansard*, ccxi. 590.

[8] *Ibid.*, ccxi. 565–99, 1332–48.

Richmond, however, did not try to destroy the bill altogether, and the government acknowledged that it could not have been carried through the Lords without the forbearance of the opposition.[1]

In the Commons, the Conservatives as a whole displayed no special concern for the interests of the licensed trade, which, indeed, found some of its stoutest defenders on the Liberal side.[2] The chief Conservative advocate of the drink interest was Watney, with support from his fellow-brewer Wethered, and from Henley and Raikes, but he was far from representative of his party. Selwin-Ibbetson did much to facilitate the bill's passage, and showed some disposition to strengthen it. He wanted to raise the rateable value required in premises to be licensed (thereby restricting the increase of houses), and, with Gurney and Straight, and in opposition to Watney and Henley, he favoured imposing penalties for repeated offences upon owners of licensed premises, as well as licensees.[3]

The Licensing Act of 1872, in fact, was the work almost as much of Conservatives as of Liberals. But the resentment which some of its provisions created in the licensed trade was vented overwhelmingly on the latter, as the party in power. The hostility of the drink interest to the government intensified: 'we shall hail with delight the advent of a Conservative Ministry', the *Licensed Victuallers' Guardian* had declared on 27 April. Whatever their sympathy with the government's course, Conservatives could hardly refrain from exploiting its unpopularity. Some were ready to go far in encouraging the political activity of the trade. The Leeds member W. St. J. Wheelhouse told the annual dinner of the York Licensed Victuallers' Association, in December 1872:

> He wanted the Licensed Victuallers all over England quietly and thoroughly to organise—to organise themselves, to work up their own interests, and to say to the Government, whether Whig, Tory, or Radical, that a certain state of things they would have, and that a certain state of things they would not have.[4]

Selwin-Ibbetson remained anxious to consolidate the advantage

[1] *Ibid.*, ccxi. 1666.

[2] W. V. Harcourt was a great opponent of the Licensing Bill. The Conservative Talbot actually rebuked Liberal opposition to the bill in behalf of the licensed victuallers, many of whom, he said, wanted it to pass, since resistance to a moderate measure would only produce an immoderate one (*ibid.*, ccxii. 1905).

[3] *Ibid.*, ccxiii. 500–8, 649–59. He did, however, help the trade by securing the desired regulation of grocers' licences (*ibid.*, ccxiii. 464–82, 677–9), and once joined Watney and Henley in trying to relax a part of the bill (*ibid.*, ccxiii. 343–5). Cawley, of Salford, was another Conservative who helped to increase the bill's rigour in Committee (*ibid.*, ccxiii. 660–2).

[4] *Licensed Victuallers' Guardian*, 21 Dec. 1872.

the party was gaining from the licensing imbroglio by constructive action. What the trade wanted, he told Disraeli at the end of 1872, was a definitive consolidation of the licensing laws, holding out the prospect of a period of peace. He wrote:

> if a really sound consolidating Act was brought in by an independent member on our side of the house, it would embarrass the government very much, and that [*sic*] if as I believe would be the case, the trade looked upon it as a boon and took it up, our party might take it up also, and it would afford us a standing ground at the coming elections on the question, instead of leaving each of our candidates to pledge himself differently according to the number of publicans in his constituency. . . . I have already had applications from the provincial trade to deal in this way with the subject, and I have every reason to believe that it would be very warmly supported . . . Both Gerard Noel [the whip] and Gorst tell me that my action last year forcing as it did the Government into this unpopular measure, has done us much good or as Noel calls it in his letter to me 'infinite service' at all the recent elections. But my hold on the Trade whether Conservative or Liberal, is simply on account of their belief that I am sincere in wishing (as I have always said was my intention) to complete the act of 1869 [his Beerhouses Act] by a consolidation and simplification of the law. And I think the Conservative feeling now undoubtedly existing in the Trade would be lost at once, if we were for a moment thought to be making political capital out of the mess without any definite plan of our own.

If the party did nothing, Selwin-Ibbetson warned,

> when the contest comes we may find those who are Liberal on other questions desert us, which they certainly will not do if they continue to believe we are working on their side.[1]

Disraeli seems to have vetoed Selwin-Ibbetson's project of a bill.[2] But during 1873 the Conservative party showed some inclination to capitalise on the licensing question by showing sympathy for the grievances of the trade. Richmond roundly condemned the Licensing Act at the outset of the 1873 session.[3] Selwin-Ibbetson took up the issue of the brewers' licence duty, a tax they greatly disliked. Their spokesman, Pryor, had told him that if the Conservatives would act, the influence of every brewer in the country would be used on their side at the elections, and he persuaded Disraeli to let him make a not very vigorous demonstration during a budget debate.[4]

[1] Selwin-Ibbetson to Disraeli, 12 Dec. [1872]: Disraeli Papers, B/XXI/I/8. By 'last year' Selwin-Ibbetson obviously means 'last session'.

[2] See Selwin-Ibbetson to Disraeli, 26 Jan. [1873]: *ibid.*, B/XXI/I/2.

[3] *3 Hansard*, ccxiv. 51. With it he coupled the Public Health Act.

[4] Selwin-Ibbetson to Disraeli, 10 and 19 April [1873], with Pryor to Selwin-Ibbetson, 18 April 1873 (Disraeli Papers, B/XXI/I/3, 4, 4a); *3 Hansard*, ccxv.

The closer an election came, the more inseparably was the drink question bound up with party politics. The licensed victuallers supported the Conservatives, Henry Stracey told Disraeli in August 1873, and many expected a Tory government to repeal the Licensing Act.[1] The Conservative party was far from wedded to the interests of brewers and publicans, and it is very doubtful whether it received from them after 1872 anything like as much financial support as has sometimes been supposed.[2] But it was unlikely to resist the temptation to court the electoral assistance which they seemed increasingly minded to give it.

The labour scene revealed a growing turbulence in 1872–3. The trade unionists were engaged in a powerful agitation for the repeal of the Criminal Law Amendment Act of 1871, whose penal provisions hamstrung their operations in trade disputes, and this broadened, after the prosecution of the London gas-stokers for breach of contract and conspiracy in December 1872, to include the demand for the amendment of the Master and Servant Act (to eliminate imprisonment for breach of contract) and of the law of conspiracy (to withdraw union activities from its purview). At the same time, increasing union strength and militancy found expression in the movement for a nine-hour day, especially strong among the engineers (who were successful) and the textile workers.[3] There was a wave of strike action, extending even to the countryside, where the agricultural labourer was at last beginning to try the effect of combination. Plimsoll's agitation on behalf of the merchant seamen was reaching its peak.

Organised labour continued to be closely allied with the Liberals, and to find its most assiduous parliamentary helpers among them. It was W. V. Harcourt and A. J. Mundella who attempted to amend the law of conspiracy in favour of the unions,[4] and Mundella, again, who introduced in 1872 and 1873 a bill to give women and children in textile factories the nine-hour day. But the Liberal party included also those of whose 'cold-blooded, economist views' Mundella was

[1] Stracey to Disraeli, 20 Aug. 1873: Disraeli Papers, B/XXI/S/616.

[2] Cf. Hanham, p. 225, controverting Ensor's view.

[3] For the nine-hour movement in the textile industry, see S. and B. Webb, *History of Trade Unionism*, 2nd ed., pp. 310–12. In 1873 the T.U.C. instructed its Parliamentary Committee to press for a nine-hours bill.

[4] Harcourt's Conspiracy Law Amendment Bill of 1873 was supported by at least one Conservative, Douglas Straight, Q.C., who had led the defence in the trial of the London gas-stokers, but Cairns helped to stultify it in the Lords (Howell, pp. 242, 300).

905–20. Selwin-Ibbetson's attack on the duty was supported by Powell, but opposed by Corrance, Fowler, and Liddell.

moved to complain[1]—men like Fawcett and Herbert, who violently opposed legislative interference with adult labour[2]—and the Liberal government would do virtually nothing to satisfy the unionists' demands. By 1873, the working men were sufficiently disgruntled with the ministry to start supporting independent candidates against the official Liberals in by-elections.[3] There was a situation here which the Conservatives might well have tried to exploit.

At the Crystal Palace, in June 1872, Disraeli did declare in favour of the reduction of hours of labour.[4] But he produced no specific proposals, and, as with sanitary reform, his party showed no enthusiasm to follow his lead. Most Conservatives were too disturbed by the new assertiveness of the working men to be willing to offer them concessions in the hope of weaning them from Liberalism. Their feeling was exemplified by the party's spokesman on labour questions, Hardy, who wrote in his diary for 5 July 1872:[5]

> All is prosperous if Labour were not so riotous. The demands become excessive & where it is to end no one seems to foresee. Strikes actual & prospective alarm all & yet while the men show how they can hold their own we spend our time in coddling them by minute legislation.

It was not until mid-1873, when a general election was looming in sight, that Disraeli again gave attention to labour matters and their political bearing. He noted in May the working men's vital concern with questions like that of master and servant.[6] In June he showed calculated interest in Mundella's nine-hours bill, and in August asked Hardy for a memorandum on the labour laws, a subject which, he said, 'will press us'.[7] He still, however, had no definite ideas for action. It is highly unlikely that, even if the general election of 1874 had not intervened, he would have fallen in with the wishes of Callender, who was planning to induce him to propose a 56-hour week for the textile industry, with the backing of the operatives' representatives, so snatching the nine-hours cause out of the hands of Mundella, and

[1] *3 Hansard*, ccxvi. 821.

[2] See especially Fawcett's assault on Mundella's 1873 factory bill (*ibid.*, ccxvii. 1287–1303). Herbert, attacking Pell's measure against truck in the hosiery trade, which was reintroduced in 1872, said that 'the tendency of this species of legislation was to unman the workpeople' (*ibid.*, ccxiii. 212).

[3] H. W. McCready, 'British Labour's Lobby, 1867–75', *Canadian Journal of Economics and Political Science*, xxii (1956), 155.

[4] Above, p. 160.

[5] Cranbrook Papers, T501/295.

[6] *3 Hansard*, ccxv. 1368. Cf. Harcourt's words to Bright, 8 Aug. 1873, quoted in McCready, p. 155.

[7] *Ibid.*, ccxvi. 827-8; Disraeli to Hardy, 10 Aug. 1873, in *Gathorne Hardy*, i. 329.

getting the Conservative leader recognised as 'the channel through which workpeople desired to express their wishes'.[1]

Deprived of specific guidance from Disraeli, the party sometimes took up attitudes on labour questions difficult to reconcile with the spirit of his Crystal Palace speech. The debates on the Mines Regulation Bill which the government carried in 1872 illustrate this. The bill's principal effects were to restrict the employment of boys and to introduce substantial safety regulations, throwing increased responsibility on owners, agents, and managers. Well represented in both parties, the mining interest exercised great influence on the ultimate shape of the measure. On the Conservative side, the most conspicuous friends of the mineowners were A. S. Hill, spokesman for the Mines Association, Sir George Elliot, member for North Durham, a pitman's son who had started life at the pit face and was now one of the biggest colliery owners in the country, Liddell, member for South Northumberland and heir to the Ravensworth estate and collieries in Durham, and Cross. These men collaborated in a series of efforts to weaken the bill,[2] and opposed Wheelhouse's attempt to enlarge it by excluding women entirely from employment in coal mining.[3] In the Lords, Richmond moved a number of amendments primarily in the owners' interest, including one which would have extended the maximum working week underground for youths under sixteen, and clashed with Shaftesbury, whose isolation on the Conservative benches was sharply revealed.[4] The conduct of the Conservatives over the Mines Bill of 1872 emulated that of their leader over the Mines Bill of 1850, and suggested that whatever he might say, they were no less the party of capital and no more the party of labour than their opponents.

Only in the movement for the protection of the merchant seamen did Conservatives show to advantage. Plimsoll's agitation, strongly backed by the trade unions, was attaining considerable proportions, and attracted much Conservative support. If the president of the committee set up to aid Plimsoll in March 1873 was the inevitable

[1] Callender to Corry, 16 Feb. 1874: Disraeli Papers, B/XXI/C/11.

[2] See, e.g., *3 Hansard*, ccxii. 183–90, 508–27, 663–4.

[3] *Ibid.*, ccxii. 29–35.

[4] For the whole debate, see *ibid.*, ccxii. 1869–83. Salisbury commented on Shaftesbury's amendment to raise the age of employment for boys in coal mines from ten to twelve years that the bill would send up the price of coal as it was. Cairns took Shaftesbury severely to task for his self-righteousness, and the quarrel had to be patched up by the Earl of Harrowby, who told Cairns: 'As a mere matter of politics, it wd. be inadvisable to establish publicly or privately a breach with him . . .' (Harrowby to Cairns, 28 July 1872 (typescript copy): Cairns Papers, vol. iv. For the reply, see Harrowby Papers, vol. xxxvii, ff. 105–10).

Shaftesbury,[1] its members included four Conservative M.P.s: Lord Henry Scott, G. W. P. Bentinck, and the sailors Hay and Elphinstone.[2] These and others gave Plimsoll valuable assistance in Parliament. His bill of 1873, designed to provide for survey and to prevent overloading, carried the names of Selwin-Ibbetson, Hill, and C. E. Lewis among its sponsors, and received enough Conservative backing for its author to declare:

> it had been painfully borne in upon his mind that the interests of the working classes, when the issue lay between them and the capitalists, were safer with the other side of the House than with his own.[3]

Plimsoll's successful motion for a Royal Commission on the merchant marine was seconded by Pakington, and had general Conservative support.[4] Pakington and Hambro joined in harrying the President of the Board of Trade with questions about wrecks and unseaworthy ships, and in the Lords Malmesbury called for the searching inspection of merchant vessels before putting to sea.[5] The government was obliged to pass a measure strengthening the power given to the Board of Trade by the act of 1871 to detain unseaworthy ships, and it was clear that further legislation would have to follow.

To the party of the land, much the most disturbing phenomenon on the labour scene in 1872–3 was the rise of trade unionism among the agricultural workers. Since the troubles of the 'thirties, the agricultural workers had been one of the more depressed and subservient sections of the labouring population, and their inertia had come to be taken for granted.[6] While claiming to represent the rural community as a whole, the Conservative party in fact represented first the interests of the landlords and second those of the farmers, and these naturally precluded any effort to raise the condition of the agricultural labourer which might threaten the existing structure of rural economy and society. The party had shown very little concern to promote rural social improvement: even the Tory paternalism of the 'thirties and 'forties had been focused overwhelmingly on the urban working class.[7] Conservatives tended, of course, to argue that the sense of social

[1] On Shaftesbury's connection with the Plimsoll movement, see Hodder, iii. 325–8.

[2] *The Times*, 24 March 1873.

[3] *3 Hansard*, ccxv. 1993. Salisbury seems to have interested himself in the bill: see R. O'Hara (apparently the bill's draftsman) to Salisbury, 5 July [1873] (Salisbury Papers, G.C., 'Political 4').

[4] *3 Hansard*, ccxiv. 1319–62.

[5] *Ibid.*, ccxv. 98.

[6] At least until the 'sixties, when, with the strengthening of their bargaining position in an increasingly tight labour market, they began to resort to strike action and unionism on an appreciable scale (E. L. Jones, p. 336).

[7] Shaftesbury took up the condition of the rural poor in a speech at Sturminster in 1843 (*Speeches of the Earl of Shaftesbury, K.G. Upon Subjects Having*

responsibility displayed by the landed interest formed an adequate guarantee of the labourer's welfare.

The fact could not, however, be ignored that all too often, despite the upward trend visible since the 'fifties, the agricultural labourer's wages were inadequate, his housing bad, and his chances of education and self-improvement scanty. By the end of the 'sixties, as growing labour shortage made it vital to keep him on the land, his social condition had become a matter for considerable discussion. The more progressive Conservative outlook on the question was exemplified by Northcote in his address to the Social Science Congress in 1869. Looking for the raising of the labourer's condition to 'the free play of individual competition under favourable circumstances, rather than to any artificial remedy', he extolled the merits of savings banks, benefit clubs, piece-work, cottage improvement, garden allotments, and better sanitary and educational arrangements.[1] But he did not want to see the labourers asserting their own claims against their masters through trade unionism, and he was as much worried as other Conservatives by the appearance of their first really effective unions in 1871–2.

That the farm worker should display such unaccustomed self-assertiveness, that unionism should intrude into the settled rural world where the Conservative party had its roots, was bad enough. Worse was the fact that the new unions had a strong nonconformist element, were immediately taken up by Radicals who hoped to use them to shatter the political torpor of the countryside, and sometimes harboured extreme social and political aspirations.[2] They threatened not simply the profits of farmers and landowners but the whole rural social order, with its dominance of squire and parson and its innate conservative feeling. Their initial success was considerable, higher wages and shorter hours being widely obtained, but the farmers, whose economic position at this period was far from easy, soon began

[1] *Transactions of the National Association for the Promotion of Social Science*, 1869, pp. 17–24 (see also pp. 566–7). Cf. Lord Colchester's article on 'Agricultural Labourers', *Imperial Review*, 5 Sept. 1868, which contends that what the labourer needs is education and knowledge of the state of the labour market, so that he can go where wages are highest. Hicks Beach was another strong Conservative supporter of better education for the rural labouring class.

[2] On the labourers' unions, see especially J. P. D. Dunbabin, 'The "Revolt of the Field": the Agricultural Labourers' Movement in the 1870s', *Past and Present*, no. 26 (1963), 68–97. The unionists were often strongly anti-clerical, and some of them looked forward to the expropriation of the farmers and the division of the land.

Relation Chiefly to the Claims and Interests of the Labouring Class, pp. 87–90), but such initiatives were rare. When Shaftesbury succeeded to his earldom in 1851 he found insanitary cottages, truck, etc. on his own estates, but had little money to remedy things (Hodder, ii. 365–70).

to concert measures against them, and the landlords were only occasionally less hostile.

The labourers' movement arose so patently out of legitimate grievances that Conservatives, however much they might dislike it, seldom felt able to condemn it unreservedly. Some, indeed, like Lord Grey de Wilton, professed sympathy for it, as did elements of the clergy.[1] Disraeli, at Manchester in April 1872, acknowledged that agricultural labourers had as much right to combine as other workers, while warning that the farmers as a body simply could not afford higher wages.[2] But many Conservatives saw the movement as essentially the work of 'agitators' and 'demagogues' practising upon simple men,[3] and set themselves to combat its influence. Viscount Barrington endeavoured to prove to his workers 'that the Union *lords* make serfs of them, rather than the lords of the soil'.[4] Carnarvon and Northcote discussed plans to counteract the activities of the 'agitators'.[5] Salisbury, in May 1873, encouraged the Hertfordshire farmers in their project of a protective association (though advising them to direct it not against unions as such, but only against those which acted 'violently or unfairly'), and offered some hints on how they might keep the labourers under control, recommending tied cottages, deferred payments, and a blacklist.[6] Though the violence of the farmers against the unions in 1873–4 caused some embarrassment to their Conservative friends, not all of whom could wholly approve,[7] the bulk of the party was far from sorry to see their counter-attack succeed and union power crumble.

The 'revolt of the field' did, however, do something to stimulate Conservative willingness to help better the labourer's condition. The party would have nothing to do with the Liberal Trevelyan's campaign to give the rural householder the vote.[8] But it was ready to

[1] Speech by Lord Grey de Wilton reported in the *Conservative*, 25 Oct. 1873; M. B. Reckitt, *Maurice to Temple: a Century of the Social Movement in the Church of England*, pp. 115–16.

[2] *Selected Speeches*, ii. 507–10.

[3] E.g., Marlborough and Adderley. F. E. Green, *A History of the English Agricultural Labourer, 1870–1920*, p. 40.

[4] Barrington to Disraeli, 28 Sept. 1872: Disraeli Papers, B/XX/Ba/16.

[5] Carnarvon to Northcote, 21 Dec. 1872, and Baker to Northcote, 27 Dec. 1872: Add. MS. 50022, ff. 195–7, and 50039, ff. 64–5. Northcote had evidently suggested a circular to Chambers of Agriculture and a series of tracts.

[6] Salisbury to C. H. Lattimore, 6 May 1873 (draft): Salisbury Papers, G.C., 'Political 3'.

[7] Lord Walsingham, for instance, deprecated talk of crushing unionism, and said that the right of combination could not be denied. Green, p. 62. Cf. Hanham, pp. 29–30.

[8] Disraeli was so little favourable to household suffrage in counties that late in 1873 he was trying, through Rowland Winn, M.P., to get up a 'Borough

consider practical social improvement. The need to provide better housing, for instance, was recognised: few labourers' dwellings, Palk admitted, 'would bear the examination of sanitary Inspectors', and Kennaway had a number of suggestions for encouraging expenditure on erecting and improving cottages, urging that the government should lend money cheaply for the purpose.[1] Pell advocated co-operation for the labourer, while Derby, like Northcote, favoured piece-work.[2]

The most positive step was taken by the tenant-farmer Read, when, in 1872, with Pell and Kennaway and two Liberals, he introduced the Agricultural Children Bill, which purported to advance the education of the labouring class by extending the factory acts, in mitigated form, to agriculture. As passed, with government help, in 1873, the measure forbade the employment of children under eight, and made employment between eight and twelve conditional on having passed the Education Department's fourth standard or having made a minimum number of school attendances in the previous year.[3] It met some opposition from the right of the Conservative party. Barttelot succeeded in largely reducing the penalties for breach of it, and Salisbury and Bath criticised it on the ground primarily that it would increase the farmers' labour troubles.[4] But it was a very innocuous measure, whose provisions could be suspended by the magistrates at certain seasons, and which incorporated no machinery of enforcement. In fact, it was something of a fraud: its real purpose, as the Central Chamber of Agriculture, which supported it, acknowledged,[5] was less to promote education than to forestall the universal introduction in the rural areas of the detested school boards, whose powers of direct compulsion would interfere far more seriously with the farmers' labour supply than the indirect compulsion of Read's act. When it came into effect in 1875 the measure proved almost totally inoperative, as many of those who acquiesced in it must all along have expected.

. . . . .

[1] *3 Hansard*, ccxii. 1259; ccx. 1903–4.

[2] *Ibid.*, ccx. 1919; speech of Derby at Preston, 5 Oct. 1872, in *Speeches and Addresses*, i. 185–97.

[3] See, for this measure, Robson, pp. 178–82.

[4] *3 Hansard*, ccxv. 1458–9; ccxvi. 719, 720. Cross, on the other hand, got the minimum age of full-time employment raised to thirteen, but it was brought back to twelve in the Lords, where Salisbury and Richmond were able to relax the bill's provisions (*ibid.*, ccxvi. 1151–6).

[5] Matthews, p. 310.

Defence Alliance' to combat it. Winn to Cross, 18 Sept. 1873: Cross Papers (seen at the India Office Library; not traced in British Museum Add. MSS.). Cf. Disraeli to Northcote, 11 Sept. 1873, in M. & B., v. 259.

Education continued in 1872–3 to be one of the most contentious of social questions, and, like licensing, acquired growing electoral implications. This was due largely to the increasing violence of Radical and nonconformist dissatisfaction with the act of 1870. The Education League and its friends were determined to achieve a 'national' system, with universal school boards and compulsion, and to destroy the denominational schools. They mounted a strong assault in 1872, the battle centring around the 25th clause of the act of 1870, which had become the symbol of nonconformist discontents. This clause empowered school boards to pay school fees for children whose parents could not afford them, the choice of school remaining with the parent. The realisation that it could be used to subsidise attendance at denominational schools out of the rates brought a storm of nonconformist anger.[1] Forster, however, would not be browbeaten, and stoutly defended his act, including the 25th clause. The main concern in his mind was by this time compulsion: now that schools were being provided all over the country, the chief task was to fill them, and he announced that he would be ready to bring in a general compulsory measure in 1873, for the enforcement of which it might be necessary to make school boards universal.[2]

The strength of nonconformity in the Liberal party made Forster's position both in Parliament and in the country dependent partly on Conservative support. This, of course, he generally received. W. H. Smith was his chief Conservative ally, and kept in close touch with him. At the beginning of 1872, at Forster's instigation, Smith was planning to get up a movement, in conjunction with men of both parties, to back the Education Act against the attacks of the League, pleasantly conscious of the political advantage that it would produce. 'Backing up the Government against its own Dissenting supporters', he told Sandon, 'means I think a very early breach between them and the Govt.'[3] Smith's educational views differed somewhat from those of the majority of his party. He was not happy with the 25th clause, and behind the scenes was urging Forster to repeal it, together with the 17th clause, which allowed school boards to remit fees in their schools.[4] He thought that aid for the education of very poor children should be administered by the guardians and should count as relief, the object being to keep expenditure on this count to the

[1] On the 25th clause controversy, see Cruickshank, pp. 41–3.

[2] *3 Hansard*, ccix. 1429–30.

[3] Smith to Sandon, 8 Jan. 1872: Harrowby Papers, vol. xxxix, ff. 189–94. Smith stated that Thomas Hughes, who had been given notice by his dissenting supporters at Frome for backing the Education Act, had said that the issue would give the Conservatives 80 or 100 seats at the next election.

[4] Smith to Sandon, 24 Feb. 1872: *ibid.*, ff. 195–8. In public, however, Smith defended the 25th clause (*3 Hansard*, ccix. 1461–2; ccx. 1743).

minimum.[1] He favoured Forster's plans for general compulsion, and on the London School Board was himself active in applying it in the Metropolis.[2]

Most of his colleagues took a different line. They staunchly upheld the symbolic 25th clause, which became an issue at by-elections. And they maintained their resistance to general compulsion, especially if it meant school boards everywhere. No object was nearer to the party's heart than to exclude, so far as possible, boards, compulsion, and rating from the rural districts, where they threatened so much damage to the interests of squire, parson, and farmer. To escape the necessity for boards, some Conservatives felt it would even be worthwhile to accept a mild degree of compulsion through the application of the half-time system of the factory acts to agriculture: this trend of thought found expression in Read's Agricultural Children Bill. Hostility to boards, compulsion, and rating largely accounts for the Conservatives' dislike of the government's Scottish education measure of 1872, which made all three universal in Scotland and was feared as setting a precedent for England.[3]

In the end, the cabinet would not allow Forster to introduce a measure for general compulsion in 1873. He did, however, bring in a bill to amend the act of 1870. Its main proposals, following, to a large extent, the views of W. H. Smith, were to repeal the 25th clause and to provide that aid for the education of very poor children should be administered by the guardians, though it was not to count as poor relief. Since the parent retained the choice of school, the new provision still allowed rates to be applied in support of denominational teaching, and could thus be regarded as a victory for the denominationalists over the League. Nevertheless, Disraeli seems to have contemplated opposing the bill, and even using it as a pretext for voting with the militant nonconformists to overturn the government.

He was stopped by the discovery that a good many of his supporters were unwilling to show hostility to Forster. A report from Winn on 'the troublesome men of the Party' told him that Smith, Birley, Powell, and others thought opposition to the government measure

[1] A number of Conservatives agreed with him in this, for instance Corrance and Pell. *Ibid.*, ccix. 1442–3; Pell to Smith, 22 Jan. 1873 (Hambleden Papers, PS 3/13).

[2] By mid-1873, however, he had grown less sanguine about direct compulsion, and hoped more from the indirect method of making a certificate of school attendance a universal condition of employment. He also advocated a half-time system. *3 Hansard*, ccxvi. 1461; ccxvii. 796.

[3] The party resented also the bill's takeover of the parochial schools, which it regarded as belonging to the Established Church. In the Lords, Richmond was able to insert a formal recognition of religious teaching into the bill, and to secure a separate (though temporary) Scottish Education Board (*ibid.*, ccxii. 1014–20, 1022–3, 1032–7; ccxiii. 160–82, 301–6).

impolitic.[1] Gorst, too, warned his leader that any party manoeuvre would alienate an important section of Conservative supporters in the very areas from which, electorally, he hoped so much.

> With country gentlemen & farmers in the agricultural counties [he wrote] such a policy might be popular: they really dislike education and school boards altogether. But in the boroughs and populous counties, our party embraces zealous and active promoters of Education, and Forster's Bill is founded on the very principles for which they have as they think so successfully contended. They look upon it as a great triumph of Conservative principles that the Govt. have felt compelled to turn their backs on the Education League & bring in such a bill as the present; and they desire to give the measure an active support and claim it as the expression of their own views. I confess that the idea of defeating the Government and having an appeal to the country on this question fills me with dismay. We cannot carry the English majority we hope for without the active help of those, who on this question will be opposed to our policy.[2]

Disraeli gave way. 'He had evidently meant hostility to it,' Hardy noted after a council on the bill, 'but saw the danger of disunion in such a course.'[3]

Forster, in the event, dropped the repeal of the 25th clause from his bill, and it remained as a rallying cry for educational and political partisans. The government measure went through, though it ran into some trouble from the local taxation men, who were determined to express their feeling against growing educational expenditure and against the clause of the bill which threatened to increase it by making the education of the children of outdoor paupers a condition of their relief. The Liberal Torrens's attack from the local taxation standpoint was supported on the Conservative side by Lopes and his friends, and of the 72 votes which Torrens mustered, 56 were Conservative.[4]

The reprieve of the 25th clause was, of course, unwelcome to W. H. Smith, and he had to be dissuaded by his colleagues and by intimations of his leader's displeasure from himself moving to abolish

[1] Report sent to Disraeli by the chief whip, Taylor: Disraeli Papers, B/XX/T/165. It and Taylor's covering note (B/XX/T/166) are undated, but must be of mid-June 1873. Powell, according to the report, professed himself unable to vote against Forster because of the feeling in his constituency (W. Riding of Yorks., N. Division) in the latter's favour.

[2] Gorst to Disraeli, 21 June 1873: *ibid.*, B/XXI/G/243.

[3] Hardy's diary, 27 June 1873: Cranbrook Papers, T501/295.

[4] For the debate, see *3 Hansard*, ccxvii. 502–87. The whips, Taylor and Winn, voted with Torrens, and Disraeli was absent from the division. Not all the Conservative speakers took a parsimonious and restrictionist line. Adderley 'looked upon this expenditure in the light of a profitable investment'.

it, together with clause 17.[1] Disraeli felt that the 25th clause had too much political value to be tampered with: it was, he told Cairns,

> the shibboleth of our party, which will be one of our symbols in the impending County election, and at a dissolution might dispose of thirty or forty votes. Mr Smith decides on the abstract merits of the case, obtained in his experience of the London Board without the slightest reference to the general political situation.[2]

Disraeli was right to regard the education question as one of the Conservatives' major electoral assets. Its effect on their opponents was such that by late 1873 Gladstone feared that it would either split or fatally cripple his party.[3]

The record of 1872–3 shows how poorly the Conservative party responded to the call to patronise social reform which Disraeli had issued at Manchester and the Crystal Palace. It dragged its feet most conspicuously in the very areas on which its leader had laid special stress: an important section of it placed the interests of the rural ratepayer above the progress of sanitary reform, and in the field of labour regulation its aid to the cause of the merchant seaman hardly compensated for its backwardness in helping the miner and the agricultural labourer. Disraeli himself, apart from his intervention on the Public Health Bill, did nothing to advance social questions, and did not seriously attempt to translate his rhetorical concern for 'the elevation of the condition of the people' into practical policies. No concerted move was made to appeal to the working-class electorate on a social reform platform, or any other platform, and the party's channel of communication with the masses through the National Union was not exploited.[4]

It was not simply that the party had little taste for appealing to the working classes. More than ever, its mind was concentrated on the middle-class vote. By 1873 there were signs of an important movement towards Conservatism among the middle classes. This was part of a European phenomenon, the reaction of the propertied bourgeoisie

[1] Sandon to W. H. Smith, 'Sunday Aft.' [July 1873]: Harrowby Papers, vol. lxv, ff. 305–6.

[2] [Disraeli] to Cairns, 'Sunday' [July 1873] (typescript copy): Cairns Papers, vol. iv.

[3] Gladstone to Granville, 3 Sept. 1873, in *Political Correspondence of Mr. Gladstone and Lord Granville*, ii. 405.

[4] The Union continued to be confined to a limited organisational rôle: it was in 1873 that Raikes stressed that it was basically 'a handmaid to the party'. He said also that its purpose was to be a 'conductor' between its constituent associations and the party leadership, but it is doubtful how much was conducted. National Union annual conference report, 1873 (Publications of the National Union, no. XXI), pp. 10, 35. Cf. McKenzie, 2nd ed., pp. 158–9.

to the advent of the mass electorate and the challenge of organised labour and socialism. In England it was to a large extent the delayed effect of 1867. The second Reform Act had created a permanent threat that the working classes would use their new political power if not to despoil the well-to-do at least to give legislative expression to fraternalist or socialist ideas which demanded the organisation of society in the interests of all its members. To resist the remodelling of society for the benefit of the numerical majority was the central preoccupation of the propertied classes, and the growing militancy of labour in 1872–3 did much to help convince them that a stout resistance was necessary. This had very damaging implications for the Liberal party. By 1873 it had largely carried out the programme of reforms for which its middle-class supporters had voted in 1868: for a good many middle-class people, economically and socially satisfied, and sated with change, the question now was how far it could be relied upon to offer a firm front to the march of labour and the influence of advanced Radical and 'communistic' ideas. The vigour of its left-wing Radical element—symbolised in September 1873 by the appearance of Joseph Chamberlain's programme of 'Free Church, Free Land, Free Schools, and Free Labour'—and the growth within a section of it of the outlook which a disapproving Gladstone was later to dub 'construction—that is to say, taking into the hands of the state the business of the individual man',[1] put the answer seriously in doubt. As an agency for the stabilisation of the economic and social order, the Conservative party had greater appeal, and as the memory of the *volte-face* of 1867 faded, and it became clear that, whatever the youthful extravagances of its leader, the party was not going to take the lead in competitive bidding for the 'democracy', the satisfied and apprehensive elements of the middle classes moved over to it in increasing numbers.[2] The conjunction of the bourgeoisie with the old landed classes for the defence of property and constitutionalism which Peel had sought to foster was taking shape under the pressures resulting from Disraeli's coup of 1867, and foreshadowing the reconstruction of politics along the horizontal lines of class.[3]

[1] Gladstone to Acton, 11 Feb. 1885, in Morley, iii. 173.

[2] This very important process has scarcely been studied. There are some remarks on it in Sir I. Jennings, *Party Politics*, ii. 128–9, and Dunbabin, 'Parliamentary Elections', pp. 89–90. For the intellectuals, see J. Roach, 'Liberalism and the Victorian Intelligentsia', *Cambridge Historical Journal*, xiii (1957), 58–81; and on the movement of the right-wing Whigs towards Conservatism in 1873–4, W. H. Maehl, 'Gladstone, the Liberals, and the Election of 1874', *Bulletin of the Institute of Historical Research*, xxxvi (1963), 60, 66–7.

[3] There were, of course, other factors than the extension of the franchise and the advance of labour conducing to political division along class lines and so to the influx of the bourgeoisie into the Conservative party: among them

In this situation, the main concern of the Conservatives was to avoid anything which might check the swing towards them. This was not the time for challenging policies of social improvement; still less for any identification of the party with working-class interests and aspirations. After the 1872 speeches, Disraeli studiously refrained from taking any positive line which might alienate some part of his actual or potential support, and continued to avoid a premature defeat of the ministry, preferring to profit by its difficulties as long as possible.[1] When, in March 1873, Gladstone resigned after a defeat on the Irish University Bill, Disraeli declined to take office, believing with Northcote that time was needed 'to mature the fast-ripening Conservatism of the country, and to dispel the hallucinations which have attached a great mass of moderate men to the Liberal cause'.[2] He used the occasion, however, to suggest to the middle-class public that the topics on which much of their support for Liberalism had depended were played out, and that the great issue now was the defence of the country's institutions.

> We are now [he said] emerging from the fiscal period in which almost all the public men of this generation have been brought up. All the questions of Trade and Navigation, of the Incidence of Taxation and of Public Economy are settled.

More fundamental matters would demand attention in the future, the position of the monarchy, of the Church, and of landed property, and it was essential that there should be at this juncture 'a great Constitutional Party, distinguished for its intelligence as well as for its organisation'.[3] Even Disraeli's frank admission that the Conservatives had no policy (an opposition, he declared, 'is essentially a critical body; it is not a constructive one, and it cannot be') was well calculated to appeal to that section of middle-class opinion which, after five years of incessant legislation, wanted nothing better than a rest.

The growing Conservative concentration on the middle-class vote came out strongly in the budget debates of 1873. The Chancellor, Lowe, proposed to reduce indirect taxation (notably the sugar duties),

[1] See *Gathorne Hardy*, i. 310, 318; Viscount Cross, *A Political History*, p. 13.

[2] Northcote to Disraeli, 14 March 1873: Add. MS. 50016, ff. 144–7 (quoted in Southgate, p. 349). 'I believe', Northcote said, 'that the disintegration of Gladstone's party has begun and that nothing but precipitancy on our part can arrest it.'

[3] *3 Hansard*, ccxiv. 1944.

were the separation of classes caused by the increase of large-scale industrial units and by urban (and especially suburban) growth, and the rise of the white-collar and professional workers, providing 'at least a potential rank and file for a non-working-class party'. J. Cornford, 'The Transformation of Conservatism in the Late Nineteenth Century', *Victorian Studies*, vii (1963–4), 64–5.

thus benefiting the working classes, on whom it primarily fell. Conservatives, however, argued that it was direct taxation, both national and local, which should have first claim to remission, and vented their irritation at the swelling burden of the rates, especially for education, poor relief, and health, pointing out that this was not the grievance of the landed interest alone—there existed, George Hamilton reminded the government, a large local taxation movement in the great towns, supported mainly by poor middle-class householders.[1] It was the poorer section of the middle class which the Conservatives seemed to have most in mind. Northcote maintained that there was as much poverty and suffering among income tax payers as among the working classes; Liddell that the working man, whose wages had greatly increased in recent years, was better able to pay his small quota to the revenue than the fixed-income man who had lost by rising prices.[2] Cave insisted that the wage-earners were well enough off, and dwelt on the sorrows of 'the poor curate or the parish doctor', paying increased rates to provide working-class schoolchildren with 'more cubic feet of air than they used to have in his time at Harrow'.[3]

Disraeli, too, took the line that it was not so much the working classes that required fiscal relief as the middle classes of London and the great towns, classes 'that we have been accustomed to look up to as the very marrow of our population', but which were feeling the pressure of taxation and high prices, 'caused by that very prosperity which has made the rich more rich, and which has given to the working classes that welfare which is universally admitted to exist'.[4] He contended that the working men were fiscally lightly burdened.

> They are now [he said] in a position to secure not only the means of existence but the means of enjoyment... They believe they have realized—I am speaking of the working classes in the great scenes of our industry, Lancashire, Yorkshire, Cheshire, and so on—the dream of their youth, 'A fair day's wage for a fair day's work', and that they have at last secured that share of profits, which, in the partnership between labour and capital, labour ought to secure. Whether they are right or whether they are wrong is another point . . .

Their real interest, he added, was not in reductions of the sugar duty, but in questions like that of master and servant.[5]

It was Disraeli's concern, as a general election became imminent, to present an essentially negative and quietist front, adapted to appeal to those elements of the middle classes which were seeking a refuge

[1] For the main debates, see *ibid.*, ccxv. 1030–1104, 1300–91.
[2] *Ibid.*, ccxv. 1066, 1315.
[3] *Ibid.*, ccxv. 1306.
[4] *Ibid.*, ccxv. 1350.
[5] *Ibid.*, ccxv. 1366–7, 1368.

from Radicalism and 'democracy'. 'As to our general policy,' he told Northcote, in September 1873, 'it is to uphold the institutions of the country, and to arrest that course of feverish criticism and unnecessary change, too long in vogue.'[1] There was nothing here for the working man as such. The party could not show special zeal for the interests of a class whose force its new bourgeois adherents were relying on it to contain. The theme of social reform, so boldly proclaimed in 1872, was now muted, though not entirely abandoned.[2] Disraeli was at pains, at the end of 1873, less to promise the working classes material betterment than to remind them of the limits beyond which governmental efforts for their welfare could not go. At Glasgow in November, he impressed upon a deputation of factory operatives that no legislation could interfere with the rate of wages, which 'must be left to those inexorable rules of political economy to which we must all bow'; and he suggested to the Conservative working men of the city that the difficulties encountered by employers and employed might be due to 'some inexorable law of political economy which cannot be resisted'.[3] When the Conservatives did appeal specifically to the working man, they did so more than ever in terms of his common interest with other classes in the maintenance of the established order. He would not be helped, a National Union pamphlet warned him in 1873, by Radical agitation, which destroyed the confidence of the upper classes and caused the withdrawal of the capital on which his livelihood depended.[4]

Making suggestions on policy in anticipation of a dissolution, that tried exponent of social paternalism Manners said nothing of social reform: he recommended Disraeli to go in for the abolition of the income tax, a cry calculated to attract middle-class, not working-

[1] Disraeli to Northcote, 11 Sept. 1873, in M. & B., v. 259.

[2] In August 1873 some interest was taken in a project for educating working-class opinion on social reform put to Disraeli by Blanchard Jerrold, editor of *Lloyd's Weekly Newspaper*. This resulted in the publication in the *Morning Advertiser* (Aug.–Oct. 1873) of a series of articles, presumably by Jerrold, under the title 'Our Social Reform Expedition', their object being to study the social legislation of the Continent with a view to contributing to the social reform movement which the writer anticipated in England. See Jerrold to Disraeli, 8, 16, and 19 Aug. 1873, and Hart Dyke to Disraeli, 'Wednesday': Disraeli Papers, B/XXI/J/43, 44, 45, 43a.

[3] *The Times*, 21 and 24 Nov. 1873.

[4] *The Political Future of the Working Classes; or, Who are the Real Friends of the People?* by 'E.B.' (Publications of the National Union, no. VII, rev. ed., 1873), p. 3 (quoted in McKenzie, 2nd ed., p. 149). Of a piece with this stress on the identity of class interests was Disraeli's declaration against the segregation of working-class Conservatives in separate associations (speech to the Glasgow Conservative working men: *The Times*, 24 Nov. 1873), which hastened the absorption of the working men into the general party associations.

class, votes.[1] It was at the bourgeoisie that the party was aiming, and even here it would rely not on any positive programme of its own but on the antipathies which its opponents had aroused and the misgivings they evoked.

When Gladstone finally went to the country in January 1874, the odds were against him. At home the government had disturbed powerful vested interests and alienated many moderates, without satisfying some of its most ardent friends. Abroad, many felt that it had asserted itself too little. About its possible future courses, and the prospective influence upon it of the Liberal party's Radical wing, there was much unease.

With the tide running in their favour, the Conservatives did not need any positive policy. They had less to appeal to the electorate than to wait for the electorate to appeal to them. Disraeli's election address[2] was cautious and negative. He remarked that Conservatives had always favoured the reduction of local taxation and abolition of the income tax which Gladstone was now proclaiming; promised support for all measures calculated to improve the condition of the people, while contending that this end was not to be advanced by 'incessant and harassing legislation'; suggested that it would have been better had there been in the previous five years 'a little more energy in our foreign policy and a little less in our domestic legislation'; opposed the assimilation of the county to the borough franchise; and reminded the electors of the antipathy of some of Gladstone's followers to the monarchy, the House of Lords, the union with Ireland, the Established Church, and religious education.

All this was meant to play primarily upon the susceptibilities of the middle classes—upon their dislike of taxation, fear of Radicalism, aversion from continual change, and hankering after international prestige. It was the 'Palmerstonian' bourgeoisie that the Conservative campaign was designed to attract, and attract with something very much like Palmerston's formula of quiet at home and greatness overseas. But care was taken not to let Conservatism appear too stationary or obstructive. On the contrary, it was suggested, the Conservatives were now the real party of moderate progress, the representatives of true liberalism as opposed to doctrinaire Radicalism, who would push forward with the useful and necessary business which the 'harassing' and 'spectacular' legislation of Gladstone's ministry had caused to be neglected.[3]

[1] Manners to Disraeli, 2 Oct. 1873: Disraeli Papers, B/XX/M/169.

[2] Printed in *The Times*, 26 Jan. 1874.

[3] The pamphlet *An Appeal to the Moderate Liberals*, written by the successful Conservative candidate at Marylebone, Forsyth (for the attribution, see the

Its anxiety to nurture middle-class support prevented the Conservative party as a whole from making any special appeal to the working men, or giving prominence to the social questions in which they were most interested. Marked readiness to make concessions to the demands of organised labour, or to embark upon expensive developments of education and sanitary reform, was not likely to recommend it to the great class of investors, employers, and rate-payers. In any case, as Disraeli and others realised, the working-men voters were not a cohesive bloc, apart from the rest of the nation and conscious only of their particular class interests. They were, to a large extent, responsive to the same considerations and arguments as the classes above them, and the 'national party' could afford to appeal to them in the same terms as to the rest of the nation, confident that they, too, would be moved by the call of patriotism and defence of existing institutions, with an unspecific promise of cautious improvement thrown in. There was every prospect that the Conservatives could secure a significant working-class vote without going much out of their way to cultivate it. Such seemed to be the implication of the Stroud by-election at the beginning of January 1874, when a predominantly working-class and hitherto staunchly Liberal constituency was won by a Conservative candidate who in 1868 had not dared hold a public meeting. Reporting to Disraeli, Hicks Beach ascribed the victory principally to the change in the political sympathies of the working class (a change more readily expressed in votes now that the Ballot Act of 1872 had diminished the intimidatory power of the mainly Liberal millowners). The most popular Conservative cry had been religious education and the 25th clause, while the publicans 'did something, but not very much: as the principal brewer in the place was against us'. Most important, perhaps, had been the attitude of 'let's try the other side' among voters sated with five years of Liberalism.[1] These factors were to be widely operative at the general election.

Conservatives could not, however, wholly refrain from paying attention to the special interests of working men, especially in the great urban and industrial constituencies, and social questions did play a considerable rôle in the contest (as they had not done in 1868). Most prominent were labour problems. Working-class exasperation

[1] Hicks Beach to Disraeli, 7 Jan. 1874: Disraeli Papers, B/XXI/B/192. The Conservatives, however, lost Stroud at the general election.

---

copy in vol. i of the National Union pamphlets in the library of the Conservative Research Department), exemplifies this line. Forsyth admitted that 'the Conservative ranks include many whom you would, perhaps, rightly call bigots and reactionaries', but insisted that these people would not determine the party's policy. The *Globe* (5 Feb. 1874) actually spoke of 'a resolute party of progress held in chains, grossly maligned, and longing to be free'.

with the government's attitude since 1871 did much to diminish the Liberals' electoral strength, even if it showed itself only on a limited scale in increased support for the Conservatives.[1] The labour movement made a far stronger effort than in 1868 to press its demands, the chief of which were the repeal of the Criminal Law Amendment Act, the alteration of the law of conspiracy in its relation to the activities of trade unions, the amendment of the Master and Servant Act, a nine-hours bill, a merchant shipping bill on Plimsoll's lines, and a bill on workmen's compensation for accidents. On these issues many candidates were forced to commit themselves at the elections, the T.U.C. Parliamentary Committee supplying a set of test questions for the purpose.[3]

Few Conservatives had much real sympathy for the working men's claims. The *Quarterly* growled, in January 1874, that the unionists wanted 'nothing less than the repeal of the whole body of law by which a dangerous and encroaching despotism is at present held imperfectly in check', and defended the Criminal Law Amendment Act, the Master and Servant Act, and the law of conspiracy.[3] A letter from Montagu Corry to Sandon suggests that the party leadership broadly concurred in this attitude.[4] But Conservative candidates in the larger boroughs, especially in the industrial north, had frequently little option but to endorse the working men's objectives. Callender, newly-elected for Manchester, told Corry:

> The elections in Lancashire have largely hinged upon 2 questions—the 9 Hours bill & the demands of the Trades Unionists. On both these points—every candidate for a borough constituency has had to promise compliance . . .[5]

[1] See especially H. W. McCready, 'The British Election of 1874: Frederic Harrison and the Liberal-Labour Dilemma', *Canadian Journal of Economics and Political Science*, xx (1954), 166–75. Howell (pp. 338–9) attests the fact that the labour leaders were much less active on behalf of the Liberals in 1874 than they had been in 1868.

[2] McCready, 'British Labour's Lobby', p. 155; Howell, pp. 278–9, 332–3.

[3] *Quarterly Review*, cxxxvi (1874), 179–200. If the unions got what they wanted, feared the *Quarterly*, the next step would be 'a demand for legislation for the purpose of giving effect to Unionist projects of social reform'.

[4] 25 Jan. 1874: Harrowby Papers, vol. lii, ff. 220–1. Corry referred Sandon, who had evidently raised the question of the labour laws, to the *Quarterly* article, and his words seem to imply that the article's case for the maintenance of the greater part of the existing law coincided with Disraeli's views.

[5] Callender to Corry, 16 Feb. 1874, cited above, p. 173, n. 1. Cf. W. Morris (chairman of the management committee of the newly-formed Employers' Confederation) to Salisbury, 31 March 1874: Salisbury Papers, G.C., 'Political 4'. Professor Beesly thought that no single fact had more to do with the Liberal defeat in Lancashire at the election than Fawcett's 1873 speech against the nine-hours bill (S. and B. Webb, *History of Trade Unionism*, 2nd ed., p. 312, n. 1).

'I gather', Frederic Harrison wrote to John Morley, 'that throughout Yorkshire and Lancashire, the Conservative candidates represent the working men's causes, the Factory Acts, Truck Acts and even the Crim. Law Amet. abolition.'[1]

Besides labour questions, two other social issues, education and licensing, played a conspicuous part in the election, and influenced both middle- and working-class votes. The education problem deprived the Liberals of the wholehearted aid of those who were normally their warmest supporters, the nonconformists, and Gladstone and Bright recognised how much it contributed to their defeat.[2] The great point at issue was the famous 25th clause. Three hundred Liberal candidates stood pledged to its repeal,[3] while the Conservatives defended it with vehemence. Disraeli declared:

> upon this matter there can be no compromise offered . . . The 25th clause may be called the symbol of the question; those that are in favour of the 25th clause are in favour of religious education, and those that are against it are in favour of secular education.[4]

Their championship of religious education and the 25th clause may have helped the Conservatives with some working men,[5] and it certainly went far to win them Catholic support.[6] It was also one factor in accounting for the considerable assistance they seem to have received from the Anglican clergy, anxious to repulse in every sphere the nonconformist offensive which had pressed the Church so hard since 1868.

The exact part played by the licensing question at the polls is not easy to assess. Gladstone's picture of the Liberals 'borne down in a torrent of gin and beer' was certainly a rhetorical exaggeration.[7] All the same, the electoral rôle of drink was not negligible. After the bill of 1871 and the act of 1872 the government could expect little sympathy from the licensed trade. It is true that the trade did not declare for the Conservatives as such in 1874: its members were urged to vote for their friends and against their enemies regardless of party,

[1] 10 Feb. 1874; quoted in McCready, 'British Election of 1874', p. 175.

[2] See Morley, ii. 495; *Letters of Queen Victoria*, 2nd Series, ii. 318.

[3] Morley, ii. 311.

[4] Speech at Buckingham, in *The Times*, 11 Feb. 1874.

[5] See J. Morley to F. Harrison, 11 Feb. 1874, in F. W. Hirst, *Early Life and Letters of John Morley*, i. 297.

[6] Gladstone and Bright thought this a not inconsiderable factor in their success (Morley, ii. 495), and Lord Denbigh told Hardy that the Conservative victory had been largely helped by Catholic votes, especially in the London boroughs—though as a Catholic he had an axe to grind (Denbigh to Hardy, 'Ash Wednesday', 1874: Cranbrook Papers, T501/63).

[7] Largely accepted by Ensor (pp. 20–2), Gladstone's view has received some cogent criticism from Hanham (pp. 222–5).

and a number of Liberals favourable to the drink interest received trade support. Nor did the Conservative party officially align itself in any way with the trade cause. But on the whole, the Conservative candidates were usually more friendly than the Liberal to the trade's demands—even Callender, a Vice-President of the United Kingdom Alliance, did his best to conciliate his local licensed victuallers, and secured their endorsement[1]—and the bulk of the trade influence came down on the Conservative side.[2] The major trade organ, the *Morning Advertiser*, was openly Conservative[3] (though the *Licensed Victuallers' Guardian* maintained a more neutral tone), and thousands of publicans worked in the Conservative interest. *The Times* (admittedly a somewhat biased witness) wrote:[4]

> Beer, one of the greatest powers in the country, has pronounced unequivocally in their [the Conservatives'] favour. The public-house windows in London everywhere displayed the placards of the Conservative candidates.

How much the support of the licensed trade contributed to the Conservative victory is a matter of controversy. Its importance was exaggerated after the event, both by Liberals, anxious to ascribe their opponents' success to a disreputable cause, and by the trade, hoping to overawe politicians; but, bearing in mind the smallness of many of the Conservative majorities, it seems possible that without it the party would have been deprived of several valuable seats.

The result of the election was a decisive victory for the Conservatives: they made a net gain of some sixty seats, and came back 351 strong, against 301 Liberals and Home Rulers.[5] It was obvious from the returns that the party had succeeded in broadening the basis of its support, both among the middle classes and among the working men.

In the larger boroughs, where the working-class vote was most heavily concentrated, and Gorst's efforts had in many cases much improved Conservative organisation, there were significant advances.

[1] He was at once taken to task by the Alliance's secretary. *Manchester Guardian*, 4 and 5 Feb. 1874.

[2] The *Licensed Victuallers' Guardian* wrote (28 Feb. 1874): 'The Trade simply returned Conservatives because in the majority of cases the views expressed by the candidates of that party were more favourable to the Licensed Victualling interests than were those of the Liberal nominations.' Both the *Guardian* (14 Feb. 1874) and the *Morning Advertiser* (12 Feb. 1874) thought that in 1868 the trade, if anything, had been Liberal.

[3] See especially its leaders of 26 Jan. 1874, and its call to the trade on 2 Feb. to oppose the ministry.

[4] 6 Feb. 1874.

[5] This is the estimate of *The Times*, 19 Feb. 1874.

In towns of over 50,000 inhabitants, the Conservatives secured 44 of the 114 seats, compared with 25 in 1868.[1] Perhaps their most striking success was in the populous London boroughs, where, besides taking the second Westminster seat, they made gains in the hitherto Radical strongholds of Chelsea, Marylebone, and Tower Hamlets.[2] Elsewhere, there were Conservative gains in Glasgow, Leeds, Manchester, Nottingham (2), Stoke, and Newcastle. The industrial Yorkshire and Lancashire boroughs increased their Conservative leanings appreciably: in addition to the gains in Leeds and Manchester, there were others in Oldham, Stalybridge, Wakefield, Warrington, and Wigan (though there were also losses in Blackburn and Bolton). Lancashire as a whole was more of a Conservative bastion than ever, now returning 26 Conservatives among its 33 members, compared with 21 in 1868.

The borough results obliged bourgeois Liberals and Radicals to admit that their grip on the working-class vote had slipped. 'There *is* a Conservative working man, both a sprinkling of the skilled, and the mass of the unskilled and rough', wrote Frederic Harrison.[3] But the extent and significance of the working-class movement away from the Liberals should not be exaggerated. Harrison thought it probably accounted for only 15 or 20 seats, and it would seem that the swing to the Conservatives in the large English boroughs may have been less than the swing to them generally.[4] The increased Conservative share of the working-class vote, moreover, did not represent wholly an increase in Conservative convictions: some of it represented temporary frustration with Liberalism, some of it reflected the new-found superiority of Conservative organisation, and some of it was due to the greater freedom of voting furnished by the ballot and by the apathy of Liberal employers, disgruntled with their party, as to the way their hands went.[5]

Perhaps more important than its increased working-class vote was the strong support the Conservative party won from the middle

[1] Hanham, p. 92, n. 2.

[2] Altogether, they won 11 out of 25 seats in London, compared with 4 in 1868. P. Thompson, 'Liberals, Radicals and Labour in London 1880–1900', *Past and Present*, no. 27 (1964), 74, n. 2 (which refers in error to the election of '1875').

[3] Harrison to Morley, 10 Feb. 1874, quoted in McCready, 'British Election of 1874', p. 175. Harrison spoke of 'the alienation of the workmen from the middle classes, a real and permanent alienation'.

[4] See the figures given by Hanham (p. 193) for a sample of 52 constituencies.

[5] The ballot probably helped the Conservatives appreciably in some places, where Liberal employers had hitherto exercised an intimidatory influence on the voting of their men (cf. Gorst, p. 120). Hanham (pp. 74, 76) regards the apathy of Liberal employers in 1874 as a considerable factor in the elections in medium-sized boroughs.

classes. The defensive reaction against the challenge of Radicalism and labour had a substantial effect on the polls.

> As far as I can make out [Lord Halifax told Gladstone after the contest] people are frightened—the masters were afraid of their workmen, manufacturers afraid of strikes, churchmen afraid of the nonconformists, many afraid of what is going on in France and Spain—and in very unreasoning fear have all taken refuge in conservatism.[1]

This movement had much to do with the Conservative successes in the larger boroughs, and showed itself also in the smaller boroughs and counties.[2] It was strikingly manifested in and around London: the Conservatives gained three seats in the City, and did remarkably well in the suburbs, taking all the county constituencies adjoining London, 'where the suburban villas poured forth their tide of voters early in the morning, before the city business began'.[3] Elsewhere, gains in places of the type of Cambridge, Cheltenham, Lewes, and Salisbury revealed the trend. The growth of the party's middle-class vote was accompanied by an increased representation of the industrial, commercial, and professional bourgeoisie on its Commons benches. Compared with 1868, Conservative members included proportionately fewer landholders and more colliery owners, merchants, and brewers and distillers, and had proportionately more financial and manufacturing interests.[4] Of course, the Liberals still had the great bulk of the industrial and commercial interests represented in Parliament, but the disparity in this respect between the two parties was a good deal smaller than in 1868.

Contemporaries noted that the influx of the bourgeoisie was

[1] Quoted in Morley, ii. 494 (cf. Edward Baines's letter of 13 March 1874, explaining his defeat at Leeds, quoted in Vincent, pp. 124–6). This mood of apprehension made it unnecessary for Conservative candidates in some places to do more than champion resistance to fundamental change. 'He had gained the confidence of his constituency in 1874', Lord Randolph Churchill later declared, 'on the cry of "Defence of our old institutions"—by which the masses enfranchised in 1867 meant beer and the Bible, but others more profound understood the Church, the House of Lords, the rights of property, the sanctity of the wills of pious founders, the law of entail, &c...' (*3 Hansard*, ccxxxviii. 901).

[2] It was probably a good deal helped by the ballot, which encouraged voting by people who in the past had been unwilling to face the turbulence of the polls. H. E. Gorst (pp. 129–30) thinks, also, that their discountenancing of bribery brought the Conservatives a large accession of support from respectable middle-class people hitherto aloof from elections.

[3] *Quarterly Review*, cxxxvi (1874), 567.

[4] See Thomas, pp. 15, 16. The percentage of landholders fell from 80% in 1868 to 73% in 1874. Colliery owners increased from one to seven, brewers and distillers from seven to fourteen.

beginning to change the face of Conservatism. *The Times* wrote, unsympathetically:[1]

> The fact is that Toryism itself is vulgarized in these days. Pushing middle-class *parvenus* cannot be kept out of it. They are its loudest, its most uncompromising, its most pretentious, its most contemptuous partisans.

The *Hour*, on the other hand, discussing 'the revolt from Liberalism of the wealth, the intelligence, and the respectability of the country', thought the Conservatives would gain much from the infusion of the moderate Liberal element, which would be

> a guarantee that the Conservatism of the future shall be a policy active, energising, progressive, and in the best sense of the word Liberal. The Conservative leaders will henceforth owe enlarged duties to an extended body of followers.[2]

There was some truth in this comment, but in one sphere, at least, the 'progressive' side of Conservatism was not likely to be enhanced. The more the party drew strength from the defensively-minded bourgeoisie, the less it would find it easy (or necessary) to sympathise with the working-class demands against which many of its new supporters were reacting. E. S. Beesly saw this, and complained in the *Bee-Hive*[3] that from the working-class point of view the Conservatives were getting worse rather than better, for their natural hostility to the interests of the labouring class had been intensified by the influx into the party of manufacturers and other capitalists, 'so that Toryism is now rather plutocratic than aristocratic'.[4]

It would be wrong, however, to overestimate the change wrought in the composition and character of the Conservative party by the increased support it received from middle and working classes in 1874. True, it had at last gained the foothold in the larger boroughs the lack of which had crippled it for a generation, and had come closer to an understanding with the world of urban industry and commerce. But it remained very largely the party of the shires and country towns. The towns of over 50,000 inhabitants, which had provided 9.1% of Conservative seats in 1868, still provided only

[1] 4 Feb. 1874.

[2] *Hour*, 9 Feb. 1874.

[3] 28 Feb. 1874.

[4] The more plutocratic aspect of the Conservative party was interestingly (though exaggeratedly) noticed in August 1875 by the New York *Herald*, which referred to the shipowning Conservative member for Plymouth, Bates, as 'a conservative of the new type—a wealthy, one-ideaed merchant, who feels that he has a stake in the country, and that he must protect his interests. The House of Commons is just now swamped with such as these . . . [Disraeli] cannot afford to irritate the plutocrats, shippers, merchants and others who are the backbone of the conservative party' (quoted in R. J. Hinton, *English Radical Leaders*, p. 202).

12.5% in 1874, while the English and Welsh counties and English boroughs of under 20,000 inhabitants provided 60%, and the Scottish and Irish counties another 10%.[1]

Nor was the Conservative advance based on solid and lasting foundations. It was really not so much a Conservative advance as a Liberal recession. In 1880, after the reaction, a Conservative supporter summed up thus:

> In fact the British constituencies were liberal even in 1874—the conservatives won then through the abstentions of many; the conversion of a few & the disgust of all moderate persons; including publicans.[2]

Gorst knew perfectly well the precariousness of the Conservative position, and as early as December 1874 was afraid lest the reaction in the English boroughs, 'which brought us into power', should prove a mere temporary revulsion against the late government, and lest the electors should revert to their 'normal allegiance' to the Liberals.[3] But on the morrow of the polls, such shadows were in the background. The Conservative party had achieved a majority for the first time since 1841, and was at last to have office with power.

It was a cabinet of familiar faces which Disraeli formed in February 1874. Eleven of its twelve members had been in the cabinet of 1866–8, six of them in the same posts. Even the seceders of 1867, Salisbury and Carnarvon, returned to the fold, as right-wing policemen, ready to restrain Disraeli from further leaps in the dark.

The sole newcomer was Richard Assheton Cross, member for South-West Lancashire, who became Home Secretary without having previously held a ministerial post. Cross was the only cabinet representative of what might be called the new Liberal-Conservatism of the industrial, commercial, and professional middle class, which had had so much to do with the ministry's accession to office. A successful barrister and provincial banker, with great experience and reputation in local government, whose family fortunes were based on the tannery business and the law, he had defeated Gladstone in South-West Lancashire in 1868, and, with his friends Sandon and Smith, had been marked as a rising man in the Parliament of 1868–74.[4] It was

[1] Percentages based on the figures given in Hanham, pp. 39, n. 2, 92, n. 2; *Pall Mall Gazette*, 21 Feb. 1874. Some county constituencies, of course, were of a largely industrial character.

[2] Political notes of 16 April 1880, apparently by one of Cranbrook's (i.e. Hardy's) sons: Cranbrook Papers, T501/275. Cf. Gorst, p. 152; Lord Eustace Cecil to Salisbury, 19 April [1880] (Salisbury Papers, S.C.).

[3] Gorst to Disraeli, 2 Dec. 1874: Disraeli Papers, B/XXI/D/463a (printed in Hanham, pp. 389–90).

[4] For Cross's background and early career, see the opening chapters of F. J.

thought in 1874 that he might get the Local Government Board, and political circles were surprised at his rise to the Home Office, to which Hardy had been expected to return. It is not known precisely why Disraeli did not put Hardy at the Home Office, but he had realised in late 1873 that labour questions would become pressing,[1] and it seems likely that he was influenced by the consideration that Hardy was too unsympathetic towards organised labour to have much chance of settling them satisfactorily. His first alternative was Hicks Beach, but finally the job went to Cross, whom he had originally destined for the Board of Trade.[2]

Cross's sudden elevation was apparently less a matter of deliberate choice than the semi-fortuitous outcome of the reshufflings inevitable when a cabinet is being constructed. But it served as a useful gesture towards the business and professional classes from which he sprang, and towards loyalist Lancashire, which in Cross and his school and college friend Derby now had two cabinet members. What effect it would have on the vital matter of the government's handling of labour questions remained to be seen. Cross was thoroughly acquainted with the problems of urban and industrial Britain, had expressed a good deal of concern, in election campaigns, for the improvement of the condition of the masses, and had agreed with Sandon's suggestion of taking up social reform in 1871; but his pronouncements on mines regulation and the labour laws in Parliament in 1871–2 had been in favour of the employers' rather than the workers' interests.[3] His 1874 election address said nothing about social problems, and it was hard to predict what course he would adopt in the office which gave him so much contact with them.

The only other department dealing with social questions represented in the new cabinet was the Council Office, where the agricultural Richmond, as Lord President, supervised education—without enthusiasm, for he had badly wanted the War Office.[4] Richmond was one of the four cabinet ministers who had had previous departmental experience of social questions, the others being Northcote, Hardy, and Manners. Pakington was no longer in the cabinet or in Parliament, having been beaten at Droitwich, to Disraeli's evident relief.[5]

[1] Above, p. 172.

[2] See the draft cabinet list in Disraeli's hand, 17 Feb. 1874 (Disraeli Papers, B/XII/A/1), and *Gathorne Hardy*, i. 335.

[3] For the latter, see, e.g. *3 Hansard*, ccxii. 29–30, 663–4.

[4] *Gathorne Hardy*, i. 335.

[5] Disraeli told the Queen that Providence had disposed of him: *Letters of Queen Victoria*, 2nd series, ii. 321. He shortly entered the Lords as Baron Hampton.

Dwyer, 'The Rise of Richard Assheton Cross and His Work at the Home Office, 1868–1880' (Oxford Univ. B.Litt. thesis 1954).

As in 1866–8, the Conservative cabinet reflected to some degree the party's relatively tenuous association with that urban and industrial Britain where the great matrices of social problems lay. Only Cross and Derby had strong current links with the manufacturing areas. Of the six seats represented by cabinet ministers, not one was a borough, and only Cross's constituency of South-West Lancashire had a largely industrial character.[1] The twelve seats which members of the cabinet had formerly held included one county, eight small or middling boroughs, and but three centres of population and industry, Belfast, Dudley, and Preston, once represented respectively by Cairns, Northcote, and Cross. Northern constituencies had seen especially little of the new cabinet: of the total of seventeen English seats which its members were holding or had held, only two, Preston and South-West Lancashire, lay farther north than Newark, and both these, of course, were accounted for by Cross.

The omission of the President of the Local Government Board from the cabinet (where he had sat under Gladstone) suggested that the emphasis Disraeli had laid in 1872 on the importance of public health had been less than heartfelt. So did the bestowal of the presidency on the Hampshire country gentleman George Sclater-Booth, a second-rank figure, who had held junior office at the Poor Law Board and the Treasury in 1867–8[2]. Another important department dealing with social questions which was left out of the cabinet was the Board of Trade. Here Disraeli made his worst appointment. The presidency, intended first for Cross and then for Sclater–Booth,[3] finally descended upon Adderley, whose previous ministerial performances had been inept, and who knew nothing of the Board's business.[4] The vital post of Vice-President of the Committee of Council on Education was more happily disposed of: it was at first meant for W. H. Smith,[5] but in the end it went to Sandon, while Smith became Secretary to the Treasury. The appointment of Sandon and Smith, like that of their close associate, Cross, was in part a gesture towards the new Liberal-Conservatism of the great centres of industry, commerce, and population.

The disposition of the junior appointments concerned with social problems was unfortunately affected by Disraeli's policy of using 'the

[1] The other five seats were Bucks., N. Devon, N. Leics., N. Northants., and Oxford University.

[2] At one point Hicks Beach was considered for the post. See the draft cabinet list of 17 Feb. 1874, cited above, p. 195, n. 2.

[3] *Ibid.*

[4] Childe-Pemberton (p. 216) says that he told Disraeli so, and received the answer: 'You know as much about it as Ward Hunt [the new First Lord] does about the Navy.'

[5] *Letters of Queen Victoria*, 2nd series, ii. 322.

minor and working places' to muzzle the men who might give trouble and form 'a Tory cave'.[1] It was through this that Selwin-Ibbetson became Under-Secretary at the Home Office (though his specialist knowledge of licensing questions made the choice appropriate), that Read, as a sop to the rural ratepayer, got the Parliamentary Secretaryship to the Local Government Board,[2] and that the Secretaryship to the Board of Trade was given to George Cavendish Bentinck, whose parliamentary speciality was turning up late at night, flushed in face, to obstruct business.[3]

Minor infelicities apart, however, it was a strong and capable government. It needed to be, as it faced the task of demonstrating that a party borne to power on a negative tide could consolidate its position by positive achievement.

[1] Disraeli to Lady Bradford, 27 Feb. 1874, in M. & B., v. 295–6.

[2] He made sure, before accepting, that his chief would not be Adderley, with his 'rather wild notions on sanatory [*sic*] matters' (Read to Disraeli, 24 Feb. 1874: Disraeli Papers, B/XII/A/58a).

[3] Sir H. W. Lucy, *Men and Manner in Parliament*, new ed. (1919), pp. 88–90.

V
THE CONDITION OF THE PEOPLE, 1874-6

MOST observers agreed that the verdict of the polls was a negative one. The election had been decided, the *Standard* held,[1] on the general issue of the defence of the constitution and the social order; and what the people wanted was what Palmerston had given them—quiet. The government had been returned on a platform of immobility, 'pledged only to silence and consideration', as Salt put it in the Commons,[2] and what was expected of it was rather the sober Conservatism of tradition than the more dashing and bizarre confections of its commander-in-chief.

It was ironic that Disraeli, the most imaginative and venturesome of politicians, should attain power at last through a reaction towards respectability and calm. But the irony was only on the surface, for the Disraeli of 1874 was no longer the Disraeli of the second Reform Act; still less the Disraeli of Young England. Nearly seventy years old, rarely free from illness, deprived by his wife's death in 1872 of the main support of his career, he was, as Lady Derby assured the nervous Carnarvon,[3] a changed man, cautious and averse from innovation. No more than his colleagues did he mistake the terms on which the electorate had summoned him to power. The tranquillity they demanded he was ready to provide.[4] He had little inclination to depart from the solid Conservatism whose observance Salisbury and Carnarvon had entered his cabinet to ensure, and which those staunch companions of the grouse moors Cairns, Richmond, and Hardy embodied to perfection. He would do nothing to endanger the security of his own position and the unity of his follow-

[1] 9 Feb. 1874; cf. 17 Feb. [2] *3 Hansard*, ccxix. 219. [3] Hardinge, ii. 63.

[4] His response in October 1874 to Cross's proposal for a reform of London government is symptomatic. 'We came in', he reminded his Home Secretary, 'on the principle of not harassing the country' (Disraeli to Cross, 22 Oct. 1874: Brit. Mus., Add. MS. 51265 (Cross Papers), unfoliated).

ing: his only fixed political principle in these years, Salisbury judged, was 'that the party must on no account be broken up'.[1]

In these circumstances, it mattered little that the Conservative victory could plausibly be represented as the vindication of the popular and progressive principles which Disraeli had proclaimed in 1867 and in 1872. A sweeping renovation of Conservatism on popular and progressive lines was beyond either the will or the power of the prime minister to attempt. Nor, indeed, had he ever had any very precise idea of what form such a renovation might take. For years he had thought in generalities and talked in slogans—'the national party', 'the elevation of the condition of the people', 'sanitas sanitatum'—leaving their translation into action to other hands and other times. The great Conservative champion of social reform and the reconciliation of classes came into office in 1874 without a single concrete proposal in his head.

> When the Cabinet came to discuss the Queen's Speech [says Cross],[2] I was, I confess, disappointed at the want of originality shown by the Prime Minister. From all his speeches, I had quite expected that his mind was full of legislative schemes, but such did not prove to be the case; on the contrary, he had to entirely rely on the various suggestions of his colleagues, and as they themselves had only just come into office, and that suddenly, there was some difficulty in framing the Queen's Speech.

Not only was Disraeli without a definite policy in 1874, he was also virtually incapable of constructing one. To convert general ideas into the detail of parliamentary bills was an exercise alien to his nature and largely foreign to his experience. The quarter of a century spent either leading the opposition or as a minister without a majority had made him a master of critical incision and tactical dexterity, but it had given him only a meagre training in the conduct of business and the conception and execution of legislation. Detail—so vital to the practical expression of policy—was beyond his grasp.

> Disraeli's mind [Cross tells us][3] was either above or below (whichever way you like to put it) mere questions of detail. When the House was in Committee he was, comparatively speaking, nowhere.

Carnarvon, in late 1874, put it even more strongly: 'He detests details . . . He is in fact unable to deal with details. He does no work. . . . M. Corry is in fact Prime Minister.'[4]

[1] A. J. Balfour, *Chapters of Autobiography*, ed. Mrs Edgar Dugdale, p. 113.

[2] *A Political History*, p. 25.

[3] *Ibid.*, p. 44.

[4] Quoted in Hardinge, ii. 78. Someone else who noted Disraeli's lack of capacity for details and the conduct of business was Bagehot: see the relevant passages (of 1874 and 1876) in *The Works and Life of Walter Bagehot*, ed. Mrs

Disraeli's rôle was to dream the dreams, not to implement them. He had conceived the vision of a national Toryism, rooted in the affections of the people and ministering to their needs, and he had proclaimed it with signal consistency for most of his political life; but in what practical works it should now issue he had only the vaguest of notions. It was thus left to his subordinates to produce measures which should demonstrate the worth of his past professions. The content of the government's domestic programme depended almost entirely on their work. Disraeli, certainly, exercised the important function of general supervision, and the weight of his approval could be vital to the success of projects of reform.[1] But he made no attempt to plan policy on either a short- or a long-term basis, and there was, as Lord Randolph Churchill later said,[2] 'no master-mind pervading and controlling every branch of the administration'. Each session's programme of legislation was drawn up *ad hoc*, by the simple process of writing round to ministers for whatever proposals they had in hand and collating the replies to form the Queen's Speech.[3] The result was not, and could not be, the progressive unfolding of a coherent policy; rather was it the haphazard production of piecemeal reforms, whose timing and details were dictated by the pressures and circumstances of the hour.

In short, the government of 1874–80 did not possess and never attempted to develop a domestic 'policy'. Disraelian Conservatism in office was found to mean much the same as other Conservatism: empiricism tempered by prejudice. Those who, like Cross, had expected their leader to unlock from the recesses of his mind a Conservative programme were forced to realise that there was no programme there. What the ministry would do in the field of social improvement would depend almost entirely on what the ministers most concerned found readiest to hand.

The government was certainly willing to undertake moderate social reforms, even if, on taking office, it had no clear idea what they might comprise. Some colour had to be given to the prime minister's past pronouncements, and some attempt had to be made to recompense the Conservative working man for his vote, and to show that Tory

[1] E.g. apparently, Cross's labour legislation of 1875 (see below, p. 215).

[2] *Fortnightly Review*, xxxiii, new series (1883), 615.

[3] See, e.g. Disraeli to Cross, 19 Jan. 1875; Northcote to Cross, 10 Jan. 1879: Add. MS. 51265 (unfoliated).

Russell Barrington, vii. 35–6, 83–4, 85–6. There is much truth in A. J. P. Taylor's comment on Disraeli (*Englishmen and Others*, p. 67): 'Power was too practical an affair to interest him. He relished the trappings of power, not the reality—the drama of great debates, the high-sounding titles, his name echoing through history.'

criticisms of Liberal neglect had been more than mere debating points. The party which for years had posed as the real friend of the working classes could hardly ignore their needs after they had helped to place it in power. Moreover, for a government which had been elected primarily to give the country a rest from 'harassing' legislation and the agitation of major political questions, and which found itself in a period of relative international calm, social problems were one of the few spheres open to its energies. Being largely non-partisan, if not uncontroversial, they might be tackled without serious upheaval, and with, Conservatives naturally hoped, substantial electoral advantage. Some of them, in any case, could hardly be put aside. Because they had played a rôle in the election and been the subject of candidates' pledges; because their internal development had reached a point at which legislative action was unavoidable; because they aroused the feeling of powerful interests and the concern of public opinion; because inquiry and discussion had rendered them ripe for treatment, a variety of social questions forced themselves upon the government's attention.

The task of dealing with them fell primarily on the shoulders of four ministers: Cross at the Home Office; Sclater-Booth at the Local Government Board; Sandon at the Education Department; and Adderley at the Board of Trade. It was they who bore the responsibility for the measures which are commonly regarded as the fruits of Disraeli's policy. Of the four, only Adderley proved a failure. The others were all competent men of business and successful in the conduct of their departments. Cross, indeed, the only one of the group with a cabinet seat, was something more. Though he fully shared his colleagues' lack of boldness and originality, he carried the virtues of application and common sense almost to the level of greatness, and made himself into one of the best of British Home Secretaries. A thorough Conservative, Cross was nonetheless a Conservative of a new stamp. He brought to government, as few had done before him, the passion for exactitude and efficiency of the professional and commercial bourgeoisie, and unlike the customary type of Conservative minister, he believed in improving activity as a positive good. Cross wanted to do much and wanted to do it well; he was the only really zealous reformer in the government, and perhaps the first cabinet minister in British history to establish a reputation on the basis of social reform. Upon him more than upon any other Disraeli relied for the translation of past words into present measures. Cross's position and function within the ministry were curiously symbolic of the place which social reform occupied in the Conservative cosmos. He scarcely moved in the same world as the great figures of the party, and his relations with them, and especially with

Disraeli, whose approval for his actions he constantly sought,[1] were deferential. He never attained to the front rank of the cabinet. He was simply the workhorse of the administration, the man whose job it was to show that the Conservative party cared for the people, while his colleagues got on with what were to most of them more important subjects.

No one can deny that the activity of Cross and his fellow ministers produced remarkable results: the largest crop of social legislation yielded by any British administration before that of 1906 was the outcome of their work. Most of it was packed into the first three years, 1874–6. In that period the Conservatives passed eleven major acts bearing on the social problems with which this study is concerned. In 1874 they dealt with licensing and factory hours; in 1875 with the labour laws, artisans' dwellings, public health, friendly societies, and adulteration; in 1876 with education, merchant shipping, and the pollution of rivers. It was a considerable performance, even when we admit that it was of rather mixed quality. But of mixed quality it was: if only the Licensing Act was a mistake, only the settlement of the labour laws was a triumph, and the remaining measures were cautious, limited, and even weak. It is not surprising. The character of the government's legislation was determined by many factors—the nature of the problems, the trend of public opinion, and the expertise of the civil service among them—but not least by the general feeling of the Conservative party, and the general feeling of the Conservative party, while it did not counsel inaction, by no means encouraged boldness in the sphere of social reform.

Few Conservatives would have denied that measures to improve the condition of the people were desirable. A section of the party was even eager for social reform. In the populous urban constituencies especially, it was impossible for Conservatives to ignore the needs of the working population. When, in 1874, the Conservative Association of Radical Finsbury (whose chairman at the time was that enthusiastic reformer Charley) began to publish its own penny monthly paper, it significantly devoted much of its attention to prospective social legislation.[2] And in more important circles the idea was sometimes expressed that social reform was the great necessity of the hour. Disraeli found this a useful argument when evading Trevelyan's county franchise proposals: in May 1874 he adduced as one reason for not embarking on 'organic change' the fact that 'the disposition of the country is favourable, beyond any

1 See his letters in Disraeli Papers, B/XX/Cr.

2 See the *Finsbury Conservative*, Oct. 1874–June 1875.

preceding time that I can recall, to a successful consideration of the social wants of the great body of the people'.[1] Similarly, some notes in Corry's hand of July 1875, directed against Dilke's proposals of electoral reform, include the following:

> From past experience, any one proposing it must contemplate a far longer Parliamentary paralysis, so far as mere social legislation is concerned, than has ever occurred. Social legislation, and not organic change in the Constitution, is the need of the day, and the question whether Parliament has time and energy to meet that need becomes daily more pressing.[2]

But the bulk of the party thought of social reform very much in the spirit of Salt, who remarked, at the end of the session of 1875, that Parliament was now going through a course of 'suet-pudding legislation; it was flat, insipid, dull, but it was very wise and very wholesome . . .'[3] Social measures were boring, yet righteous; and were accepted as an essential insurance against the dangerous fermentation of working-class discontents. There was little enthusiasm for them, and a strong concern to see that they were not too extensive in scope.

Conservative reservations about the extension of governmental interference in economic and social life were, if anything, increasing rather than diminishing. The delayed impact of 1867 was making itself felt, as working-class political consciousness and influence grew. State intervention was one thing when directed by the upper and middle classes in conformity with their interests or with their interpretation of the general interest; it was another when the prospect seemed to loom that it would be carried out more and more at the behest of the working classes, and that under pressure from the mass electorate its principles would be given a development fatal to the security of property and the stability of the social order. Moreover, the attitude of the party could not fail to be affected by the influx of the apprehensive and defensive sections of the bourgeoisie, anxious to reassert against the advance of fraternalist and collectivist concepts of society their individualistic tenets of freedom and free enterprise. The tendency of this movement was naturally to reinforce those elements in the party whose existence had helped to encourage it. It reinforced the rigidly anti-democratic Toryism of Salisbury, the Conservatism of Coblence, still embattled against the French Revolution. But much more strongly and directly, it reinforced the Liberal-Conservatism of men like Derby, Northcote, Cross, and W. H. Smith, men of Peelite or Palmerstonian stamp, who had always

[1] *3 Hansard*, ccxix. 259.
[2] Disraeli Papers, B/XII/B/1b.
[3] *3 Hansard*, ccxxv. 1064.

accepted the basic principles of the individualist creed, and were scarcely distinguishable on many issues from moderate Liberals. It was in their image that the party came increasingly to be moulded. The paternalist strain of Toryism, with its stress on the obligation of government to secure the welfare of the people by positive action, faded still further as the Conservative party quickened its absorption of the bourgeois disciples of 'freedom' and non-intervention, and became more and more, in composition and outlook, what Peel would have made it a generation earlier—the great party of property and of the respectable middle classes. The result of Disraeli's gamble of 1867 was turning out to be not the flowering of the popular, national Toryism of his early dreams, but the resurgence of that 'Peelite' Conservatism by destroying which he had risen, and towards whose reconstruction the facts of political life had almost ever since compelled him to manoeuvre. The process to which he owed his final lease of power was creating a party penetrated through and through with the ideology that the older Toryism had so often denounced and the newer Liberalism was beginning to discard. The Conservatives looked less than ever like the trustees of paternalism and the organic view of society, as they took up the cudgels of individual liberty and freedom of enterprise against the bogies of collectivism and socialism.

This trend could scarcely fail to have a restraining effect on Conservative activity in the field of social reform. Its influence was perceptible in the pronouncements of Conservative politicians on social questions, and especially on the general issue of the rôle of the state in economic and social affairs. Conservatives increasingly assumed the defence of what had been classically Liberal positions against the exponents of governmental intervention and collective welfare. It was a Conservative, Mills, who told the Commons in June 1876 that 'The province of legislation was simply to maintain law and order',[1] and in the course of the same debate (on the Permissive Bill), another Conservative, Storer, remarked on the 'extraordinary fact' that all the arguments in favour of free trade had come from the Conservatives and all those in favour of the destruction of individual liberty from the Liberals.[2] The enemy, in Conservative eyes, was more and more the fraternalist and collectivist concept of society held by the organised working class and their Radical allies. Magee, the Tory bishop of Peterborough, made this very clear in the course of defending his celebrated preference for freedom over enforced sobriety in a debate of June 1876. There was, he asserted,

> too great a tendency on the part of those who were gaining political power in the State to believe that legislation could do everything for

[1] *Ibid.*, ccxxix. 1839.
[2] *Ibid.*, ccxxix. 1862–3.

> them, and that as little as possible was to be done by themselves. And this very class, from their habits and many of their associations, were perhaps less sensitive upon the point of personal liberty than others. So far from working men being jealous of their personal freedom, the habits acquired in Trades Unions led them to sacrifice that feeling for other things. They were, from their connection with Trades Unions, too apt to regard the State as a great Union, and were too willing to give up their own freedom and endanger the freedom of their neighbours by bringing about some larger and sweeping action on the part of the State.[1]

In face of the threat depicted by Magee, paternalistic reform seemed to some dangerously like opening the sluice-gates to the flood. Salisbury, in July 1874, explicitly warned against entering 'the regions of paternal Government' and

> laying down new principles of legislation which, upon other subjects[2] and under a political system where power resided with the greatest numbers, would some day be used most disadvantageously against them.[3]

Even while the ministry was carrying through important measures of social amelioration, scepticism of the value of legislative interference was voiced, and emphasis was laid on the necessity of promoting self-help and respecting individual liberty in the pursuit of social progress.

> How small, of all that human hearts endure,
> That part which laws or Kings can cause or cure!

recited Edward Stanhope,[4] moving the Commons' Address of 1875, in reply to a Queen's Speech which had promised six bills on social subjects. And at the end of that great session of reforming legislation, Northcote, writing to the working-class leader G. J. Holyoake, stressed enlightenment and self-help, not government intervention, as the means of elevating the condition of the people:

> The three things to which I attach importance in efforts to assist the working classes are (1) to endeavour to get a clear insight into their wants and feelings from their own point of view; (2) to assist them to obtain an equally clear insight into the matters in which they are brought into contact with other classes from the point of view taken by those classes; and (3) to get them to work out their own improvement for themselves.[5]

Disraeli was careful to maintain that in a free society progress must come by inducement rather than by direction from above. Defending the principle of permissive legislation, he said:

[1] *Ibid.*, ccxxx. 724–5.
[2] He was speaking on licensing.
[3] *3 Hansard*, ccxx. 1190. Cf. *ibid.*, ccxxx. 730.
[4] *Ibid.*, ccxxii. 43.
[5] Northcote to Holyoake, 30 Oct. 1875 (copy): Add. MS. 50052, ff. 142–3.

> permissive legislation is the characteristic of a free people. It is easy to adopt compulsory legislation when you have to deal with those who only exist to obey; but in a free country, and especially in a country like England, you must trust to persuasion and example as the two great elements, if you wish to effect any considerable change in the manners and customs of the people.[1]

In such a climate of thought, the social reforms of 1874–6 were bound to be cautious and limited. Indeed, it is remarkable that they went as far as they did. Empiricism and pressure of circumstances combined to produce a certain dichotomy between what ministers and their followers would have allowed to be theoretically desirable and what they were prepared to countenance in practice. At grips with the insoluble problem of exactly how far state interference might properly go, the government constantly found itself permitting it to go a little further. But upon the scope and nature of its reforming activities, the increasing acceptance by the Conservative party of the individualist bourgeois ethic of freedom and self-help could not fail to leave its mark.

One severely practical consideration, too, tended to limit the government's activity in the social field. This was the cost of social reform, both at the national and the local level. Nationally, the difficulty did not prove serious in 1874–6, but it was always present in the background. Northcote and his colleagues, hoping to avoid the customary Liberal charge of extravagance against a Conservative government, were anxious to keep expenditure down, and as early as January 1875 the cabinet was setting its face strongly against increased estimates.[2] A great deal of concern was displayed by the Chancellor from 1874 onwards about the growth of loans to local authorities for social improvements;[3] though he was prepared to admit the propriety of encouraging local authorities to borrow 'where the works for which they borrow are of general utility by which a large number of persons benefit who are not called on to pay rates'.[4]

[1] *3 Hansard*, ccxxv. 525 (June 1875).

[2] See Hunt to Hardy, 12 Jan. 1875, reporting a cabinet meeting: Cranbrook Papers, T501/260.

[3] See Northcote to Sclater-Booth, 8 Sept. and 27 Nov. 1874; to Derby, 5 Oct. 1874; to Hubbard, 28 Nov. 1874; and to Welby, 30 Nov. 1874 (copies; Add. MS. 50052, ff. 40–1, 47–8, 60–2); also *3 Hansard*, ccxxviii. 1110–14. The loans in question were made by the Public Works Loan Commissioners under such acts as the Public Health Act, 1872. The trouble was that advances were gaining on repayments, and the exchequer balances were going down.

[4] Northcote to Thomson Hankey, 28 Dec. 1875 (copy): Add. MS. 50052, ff. 156–7.

By 1876 the pressure for economy was reaching considerable proportions, as the weakening of the country's prosperity began to affect the revenue, and as Liberal criticisms of Tory improvidence broke out in force.[1]

A greater threat to measures of social reform was, as usual, the local taxation question. Unless the new ministry could give its supporters some satisfaction on this issue, their assiduous sabotage of all bills laying additional charges on the rates was likely to continue, in spite of Disraeli's attempt to muzzle their leaders by making Lopes a Civil Lord of the Admiralty and putting Read at the Local Government Board. The cabinet was obliged to treat local taxation as a matter of urgency, and Northcote's first budget provided for the giving of £1,250,000 *per annum* in relief of local charges for lunatics and police. The Chancellor stressed that if Parliament wanted to promote by legislation an improvement in the dwellings, sanitary arrangements, and education of the people, this could be done satisfactorily only through local agency, and for this reason it was essential to remove the local taxation grievance.[2] The concessions of 1874, however, were far from ending the matter. Conservative backbenchers were not satisfied, and continued to look jealously at any proposal tending to increase the rates. Fawcett, in May 1875, was able to dwell at length on the hostility to social improvements which the local taxation question bred among Conservatives, and to point out that the Local Taxation Committee of the Central Chamber of Agriculture, the centre of resistance to measures imposing local charges, included sixty-two Conservative members of Parliament and thirteen members of the government.[3] At the end of 1875 and the beginning of 1876 the pressure on ministers to take further action became severe: should nothing be done, Lord Eustace Cecil warned Salisbury, 'it does not require a prophet to foresee that the coming Session will be the

[1] See the budget debate of 3 April 1876, in *3 Hansard*, ccxxviii. 1100–47; and W. H. S[mith] to Northcote, 14 June 1876 (Add. MS. 50021, f. 13). Financial difficulties were a factor in preventing the government from seeking to help the working classes by lightening their fiscal burden, but it was not inclined to go far in this direction anyway. Northcote, in order to 'take the most plausible cries out of the mouths of the demagogues', favoured the reduction of those indirect taxes which bore heavily on the working classes, and in his first budget he repealed the sugar duties, a step encouraged by Disraeli on the ground that it would 'satisfy the free traders and the democracy' (Northcote to Hunt, 17 March 1874 (copy), Add. MS. 50052, ff. 7–8; Disraeli to Northcote, 4 April 1874, in M & B., v. 307). But the main fiscal change of 1874—a penny off the income tax—was designed to please the middle, not the working, classes.

[2] *3 Hansard*, ccxviii. 652–3, 1018–19.

[3] *Ibid.*, ccxxiv. 802–19. For the Local Taxation Committee's work in 1874–80, see Matthews, pp. 90–5.

beginning of the end'.[1] To many Conservative backbenchers local taxation was probably more significant than any other question. The government had little option but to purchase with further adjustments if not the euphoria at least the quiescence of its agricultural stalwarts, and this it did.

Being without specific ideas when it came into office, Disraeli's government needed time to develop its projects of social reform. Two important questions, however, licensing and the labour problem, demanded attention at once, and with both Cross grappled in the session of 1874.

The licensed victuallers confidently expected that their grievances against the act of 1872 would be removed by a government which, they argued, owed its existence partly to their support. The Conservative leaders had never committed themselves to the cause of the trade, but the alacrity with which they moved to satisfy it in 1874 suggests that they, too, were conscious of a debt, and anxious to retain the publicans' favour. The first important social measure they introduced was the Intoxicating Liquors Bill which Cross explained to the Commons in April. It was proposed to put back the closing time of public houses in London and large towns by half-an-hour; to remove the magistrates' discretion as to hours of closing, whilst giving them discretion as to the endorsement of publicans' licences upon conviction for offences; to repeal the much-resented adulteration clauses of the 1872 act;[2] and to reduce sharply police powers of entry on to licensed premises. The bill, in fact, gave the licensed victuallers a large instalment of what they had demanded during the election campaign.

Cross did his best to defend the production of a bill increasing facilities for drinking at a time when, as he admitted, liquor consumption and convictions for drunkenness were rising. He attributed increased consumption and drunkenness largely to the inability of the working classes to find other pleasurable outlets for their newly-increased means and leisure, and suggested that sobriety would be better advanced by improving their material conditions of life

[1] Cecil to Salisbury, 1 Feb. [1876]: Salisbury Papers, S.C. Pell had been threatening an independent motion, and Corrance had been trying to raise an agitation in his county. See Pell to Northcote, 20 Oct. 1875 (Add. MS. 51265; unfoliated), and Barrington to Corry, 16 Jan. 1876 (Disraeli Papers, B/XX/Ba/32).

[2] Cross pointed out that a general act covering adulteration had been passed in 1872, and contended that the provisions of Bruce's act were useless (*3 Hansard*, ccxviii. 1241–2). But Ensor notes (p. 35, n. 4) that when the government itself passed a measure against adulteration, in 1875, its provisions were less stringent than those which Bruce's act had contained.

(especially housing) than by restricting the sale of drink.[1] He looked to enlightenment and self-help, rather than repressive legislation: 'what I want to see brought about', he said, 'is, that people should look upon being drunk as a matter of disgrace'; and he added:

> I have always said that the people of England have no right to come to this House for legislation for the mitigation of an evil, until they have done their best to cope with it without legislation; and in this case, the working men in their building societies and clubs have the remedy in their own hands if they choose to make use of it. They can, if they please, form themselves into building societies, build their own homes, and not allow a public-house to be among them.[2]

This last passage was not, perhaps, very realistic, but there was much sense in Cross's arguments. He was right to stress what temperance reformers too readily forgot, that drink as such was not the cause of drunkenness, and that the drink problem could not be treated in isolation from the general moral and material condition of the working class, or solved simply by closing public-houses earlier. But in the context of his bill, these points inevitably seemed—and, indeed, were—excuses to justify unwarrantable concessions to the licensed trade.

The representatives of 187 local organisations in connection with the Licensed Victuallers' Protection Society passed unanimously a resolution thanking the government for its measure.[3] Elsewhere there was less enthusiasm. In the Conservative party itself minds were troubled by the extension of hours (though the other concessions were felt to be fair). The Liverpool Conservatives decidedly opposed it,[4] and when the bill came up for second reading increased hours were criticised by five of the six Conservative backbenchers who spoke.[5] Assheton represented a good deal of feeling on his benches when he said that the act of 1872 'had done untold good throughout the country; but it did not receive fair play . . .'[6] The merits of the

[1] *3 Hansard*, ccxviii. 1230–1.

[2] *Ibid.*, ccxviii. 1231–2.

[3] *Morning Advertiser*, 6 May 1874. They wanted in addition, however, uniformity of hours outside London and the regulation of grocers' licences.

[4] See J. Torr, M.P. to Sandon, 'Thursday' [early 1874], and 13 March [1874]; and E. Whitley to Sandon, 29 April 1874: Harrowby Papers, vol. 1, ff. 220–1, 226–7, 237. A temperance crusade was beginning in Liverpool, somewhat to the embarrassment of the Conservatives, many of whose most active supporters were connected with the licensed trade (see Sir W. B. Forwood, *Recollections of a Busy Life, being the Reminiscences of a Liverpool Merchant 1840–1910*, pp. 207–8).

[5] The exception, Greene, was a brewer. For the second reading debate, see *3 Hansard*, ccxix. 75–150.

[6] *Ibid.*, ccxix. 110.

1872 act were also being impressed upon the Home Office by the returns it was receiving from the borough authorities. These showed clearly that there was little public feeling against the hours fixed by Bruce, and little demand for any extension.[1]

It seemed wisest to retreat, and in the course of the second reading debate an obviously unhappy Selwin-Ibbetson declared that the government would consult members on the question of hours.[2] In cabinet, Cross put before his colleagues the proposals which he felt would satisfy the party, removing the extra half-hour which he had given in towns (though retaining it for London), and advancing the closing-time in country districts by an hour. Only Salisbury demurred,[3] and the new hours were introduced when the bill went into Committee, with a warning by the embarrassed Cross against trying to 'insist by Act of Parliament on the sobriety of the people'.[4] The government was able to carry its main proposals, but the Committee debates gave rise to the greatest confusion and caused ministers much humiliation. Conservatives, like Liberals, were a good deal divided. For some, the revised bill still offered excessive facilities for drinking. The half-hour extension for London was strongly opposed by Forsyth and others, the distiller Boord contending that the licensed victuallers did not want the change.[5] Laird, of Birkenhead, led a group of northern Conservatives in an unsuccessful attempt to secure later opening in large towns.[6] There were, however, those who thought the bill too restrictive. If it was a Liberal, Knatchbull-Hugessen, who took the lead in trying to make it kinder to the interests of the trade, he was vigorously seconded by the Conservative brewers, Greene, Watney, and Hall. The harassed ministry was obliged to give some ground in Committee, on Sunday hours and on the question of where and how, for closing purposes, the line was to be drawn between town and country.

[1] 'Reports from Borough Authorities in England and Wales Relating to the Licensing Act, 1872' (*P.P.* 1874, liv. 243).

[2] *3 Hansard*, ccxix. 99–100. Selwin-Ibbetson was hard put to it to find plausible reasons for destroying Bruce's act, for which, as Harcourt pointed out, he had himself been largely responsible.

[3] 'I regret it exceedingly but am obviously in a minority' was his comment on the paper containing the new hours which Cross passed round the cabinet, and which survives in the Cross Papers (Add. MS. 51265: unfoliated).

[4] *3 Hansard*, ccxix. 968.

[5] See *ibid.*, ccxix. 1003–16. Boord was contradicted by Russell, who, with the brewer Watney, supported the extension, which was carried by 161 votes to 126.

[6] See *ibid.*, ccxix. 1091–1105. The northern members were altogether divided on this issue: Eslington, Birley, Greenall, and Torr backed Laird, while Cawley and Wheelhouse supported the government. For the strong feeling of the Liverpool Conservatives on the hours question, see E. Whitley to Torr, 15 July 1874 (Harrowby Papers, vol. 1, f. 59). They were anxious to avoid the charge that their party was pandering to the beer interest.

No one was really happy with the measure as it emerged from the Commons. Ministers wanted only to hear the last of it. Salisbury clearly disliked its remodelling. He was showing all his habitual impatience of efforts to promote morality by legislation, and in the Lords he issued warnings against paternalism and lashed the Bishops of London and Peterborough (who opposed the half-hour extension in the Metropolis) for

> calling in the secular authority to carry out those objects which, if right, they ought to attain by their own preaching and ministrations. Sobriety was no doubt a very good thing, but it ought to be enforced not by Act of Parliament, but by moralists and preaching and admonition.[1]

In the liquor trade feelings were mixed. Callender assured Salisbury that the licensed victuallers in his constituency were fully satisfied with the measure,[2] and it did undoubtedly give the trade the greater part of what they wanted. But there was annoyance at the government's withdrawal over hours, even though, as the *Morning Advertiser* admitted, this might be considered 'a public far more than a publicans' question'.[3] The *Licensed Victuallers' Guardian*, after declaring on 20 June that the Government had fairly redressed all the trade grievances, grumbled on 18 July:

> How the Trade would have fared had it not been well and zealously represented in the lobby of the House during the progress of the Bill, we dare not reflect upon; for never in Parliamentary history has a party shown so little disposition to remedy a class and public grievance as the party which now holds the helm of the State ship.

In its effort to appease the licensed trade the ministry had got itself into an unedifying mess. The act of 1874, badly conceived and ingloriously carried through, was the worst possible start to its programme of social legislation. 'I have not much to be proud of in this matter', was Cross's final verdict on the measure.[4] But at least the act laid the licensing question to rest for some time, so far as legislative action was concerned. Of course, both the drink and the temperance

[1] *3 Hansard*, ccxx. 1201. Knowing Salisbury's feelings on licensing matters, both Knatchbull-Hugessen and the Hon. Sec. of the Brewers Union, Hallett, made efforts to get him to protect the interests of the trade. See Knatchbull-Hugessen to Salisbury, 25 June 1874 (Salisbury Papers, S.C.); W. H. Hallett to Salisbury, 9 July 1874 (*ibid.*, G.C., 'Political 4').

[2] Callender to Salisbury, 27 June 1874 (*ibid.*, S.C.)—a letter which illustrates clearly the anxiety of some Conservative members to keep the favour of the trade (though Callender was a member of the United Kingdom Alliance).

[3] 17 June 1874. On 9 June the *Morning Advertiser* had remarked that a large majority of publicans had given up the question of hours, 'or, indeed, intimated their feelings in favour of restriction'.

[4] Cross, p. 25.

interests continued to exert political pressure for their respective ends, the former putting its trust mainly in the Conservatives, the latter relying more than ever upon the Liberals, who included nearly all its best friends. Neither was very successful, for the Home Office was anxious to avoid concessions which would re-open the main question. The efforts of the brewers to secure the repeal of their licence duty evoked more irritation than sympathy from Northcote.[1] On the other hand, the government would have nothing to do with the various schemes of local control propounded by the temperance Liberals. Though Birley and Callender and some Irish Tories went on voting for the Permissive Bill or supporting Sunday prohibition, the general feeling of the party was extremely hostile to further drastic restriction of the trade. The typical Conservative view was that of Mills, who attacked the Permissive Bill because

> temperance would be more advanced by providing suitable dwellings, wholesome water, and pure air for the people, than by enacting penal laws, which were sure to provoke a just reaction. It was a transgression of the limits of legislation to interfere with the morals of the people in this manner. The province of legislation was simply to maintain law and order.[2]

When in 1876 the Archbishop of Canterbury, impelled by the growth of the temperance movement in the Church of England, raised the drink question in the Lords, Salisbury and Bishop Magee simply reiterated these ideas.[3] In licensing as in other spheres, it was increasingly the notion of freedom and non-interference which shaped Conservative attitudes.

All the same, there remained a realisation among many Conservatives who detested temperance fanaticism that the drink problem was serious, and that some further measures might be necessary to cope with it.[4] At the Home Office, Selwin-Ibbetson was especially worried by the evil effects of the almost unrestricted issue of off-licences, and was ready to support a measure to give the magistrates the power of regulating 'what they believe to be the most fruitful

[1] See Northcote to Pryor (until 1875 chairman of the Brewers' Association), 28 April 1874, 12 May 1875, 3 Feb. and 7 July 1876 (copies; Add. MS. 50052, ff. 20–1, 116, 171; Add. MS. 50053, f. 16); and *3 Hansard*, ccxxiii. 370–92. A Conservative brewer, A. Payn, complained bitterly to Lord Eustace Cecil about the party's omission to support 'those who sent 50 members at least to this Parliament' (Payn to Cecil, 22 April 1875: Salisbury Papers, G. C., 'Political 4').

[2] *3 Hansard*, ccxxix. 1839.

[3] *Ibid.*, ccxxx. 723–33. Magee was a supporter of the recently-formed Church of England Temperance Society.

[4] See, e.g., Earl Percy's speech, *ibid.*, ccxxix. 1844–8.

source of crime with which they have to contend'.[1] An effective attack on drunkenness, he told the Commons, would involve giving magistrates 'a more complete control over all the houses so as to limit them to the wants of the district'.[2] But these were steps, apparently, which his colleagues did not care to take, and upon the legislation of 1874 the licensing question for the moment rested.

If the government's first concern in 1874 was to conciliate the drink interest, its second was to establish friendly relations with the growing power of organised labour.[3] It was obvious that the artisans' demands could not be ignored, for the general election had emphasised their political strength. In the north, especially, labour questions had greatly aided the Conservative victory, and a number of Conservative members were pledged to seek satisfaction for the working men over hours, the law of master and servant, and the law governing trade unions. Disraeli had not even formed his cabinet before Callender was urging action on the nine-hour day in the textile industry—which he thought a more pressing problem than the trade union question. Callender was anxious that the government should take the matter out of the hands of Mundella, the champion of the nine-hours bill in the last Parliament:

> we are all [he wrote] so deeply pledged to it that it could not alienate our friends—& may I venture to add—it would strengthen all we have said as to the policy of the Conservative party—attending to the health & comfort of the nation rather than wretched political agitation.... it would give us immense influence here for many years to come.[4]

Cross, as a Lancashire member, was well aware of the political significance of the hours question and ready to grapple with it. There was no real reason to hold back: the textile manufacturers showed small anxiety to retain the existing sixty-hour week, and a Local Government Board inquiry in 1873 had produced a recommendation in favour of 54 hours and the raising of the ages of half-time and full-time employment.[5] Consequently, when Mundella, with Callender's support, once again brought in his nine-hours bill of 1872–3, Cross

[1] Printed memorandum by Selwin-Ibbetson, n.d., but printed 8 May 1876: P.R.O. 30/6/72, pp. 365–6. Selwin-Ibbetson was recommending government backing for the bill of a Liberal, Johnstone, on the subject.

[2] *3 Hansard*, ccxxix. 1882.

[3] The trade unions were undergoing rapid development in the early 'seventies: the T.U.C. of 1872 claimed to represent 375,000 men, that of 1874 1,200,000. S. and B. Webb, *History of Trade Unionism*, 2nd ed., p. 326.

[4] Callender to Corry, 16 Feb. 1874: Disraeli Papers, B/XXI/C/11.

[5] See the report to the Local Government Board on proposed changes in textile factories, by J. H. Bridges and T. Holmes, 7 April 1873: *P.P.* 1873, lv. 803.

responded by taking the matter into the hands of the government and producing a measure of his own. He proposed to give women and children in the textile industry a week of 56½ hours (instead of Mundella's 54 hours), and (like Mundella) to raise the age of half-time employment from eight to ten, and of full-time employment from thirteen to fourteen (unless the child could produce an educational certificate). Reducing the hours of women and children meant in practice reducing the hours of men also, but this Cross was reluctant to state plainly, for, hoping to avoid the wrath of the political economists, he still paid lip-service to the accepted doctrine that while women and children might be protected as not being absolutely free agents, 'so far as adult males were concerned, there could be no question that freedom of contract must be maintained, and men must be left to take care of themselves'.[1] It was a good case of a Conservative minister doing in fact what he would hardly have attempted to justify in theory.

The operatives made some difficulty at first about accepting Cross's proposals, but this was overcome, and the bill passed both Houses with general acclaim, notwithstanding some sharp attacks by Fawcett on political economy grounds.[2] Its only serious critic on the Conservative side was the Yorkshire woollen manufacturer Starkie, who thought it would reduce the value of property and limit profits.[3] The Factory Act of 1874 was perhaps the only really paternalist social measure which the ministry was to pass. A moderate settlement of a long-agitated question, motivated in large part by considerations of political advantage, it paid small attention to the tenets of freedom and non-intervention to which its author felt obliged to genuflect even as he transgressed them.

To organised labour as a whole, however, the salient question was what the government would do about the law of conspiracy, the Criminal Law Amendment Act, and the Master and Servant Act. The unionists hoped for quick concessions, and they were angry when Cross decided to appoint a Royal Commission to review the subject. They regarded this as a device for evading action, and the T.U.C. Parliamentary Committee refused the Commission its co-operation.[4] Nor did the Commission's report, when it finally appeared

[1] *3 Hansard*, ccxviii. 1793–4. Subsequently Cross pleaded that his bill would at least infringe the principles of political economy no further than existing factory acts had done (*ibid.*, ccxix. 1420).

[2] Fawcett, using exactly the same arguments as had been used against the factory legislation of the 'thirties and 'forties, mustered 79 votes against the second reading. For his main speech, see *ibid.*, ccxix. 1421–31. To Fawcett, Callender's views were 'Socialism' (*ibid.*, ccxviii. 1802).

[3] *Ibid.*, ccxix. 1480–2.

[4] On the attitude of the unionists, see Howell, pp. 340–8. Alexander

George Sclater-Booth

Sir Charles Adderley

in 1875, give them much cause for satisfaction. Though it recommended amendment of the Master and Servant Act in the sense desired by the unionists, it proposed only minor alterations of the Criminal Law Amendment Act and of the law of conspiracy.[1] There was, however, a dissenting report by Alexander Macdonald, one of the two working-class leaders now in Parliament, who advised the total repeal of the Criminal Law Amendment Act, and endorsed the words of Hughes and Harrison in the minority report of 1869 against exceptional penalties for working men and their combinations.[2] The main report, signed not only by Conservatives like Winmarleigh, Goldney, and Gurney, but also by Roebuck and Thomas Hughes, undoubtedly represented the bulk of middle-class opinion. Yet Cross felt dissatisfied with it. He seems genuinely to have doubted its fairness, and he certainly realised that legislation based upon it would cause the artisans to feel severely disappointed in the government.[3]

His response was largely to disregard it, and to give the working men something much closer to what they had demanded. The line he took in his labour legislation of 1875 was an advanced one, and it was apparently only his leader's approval which overcame the objections of his colleagues. That, at least, is the story which Disraeli himself told Lady Bradford:

> when Secy. X explained his plan to the Cabinet, many were agst. it, and none for it but myself; and it was only in deference to the P. Min[iste]r that a decision was postponed to another day. In the interval the thing was better understood and managed.[4]

Cross's proposals were embodied in two bills which he introduced in June 1875—the Employers and Workmen Bill and the Conspiracy and Protection of Property Bill. The first measure, which replaced the Master and Servant Act (the verbal change from 'Master and Servant' to 'Employers and Workmen' being in itself significant),

[1] Royal Commission on the Working of the Master and Servant Act, 1867, and the Criminal Law Amendment Act, 34 & 35 Vict. Cap. 32, etc., Second Report: *P.P.* 1875, xxx. 1.

[2] Royal Commission, Second Report, pp. 28–9.

[3] One would like to know how far he was influenced at this moment by the Home Office counsel, Godfrey Lushington. Lushington, a positivist and an old friend of trade unionism (see his essay, 'Workmen and Trade Unions', in *Questions for a Reformed Parliament*, 1867, pp. 37–64), apparently passed semi-confidential information to Beesly, and had a good deal to do with the triumph of the labour laws agitation. R. Harrison, 'E. S. Beesly and Karl Marx', pt. II, *International Review of Social History*, iv (1959), 218–19.

[4] Disraeli to Lady Bradford, 29 June 1875, in M. & B. v. 372.

Macdonald joined the Commission after an assurance from Cross that 'it was intended to facilitate legislation'. The fairness of the Commission was not in question: the inclusion of Russell Gurney alone guaranteed that, says Howell.

removed breaches of contract from the purview of the criminal law, except where the vital public services of gas and water were concerned, or where there was danger to life or serious damage to property. The second altered the law of conspiracy so as to free the activities of trade unions from its operation, where the acts involved were not in themselves criminal. Both bills were conceived by Cross in the spirit of classic economic liberalism: their purpose was, he later wrote, 'to place master and servant on an equal footing before the law . . . and to maintain the most absolute freedom of will between the master and the servant', and 'to maintain the most absolute freedom of will between the servant and his fellow servants . . .'[1] The two together gave the unionists a large instalment of what they wanted. Only on one point was there dissatisfaction: Cross declined to repeal or revise the Criminal Law Amendment Act, contending that it did not, as many thought, make peaceful picketing a crime.[2]

In the Commons the bills were generally approved. Mundella and Elcho, Forster and Lowe, and the working men's representatives, Macdonald and Burt, all spoke in their favour,[3] and few copied Newdegate in expressing apprehension at the increasing power of the unions and suggesting that Parliament would ultimately have to regulate them and render them corporately responsible for damage inflicted.[4] The unionists themselves were pleased with proposals far more generous than they had expected. But strong pressure was exerted to render the settlement complete by dealing with the Criminal Law Amendment Act and removing the obstacles which it placed in the way of picketing. It was Lowe who took the lead, from the Liberal benches, in urging the removal of all special legal restrictions on working-class action, and by the middle of July the cabinet and the Conservative party at large had recognised the desirability of acceding to his point of view.[5] The final step was taken: Cross announced the repeal of the Criminal Law Amendment Act and the introduction of

[1] Cross, p. 35. The unionists' agitation had made considerable use of 'freedom' arguments (see S. and B. Webb, *History of Trade Unionism*, 2nd ed., pp. 294–7), and D. Simon points out (p. 199) that the cause of reform of the master and servant law was in effect the cause of free trade in labour. Simon thinks (pp. 190–5) that the abandonment of the law of master and servant was facilitated by the decline of the small employer, whose weapon it principally was: for the most wealthy and influential section of the capitalist class, it was, by 1875, no longer worth preserving in face of militant opposition.

[2] *3 Hansard*, ccxxiv. 1679–82.

[3] See the second reading debate, *ibid.*, ccxxv. 651–86.

[4] *Ibid.*, ccxxv. 684–5.

[5] See Richmond to Hardy, 15 July 1875, reporting a cabinet meeting of the previous day (Cranbrook Papers, T501/257); *Standard*, 13 July 1875. Cross consulted with the Secretary of the T.U.C. Parliamentary Committee, George Howell, at this juncture (Howell, pp. 374–5).

provisions which legalised picketing where only peaceful persuasion was in question.

The labour legislation of 1875[1] was a remarkable stroke, and easily the most important of the government's social reforms. It gave the working class everything for which they had striven at the general election, and which Gladstone's ministry had steadily refused them. No longer (but for some special cases) need artisans fear imprisonment for breach of contract. No longer was the action of unions in trade disputes liable to be hamstrung by proceedings for conspiracy or by the prohibition of picketing. The unions had secured a charter which, until the legal decisions of the late 'nineties, seemed to guarantee them in the free and effective exercise of their functions. The labour question looked as though it had been definitively put to rest by the Conservative coup. The working men's leaders were delighted with the bills, and with Cross, whose readiness to listen to their representations during the passage of the measures had won him much goodwill.[2] The Trade Union Congress, in October 1875, carried a motion of thanks to the Home Secretary by a large majority.[3] And if the employers were inclined to be disgruntled at the extent of Cross's concessions,[4] the Conservative party hardly heeded them in its gratification at having disposed of a major cause of social conflict in what promised to be an electorally rewarding manner.

Disraeli, who had for some time rightly regarded the labour laws as the topic about which the working classes were most keenly concerned, undoubtedly hoped that the measures of 1875 would win his party the gratitude of the people and enable it to maintain the position which it had established in the populous constituencies in 1874. After the second reading he wrote jubilantly to Lady Bradford:

> . . . I cannot express to you the importance of last night. It is one of those measures, that root and consolidate a party. We have settled the long and vexatious contest bet[wee]n capital and labor.

And to Lady Chesterfield:

> This is the greatest measure since the Short Time Act and will gain and retain for the Tories the lasting affection of the working classes.[5]

[1] Rounded off in 1876 by a Trade Union Act Amendment Act, embodying minor adjustments of the law on the registration and friendly benefits of unions.

[2] See the tributes of Mundella and Macdonald in *3 Hansard*, ccxxv. 1581–2; G. Howell to Cross, 20 June 1876 (Add. MS. 51271; unfoliated); Howell, p. 381.

[3] *The Times*, 13 Oct. 1875.

[4] Even his original proposals alarmed them: see, for instance, two articles in their journal, *Capital and Labour*, 30 June 1875.

[5] Disraeli to Lady Bradford, 29 June 1875, in M. & B., v. 371; to Lady Chesterfield, 29 June 1875, in *The Letters of Disraeli to Lady Bradford and Lady Chesterfield*, ed. the Marquis of Zetland, i. 260. Cf. his letter to the Queen, 29 June 1875, in M. & B., v. 372.

Cross's bills may, perhaps, have done something to assist the growth of working-class Conservatism, but their recognition of the new status of working men and their unions within British society could be seen as an acknowledgement of established fact and as a concession to power, rather than as a free act of grace, and in one sense they did the Conservative party as much harm as good. The labour laws had been the main cause of the tension between the working classes and their traditional Liberal allies in 1871–4, and the main obstacle to the removal of that tension. Their disappearance from the arena of political controversy in 1875, albeit at the wave of a Conservative wand, tended to facilitate the return of organised labour to the Liberal fold.

The settlement of the labour laws was only one of a galaxy of social reforms which marked the year 1875. Having had time to mature its plans, the ministry devoted the session to social legislation, introducing no fewer than eight important bills, of which it succeeded in passing six. It was perhaps the first time in British history that Parliament had been called upon to devote the great bulk of its energies to questions concerning the condition of the people,[1] and it was an impressive earnest of the will of Disraeli's government to show that Conservatism could satisfy the needs of the working population. But the measures of 1875 in no sense constituted a 'programme' or embodied a 'policy': each was an empirical response to a more or less pressing problem, undertaken out of necessity, or because investigation and discussion had made the time ripe for action; and though all aimed at the amelioration of social life, it is difficult to regard them as the expression of any common underlying philosophy.

Perhaps the most important, after the labour laws, was the Artizans Dwellings Bill. The problem of working-class housing was attracting considerable attention when the Conservatives took office in 1874, and had recently been the subject of an important report by a committee of the Charity Organisation Society.[2] This committee, set up to study the situation in London, numbered among its members Shaftesbury and twenty-one M.P.s, four of whom gained office in Disraeli's ministry—Hardy, Northcote, Adderley, and W. H. Smith. Its report concluded that it was essential to provide the poorer classes with adequate housing near to their work, and that this could only be

[1] This signalised the greatly enhanced importance of social questions in national politics; they had become, noted Shaftesbury, 'Imperial' subjects (diary, 11 Jan. 1875, in Hodder, iii. 355).

[2] *Dwellings of the Poor: Report of the Dwellings Committee of the Charity Organisation Society, presented to the Council November 3, 1873.* See, on this report, C. L. Mowat, *The Charity Organisation Society 1869–1913*, pp. 55–7.

done by municipal government, acting with enlarged powers and through commercial enterprise. Stressing the difficulty experienced in obtaining sites for artisans' dwellings, the committee urged that large powers of compulsory purchase should be conferred upon the municipal authorities.

Both the Charity Organisation Society and the Royal College of Physicians memorialised the new ministry on the subject, and in May 1874 it was brought forward in the Commons by the Liberal Kay-Shuttleworth, a member of the C.O.S. committee, who pressed for action on the lines of the committee's report, contending that if only the sites could be obtained, philanthropic and private enterprise would build the dwellings.[1] He was supported from both sides of the House: even the idea of compulsory purchase found favour, the Conservative member for the City, Hubbard, remarking that 'Nothing short of a severe despotism would meet these cases'.[2] Cross was already giving his mind to the problem, and he promised legislation. Meanwhile, he assisted the passage of a Liberal bill designed to facilitate the erection of artisans' dwellings on land belonging to municipal corporations, and attempted to check the evil resulting from the demolition of existing dwellings to make way for railways by introducing new standing orders, requiring the promoters of private bills which destroyed working-class housing to procure alternative accommodation for those displaced.[3]

It was upon the problem in the large towns that attention was focused. The housing of the rural working class, though also inadequate, received much less consideration, in spite of the efforts of the Devon Tory, Palk, who reminded his colleagues in the budget debate of 1874 that 'if cottages were not built in which labourers could live in decency and comfort, it was natural they would become members of Agricultural Labourers Unions and listen to agitators'.[4] Cross seems to have thought entirely in terms of the great urban areas when he came to formulate his measure. His task was difficult, for legislation on working-class dwellings raised in acute form the problem of the proper scope of state interference in economic and social matters. There were, of course, precedents for legislation in this field—Shaftesbury's Lodging Houses Acts of 1851, the act of 1866 authorising government loans for working-class housing, and the Torrens Act of 1868 (which but for its mangling by the Lords would have given local authorities powers of compulsory purchase). But

[1] *3 Hansard*, ccxviii. 1943–67.

[2] *Ibid.*, ccxviii. 1978.

[3] See *ibid.*, ccxxi. 964. But according to Dyos ('Railways and Housing', p. 18) the railway companies succeeded in evading this provision for a decade.

[4] *3 Hansard*, ccxviii. 1190.

how far could the government go now? Opinion in the cabinet was cautious. Derby wrote of the projected bill:

> a good subject to take up, but which will require cautious handling if we are not to carry State interference beyond its legitimate limits.[1]

Northcote looked at the question from a financial point of view: the sanitary acts had led to large calls on the Public Works Loan Fund, and if artisans' dwellings were to involve demands upon it as well (as was being suggested), the government would have to borrow heavily, 'while our policy', complained that orthodox economist, 'ought to be in the direction of reducing Debt'.[2] It was perhaps the influence of the prime minister that was decisive in quieting these doubts: the benevolent interest in the housing question which he had displayed over Torrens's bill in 1868 was still active in July 1874, when he visited the Shaftesbury Park housing scheme, and saw 'an astonishing spectacle, which may change England more than all the Reform Bills—and change it always for the better'.[3]

Cross was no more anxious than his colleagues to offend against what he called 'those laws of political economy by which they ought to be bound'.[4] But his action was necessarily determined more by the facts of the problem before him than by nice calculations of theoretical merits. He was impressed by the proposals of the Charity Organisation Society's committee, and even more, apparently, by the similar recommendations of the Medical Officer of Health for the City of London, Dr Letheby, in his report on the sanitary condition of the City of London for 1872–3. In the memorandum in which he explained his bill to the cabinet,[5] Cross quoted at length Letheby's contention that what was wanted was a process whereby local authorities could get hold of sites and dilapidated property, with power to dispose of them to people who would build dwellings suitable for the labouring classes. Should this be provided, thought Letheby,

> there would soon arise a class of investors, actuated as much by sound commercial principles as by benevolent considerations, who would be willing to engage in judicious building schemes for the better housing of the poor.

To Cross this made sense, and the prospect of yoking together for the purpose of social improvement 'sound commercial principles'

1 Derby to Disraeli, 13 Oct. 1874: Disraeli Papers, B/XX/S/936.

2 Northcote to Disraeli, 14 Oct. 1874: Add. MS. 50016, ff. 254–9.

3 Disraeli to Lady Bradford, 19 July 1874, in *Letters to Lady Bradford*, i. 124. Cf. M. & B., v. 371.

4 *3 Hansard*, ccxix. 264.

5 Printed memorandum on Artizans Dwellings Improvement Bill, 28 Jan. 1875: P.R.O. 30/6/72, pp. 235–8.

and that municipal initiative whose potentialities had been revealed to him by his examination of the slum clearance schemes already carried through by the cities of Edinburgh, Glasgow, and Liverpool, was highly attractive. Accordingly, the Artizans Dwellings Bill which he introduced in February 1875 was drawn on the lines which Letheby and the C.O.S. committee had advocated. Municipal authorities in London and the larger towns (to which the operation of the bill was confined) were empowered to draw up improvement schemes for such districts as might be certified to be unhealthy by a medical officer of health, to purchase the land involved, compulsorily if necessary, and to let or sell it for the provision of working-class housing, rehousing those displaced in or near the same district. They were also to be able to obtain cheap loans for these purposes from the Public Works Loan Commissioners.[1] The actual building of new dwellings was, of course, to be undertaken by private enterprise.

Submitting his measure to the Commons, Cross stressed the basic importance of the housing problem. 'We may take it as an axiom', he said, 'that what the homes of the people are the people themselves will be found to be.'[2] But he was careful to stress also that in tackling the question he was proposing nothing which would overstep the accepted limits of state action or undermine the self-reliance of the lower orders.

> I take it as a starting-point that it is not the duty of the Government to provide any class of citizens with any of the necessaries of life.[3]

He was a little uncomfortable, all the same, about even the very moderate degree of legislative interference which his bill embodied, and sought to evade the issue by presenting the question as essentially one of sanitary reform—thus transferring it to a sphere where a large measure of state action had long been sanctioned. He asked 'the political economist who may be disposed to scan this kind of legislation too closely' to remember that health was wealth, and argued that where they could, 'without any inroad upon the sound principles of political economy', use legislative means to prevent the waste caused by disease, it was their duty to do so.[4]

Cross was not entirely successful in escaping the criticisms of the political economists. Fawcett kept up a steady fire against the bill, which he regarded as 'class legislation'.[5] On the Conservative side, Cawley, of Salford, was worried about the possibility of local authorities setting out eventually to build working-class dwellings them-

[1] Though Northcote had yielded on this point, he was far from happy about it: see his letter to Follett of 11 March 1875 (copy; Add. MS. 50052, ff. 105–6).
[2] *3 Hansard*, ccxxii. 99. [3] *Ibid.*, ccxxii. 100. [4] *Ibid.*, ccxxii. 100–1.
[5] *Ibid.*, ccxxiii. 39.

selves, and disliked the proposal to pay compensation to owners of property according to existing rather than potential values; while the City member Hubbard objected to the government's lending money for social purposes at less than the market rate.[1] In general, however, both Liberals and Conservatives approved the aims of the bill, and their copious criticisms were concentrated not against its principles but against its glaring weaknesses. The measure, it was frequently pointed out, was entirely permissive. The Conservative Salt was not the only member who 'did not quite see where the strength lay which was to bring it into practical operation'.[2] Much doubt was expressed as to whether the medical officers and local authorities upon whose initiative the measure depended would be likely to condemn the ratepayers' property and purchase it at the ratepayers' expense. Then, as Shaftesbury, among others, remarked,[3] the displacement of working-class people to make way for improvement schemes would simply worsen the immediate overcrowding problem, and there was no security that the new dwellings to be provided would be adapted to the means of those displaced. Many could not see why the bill should not apply to the smaller towns, or even to villages.

Though he accepted a number of suggestions for the improvement of the measure (including some from the Radical mayor of Birmingham, Joseph Chamberlain[4]), Cross could not make fundamental alterations. The amount of interference which the bill embodied was all he thought permissible. The government must not attempt to provide the necessaries of life; it could only try to facilitate individual and corporate enterprise. Cross was convinced that the local authorities on the one hand and private capitalists on the other would set to and work his bill.[5] Compulsion, in the context of 1875, seemed neither possible nor necessary; it was upon the operation of the principles of freedom, voluntaryism, and the education of public opinion that the housing of the people must depend.

'Our chief measure', said Disraeli in May 1875.[6] The Artizans Dwellings Act was certainly important. It was the first major attempt to tackle the problem of working-class housing in the great towns. It focused public attention on the question, and it asserted the principle that in the last resort the right of property must give way before the need of social improvement. By providing for cheap loans it even

[1] *Ibid.*, ccxxiii. 31–6, 1238. [2] *Ibid.*, ccxxii. 352. [3] *Ibid.*, ccxxiv. 453–9.

[4] J. L. Garvin, *The Life of Joseph Chamberlain*, i. 195. Among others concerned with the housing problem whom Cross consulted was Octavia Hill (W. J. Hill, *Octavia Hill*, p. 95).

[5] For instance, he expected a great effort in London as soon as the bill became law. See his letter to Disraeli, 22 June 1875: Disraeli Papers, B/XX/Cr/25.

[6] Letter to Lady Bradford, 7 May 1875, in M. & B., v. 377.

embodied a form of government subsidy for housing schemes. Yet it was a tentative measure, relying entirely upon an uncertain local initiative and upon the equally uncertain workings of the commercial and the philanthropic instincts, a measure which, while it extended the area of state interference and collective action, remained shot through with the bourgeois creed of freedom of which its author (whatever bills he might pass) was so typical an exponent. It was neither collectivist nor really paternal, yet it was irreconcilable with principles of non-intervention. Passed by a Conservative ministry, it was, with its stress on removing the obstacles to enterprise, in many ways a classically liberal measure. There is no better illustration of the confused and nervous empiricism which lay at the heart of Disraelian social reform.

Cross was far from being the only minister at work on social reform in 1875. Sclater-Booth, in particular, at the Local Government Board, had much in hand. Having carried in 1874 an amendment of the sanitary laws increasing his department's power to coerce local authorities, he produced in 1875 three important bills concerning the public health. The largest of these was a general Public Health Bill which completed the work begun in 1871–2 of putting into effect the recommendations of Adderley and his colleagues of the Sanitary Commission. It carried out the long-needed consolidation of the sanitary laws, together with some minor amendments, and thus furnished one of the basic prerequisites for the proper implementation of the legislation in this field. It did not develop the principles of sanitary legislation, as the Public Health Act of 1866 had done, and its reputation is exaggerated compared with that of the earlier measure,[1] but it was a landmark in public health administration, and was to remain in use for sixty years.

Sclater-Booth's second measure in 1875 was concerned with the adulteration of food and drugs. A Select Committee which sat in 1874 had found that the main act on the subject, that of 1872, had not been generally adopted, and had recommended that it should be repealed and replaced by a new act, compulsory in operation.[2] Sclater-Booth, however, apparently shared Disraeli's preference for permissive legislation as 'the characteristic of a free people', and though the Sale of Food and Drugs Bill which he produced in 1875 contained comprehensive provisions against adulteration, it did not

[1] As Lambert says (*Simon*, p. 560) it 'marked, *in legislative terms*, not so much a beginning as an end, not so much an extension as a consolidation of terrain already gained by the three previous decades of legislative advance'.

[2] Report of Select Committee on the Adulteration of Food Act (1872): *P.P.* 1874, vi. 243.

render it compulsory on local authorities to appoint the analysts who alone could make the measure effective. Sandford, Conservative member for Maldon, who had sat on the Select Committee, was highly critical of the bill, complaining that it had been framed rather in the wholesaler's than in the public interest. He pointed out that the town councillors to whom it entrusted the appointment of analysts were often themselves among the culprits, and that the provision which made it necessary to prove that a vendor of adulterated goods knew them to be adulterated, in order to obtain a conviction against him, would cripple the measure.[1] This latter requirement, which had done much to hamstring earlier measures, was struck out in the Commons, re-inserted by the government in the Lords, and finally abandoned.[2] As passed, the act was certainly useful, but its failure to compel the appointment of analysts was bound to limit its efficacy.[3]

The third topic which Sclater-Booth took up was the pollution of rivers, on which a Royal Commission appointed by the government of 1868 had just concluded its work.[4] Though an obvious menace to public health, pollution of rivers by sewage and factory waste was very hard to stop, for the local authorities and manufacturers responsible were liable to offer a sharp resistance to any measure forcing them to undertake the complicated and expensive task of disposing of their effluent products elsewhere. The problem had defeated the efforts of the Liberal ministry and of Shaftesbury in 1872–3,[5] and there was nothing to render it easier in 1875.

The Pollution of Rivers Bill, introduced in the Lords by Salisbury, reflected the government's unwillingness to deal too stringently with the interests affected. It was a tentative measure, much milder than the recommendations of the Royal Commission. The pollution of streams by noxious liquids was forbidden, but it was to be left to the county court judges to decide what liquids qualified as noxious. The provisions on pollution by manufacturers and mine owners were especially odd: offenders who had polluted streams for not more than twelve years would have to render their effluents harmless within

[1] *3 Hansard*, ccxxii. 599–601.

[2] *Ibid.*, ccxxiii. 1263–6; ccxxiv. 1894–5; ccxxv. 944.

[3] In the Commons in March 1876 it was alleged that in many places local authorities had not appointed analysts under the act, and that in others nothing had been done because of the absence of any provision for payment of a specific salary to the analyst. But Sclater-Booth was not ready to use the powers of compulsory appointment vested in the Local Government Board, or to recommend any uniform system of payment for analysts (*ibid.*, ccxxvii. 1293–4). Not until 1879 was the appointment of analysts made compulsory.

[4] The Commission on the prevention of rivers pollution issued its final reports in 1874 (*P.P.* 1874, xxxiii. 1, 311).

[5] The Public Health Bill of 1872, in its original form, had included clauses on river pollution, and Shaftesbury had introduced a bill on the subject in 1873.

two years, or stop the flow altogether, but as to those 'who might be said to have a longer prescription', Salisbury explained that the government felt it could not well do more than require them to use 'the best practicable and available means' for rendering their outflow innocuous.[1]

Both the lack of a definition of pollution and the twelve years distinction were severely criticised. The latter was the focus of a disagreement within the government as to how rigorously pollution should be attacked. It had not been in Sclater-Booth's original bill, and seems to have been thrust on him by Cross and Salisbury. Sclater-Booth disliked it, not as operating too leniently but as being too harsh: he was opposed to the total prohibition of even the more recent pollutions, and wanted the 'best practicable and available means' clause applied to new pollutions as well as old.

> The requirement of the 'best practicable means' [he wrote] is the mildest remedy possible for all cases, and when that has been enforced without result there is nothing left but confiscation, which is too severe for any case.[2]

Salisbury, however, wanted more vigorous action: his dislike of state intervention faded in a matter which affected the interests of himself and his fellow landowners as riparian proprietors. He refused to abandon the twelve years clause, telling Cross:

> I think the bill is more likely to be found fault with because the 12 years is not 30. What the President calls 'confiscation' is a process strictly analogous to turning out a squatter who has built on somebody else's land. These men who foul the water of which the use belongs to riparian occupiers lower down are simply wrong doers—& have no more right to any rent than a pickpocket who is made to give up his neighbour's pocket handkerchief.[3]

But Salisbury's enthusiasm for strong action was very soon modified by vigorous representations from the northern manufacturing interests which the bill threatened. These convinced him of the extreme difficulty of dealing with the effluents of mines and factories, and in a cabinet memorandum[4] he set out his doubts as to the practicability of the bill. Sclater-Booth, who was anxious to get a measure passed, countered with another memorandum,[5] rejecting Salisbury's

1 *3 Hansard*, ccxxiii. 1889.

2 Sclater-Booth to Salisbury, 2 May [1875]: Salisbury Papers, S.C. Cf. Sclater-Booth to Cross, 2 May [1875] (*ibid.*, with letters from Cross), and Sclater-Booth to Salisbury, 29 May 1875 (*ibid.*).

3 Salisbury to Cross, 3 May 1875: Add. MS. 51263 (unfoliated).

4 Copy (undated) in P.R.O. 30/6/72, pp. 97–9.

5 Dated 12 June 1875; copy *ibid.*, pp. 93–6.

idea that the bill might be made a weapon for trying to enforce the impossible at astronomical cost, but the cabinet was evidently more impressed by Salisbury's arguments, and the provisions relating to pollution from mines and factories were dropped from the bill, which now became concerned solely with pollution by sewage and solid matter, though legislation on mining and manufacturing pollution was foreshadowed for the following year. And in the press of business at the end of the session even this emasculated measure was abandoned.

In 1876 Sclater-Booth tried again, with a bill carefully framed to escape the wrath of the manufacturing interests. Pollution of rivers was made an offence, but, in the case both of manufacturing and mineral pollution and of sewage, ample time was to be given for the nuisance to be cured, and no prosecution was to be instituted in regard to the former without the sanction of the Local Government Board. Industrial interests were to be 'duly considered'.[1] Still further concessions had to be made during the bill's passage in order to satisfy the manufacturers, and there were loud complaints from the Liberal benches that the public interest was being ignored. Cross's reply, for the government, was simply that in relation to existing manufacturing pollution, where vested interests were involved, Sclater-Booth had gone as far as the public would allow him to go,[2] and this was perhaps true.

The Rivers Pollution Act marked the end of the government's main initiative in the field of public health.[3] The limited scope and vigour of the measures of 1875–6 reflected the unwillingness of ministers to push central intervention and control too far, or to deal too stringently with vested interests. They reflected also, no doubt, the position at the Local Government Board, where, since its creation in 1871, Simon and the medical experts, the driving force of advance in public health administration, had been subordinated to the officials of the old Poor Law Board. Sclater-Booth, a former Parliamentary Secretary to the Poor Law Board, and very much dominated by his permanent secretary, Lambert, another Poor Law Board man, did little to help the medical section.[4] Indeed, the beginning of 1875 found him concurring in Salisbury's complaints about 'the tyranny and impracticability of the doctors', and declaring that the great trouble of his life was to repress their 'centralising and bureaucratic

[1] *3 Hansard*, ccxxix. 1600.

[2] *Ibid.*, ccxxxi. 559. The bill did contain provisions to stop pollution from new manufactories.

[3] To the measures mentioned should perhaps be added Cross's Commons Act of 1876, designed largely to preserve open spaces around centres of population, for the health and recreation of the working classes.

[4] On the situation in 1874–6, see especially Lambert, *Simon*, c. xxiii.

tendencies'.[1] When the issue of the status and functions of the medical experts came to a head in 1876, he rejected the ultimatum presented to him by Simon, and the latter's resignation in May weakened severely the prospects for further advance in public health. With the legislation of 1875–6, 'sanitas sanitatum' had had its hour, and henceforth receded from the foreground of Conservative policy.

The last of the government's successful social measures in 1875 was concerned with the friendly societies. The importance of this subject should not be underestimated. With perhaps four million members, the friendly societies were an even greater organ of working-class self-help than the trade unions or the co-operatives. An enormous sum of hard-earned money was invested in them, and their financial stability was a matter of deep significance for the poorer classes, who so largely depended on them in sickness and old age.

There was a scheme of state registration for the societies, but many of them did not take advantage of it, and in any case it did nothing to ensure their soundness. A large number of societies were, in fact, unsound, and the problem was thought serious enough for the Liberal ministry to appoint a Royal Commission on the societies in 1870, with Northcote at its head.[2] The Commission's final report[3] appeared in 1874. It displayed a predictable reluctance to countenance any kind of state interference with the actual management of the societies, but it recommended that the government should prepare and publish model tables of premiums, as a guide for the societies, and that provision should be made for regular valuation of the societies, and for the proper keeping and audit of their accounts. Another recommendation, destined to rouse high feelings, was the prohibition of the insurance of infant lives, a practice thought to invite parental carelessness and worse. There was also a minority report, signed by Northcote's fellow Conservative M.P. on the Commission, Hicks

[1] Sclater-Booth to Salisbury, 18 Jan. [endorsed '1875']: Salisbury Papers, S. C. Sclater-Booth wanted to build up the status of the local medical officers of health (whose existence, however, he regretted) so that they could hold their own against 'the doctors at head quarters'.

[2] On Northcote's work on the Commission and subsequently, see Lang, ii. 40–51.

[3] Fourth Report of the Royal Commission on Friendly and Benefit Building Societies: *P.P.* 1874, xxiii. 1. This report contains (pt. I, pp. 112–15) the interesting 'Memorial on Government Insurance' presented to the Commission in December 1872, which proposes a self-supporting system of insurance for sickness and old age for the labouring classes, administered under government supervision through the Post Office. Among the memorialists were both archbishops, Shaftesbury, and a number of Conservative and Liberal M.P.s, including Hardy and Sclater-Booth.

Beach, which argued that if the stability of the societies was to be secured, the government should do something more to get sound tables adopted than merely publish them, notwithstanding the objection that this would lead to excessive state responsibility.

The question of how far the state should interfere was the crux of the problem. Public opinion generally held that it should not interfere much: the friendly societies were after all one of the most striking examples of that spirit of self-reliance which the comfortable classes delighted to praise and to inculcate upon the poor. The ministry fully agreed with the non-interventionist tenor of the Commission's report, and a bill to give effect to it was brought in at once by Northcote. But when it became obvious that the Commissioners' proposals would give rise to some debate, the Chancellor thought it better to delay and bring in a revised bill in 1875.[1]

The preparation of the Friendly Societies Bill of 1875 gives us an interesting glimpse of Conservatism at grips with the recurrent difficulty of deciding exactly where the limits of governmental intervention should be drawn. Northcote's approach was the incarnation of the individualist ethic of freedom and self-help. His objects were simply to assist the societies by giving them useful information (such as model tables), and to make them in their turn provide such information as would enable the public to judge their soundness for itself.[2] But even this very mild degree of interference seems to have been questioned by Cross, who co-operated with Northcote in the framing of the bill, and was evidently anxious to avoid any suggestion of the state's assuming responsibility for the stability of the societies. Northcote, however, successfully defended his attitude, telling his colleague:

> I cannot help thinking that you make too much of the bugbear Responsibility. These Societies are in great need of guidance; and, if we have it in our power to guide them ought we to shrink from doing so on the ground that if anything goes wrong we shall be held responsible? Here is a piece of ice, and a lot of people are going to skate on it: I know that certain places are dangerous: ought I to hesitate to mark those places for fear an accident should happen somewhere else and I should be held responsible? If you like to say, This whole business of Friendly Societies is one with which the State ought not to concern itself any more than with any other arrangements made by the working classes, then repeal all your F.S. Acts, do away with your Registrar, abolish all the privileges which the registered Societies enjoy, and let the people shift entirely for

[1] One difficulty was that the 1874 bill proposed to repeal the Trade Union Act of 1871; and a protest was organised by George Howell. Howell, pp. 352–4.

[2] See Northcote to Sotheron Estcourt, 11 Nov. 1874 (copy; Add. MS. 50052, ff. 52–3); Northcote's memorandum on the bill for the cabinet, 26 Dec. 1874 (copy in P.R.O. 30/6/72, pp. 381–90; partly printed in Lang, ii. 43–9).

themselves. If you stop short of this, you do recognise, and do (whether you like it or not) to some extent make yourself responsible for, the Societies which you favour in the sight of all the people.[1]

The distance between the two ministers was really minimal. If Cross doubted the propriety of any state action in this field, Northcote doubted the propriety of all but the barest modicum. He was willing to help people to help themselves, but no more: he did not dream of forcing the societies to adopt his model tables, and, like Cross, was decidedly against making the registration of societies compulsory.[2]

The bill of 1875 lessened the powers granted to the registrar of friendly societies in the bill of 1874, in deference to the societies' feeling. It carried out Northcote's aim of giving useful information to and requiring adequate information from the societies, and it also contained a limitation on the amount of insurance for children under three. It was not received with great enthusiasm, and criticisms of its weakness were many. A number of Conservatives thought it inadequate. Barttelot declared that more effective means must be taken to protect the savings of the working classes, and demanded a stronger bill, enforcing registration and audit and a sound scale of contributions on all societies; and he was supported from both sides.[3] Northcote, however, stubbornly maintained that it was not the government's business to give anything approaching a guarantee of the societies.

A good deal of excitement was caused by the limitation on infant insurance, which the working classes in the north, where the societies were especially strong, took as a slur on their parental honour. The point acquired enough significance for Callender to approach Disraeli about it. Many working people in the north, said the member for Manchester, would be angered by this limitation, 'proposed by the Tory government which has been held up for years as the true friend of the working classes!'

If the clause pass in its present shape [he continued], it will have a most injurious effect on our future political prospects. Yet as matters stand now—we are to have a discussion [in the House] in which we must speak out & probably nearly all the representatives of the great constituencies which at all events assisted to place the present Government in office will be compelled to walk into the same lobby with the opposition . . . I am not overstating the case by saying that nearly every Lancashire

[1] Northcote to Cross, 19 Jan. 1875: Add. MS. 51265 (unfoliated).

[2] See Northcote to Cross, 13 Jan. 1875, with Cross's marginal comments: *ibid*. Northcote even contemplated at one stage leaving compulsory valuation out of the bill: see his letter of 22 Jan. to Cross (*ibid*.).

[3] See especially, *3 Hansard*, ccxxiv. 1186–99.

> borough seat will be endangered if its representatives vote for this 27th clause as it now stands.[1]

Callender's alarm was heeded, and the monetary limit on infant insurance was raised.

The Friendly Societies Bill provided almost as good an example as the dwellings bill of the way in which Conservative social legislation tended to be dominated by those ideas of freedom and self-reliance whose expression had hitherto been more commonly associated with classical Liberalism. The stability of the societies was a matter of national interest, but that the government should guarantee it was a proposition which neither Northcote, one of the last of the Peelites, nor Cross, one of the first of the new bourgeois Conservatives, could admit. A measure of state responsibility they were unable to avoid, but from the full paternalism which Barttelot and some others of their supporters had suggested, they shrank, both in principle and in fact.

The social reform bills of 1875 included two failures. One was the Rivers Pollution Bill; the other was the Merchant Shipping Bill. The prevention of loss of life at sea was possibly the most difficult of all the problems with which the government had to deal, and one which far outran the capacity of its President of the Board of Trade, Sir Charles Adderley.

When the Conservatives took office, the merchant shipping question was still dominated by the figure of the Liberal member for Derby, Samuel Plimsoll. The act of 1873, strengthening the power of the Board of Trade to detain unseaworthy ships, and the appointment in the same year of a Royal Commission, had by no means appeased Plimsoll, who continued to lead a vigorous agitation for compulsory survey of merchant vessels and the adoption of a load-line, as the only means by which the safety of the seamen could be adequately protected. Plimsoll was virtually at war with the Board of Trade: he attacked its officials for obstructiveness and questioned their integrity, while they spurned his proposals as impracticable and harmful, and regarded him as mendacious and irresponsible.[2] Neither side, in fact, was wholly unjustified in its allegations. Plimsoll, though his case was basically sound, was much prone to exaggeration and carelessness over details, and his methods were not always scrupulous. The Board's officials were highly conservative in outlook, mistrusted any increase

[1] Callender to Disraeli, 29 April 1875: Disraeli Papers, B/XXI/C/16. Callender thought 'at least 30 or 40' Conservatives would have to oppose the clause.

[2] On the Board's attitude to Plimsoll in 1873–4, see the papers in M.T. 9/70/M. 1856/73.

"DOING PENANCE."

Viscount Sandon

in legislative interference with merchant shipping, and were reluctant to work the act of 1873 with any rigour.

Having no knowledge of, and no gift for comprehending, the technicalities of the merchant shipping question, Adderley was very much in the hands of the officials, especially Farrer, the permanent secretary of the Board, and Gray, secretary of the Marine Department.[1] He accepted their *immobilisme* and detestation of Plimsoll, and he concurred with them in limiting drastically the operation of the act of 1873.[2] When Plimsoll again brought forward, in 1874, a bill for survey, load-line, and the prohibition during winter of the dangerous practice of deckloading, Adderley denounced it as 'a wild assumption on the part of Government of all responsibility on the subject'.[3] The argument of 'responsibility' was, as usual, employed by nearly all Plimsoll's opponents: to transfer responsibility for the safety of shipping to the state, it was held, would merely produce indifference in the individual, and so aggravate the evils complained of. A leading exponent of this point of view was a Tory member of the Royal Commission, Lord Eslington,[4] who deprecated encouraging seamen to go to the House for protection, and thought that the proper path was to make them more self-reliant.[5] But the debate made it clear that in face of the waste of human lives which Plimsoll was trying to stop, many members felt inclined to question the views of Adderley and Eslington. The second reading of Plimsoll's bill was lost only by 173 votes to 170, and in spite of the government whips there were 44 Conservatives in the minority.[6]

This division ought to have warned the government that it would meet trouble if it persisted in its refusal to sanction a greater degree of state intervention on behalf of the seamen. The influence of the Board of Trade, however, was strong, and was powerfully reinforced by the final report of the Royal Commission, which appeared in July 1874. The report insisted that the responsibility for the safety of shipping should not be transferred from the shipowners to the government, and rejected all Plimsoll's main proposals—compulsory survey and load-line, and the prohibition of deck cargoes.[7] Adderley and his ministerial colleagues were naturally inclined to accept the Commissioners' views. They had no desire to extend the area of government interference with private enterprise more than they could help, and

[1] Adderley's minutes on the papers of the Marine Department rarely consist of more than his initials.

[2] See especially his directive of 23 Nov. 1874, in M.T. 9/98/M.15576/74.

[3] *3 Hansard*, ccxx. 377.

[4] Formerly H. G. Liddell.

[5] *3 Hansard*, ccxx. 363.

[6] Another, Forsyth, was a teller.

[7] Final Report of Royal Commission on Unseaworthy Ships: *P.P.* 1874, xxxiv. 1. For the Commission's highly inconclusive preliminary report, of Sept. 1873, see *P.P.* 1873, xxxvi. 315.

much preferred to follow the policy, embodied in the acts of 1871 and 1873, of placing responsibility squarely on the individual and punishing him where he defaulted—the classical liberal policy of which Farrer was the high priest. Their aim, therefore, was not to make it impossible but to make it disadvantageous for owners to send unseaworthy or overloaded ships to sea. A good deal of opinion held that the best way of doing this was to tackle the question of marine insurance, and check that over-valuation which too often gave owners an interest in the loss of their vessels, and to this point Cairns and Northcote, with Farrer's backing, were giving careful attention at the beginning of 1875.[1] But the handling of marine insurance required ability in the responsible ministers, and what Northcote heard from his brother-in-law, Farrer, suggested that this was conspicuously lacking.

> The truth is [the Chancellor told Cairns] that the B. of Trade is very badly represented in the House of Commons. Adderley is a charming fellow, and willing to work, but has really no head for the kind of business with which he has to deal. And G.C.B.[2] is rather worse than useless to him. . . . Farrer is continually writing to me in great alarm at the prospects of the next Session . . . He likes Adderley personally, but complains that he cannot get him to understand questions, and that when they are brought forward in the House the shipowners or others get hold of him and lead him altogether astray.[3]

Perhaps because of these misgivings, the government's Merchant Shipping Bill, when it appeared in February 1875, did not deal with insurance, though Adderley confessed that this was 'at the root of the whole matter'.[4] Its main proposal was an attempt to bring the responsibility for safety home to the individual shipowner by subjecting him to unlimited liability in respect of damage to persons or property caused by knowingly sending unseaworthy ships to sea. Of the other provisions, perhaps the most important was that which, in accordance with the recommendations of the Royal Commission, made the advance note illegal.

The measure naturally incurred the contempt of Plimsoll and his allies, who went on pressing for survey and load line, and for the regulation of deck and grain cargoes. But it also incensed the shipowners: now that the government proposed stringently to enforce

[1] See Northcote to Cairns, 5 Jan. 1875, and Farrer to Northcote, 9 Jan. 1875 (typescript copies): Cairns Papers, vol. vi. Northcote had been entrusted by Disraeli with the task of maintaining liaison between Adderley and the cabinet (see Northcote to Adderley, 7 March 1874; copy, Add. MS. 50052, f. 3).

[2] George Cavendish Bentinck, Adderley's Parliamentary Secretary.

[3] Northcote to Cairns, 10 Jan. 1875 (typescript copy): Cairns Papers, vol. vi.

[4] 3 *Hansard*, ccxxii. 125.

their responsibility, many of them veered round to Plimsoll's ideas, which—since they partially transferred responsibility to the state—appeared as the lesser of the two evils.[1] Adderley was caught between the sailors' friends on the one hand and the representatives of the shipowning interest on the other, and as amendments to his bill showered down upon the notice paper, it became evident that the passage of the measure would be rough. Northcote told Disraeli on 2 April:

> The bill is one of a most critical character, politically speaking, and there are dangers on every side. Our shipowners hate it; and they distrust Adderley. Plimsoll and his followers mean to trip us up if possible; and he has a great many friends in our own ranks. . . .
>
> What is to come of it all I cannot foresee. If it were not for Plimsoll we might shunt the bill; but in face of his rival bill that is impossible.[2]

The prime minister was sufficiently impressed by the danger to give his personal attention to the bill (probably for the first time): after the second reading, he described complacently to Lady Bradford how he had been compelled to undertake 'the management of the whole case: a vast and most complicated case, and of wh. then I knew little', and how his exertions had resulted in a government triumph.[3]

However, it seems that it was Adderley and his officials who were directly responsible for the two important amendments announced on the second reading.[4] The first placated the shipowners by removing their unlimited liability; while the second threw a sop to the Plimsollites by providing for the voluntary observance of a load line. This was as far as the government was prepared to yield. Against a compulsory load line and compulsory survey Adderley remained firm, voicing a warning about mistaken legislation which 'might supple-

[1] See, e.g., the views of the shipowning Liberal member for Sunderland, Gourley, who complained that under the government scheme of unlimited liability 'the result of a single accident might be to reduce a millionaire to poverty' (*ibid.*, ccxxii. 134–5). He was supported by two more Liberal shipowners, Wilson (Hull) and Jenkins (Penryn) (*ibid.*, ccxxii. 136–7).

[2] Northcote to Disraeli, 2 April 1875: Add. MS. 50017, ff. 21–2. Northcote added that matters were not helped by Bentinck, who was talking 'freely and pretty loud' in the lobbies against the faults of the bill, and, apparently, against Adderley, with whom his relations were poor. Northcote was returning a complaining letter from Bentinck to Disraeli, of 29 March, which is to be found in the Disraeli Papers (box B, 'Miscellaneous—3rd Period', in old classification; not traced in new classification).

[3] Disraeli to Lady Bradford, 10 April 1875, in M. & B., v. 382. Cf. Disraeli to Lady Chesterfield, 9 April 1875, in *Letters to Lady Bradford*, i. 231.

[4] See Adderley to Disraeli, 6 April [1875], and the memorandum on the bill prepared for Disraeli on 7 April, accompanied by notes by Farrer and Disraeli, of 7 and 8 April respectively (Disraeli Papers, B/XXI/A/106; B/XII/B/2c, 2b, 2a).

ment the necessary perils of the sea by the graver perils of a Government protection still more treacherous and disastrous than the sea itself'.[1]

The changes did something to moderate opposition to the bill, and enabled it to pass the second reading without a division and with a large measure of favour. But Disraeli was premature in talking of triumphs, for neither the owners nor the Plimsollites were satisfied, and a long struggle was inevitable in Committee. Nor was it certain that in that struggle the solidity of the government majority could be maintained. As Northcote had said, Plimsoll had many friends on the Conservative benches. Sympathy for the hardships of seamen was just as widespread among Conservative members as among other sections of the community, and a number of Conservatives were driven to conclude that the interests of the men could be protected only by Plimsoll's recipe of compulsory load line and survey. The most vocal supporter of Plimsoll's proposals was David MacIver, member for Birkenhead, and a former partner in the great shipowning firm of Cunard. In the House and in a series of letters to Corry for Disraeli's eye, MacIver insisted that load line and survey would have to be introduced. The responsibilities which the Royal Commission and the Board of Trade wanted to lay upon owners were, he contended, 'a mere shadow that never had been, or could be, enforced'.[2] MacIver warned Corry that the government bill was inadequate, and would settle neither of the main questions—overloading and unseaworthiness—though they were easily capable of settlement.[3] He sought anxiously to dissuade ministers from capitulating to the self-interested representations of the less reputable owners, and preferring a sham 'responsibility' to genuine reform.

> To everybody with 'doubtful' shipping property [he wrote] the principle of 'survey' is—obviously—harassing and inconvenient. And the greater the necessity for Government supervision, the more such supervision is disliked.
>
> That is Sir Charles Adderley's difficulty; and, do what he will, he cannot equally please those interested in inferior shipping property and those who desire to stop needless waste of life at sea. Clause 33[4] of the Government Bill never could have originated with anybody who really wished to help Sir Charles to a solution of the 'load line' and 'survey' difficulties. They are *technical* questions involving (as I believe) no real difficulties to any practical steamship owner. We all know perfectly well that Mr Plimsoll's suggested remedies are in the right direction; but Mr Plimsoll's remedies are not agreeable—nor likely to be—to those whose property would be reached.

[1] *3 Hansard*, ccxxiii. 474a. [2] *Ibid.*, ccxxii. 1751.
[3] MacIver to Corry, 11 May 1875: Disraeli Papers, B/XXI/M/35.
[4] On load line.

> They prefer—naturally—the recommendations of the Royal Commissioners; and, simply, because those recommendations do *not* solve the difficulty. *They don't want it solved*, or the solution would be easy enough.[1]

MacIver's desire for real reform owed something to the feeling of his working-class constituents, who were strong for Plimsoll.[2] Gorst, too, doubtless had the opinions of the Chatham working men in mind when he lent his support to survey and load line.[3] But it was not mere vote-catching which gave rise to Conservative sympathy with Plimsoll, and moved the *Standard*, on 15 July, to press Adderley to accept compulsory survey, make further concessions on load line, and refuse to be trammelled by the obstructiveness of his permanent officials.

In spite of the unease behind them, however, ministers had no intention of changing their policy. The question was whether they could fight it through. When Committee was reached their bill immediately got into serious difficulties. The shipowning interest was out to smash it, Plimsoll and his friends to transform it, and 178 amendments stood to be discussed. It rapidly became clear that Adderley was incapable of coping with the situation.[4] The first serious challenge, on the proposal to abolish advance notes, saw the President retreating ignominiously step by step in face of criticism from both sides of the House on the ground of interference with freedom of contract, until Disraeli himself had finally to announce the abandonment of the clause, with a profession of his belief that 'the maintenance of freedom of contract is one of the necessary conditions of the commercial and manufacturing greatness of the country'.[5]

Northcote had foreseen the mess, and even before Committee began had, under Farrer's impulsion, recommended Disraeli to move Adderley and defer the bill.[6] The prime minister hesitated to do the first, but as the session advanced and the Merchant Shipping Bill came into competition for parliamentary time with the Agricultural Holdings Bill, which he was anxious to pass, he agreed to do the

1 MacIver to Corry, 10 July 1875: Disraeli Papers (box xvi, packet 24, in old classification; not traced in new classification).

2 In June he presented to the House, with full approval, a petition from the United Shipping Trades Council of Liverpool, calling for government inspection of shipping and a measure against overloading (see *3 Hansard*, ccxxiv. 1294–5, and MacIver to Corry, 3 June 1875, in Disraeli Papers, B/XXI/M/36).

3 *3 Hansard*, ccxxv. 109. He opposed, however, the abolition of advance notes.

4 For his incompetent handling of the bill in the House, see H. W. Lucy, *A Diary of Two Parliaments: the Disraeli Parliament 1874–1880*, pp. 93–5.

5 See *3 Hansard*, ccxxv. 133–8, 161–75.

6 Northcote to Disraeli, 15 June 1875: Add. MS. 50017, ff. 29–30.

second. On 22 July he announced that the bill could not be passed in that session.

The result was spectacular. Plimsoll staged a violent demonstration on the floor of the House, and his followers quickly raised a substantial agitation in the country. The government was represented as having callously chosen to put its Agricultural Holdings Bill before measures to save the lives of seamen. Disraeli and his colleagues had never grasped the depth of public feeling on the question, and they were surprised and disturbed by the clamour. Some members of the cabinet were for digging in their heels,[1] but it was finally decided that the only safe course was to bring in a limited measure designed to check loss of life until the whole problem could be tackled again in the next session.

There was still no question of accepting Plimsoll's policy. Disraeli looked upon 'the Sailors' Friend' as 'a Moody and Sankey in politics: half rogue and half enthusiast', and agreed with those who felt that his proposals 'wd. injure, not to say destroy, our mercantile marine'.[2] But for a moment it seemed doubtful whether Parliament and the country would tolerate anything less than Plimsoll's policy. The Conservative party itself could not be altogether relied upon: some, like Pell, thought Plimsoll's outburst in the Commons had been justified and necessary;[3] a number, like MacIver, were under pressure from their working-class constituents to give Plimsoll extended support.[4] Northcote warned his chief that the government would have to underplay the divergence between its approach and Plimsoll's.[5]

The Unseaworthy Ships Bill which Adderley introduced on 28 July increased the powers of the Board of Trade to stop unseaworthy vessels, and provided for the intensification of survey, which it allowed to be requisitioned by a quarter of a ship's crew. Its operation was limited to one year. The Plimsollites, of course, demanded something much stronger. MacIver complained that the bill would 'worry the shipowners without protecting the men',[6] and some pressure seems

[1] See Disraeli to Lady Bradford, 27 July 1875, in M. & B., v. 383–4. This and subsequent letters to Lady Bradford (*ibid.*, v. 385–7) give a vivid description of the alarms and excursions of the crisis.

[2] Disraeli to Lady Bradford, 10 April and 29 July 1875: *ibid.*, v. 382, 386. Zetland's version of the second letter (*Letters of Disraeli to Lady Bradford*, i. 269) makes Disraeli himself use the words quoted about Plimsoll's proposals.

[3] See Pell's *Reminiscences*, p. 285 (where the Plimsoll incident is misdated 22 June, instead of 22 July).

[4] See the report of a meeting of Birkenhead working men, 25 July 1875, in Disraeli Papers, B/XXI/M/40a.

[5] Northcote to Disraeli, 26 July 1875: Add. MS. 50017, ff. 42–3.

[6] *3 Hansard*, ccxxvi. 264. In a letter to Corry of 4 Aug. 1875, MacIver wrote: 'The Bill really contains the material which, unless modified, will "keep going"

to have been exerted on Conservative members by their constituents to get the government to revive the provisions of the abandoned bill.[1] Disraeli dared not risk defeat,[2] but he was unwilling to give much ground. The point of crisis came in Committee on 2 August, when the government was strongly pressed from both sides of the House to provide for some kind of load line, and finally agreed to a load line fixed by the owner, as in the original bill.[3] This concession saved the day, but it was touch and go: the Conservatives in the House, Disraeli wrote,[4] were 'Plimsollised *too* much', and had the opposition realised the state of the Conservative camp, they might have substituted their policy for his. As it was, the government succeeded in saving its face, and the emergency bill went through.

Disraeli and his colleagues put the principal blame for the *débâcle* of the Merchant Shipping Bill upon Adderley,[5] and determined to remove him from his post. But the substitution of Hicks Beach—Disraeli's first plan—involved too awkward a reshuffle, and Cave, the second choice for the job, declined.[6] Meanwhile, informed of his imminent supersession, Adderley ceased to attend to Board of Trade business, and the department's work therefore fell into confusion. Carnarvon told Salisbury on 3 October 1875:

[1] See a note by 'M.C.' [Corry] of 1 Aug. 1875: Add. MS. 50017, ff. 49–50.

[2] He told Lady Bradford on 28 July (M. & B., v. 385) that if defeated, he could not dissolve, 'for, in the present fever, I shd. probably get worsted . . .' Two days later, however, he noted with satisfaction the failure of 'Bradlaugh & Co.' to raise 'a Clerkenwell mob, as the people said they wd. not go agst. me, who had passed the Labor Laws for them' (*ibid.*, v. 387).

[3] See *3 Hansard*, ccxxvi. 379–431. Northcote and Adderley (the latter misunderstanding the point at issue) both resisted a load line, which was yielded ultimately by Disraeli in person.

[4] To Lady Chesterfield, 3 Aug. 1875 (*Letters of Disraeli to Lady Bradford*, i. 271–2). Cf. his letter of the same date to Lady Bradford, in M. & B., v. 387, where he says: 'it needed much tact and vigilance to mitigate, or conceal, our concessions . . .'

[5] This was perhaps not entirely fair. Though Adderley's handling of the measure was inept, he was much hampered by the failure of the cabinet (to which, of course, he had no direct access) to push the bill forward (see Childe-Pemberton, pp. 219–20). Farrer complimented him on 'the single-heartedness, unfailing temper, and unwearied zeal with which, under every discouragement, you have worked at the most difficult and delicate business I have ever known at the Board of Trade' (*ibid.*, p. 221). But Farrer had all along been criticising Adderley severely to Northcote. Disraeli was apparently inclined to think that Adderley had been badly treated by his officials (see Northcote to Disraeli, 25 July and 3 Aug. 1875: Add. MS. 50017, ff. 40–1, 53–5).

[6] There are a number of letters on this subject in the papers of Disraeli, Cairns, Hardy, Northcote, Salisbury, and Sandon. See also Childe-Pemberton, pp. 222–7; M. & B., v. 395–6.

---

a general growl against the Conservative party at every port in the Kingdom' (Disraeli Papers, B/XXI/M/41).

> Adderley has not been to the Office, everything is I hear getting into disorder *& nothing is being done to carry the Act of last Session into effect*![1]

In the upshot, Adderley had to be retained in the Presidency, despite the fact that his position was ridiculed even by his own party.[2] The Board was however somewhat strengthened by the removal of Bentinck and the appointment to the Parliamentary Secretaryship of the rising Edward Stanhope.

Adderley's resuscitation enabled a beginning to be made with the implementation of the provisions of the Unseaworthy Ships Act,[3] and preparations were set in train for comprehensive legislation in the session of 1876, Cairns, Cross, and Northcote being assigned to supervise the President over its details.[4] The force of the Plimsoll agitation had left its mark, and though ministers were still firmly opposed to Plimsoll's policy—being, for instance, determined not to carry load line any further than in the temporary act[5]—they had come to recognise that reliance on the principle of 'responsibility' alone would not do, and that a significant degree of government regulation was necessary. Northcote wrote to Farrer:

> The principle on which, as I conceive, we must legislate is that of bringing both classes of force, Government interposition and Shipowner's responsibility, fairly into play.

[1] Salisbury Papers, S.C. Cf. Northcote to Disraeli, 25 Sept. 1875, and Adderley to Northcote, 29 Sept. 1875: Add. MS. 50017, ff. 62–6, 68. Carnarvon thought Disraeli's lack of energy to blame for the situation, and spoke of 'how absolutely nerveless the hands on the reins are'.

[2] As Noel told Disraeli in a letter of 18 Nov. [1875]: Disraeli Papers, B/XXI/N/141.

[3] There was some difficulty with the civil servants over this. They disliked the increased interference with shipping contemplated by the act, and were unwilling to work it forcefully. When the bill was first introduced, Farrer told ministers that its operation, 'to be useful, must be limited'. 'It would be sanguine', he admitted, 'to expect that so limited it would do much to save life', but were it not limited, he did not see his way to taking any part in working it (memo. by Farrer, for Adderley, Bentinck, Northcote, and Cross, n.d. but circa 28 July 1875: M. 10973/75, in M.T. 9/122/M. 3069/76). Cf. Northcote to Disraeli, 3 Aug. 1875 (Add. MS. 50017, ff. 53–5), on the divergence of view between Farrer and the government as to the operation of the bill. When Plimsoll advised Adderley (in a letter published in *The Times*, 6 Aug. 1875) not to put the administration of the new measure in the hands of Farrer and Gray, because they were 'far too deeply committed to resistance of all preventive legislation for it to be anything but foolishness to trust them', he was not far wrong.

[4] See Northcote to Adderley, 7 Nov. 1875 (typescript copy; Add. MS. 50063 C, ff. 161–2), and Northcote to Cairns, 1 Nov. and 13 and 15 Dec. 1875 (typescript copies; Cairns Papers, vol. vi). According to his entry in the *D.N.B.* (xviii. 896), the Parliamentary Secretary, Stanhope, largely directed the drafting of the main government bill.

[5] Northcote to Adderley, 20 Nov. 1875, stating the views of the cabinet (copy): Add. MS. 50052, f. 146.

> I am not disposed to rely exclusively on either. Even if there were no excitement, I should favour a certain amount of Government interposition; and under existing circumstances I have no doubt that it is inevitable, and that the true policy even of the *laissez faire* school would now be, to endeavour to guide the Plimsoll movement, not to try to stem it; and at the same time endeavour to enforce the Shipowner's responsibility, concurrently with the strengthening of official control. I want to say to the Shipowners, in the face of the nation, we mean to do our part, and at the same time to insist on your doing your part, to prevent preventible evils: we recognize your general merits, and wont endorse all that is said against you: we recognize the immense importance of your industry, and desire,—not only in justice to you but on behalf of national interests and those of all classes (including sailors themselves) which are connected with you,—to get you fair play and secure you from needless restrictions: we desire, too, to help you to improve the character of your seamen, and to meet the difficulties of carrying on your business with imperfect means of enforcing discipline: but on the other hand we must insist that you shall not evade your responsibilities under the specious plea of freedom of contract, which is (or may be) a good enough plea as between the contracting parties, but is one to be very jealously scrutinized when it affects the lives of other persons.[1]

It is a noteworthy statement: its thought, shaped in the classical liberal mould, yet shows the effects of an empirical criticism of classical liberal tenets. The insistence on 'fair play' and no 'needless restrictions' mingles with the acceptance of stronger government action and the sceptical attitude towards 'freedom of contract' to create a frame of mind not uncommon in these years among Conservatives brought face to face with practical problems of state intervention in the economic and social sphere.

The dual approach favoured by Northcote found expression in two bills brought in at the beginning of 1876. One, devised by Northcote and Cairns, and handled by the former in the Commons, was designed to deal with the root question of marine insurance, and in particular to check over-valuation of ships for insurance purposes. The Chancellor recognised the seriousness of interfering with full freedom of contract, but asserted that when contracts involved the interests of third parties, it became the duty of the legislature to protect the latter's rights.[2] The other bill, in the hands of Adderley, was a general Merchant Shipping Bill, which made permanent the provisions of the temporary act of 1875, and among its new clauses included one to discourage the carrying of deck loads. Because of the inherent difficulties of the subject, and pressure of business, the

[1] Northcote to Farrer, 20 Nov. 1875 (copy): *ibid.*, ff. 146–7 (briefly quoted in Lang, ii. 81–2).

[2] *3 Hansard*, ccxxvii. 147.

insurance bill was not pushed through, but its companion measure gave rise to long and vigorous debates.

The Merchant Shipping Bill was strongly attacked by Plimsoll for its failure to incorporate compulsory survey and an officially-fixed load line. Adderley insisted that between Plimsoll's view and the government's there could be no compromise. Defending the ministry's preference for trying to prevent loss of life by enforcing judicial liability, instead of by tightening government regulation, he argued that the former plan

> was the ordinary mode of Government action in this country. In other matters the Government did not search every honest man, in order to catch offenders; but the principle was to lay hold of malefactors, and to leave all men to manage their own affairs, under the necessary conditions of responsibility to others for the consequences of any carelessness or neglect on their part.[1]

As before, there were those on Adderley's own benches who felt his line of policy mistaken, and preferred Plimsoll's ideas. MacIver, continuing to oppose reliance on the principle of enforcing owners' responsibility, protested strongly against the clause of the new bill which reaffirmed the legislation of 1871 by penalising those who despatched unseaworthy ships, on the ground that as framed it would strike the innocent and respectable owners rather than the guilty, and he asserted that it had been pushed on the government by a section of the owners, who wanted to avoid the regulatory legislation which was really required.[2] Gorst gave support to Plimsoll,[3] and urged the government to relieve the seamen from the harsh laws to which they were subject in their relations with their employers by applying to the merchant service the principles of Cross's labour legislation—a demand which Adderley resisted on the ground that the labour of seamen was a special case, adding, rather curiously, that 'there was no class of workmen so nursed by the law, and who had so many advantages given them'.[4]

[1] *Ibid.*, ccxxviii. 640–1. For Adderley's conduct of the bill, see Lucy (*Diary of Two Parliaments*, pp. 141–4, 145–8), who says that Disraeli kept away from the Committee debates to avoid the embarrassment.

[2] See *ibid.*, ccxxviii. 544–7, and MacIver to Corry, 29 March 1876 (Disraeli Papers, B/XXI/M/36c). MacIver's opposition to the clause was greatly sharpened by a legal case which, he told Corry, had awakened the respectable shipowners to the fact that 'the legislation which we thought was waste paper—and therefore harmless—may any day become an unpleasant reality; and a reality only as against respectable people and *not* as against the premeditating rogue'. He was satisfied with the owners' load line provided by the act of 1875, and held that the government should now provide for survey at the owner's request.

[3] *3 Hansard*, ccxxviii. 660–2.

[4] See *ibid.*, ccxxvii. 435–7; ccxxviii. 519–39; ccxxix. 221–7. Gorst received

In spite of considerable criticism, however, the bill did not run upon the quicksands which had swallowed up its predecessor. The main challenge to the government's policy, by Plimsoll on 27 March, was crushed by 247 votes to 110. The major ministerial reverse came on deck loads. The government's provisions against these were regarded by a number of its own supporters as too weak, and Plimsoll eventually carried an amendment designed to prohibit the dangerous practice of deck-loading timber during the winter months by 162 votes to 143.[1] Some sharp practice followed: ministers used the Lords to alter this and other clauses, and Northcote suggested to Richmond that he should delay the passage of the bill in the Upper House so as to shorten the interval for agitation against these changes between their passage by the Lords and their review by the Commons.[2] When the amended bill did reach the Commons, Gorst and Plimsoll accused the government of getting the Lords to implement the wishes of the Board of Trade officials, and supported MacIver in moving the rejection of the measure on the ground that the Lords' amendments were unacceptable.[3] But this final challenge could not prevent the bill from passing into law.

The handling of the merchant shipping question in 1875–6 provides yet another example of the way in which the social legislation of the ministry was permeated less by paternalistic ideas than by the notions of freedom and individualism characteristic of classical liberalism. There can be little doubt that the problems at issue really required a paternalistic solution: Plimsoll was right in contending that only largely increased state intervention could secure the safety of the merchant service. Yet increased state intervention in the concerns of private enterprise was just as abhorrent to Disraeli and his colleagues as to their Liberal predecessors, and, like their Liberal predecessors, they clung in preference to the dubious principle of

[1] See *3 Hansard*, ccxxviii. 1590–1622, 1921–43; ccxxix. 1077–9. The Conservative critics included Eslington, MacIver, Read, and Ritchie. Plimsoll also got the government to accept an amendment penalising submergence of the load line (*ibid.*, ccxxviii. 1880–3).

[2] Northcote to Richmond, 1 July 1876: Goodwood Papers, box 31.

[3] For the debate, see *3 Hansard*, ccxxxi. 1162–84. Other Conservatives who supported MacIver's motion for rejection were Pim and Cavendish Bentinck. The objection to the amendments was, in general, that they weakened the bill, but one which strengthened it in the matter of detention of unsound vessels by the Board of Trade also came under fire from MacIver and Gorst, and from Henley and Bates.

strong backing from such Liberals as Forster, Mundella, Burt, and Macdonald, but no Conservative supported him. The extension of Cross's legislation to seamen was being demanded by the trades unionists: see G. Howell and H. Broadhurst (Chairman and Secretary of the T.U.C. Parliamentary Committee) to Disraeli, 25 April 1876 (Disraeli Papers, B/XII/C/88f).

enforcing responsibility on the individual—that is to say, letting him commit as many misdemeanours as he liked, subject to an uncertain retribution afterwards. This policy was accepted by ministers primarily because they conscientiously agreed with it; not because it was the only one which that dogmatic free-trader and departmental dictator Farrer was prepared to work loyally. Most of the party concurred: MacIver and Gorst were certainly in a minority. The policy was patently inadequate, and it involved ministers in a head-on collision with a public opinion of which they had hitherto been almost unaware. Nonetheless, they preserved it virtually intact, even in the *débâcle* of July–August 1875. The only serious concession made to Plimsoll's views was the introduction of owners' load line—a weak provision, and very different from the load line Plimsoll wanted. The act of 1876 was far from ensuring the safety of the merchant seaman, and it did very little to promote his general welfare.[1] It was, in fact, a prime instance of Liberal-Conservatism in its most liberal mood.

'Upon the education of the people of this country the fate of this country depends', said Disraeli in June 1874.[2] His supporters were in no doubt of it, and the education question was, as usual, the social problem about which the Conservative party as a whole showed most concern. Convinced of its importance as a fundamental prop of the established order of society, Conservatives were determined to maintain the voluntary, denominational system—which still provided much the greater part of the nation's elementary education[3]—against the challenge of the new school board system, a mission for which, it could be argued, the result of the general election had given them a mandate. Especially were they anxious to minimise the spread of the board system in the rural areas, upon which, as always, their thoughts principally centred, and where the intrusion of elected boards, with their powers of compulsion and rating, meant, in their eyes, fresh burdens on real property, interference with the labour supply, a threat to the dominance of squire and parson, and an unwelcome outburst of political activity among hitherto quiescent populations.

[1] The government all along showed small inclination to deal with the demands of the seamen themselves, which included not only safety measures but such points as better diet, abolition of advance notes, speedier payment of wages, and a national pension fund (see the memorial of the Liverpool Seamen's Protective Society to Disraeli, 28 Feb. 1876, in M.T. 9/123/M.4251/76).

[2] *3 Hansard*, ccxix. 1618.

[3] Sandon told the Commons that in August 1875 there were in England and Wales 12,081 voluntary public elementary schools, with an average attendance of 1,600,000, and 1,136 board schools, with an average attendance of 227,000 (*ibid.*, ccxxvii. 1204–5).

As the 'seventies wore on, it was increasingly obvious that the contest between the voluntary and board systems was heavily weighted in favour of the latter. Hampered by rising costs, poor attendance, and the difficulty of securing subscriptions, the voluntaryists were at a severe disadvantage compared with boards backed by rates and the power of compulsion. Sir Massey Lopes voiced a general Conservative worry when he told Sandon in January 1875:

> I am satisfied that Voluntary Schools will not be able much longer to hold their own in the Rural Districts, on account of increasing expences [*sic*], & not being able to secure a [? proportionate] amount of Government assistance owing to the attendance of children being so small & so irregular.[1]

How best to aid denominational education in its struggle was a question which engaged much Conservative attention. It was generally acknowledged that whatever was done must be done within the broad confines of the settlement of 1870: only a few right-wing optimists like Beauchamp, Thomas Collins, and Sir William Heathcote seriously hoped that a Tory Government would overturn that settlement, and by repealing the Cowper-Temple clause allow denominational teaching to be given in the board schools.[2] A favourite project for helping the voluntaryists was to allow the ratepayer either to allocate his education rate to a voluntary school or to deduct from the rate the amount of his voluntary subscriptions. This would shore up the voluntary schools in areas where they were in direct competition with board schools, and were suffering from the reluctance of their friends to pay subscriptions on top of rates, and would dispose of the grievance created by churchmen being obliged to pay rates for undenominational or secular teaching. But it was clear that for voluntary schools in general the best stimulant would be a substantial increase in attendance, with its concomitant rise in income. It was this consideration which was largely responsible for the change perceptible by 1875 in Conservative attitudes towards the question of general compulsion.

Forster's act was doing its work: soon, Sandon told the Commons in June 1874, the whole country would be adequately provided with schools; the great need now was to raise the deplorably low level of attendance.[3] The central issue of educational politics in the middle

[1] Lopes to Sandon, 8 Jan. 1875: Harrowby Papers, vol. liii, ff. 151–2. Cf. Heygate, *3 Hansard*, ccxxv. 835 ff.

[2] See Beauchamp to Disraeli, 9 Nov. 1874, with pamphlet by Canon Gregory (Disraeli Papers, B/XX/Ln/68, 69); Collins to Salisbury, 22 Feb. 1874, and Heathcote to Salisbury, 11 Dec. 1875 (Salisbury Papers, S.C.).

[3] *3 Hansard*, ccxix. 1638, 1640.

of the 'seventies was whether the time had come to fill the schools by the universal application of compulsion—already, of course, widely in operation under the auspices of the boards.[1] The Liberals thought that it had: Forster was strong for general compulsion, and Dixon brought in bills in 1874, 1875, and 1876 providing for its application through the agency of universal school boards. On the Conservative benches, the traditional hostility to compulsion began to wane as the conviction grew that in order not only to advance education but also to save voluntaryism it had become essential to drive the children into the schools.

Some Conservatives, certainly, were still strongly opposed to compulsion. Eslington and others attacked the enforcement of compulsory bye-laws on poor people who needed their children's earnings.[2] Rodwell believed that in the agricultural districts compulsion would be impossible to carry out.[3] The bulk of the party, however, was turning the other way. More and more Conservatives were heard to support compulsion. They resisted, of course, Dixon's method of securing it—universal school boards. Birley, spokesman of the Education Union, suggested that the principle of the factory acts might be generally applied and a certain educational standard made a condition of children's employment.[4] Others wanted compulsory powers to be entrusted to the voluntary schools or to local bodies other than school boards.[5] But whatever the means, the end was increasingly accepted as inevitable.

It was against this background that Richmond and Sandon presided over the Education Department. The former was a man of little calibre with no particular interest in education, an aristocratic amateur of the old type, whose main concern seems to have been to get the business of the session over and depart to the Scottish moors

[1] By 1873 40% of the population was under compulsory bye-laws, and by 1876 50% (84% in boroughs) (Smith, p. 296). Compulsion was also applied by Forster's act of 1873 and by the factory acts, though, according to Cross in Feb. 1875, the amount of attendance enforced under the latter was 'a mere shadow' (*3 Hansard*, ccxxii. 562).

[2] *Ibid.*, ccxxiv. 156, 1389–93; ccxxv. 799–813. As the Earl of Stradbroke pointed out to Richmond in a letter of 17 Jan. 1875 (Goodwood Papers, box 31), depriving poor families of their children's earnings often meant that they came upon the poor rate, thus increasing the burdens on real property.

[3] *3 Hansard*, ccxxv. 847–8.

[4] *Ibid.*, ccxix. 1645; ccxx. 813. W. U. Heygate took the same view: see his letter to Sandon, 20 Dec. 1875 (Harrowby Papers, vol. liii, ff. 76–7).

[5] See *3 Hansard*, ccxx. 834–5 (Grantham); ccxxii. 1089–90 (Brise); and Rev. G. Portal to Carnarvon, 18 Nov. 1875 (P.R.O. 30/6/22, no. 124). Salt, Lord Francis Hervey, and Hermon produced early in 1875 a School Attendance in Towns Bill (*P.P.* 1875, vi. 155), providing that where a town had no school board, the municipal or urban authority might exercise compulsory powers.

with that other hammer of the grouse, Lord Cairns.[1] To Sandon and Carnarvon he seemed to possess 'no knowledge of the feeling of the Country, or sympathy with the people, or anything approaching to intellectual grasp',[2] and his insistence, against custom, on regarding himself, rather than Sandon, as the minister of education, and exercising control of the department, was irritating to the latter, who had to bear the whole responsibility for educational affairs in the Commons, and was looked on by the country as the man responsible for educational policy. Sandon was an enthusiast for educational advance, and a very stout supporter of the denominational system. He aimed to steer a middle course between the demands of the Liberal activists on the one hand and the Conservative rank and file—of whose judgement in educational matters he had no great opinion[3]—on the other, and soon succeeded in winning plaudits from opponents as well as friends for his diligence and goodwill.

At first the new ministers did not appear eager to promote educational progress. They lowered the educational standard at which pauper children educated under the 1873 act were released from school,[4] and resisted Lord Hampton's (i.e. Pakington's) call for a separate Education Minister.[5] But beneath the surface Sandon, at least, impressed by the necessity of simultaneously improving attendance and revivifying the voluntary schools, was maturing large plans, and in November 1874 his scheme for a general compulsory measure was circulated to the cabinet.

[1] See his letters to Cairns of 29 July 1875 and 25 July 1876 (typescript copies): Cairns Papers, vols. vi and vii.

[2] Memo. by Sandon of conversation with Carnarvon, 18 Jan. 1876: Harrowby Papers, vol. lv, ff. 181–2.

[3] Years later, as Earl of Harrowby, he told Cranbrook (i.e. Hardy): 'I care nothing for the temporary feeling of our Conservative rank & file in the House of Commons—they have been always, as I am informed they still are, completely ignorant of the Education question & all its difficulties & dangers . . .' (letter of 27 June 1891: Cranbrook Papers, T501/146).

[4] See *3 Hansard*, ccxviii. 1707–35. Sclater-Booth, who had pressed for the alteration, said it was desirable that education under the 1873 act should be of an inferior kind.

[5] See *ibid.*, ccxix. 682–96, 1589–1623. In a letter of 15 June 1884, Sandon (now Harrowby) told Salisbury that he opposed the idea because 'the danger of a single Minister during Liberal rule would be most serious—the Liberals are keeping steadily in view universal school boards, the extinction of the Voluntary Schools, and the control from Whitehall of secondary & higher education. When they are in office, either a revolutionist or an educational "prig" (so to speak) will always be Education Minister in the Commons—hitherto the Lord President has been (& would probably continue) without any special Educatl. knowledge—you have therefore had the check of a layman on professional vagaries. . . . The subject is of much wider importance to Church and State than our ordinary men would see' (Salisbury Papers, S.C.).

In his memorandum on the scheme,[1] Sandon argued that general compulsion required immediate consideration for three reasons, 'looking at it from a political point of view'. Firstly, there was enough Conservative support for general compulsion to make the issue of a division doubtful if (as expected) Liberals introduced a well-planned compulsory measure in the next session—'I know', Sandon wrote, 'that many supporters of the Government are in favour of such a measure in the interest of the Voluntary schools, as well as on its educational merits.' Secondly, the confusion of the various acts on the labour and school attendance of children was becoming intolerable. Thirdly, and most important, was the urgency of propping up the voluntary schools in order to keep the school boards out of the countryside. Sandon explained, with a frankness impossible in public, why boards were so undesirable:

> School Boards (or some such agency) were, I believe, necessary for the large towns, and are productive of no political evil; but in the smaller country towns and in villages (besides their acknowledged inconveniences) I am convinced they will produce very serious political results. They will become the favourite platforms of the Dissenting preacher and local agitator, and will provide for our rural populations, by means of their triennial elections and Board meetings, exactly the training in political agitation and the opportunity for political organization which the politicians of the Birmingham League desire, and which will be mischievous to the State.

No clearer illustration of the determination of Conservatives not to let anything threaten the roots of their power in the inert and subservient rural communities was ever penned. Sandon went on to show that without the financial benefits resulting from increased attendance, the voluntaryists would be unable to carry the burden of providing for the educational needs of the rural areas, and would have to give way to boards. The Inspectors of Schools reported the voluntary school managers and clergy strong for compulsion, and the labouring class as 'generally not unfavourable', though many of the farmers were 'hostile to all education'.[2]

Sandon proposed to prohibit at first the employment of children

[1] 'Memorandum on the Political Effects of School Boards as Bearing Upon the Question of Fresh Legislation Respecting Compulsory Education', Nov. 1874. Printed copy in P.R.O. 30/6/72, pp. 151–65.

[2] The farmers were increasingly worried that the labouring class might become better educated than some of their employers. A committee on middle-class education in rural districts appointed by the council of the Central Chamber of Agriculture, and chaired by Hicks Beach, had noted in November 1873 that the extension of elementary education might shortly provide better education for labourers' children than the children of the middle classes could obtain (Matthews, p. 310).

under nine, and later of children under ten, during school terms, and to require such children to attend school full-time. Their education might be continued half-time up to thirteen, at the discretion of the local authorities, which were to be town councils, improvement commissioners, and local boards in urban areas, and school attendance committees in rural areas. Parents unable to pay school fees were to apply to the relieving officer.

> By a Bill of this kind we shall have made general School Boards unlikely, if not impossible, hereafter; shall probably have paved the way for the abolition of the minor existing School Boards, and shall, I am pretty confident, secure, by gradual local pressure, the early and steady training of all the population, more important than their actual learning, as well as the maintenance of the great bulk of the Country Voluntary Schools, to whom the question of general compulsion has become under the Education Act of 1870 a matter of life and death.

Sandon's proposals were too drastic for the cabinet. Richmond—while telling Disraeli: 'I confess he has made out a stronger case than I thought was possible'[1]—was averse from general compulsion, and Malmesbury commented:

> . . . I think that if it is stretched as far as Sandon's opinions there will be a row among the labourers or the ratepayers or both before it has been long in force.[2]

In face of the cabinet's caution, the backing accorded to Sandon's ideas by such junior members of the government as W. H. Smith and Massey Lopes[3] availed little. No bill was framed, and the ministry's action on the educational front in 1875 was limited to the introduction of a new Education Code, whose general effect was to raise the standards necessary for the attainment of government grants and to encourage the teaching of subjects beyond the three Rs.

Nevertheless, the question of compulsion was impossible to evade for long. Governmental inaction became even more difficult to justify after Fawcett's motion on the school attendance of children employed in agriculture had drawn attention to the extreme deficiencies of rural education, and to the fact that Read's Agricultural Children Act of 1873 was in most places proving a dead letter, for lack of any machinery of enforcement or attempt on the part of the

[1] Richmond to Disraeli, 18 Nov. 1874: Disraeli Papers, B/XX/Le/58.

[2] Malmesbury to Richmond, 23 Jan. 1875: Goodwood Papers, box 31. From Malmesbury to Richmond, 10 June 1875 (*ibid.*), it transpires that the Queen was much concerned about compulsion: 'Upon an excess of this', Malmesbury wrote, '& on vivisection there can be no mistake as to her feeling . . .'

[3] See Smith to Sandon, 21 Nov. 1874, and Lopes to Sandon, 8 Jan. 1875: Harrowby Papers, vol. liv, ff. 150–3, vol. liii, ff. 151–2.

government to have it enforced.[1] By the autumn of 1875, while Richmond was hoping that the ministry would do as little as possible in the educational field,[2] Cross was strongly advocating compulsion,[3] and Sandon was preparing a second scheme for a bill.

The Vice-President put his case to the cabinet in a memorandum of November 1875.[4] He contended that the failure of the Agricultural Children Act placed the government in a difficult position. The Conservative party, which took credit for having promoted the factory legislation which provided education for children employed in industry, was now allowing to be inoperative the only act covering agricultural children, 'in whose labour we may be held to be principally interested as employers', and, continued Sandon,

> we refuse to support or to propose any other measure for securing for the rural working population that education which we lose no opportunity of pluming ourselves upon having made indispensable for the same class in the towns.

Sandon did not see what answer could be made in the forthcoming session to appeals to enforce Read's act, and was doubtful of the result of a division on any scheme for securing attendance without the use of school boards.[5]

> All must agree, I imagine [he wrote], that it is not worth while now to enter upon an argument as to whether it is desirable or not that the working people in Town or Country should have instruction (though one cannot ignore the fact that a distrust of the effect of universal education still underlies the opposition of some of our friends in Parliament to any action on these matters); the general policy of the country must, I take

[1] For the debate on Fawcett's motion, see *3 Hansard*, ccxxii. 1054–1123, and on the failure of Read's Act, Robson, pp. 181–2. Many Conservatives were hostile to the implementation of Read's act because of the way in which it would interfere with the farmers' labour supply, but others hoped that if put into effect it would obviate the need for general compulsion and school boards. Disraeli, apparently, as a Bucks. magistrate, opposed the enforcement of the act in his county, and so drew a reproach from Pell (see *3 Hansard*, ccxxvii. 130, 131–2; ccxxviii. 1282), but his action may have been due to the knowledge that the government was preparing to deal comprehensively with the compulsion question.

[2] Richmond to Disraeli, 8 Oct. 1875: Disraeli Papers, B/XX/Le/83.

[3] See his speech in Lancashire reported in *The Times*, 22 Sept. 1875.

[4] 'Memorandum on the Position of the Agricultural Children's Act, and the further Legislation which it seems to require', followed by 'Memorandum on various other Proposed Amendments of the Education Acts' (printed copy, dated in MS. 4 Nov. 1875, in P.R.O. 30/6/72, pp. 189–211). A draft of this memorandum (with small divergences) exists in the Harrowby Papers, vol. lv, ff. 136–80.

[5] He noted that three Conservative M.P.s (unnamed) were preparing a bill for compulsion without boards.

> it, be considered settled, and that—for good or for evil—instruction is to be universal. In this case, the sooner elementary instruction becomes universally a matter of course, the sooner will the conceit of the exceptional possession of elementary knowledge be got rid of, and the safer will it be for the community at large. I cannot see that we shall secure any adequate compensating advantage to the Nation, or any Party in it, by allowing, in obedience to the most timid section of our Supporters, the Country to become possessed with the notion that it is the policy of the Conservative party to grudge and to restrict the education of our people.

The government's proper course, Sandon argued, was 'to make the education given as sound, as sensible, as moral and religious, as universal as possible', and to keep the leadership of the education movement out of the hands of its opponents, who might use it 'for purposes which we believe to be mischievous to the Country, and which timely action on our part may make impossible'.

Sandon went on to list in detail the educational objects which he felt the ministry should pursue. One of them was to minimise the number of school boards.

> It cannot be too often repeated that School Boards, though politically harmless and often highly necessary in large towns, are of the worst political effect in small communities, where they afford the platform and the notoriety specially needed by the political Dissenting Ministers (many of them, to my mind, the most active and effective revolutionary agents of the day), and also provide a ready machinery for lowering the legitimate and useful influence of the leading personages of the place.

Another great object was, of course,

> To preserve the Voluntary School System—as being much less costly than that of the Boards; as having an important social influence in the country; as offering a better security for moral and religious teaching; and as being indirectly a great and legitimate source of strength to the Church.

As to the method of securing attendance, Sandon wished

> To avoid the machinery and vexation of direct compulsory attendance at school (unless adopted by the free choice of a locality), for the children of the industrious poor, and to work, by indirect compulsion and the offer of advantages for school attendance and success, instead of by penalties and attendance officers.

This preference for indirect compulsion was embodied in Sandon's concrete proposals. He wanted to forbid the employment of children under ten, and make the possession of a certificate either of school attendance or of having passed a given standard a condition of employment at ten. To encourage attendance after ten, he suggested offering to children who reached a certain standard prize free education up to fourteen. In areas without school boards these measures were to be enforced by school committees, elected by existing local authorities, with power to make compulsory bye-laws.

Such a scheme, Sandon hoped, would reinvigorate the denominational schools by forcing the children into them. Some other proposals for helping denominationalism, however, he felt obliged to reject—allocation of rates and the counting of subscriptions in lieu of rates among them.[1] He rejected, too, the repeal of the Cowper-Temple clause, but he was deeply worried by what he held to be the declining position of religious instruction under the act of 1870, and wanted to make the use of the Bible compulsory in all schools, so as to provide some security for the moral and religious training of the working classes.

With the circulation of Sandon's memorandum, discussions began again on the possibility of an education measure. Richmond took issue with the views of his subordinate, and argued that the best plan would be to give rural districts the option of adopting compulsory bye-laws worked by the guardians, rather than to introduce

> what would be called by our opponents a retrograde proposal to enforce school attendance on agricultural children *only up to ten years of age.* For the boon of Free Schooling (10s. per annum) would be illusory in the case of poor parents, who require, not relief from the payment of the school fee of 2d. a-week, but the wages earned by their children; while the greater part of the 150,000*l.* to be paid out of the Consolidated Fund for Queen's Scholars[2] would merely go into the pockets of the town artizan and shopkeeper class, whose children attend Public Elementary Schools, and who certainly do not need such relief. The proposal, moreover, would be regarded as the first step to a system of universal Free Schooling.[3]

The cabinet, however, was more impressed by Sandon's arguments, and on 17 November took the decision to introduce a bill embodying his leading principles.[4] The framing of this measure caused some trouble. Richmond kept it very much under his own control, and Sandon, easily excitable, felt that he was not being sufficiently consulted, and tried to assert his position.[5] On the precise content of the

[1] He actually favoured the second idea, but could not see how to work it.

[2] The title proposed by Sandon for those in receipt of prize free education.

[3] Cabinet memorandum by Richmond, 8 Nov. 1875 (printed copy in P.R.O. 30/6/72, pp. 185–8).

[4] See Sandon's note of 7 Jan. 1876 on a letter from Richmond of 17 Nov. 1875: Harrowby Papers, vol. liii, f. 331.

[5] See Sandon to Richmond, 23 and 25 Nov. 1875 (Goodwood Papers, box

bill, it proved difficult to reach agreement, largely because of the determination Sandon showed to press his point about compulsory religious instruction.

The work of formulating the measure was in the hands of a committee consisting of Richmond, Sandon, Salisbury, and Hardy.[1] In January 1876 Sandon circulated a paper on the religious instruction issue,[2] in which he contended that the existing educational system operated in such a way as positively to discourage religious instruction, and that their proposed legislation would tend to aggravate the evil. He wrote:

> we have every prospect of seeing shortly between three and four millions of the Children of the Country trained by an army of some 20,000 skilled Teachers, aided by some 30,000 Pupil Teachers—having received no special Religious and Moral teaching themselves, uncontrolled like the regular Civil Service by the conditions of Pensions, restless, over-educated, and dissatisfied with their position—a serious danger to the State and to Society—and not unlikely to communicate their feelings to their pupils—and all this the result of State action, and contrary to the evident wishes of the country . . .

In order to ensure the religious and moral training of the working population, Sandon wanted to prescribe religious instruction in all schools. To him, this question was more important than anything else,[3] and he believed that his proposal would not only serve religion and morality but also be a shrewd move politically, for, he assured Corry, it would be popular with the party and the country, and would 'split every Dissenting Community, & be checkmate to Forster, whose position would be an awkward one'.[4]

Sandon's views were supported, apparently, by Salisbury, Hardy,

[1] See Hardy's diary, 20 and 26 Jan. 1876: Cranbrook Papers, T501/296.

[2] Printed copies, with MS. additions and corrections, in P.R.O. 30/6/72, pp. 51–4, and Disraeli Papers, B/XXI/S/42b.

[3] See, e.g. his letter to his wife, 23 Jan. 1876: Harrowby Papers, vol. xlv, ff. 123–4.

[4] Sandon to Corry, 26 Jan. 1876: Disraeli Papers, B/XXI/S/42. The blending (without conscious hypocrisy) of sacred and profane motives is characteristic of Sandon.

31), and Richmond to Sandon, 23 Nov. and 1 Dec. 1875 (Harrowby Papers, vol. liii, ff. 332–7). Richmond put the matter before Disraeli, writing of his subordinate: 'He is by nature a fidgetty fussy fellow, and is more than commonly interested upon the subject of Education' (Richmond to Disraeli 24 and 28 Nov. 1875; Disraeli Papers, B/XX/Le/90, 92). Disraeli himself felt that Sandon was 'a little impetuous, with the best meaning in the world' (to Richmond, 27 Nov. 1875; Goodwood Papers, box 31). See also W. H. Smith to Sandon, 30 Nov. and 13 Dec. 1875: Harrowby Papers, vol. liv, ff. 163–7.

Northcote, and Carnarvon,[1] but the cabinet finally baulked at the step suggested, though leaving open the question of what was to be done if it was proposed from the Conservative back benches.[2] Over the bill as a whole, however, Sandon got what he wanted, after some dissensions.[3] As finally drawn, the measure followed closely his November memorandum, somewhat to the unease of Richmond, who grumbled to Hardy: 'I am afraid we have gone much nearer direct and universal compulsion than we intended at first.'[4]

The ministry's resolve to legislate was reinforced by growing pressure from its supporters to do something effective for the voluntary schools. Talbot urged action on behalf of the Churchpeople, who were disappointed with the fruits of Conservative government.[5] A conference of Conservative provincial leaders passed unanimously a resolution summoning the ministry to bring in a measure to aid the denominationalists, and favoured the granting of compulsory powers to local authorities in districts without school boards.[6] And in

[1] See Sandon to Lady Mary Sandon, 17 and 23 Jan. 1876, and Salisbury to Sandon, 23 Jan. 1876: Harrowby Papers, vol. xlv, ff. 121–4; vol. liv, ff. 3–4. Hardy was especially keen to do something for religious education and the denominational schools. In November, he had proposed even that the condition requiring voluntary schools to raise a certain sum in subscriptions in order to get a government grant should be removed, and had told Richmond that he thought the Conservative majority in many boroughs might turn upon support for the voluntary against the board system. Richmond thought his proposal impolitic (see Hardy to Richmond, 26 Nov. 1875, and Richmond to Sandon, 1 Dec. 1875; *ibid.*, vol. liii, ff. 334–9).

[2] Sandon to Lady Mary Sandon, 3 Feb. 1876: *ibid.*, vol. xlv, ff. 129–30.

[3] See Sandon to Lady Mary Sandon, 31 Jan., 1 and 3 Feb. 1876: *ibid.*, vol. xlv, ff. 126–30. From Hardy's diary, 26 Jan. 1876 (Cranbrook Papers, T501/296) it emerges that 'Salisbury & Sandon were for rather stronger measures than Richmond & self'. Sandon's tendency to change his mind about points already agreed irked Richmond, who traced the trouble to the fact that the Vice-President's private secretary had been Forster's secretary, 'and he discusses the matter over with him and gets the Forster view and what Forster will say to this that and the other proposal as we make them' (Richmond to Hardy, 27 Jan. [1876]: *ibid.*, T501/257). The official referred to was presumably Patric Cumin, a strong supporter of the board system, with Liberal and anti-denominational sympathies, on whom see W. H. G. Armytage, 'Patric Cumin, 1823–1890', *Bulletin of the John Rylands Library*, xxx (1946–7), 271–7.

[4] Richmond to Hardy, 25 Jan. 1876: Cranbrook Papers, T501/257.

[5] Talbot to Salisbury, 2 Nov. 1875 (Salisbury Papers, S.C.); to Carnarvon, 2 Nov. 1875 (P.R.O. 30/6/22, no. 159; for Carnarvon's non-committal reply, see *ibid.*, no. 160).

[6] See Gorst to Sir W. Hart Dyke (the whip), 21 Dec. 1875 (Disraeli Papers, B/XXI/D/466a); Gorst to Salisbury, 30 Dec. 1875 (Salisbury Papers, S.C.). Gorst did, however, report misgivings in some minds: Conservative members of school boards in Hull and Sheffield, where the voluntaryists were in a strong position, had no wish to disturb the *status quo*, and a number of Yorkshire Conservatives feared that a move in favour of the voluntary schools would

February 1876 a powerful deputation to Richmond, headed by the Archbishop of Canterbury, and including a number of Conservative members of Parliament, requested help for the voluntary schools and the extension of compulsory powers.[1] At the same time, a Royal Commission which the government had set up to inquire into the working of the factory acts produced a report which, in effect, recommended direct compulsion, with full-time education up to the age of ten and half-time after ten.[2] Even the National Society now accepted compulsion as inevitable,[3] and the council of the Central Chamber of Agriculture was prepared to support not only the granting of compulsory powers to sanitary authorities but also permissive rating in districts without school boards.[4]

The ministry's Education Bill was introduced by Sandon in May 1876. It forbade the employment of children under ten, and made a certificate either of the attainment of a certain standard or of a certain amount of attendance a condition of the employment of children between ten and fourteen.[5] This was the core of the measure, designed, Sandon said, to fix the responsibility for education primarily on the parent, by making it his interest to send his child to school.[6] The enforcing authorities were to be school boards, where they existed, and elsewhere town councils and boards of guardians, which might act through school attendance committees, and which were to have power to pass compulsory bye-laws. There was special provision for action against parents who neglected the education of children under ten. Children who, at ten, passed the required standard and possessed the attendance certificate were to be offered free education for the next three years. In districts without school boards, the guardians were empowered to pay fees for poor children. Government aid to the poorer schools was to be increased, and a great fillip was given to the finances of the voluntary schools by the raising of the maximum *per capita* grant and the abolition of the rule that the parliamentary grant must not exceed a school's income from fees and subscriptions.[7]

Not surprisingly, the measure attracted fire from several quarters.

[1] *The Times*, 18 Feb. 1876.

[2] For this report, see *P.P.* 1876, xxix. 1. There is a summary of its educational findings in Robson, pp. 210–13.

[3] See its organ, the *School Guardian*, 11 March 1876.

[4] Matthews, p. 311.

[5] These provisions were to come into operation by stages, reaching full force in 1881.

[6] *3 Hansard*, ccxxix. 943.

[7] On the new grant regulations, see *ibid.*, ccxxx. 1640–59, and W. H. Smith to Northcote, 17 July 1876 (Add. MS. 50021, ff. 15–20).

---

simply unite the opposition. Gorst himself was for action, and took part in getting up a memorial to Disraeli (see his letter to Salisbury, 13 Jan. 1876: *ibid.*).

The Liberals felt that it did too little for compulsion and rather too much for the voluntary schools. Men like Forster, Dixon, and Mundella wanted direct compulsion, and backed the recommendations of the Factory Acts Commission. Others fastened on the boost which the bill would give the voluntaryists, by increasing their attendance figures, and thus their income from school fees and government grant. This, it was suggested, coupled with the abolition of the rule that the parliamentary grant to a school was not to exceed its income from other sources, and with the provision of special grants for small schools, might enable some voluntary schools to subsist wholly on the grant and their fees (the latter paid, perhaps, by the guardians out of the rates), without any voluntary subscriptions at all.[1]

On the Conservative benches, there were some who thought more might have been done for compulsion, especially among the representatives of the large urban constituencies. Knowles, of Wigan, criticised the bill as 'too permissive', and, supported by Hamond (Newcastle), Ritchie (Tower Hamlets), and Brise (East Essex), he secured 165 votes for an attempt to make it obligatory on the local authorities to enforce compulsion.[2] Many, however, felt that compulsion had been carried too far, and aid to voluntaryism not far enough. The members for agricultural constituencies were especially worried about the effect of the bill on the rural labour supply. Several of them would even have preferred direct compulsion up to ten or twelve to the scheme of making employment at ten dependent on the possession of certificates,[3] and Rodwell got 108 votes for the reduction of the age when children might be employed without certificates from fourteen to thirteen.[4] It was the agricultural Tories, too, with their engrained suspicion of the ultimate results of education in the countryside and their tenderness for the rates, who showed most hostility to prize free education.[5] The fervent supporters of religious education and the voluntary system were more disgruntled than anyone with the bill. There was a strong back-bench demand for religious instruction to be provided in all schools, and for the granting of powers to enable districts to get rid of school boards which were no longer required.[6]

1 *3 Hansard*, ccxxxi. 10–22.

2 *Ibid.*, ccxxx. 48–51, 1400–8. Most of the 165 votes, of course, were Liberal.

3 See *ibid.*, ccxxx. 1290–3.

4 *Ibid.*, ccxxx. 1511–14.

5 *Ibid.*, ccxxx. 1451–6. Prize free education was, however, criticised by Liberals as well as Conservatives, even Forster being afraid of it as a step towards universal free education. Sandon stuck to the scheme, which he described as one of his 'particular fancies' (letter to his wife, 11 Aug. 1876: Harrowby Papers, vol. xlv, ff. 135–6).

6 See e.g., *3 Hansard*, ccxxix. 954 (Kennaway), 958 (Mills), 962 (Talbot), 962–3 (Lloyd), 1940 (Birley), 1958 (Stewart); ccxxx. 1216–22 (Hubbard), 1242–3 (Paget), 1248–9 (Hall).

The government saw the need to make concessions to its various critics. To placate the enthusiasts for compulsion, Sandon made it obligatory on town councils and boards of guardians to appoint attendance committees to administer the act, and inserted a declaration that it was the duty of the parent of every child over five to secure for it efficient education. He insisted that the clause dealing with children under ten whose education was neglected was meant to be stringently enforced and to provide a degree of compulsion over such children, and accepted its strengthening in Committee.[1] The effect of these changes was very important: they meant that the bill in its final form was, as Forster said,[2] really a measure of direct compulsion.

To meet the fears of those who felt that the bill would upset the labour market, Sandon agreed to let children work at ten without certificates, if they were employed and attending school half-time under the factory acts or local bye-laws,[3] and he allowed local authorities to suspend restrictions on the employment of children over eight for agricultural purposes for up to six weeks in the year.[4] But the great question was what the government would do for its keenly-disappointed champions of religious education and voluntaryism. Sandon refused to insist on religious teaching in all schools (though this had been, of course, his own desire),[5] but he accepted an amendment from Pell providing for the dissolution of unwanted school boards,[6] and provoked a storm of Liberal anger at what was taken to be a reactionary assault on the board system.

The Conservatives were determined to have Pell's clause, the Liberals to stop it, and the conflict threatened the progress of the bill sufficiently for the prime minister to step in. Disraeli's attitude revealed how completely out of touch he was with the feeling of his rank and file. He regarded their anxiety to strike a blow at school boards with contempt, as his words to the Queen make plain:

> the Ministry [he told her] fell into one of those messes of ecclesiastical weakness, which seems inevitable, every now and then, for the Conservative party. The whole of yesterday was consequently wasted on an

[1] *Ibid.*, ccxx. 1413–18. The Conservative party was apparently generally in favour of strengthening the clause: see Northcote to Salisbury, 14 July 1876 (Salisbury Papers, S.C.).

[2] *3 Hansard*, ccxxxi. 610–11.

[3] *Ibid.*, ccxxx. 1294–6. This amendment, moved by a Liberal, was supported from both sides.

[4] *Ibid.*, ccxxx. 1418–20, 1435–49. One Conservative, Hamond, of Newcastle, protested: 'they were debating this clause as if the object of the Bill were to provide labour for the farmers at the cheapest rate, and not to carry education to the rural districts' (*ibid.*, ccxxx. 1420).

[5] A Conservative amendment for this was beaten by 190 votes to 96 (see *ibid.*, ccxxx. 2010–20).

[6] *Ibid.*, ccxxx. 1666–75.

idle Education clause, which conveyed a petty assault on the Nonconformists.[1]

Disraeli intimated to Sandon that the clause must be abandoned.[2] But Sandon, who had acted with the full approval of the cabinet, was convinced that the whole party and most of the country approved what had been done, and that to retract would be a serious error. Salisbury wrote in strong terms to Disraeli to discourage retreat; and Northcote, too, defended the clause, which, he believed, could not be abandoned 'without seriously damaging and probably breaking up our party'.[3] From the back benches, Beresford Hope and Lord Henry Scott added their voices.[4] Disraeli gave way, and Pell's clause (with some conciliatory modifications) was carried through.[5] It did something to lessen the frustration of the militant voluntaryists, but unaccompanied by any provision giving security for religious teaching in all schools, it left many Conservatives feeling that the government had let its best supporters down.[6]

The Education Act of 1876 was a political rather than an educational measure. Its aim, as Sandon's memoranda show, was to maintain the primacy in elementary education of that voluntary and denominational system which Conservatives rightly regarded as a basic prop of their social and political power. In particular, it was designed to prevent the incursion of the rival board system into the deferential torpor of the Tory shires. The improvement of national education was a secondary object, accepted by most Conservatives without enthusiasm. Compulsion was swallowed by those who had so long fulminated against it not in order to help the children but in order to help the voluntary schools, and so keep out the boards. There was no desire that the education of the working population should be raised above the most elementary and functional level. The object of education for the great mass of the people, Cross had declared, was 'to make them more fit to do their duty in that station of life to

[1] Disraeli to Queen Victoria, 22 July 1876, in M. & B., v. 483.

[2] See Sandon to Salisbury, 22 July 1876: Salisbury Papers, S.C.

[3] Salisbury to Disraeli, 22 July 1876 (Disraeli Papers, B/XX/Ce/80); Northcote to Salisbury, 22 July 1876 (Salisbury Papers, S.C.). 'The Chief', Northcote wrote, 'really does not know the feeling of our friends on the subject.'

[4] See Hope to Disraeli, 23 July 1876, and Scott to Disraeli, 23 July 1876 (Disraeli Papers, B/XXI/H/647; B/XXI/S/75); Scott to Salisbury, 23 July 1876 (Salisbury Papers, S.C.).

[5] Sandon told Salisbury: 'I believe the opposition and discussions on it will be a very solid gain to us politically in the Country' (letter of 29 July 1876; *ibid.*). For Disraeli's comments on the final stages of the Education Bill, in letters to the Queen and to Lady Bradford, see M. & B., v. 483–5.

[6] The Church accepted the bill only with reluctance: they wanted, said the Archbishop of Canterbury, 'a great deal more' (*3 Hansard*, ccxxxi. 797).

which they are called . . .'[1] Sandon assumed the country to wish that 'all children of talents should have an open career before them', and was willing to consider enabling the best elementary school children to go on to higher schools,[2] but he rejected the notion of creating

> a whole population whose great ambition would be merely to wield the pen instead of the plough or the shuttle, as if the former occupation were superior to the latter.[3]

The helots might be made better and happier helots, but helots they must, in the nature of things, remain.

It is significant that when the government decided for general compulsion it decided for the indirect variety. The 'paternalist' solution would have been direct compulsion, but this was rejected: it might, Sandon declared, affect 'the national character of the English people, who had always prided themselves on their independence'.[4] Instead, ministers proceeded on the principle of trying to enforce responsibility on the individual, just as they did in the case of the Merchant Shipping Bill. Parents were not obliged to send children to school, but it was made disadvantageous for them not to do so. It was only when altered under pressure that the bill became virtually one for direct compulsion; in its original form it was strongly tinctured by those ideas of individual freedom and personal responsibility which increasingly dominated Conservative thought, and which its permissive terms expressed.

The social legislation of 1874–6 was doubtless, in part, a conscious attempt to show that Conservative protestations of concern for the condition of the people, and criticisms of Liberal neglect, had been more than empty words. The party had said that it would substitute long-needed measures of social improvement for the 'sensational' and 'harassing' legislation of Gladstone's ministry, and Disraeli's lieutenants saw to it that the promise was kept. Their work cannot, however, be viewed as the embodiment of any Conservative social 'policy'. It was empirical, piecemeal reform, dealing with problems as and when they were pushed into prominence by their inherent size and urgency, by agitation and the pressure of public opinion, by investigation and discussion, and by the exigencies of party politics. Questions like licensing, the labour laws, education, and merchant

[1] Speech reported in *The Times*, 22 Sept. 1875. Cf. Adderley, *A Few Thoughts on National Education and Punishments* (1874), pp. 23, 30–2; speeches by Pell, Mills, Sandford, and W. H. Smith, *3 Hansard*, ccxxii. 1072, ccxxvii. 1808, ccxxviii. 1268–9, ccxxx. 69–70.

[2] *Ibid.*, ccxviii. 1541–5; ccxix. 1653. Both Goldney and Birley had pressed this on him.

[3] *Ibid.*, ccxxix. 933–4.

[4] *Ibid.*, ccxxix. 940.

shipping were taken up not because Conservative ministers possessed and were anxious to implement a policy for them, but simply because they could scarcely be avoided. The direct pursuit of political advantage was a strong factor in the case of the Licensing Act (designed to satisfy the drink trade), the labour laws and the Factory Act (designed to win the working men, and, in the latter instance, to forestall Mundella), and the Education Act (designed to preserve one of the main agencies of Tory supremacy in the countryside).

No more than other measures under other governments did the bills of 1874–6 spring from the will and imagination of ministers alone. The Merchant Shipping, Friendly Societies, Public Health, and Pollution of Rivers Bills all followed upon the work of Royal Commissions, the Sale of Food and Drugs Bill upon that of a Select Committee, the Artizans Dwellings Bill upon that of Letheby and the Charity Organisation Society; and in all cases, too, there was the influence of the permanent officials, within the limits of whose outlook departmental policies were almost necessarily confined, and of whom Farrer was only the most obtrusive and powerful. Most of what Disraeli's ministers did (like most of what any minister does) had been long in preparation in the corridors of other minds, and most of it would probably have found its way on to the statute book under any government. Only in the Licensing and Education Acts did the Conservatives pursue courses which their opponents certainly would not have pursued; only in the settlement of the labour laws did they go further than the temper of the times might have seemed to dictate.

Their measures bore the imprint of no common philosophy. The spirit in which they were conceived was hardly Tory paternalism, if by that term is meant the kind of attitude of which Shaftesbury was the leading exponent.[1] It was rather a mixture—the ingredients ill-defined and the proportions variable—of paternalistic benevolence with empiricism and Peelite liberalism. The last element was perhaps the strongest. Everywhere in the social legislation of the Disraeli ministry can be seen the mark of the Liberal-Conservatism which men like Cross, the new bourgeois Conservative, Northcote, the old Peelite, and Sandon, the ex-Palmerstonian, incarnated, which country gentlemen like Adderley and Sclater-Booth accepted, and which Disraeli himself endorsed. Its characteristics included a firm (though not altogether uncritical) faith in the fundamental teachings of political economy, and a strong belief in the creed of freedom and individualism, with, as a corollary, a tendency to distrust govern-

[1] Still less was it paternalistic Tory Democracy, as Professor S. H. Beer (who overestimates the measures' 'vigor and originality') seems to think (*Modern British Politics*, pp. 262–70).

mental intervention and 'welfare' legislation. Accordingly, the labour laws were devised to establish 'freedom' between employer and workman and between workman and workman; the Merchant Shipping and Education Bills put their trust in individual responsibility; the Artizans Dwellings Act enshrined the permissive principle, that 'characteristic of a free people'; and the Public Health, Sale of Food and Drugs, Pollution of Rivers, and Friendly Societies Acts applied the power of the state in a manner so gentle as sometimes to be almost imperceptible. The Factory Act was the only measure which was really thoroughly paternalist, and even this ran on lines long since accepted by the proponents of liberal theory.

Of course, the measures of 1874–6 did represent legislative interference in economic and social matters. They did not significantly widen its area, but they did, though only to a small extent, increase its degree, and with the more extreme forms of the individualist creed they were not compatible. To those most rigidly determined to repulse the advance of 'socialistic' ideas, they were unwelcome,[1] and it is conceivable that they lost the Conservatives a little sympathy among some middle-class devotees of property and self-help. They marked yet another step in a process the direction and even the existence of which their authors were reluctant to acknowledge or approve. But it was a process that did not go unnoticed. As the *Standard* put it, on 5 June 1876:

> That a reaction has for some time been in progress against that rigid school of political economy whose edicts twenty years ago it was heresy to question, a good deal of our recent legislation sufficiently testifies. We do not, of course, mean that any one disputes the principles of that science to which we owe so much, but only that its claims to ride rough shod over every counter consideration and to drive a ploughshare, so to speak, through all the complex social conditions of the present age, regardless of surrounding circumstances, are no longer submitted to in silence.

Significantly, the *Standard* was unsure whether this trend had not been carried too far.

There is one more point to be made about the measures of 1874–6. As one would expect of piecemeal reforms carried out in a mood of cautious quasi-liberalism, their efficacy was mixed. The mere recitation of their titles tends to give an exaggerated impression of their practical significance. It is true that all of them except the Licensing Act were useful and commendable, and that two of them, the acts dealing with the labour laws, were a striking success. But it is also true that several

[1] Dr Southgate points out (p. 367) that to men of the stamp of A. V. Dicey or Lord Elcho measures like the Merchant Shipping or the Education Act set bad precedents for the Radicals to follow.

of them were too tentative and weak adequately to subdue the problems with which they were concerned, even if some of their deficiencies can be excused on the ground that public opinion in the mid-'seventies would take nothing stronger. The Merchant Shipping and Friendly Societies Acts were very lame. So, too, were the three public health measures, especially the Rivers Pollution Act, which had not been passed twelve months before Sclater-Booth was admitting that its full enforcement would require further legislation.[1] As for the Artizans Dwellings Act, commonly regarded as one of the most important moves of Disraeli's ministry, its provisions were so difficult and costly to work that it had very limited results.[2] So reluctant was the government to interfere forcefully in economic and social affairs that it did not always exert itself to make its own legislation effective. Section 12 of the Factory Act of 1874, for instance, which prevented children from undertaking full-time labour at thirteen without an educational certificate, was not initially enforced, because the Home Office had been persuaded that it would disrupt the labour market.[3] The impact of the legislation of 1874–6 on the condition of the people was doubtless beneficial, but it was hardly resounding.

> I have, for forty years, been labouring to replace the Tory party in their natural and historical position in this country. I am in the sunset of life, but I do not despair of seeing my purpose effected.

Thus Disraeli, in January 1874.[4] Among his efforts to restore that 'natural and historical position', social legislation occupied an important place. He saw the reforms of 1874–6 as a means at once of damping down social discontents and reconciling classes and of associating his party with the advancement of the welfare of the people. What was passing through his mind is illustrated by his letters during the reforming session of 1875. He told Lady Bradford that the Friendly Societies and Artizans Dwellings Bills 'indicate a policy round wh. the country can rally',[5] and spoke of the labour

[1] *3 Hansard*, ccxxxiii. 718 (6 April 1877).

[2] See below, p. 289.

[3] The Home Office tried to put the responsibility for non-enforcement on to the Education Department, which had to arrange for the issue of certificates under the section, but the Education Department firmly passed the buck back, and in the end Cross simply had to instruct his factory inspectors to be 'very careful & tender' in dealing with the act. The whole story can be found in H.O. 45/9308/12500 (for the official copy of Cross's instructions to the inspectors, see H.O. 87/6, p. 334). It should be added that the Royal Commission on the Factory and Workshops Acts (for whose report see *P.P.* 1876, xxix. 1) also came to the conclusion that section 12 should be temporarily suspended.

[4] Letter to the Rev. A. Beaven, 17 Jan. 1874, in M. & B., i. 222.

[5] Disraeli to Lady Bradford, 26 Feb. 1875: *ibid.*, v. 374.

laws as 'one of those measures, that root and consolidate a party'.[1] To the Queen, he wrote of the labour laws:

> they will greatly content the mass of the people; and reduce the materials for social agitation.
>
> Sir George Elliot, the greatest employer of labour in your Majesty's dominions, assured Mr. Disraeli yesterday, that a very great and beneficial change had come over the feelings of the working classes; perceiving, as they do, that the object of all the measures of the present Ministry is really to elevate their condition and mitigate their lot.[2]

It was natural that Disraeli should hope that his government's social measures would bind the working classes to the Conservative party. But there seems to be little evidence that the work of 1874–6 did, in fact, substantially strengthen the ties between Conservatism and the people. No doubt the Conservative working men who had shown themselves in 1874 were confirmed in their faith by the ministry's social reforms, which certainly offered the mass of the people more than five years of Liberal rule had done. Of any influx of fresh converts, however, there is no sign. Most working men, while taking the gifts, continued to mistrust the Greeks. No surge of popular enthusiasm accompanied the passage of the government bills, and it is doubtful how far they counted, in the eyes of the working class, as scores to the Conservative party's political credit. Most of them, being relatively uncontroversial and supported as much by Liberals as by Conservatives, were virtually divorced from party politics, and could scarcely affect the balance of party advantage.[3] The Factory Act and the labour laws were perhaps the only measures which improved the lot of the working population sufficiently obviously and directly to rouse feelings of gratitude.

In any case, social legislation alone could not win the masses for the Conservative party. If the Conservatives were to root their power in the support of the people, it was essential that they should try to establish more intimate relations with the working classes. They would have to cultivate their applause more directly and take closer account of their feelings and aspirations. But for this they had little inclination or ability. Even while they passed their measures of reform, the Conservative leaders made small attempt to carry to the masses

[1] Above, p. 217.

[2] Disraeli to Queen Victoria, 17 July 1875: *Letters of Queen Victoria*, 2nd series, ii. 414.

[3] It is interesting to note that the 1875 annual conference report of the National Union (Publications of the National Union, no. XXVI) mentions (p. 7) a certain 'lack of interest in political questions' in the year under review. The year in question, July 1874–June 1875, had seen the passage or introduction of several major social measures: evidently they did not arouse great interest, or were not counted as 'political' questions, or both.

the image of a party solicitous of their approbation and sympathetic to their interests. Whatever they might do for the working man, they could not conceive of a relationship with him which should be other than *de haut en bas*.[1] Their dislike of appealing to the people was such that it was difficult to get them even to recognise the efforts of their working-class supporters. After a conference of Conservative agents in December 1875, Gorst reported to Hart Dyke, the whip:

> Some very strong remarks were made as to the importance of the leaders of the Conservative party taking a more active part in Conservative demonstrations . . .[2]

Disraeli set a poor example in this respect. He had no gift for arousing tides of popular enthusiasm, and, indeed, agreed with the convention of the age which regarded such endeavours on the part of the chief minister of the crown as inadmissible demagogy. Nor did his physical condition by this time permit the efforts necessary to carry the banner of a progressive and popular Conservatism to the working population.

Conservatives were, moreover, well aware that too overt a bid for working-class support might do them as much harm as good. They could hardly identify themselves with the special interests of the working class and court the favour of the 'democracy' without alienating a portion of the middle-class support which they were so anxious to maintain and extend. Nor was it part of the philosophy of the 'national' party to look to any one class of the community more than another. Consequently, when the Conservative leaders did appeal to working men, they appealed to them not in terms of their interests as working men, but in terms of their community of interests with the other classes of society. Working men should be Conservative, it was suggested, not because they were the special objects of the party's care, but because they had as much interest as anyone in the stability of the existing social order, which the party existed to preserve. As Derby told the Edinburgh working men, in December 1875, in a speech which the National Union published:

> Whatever troubles the waters of society, whatever frightens the timid and the rich—and money is always timid—the artisan and the labourer are the first sufferers. The shopkeepers or the manufacturers lose their profit, but he loses his daily bread.[3]

[1] They failed to recognise what Shaftesbury recognised (diary, 11 Jan. 1875, in Hodder, iii. 355): 'The working classes have become patrons instead of clients; and they both can and do fight their own battles.'

[2] Gorst to Hart Dyke, 21 Dec. 1875: Disraeli Papers, B/XXI/D/466a.

[3] *The Conservative Working-Man. Speech of the Earl of Derby at Edinburgh. December 17th, 1875* (Publications of the National Union, no. XXVII), p. 5. Also quoted in McKenzie, 2nd ed., p. 148, where, however, the author confuses the 14th and 15th Earls of Derby.

The party's determination to deal with the working men on its own terms precluded any real lessening of the gulf which separated it from the organised labour movement. Nor was such a lessening sought, though Cross's legislation of 1875 might have furnished a basis for it. The representations of labour, even on those subjects which specially concerned it, were seldom treated with much respect. An instructive case is that of the memorial on shipping which the Trade Union Congress adopted at Liverpool in January 1875, for presentation to Disraeli. The president of the Congress, Fitzpatrick, sought an interview with the prime minister through his local M.P., MacIver, but was refused. When he made a second approach, MacIver wrote to Corry in terms eloquent of the position which Fitzpatrick and his friends occupied in Conservative estimation:

> When we were talking the other day in the House of Commons, my feeling was that it would not be right to let these people be a trouble to Mr. Disraeli, even if he were willing to receive them.
>
> It is just possible, however, that Mr. Disraeli might like to see them. But his seeing them would not help me in any future election—perhaps rather the contrary. . . .
>
> What *is* certain, however, is that Mr. Disraeli's receiving these Trades' Unionists would have a certain amount of effect upon working people all over the country; but whether of a kind that Mr. Disraeli desires, you will know better than I. . . .
>
> In the meantime, I have told Fitzpatrick that he can't have an interview; but that, if he gives me his memorial, I shall be glad to write to Mr. Disraeli with it.[1]

In view of the disinclination of the party leaders to make any real effort to court the working classes, it is not surprising that the machine through which they might have attempted such an enterprise was allowed to rust. The central organisation which Gorst would so willingly have employed for a campaign of popular Conservatism began to decline immediately after the general election it had helped to win.[2] Party management slid increasingly back into the hands of the whips, who had none of Gorst's enthusiasm for spreading the gospel to the working men. Gorst watched with dismay the weakening of the position which the Conservative party had achieved in the

[1] MacIver to Corry, 20 Feb. 1875, enclosing Fitzpatrick to MacIver, 19 Feb. 1875: Disraeli Papers (box xvi, packet 24, in old classification; not traced in new classification). See also the letter of Howell and Broadhurst to Disraeli, 25 April 1876 (cited above, p. 240, n.4), putting the views of the trade unionists on the Merchant Shipping Bill. In this case also Disraeli had refused to see a deputation, and the papers accompanying the letter suggest that little notice was taken of its representations.

[2] On this, see Feuchtwanger, 'J. E. Gorst', pp. 199–202; McKenzie, 2nd ed., p. 160.

boroughs in 1874, as it was reflected in the municipal election results of 1874 and 1875, and pressed the problem on Disraeli's attention. He felt that the prime minister's colleagues (none of them, he noted, borough members) either did not see the need to take steps to build up Conservative strength in the boroughs or else simply despaired of maintaining the party's position in the boroughs permanently. 'At any rate,' he wrote, 'little has been done to strengthen & consolidate our friends in the Boroughs and much to alienate and discourage them'.[1]

Gorst's warnings, however, went unheeded. As he suspected, the attitude of the party leaders towards the boroughs was defeatist,[2] and sometimes indifferent. Nothing was done to consolidate or enlarge the foothold gained among the great urban populations by 1874. Disraeli, it is true, made a gesture towards the large boroughs by inviting some of their new Conservative members to second the Commons' Address at the opening of successive sessions—Callender, of Manchester, in 1874, Whitelaw, of Glasgow, in 1875, Torr, of Liverpool, in 1877, Tennant, of Leeds, in 1878, and Corry, of Belfast, in 1880. But more than this was needed. The impression remained that the Tory party was not really interested in the great centres of the working-class vote and not inclined to take pains to hold their allegiance. Conservative borough members were sometimes made uncomfortably aware of the low position which they and their concerns occupied in the party's councils. When Callender, in April 1875, called the prime minister's attention to the damage which the Friendly Societies Bill was likely to do to the prospects of the Lancashire borough members, he felt impelled to write to Corry:

> . . . surely the unanimous opinion of the large towns should not be disregarded. On all questions affecting land or finance, we give the Government all support, and there is a very strong feeling which I hardly like to express that it is hardly advantageous for the interests of the party that in a matter specially of local interest our experience is not consulted & our wishes appear likely to be disregarded.[3]

[1] Gorst to Disraeli, 2 Dec. 1874 (Disraeli Papers, B/XXI/D/463a; printed in Hanham, pp. 389–90). Gorst's recipe for holding the boroughs was to create by patronage a corps of Tory borough leaders. 'I do not dissent from your view', he told Disraeli, 'that the mass of the people is, or may be made, Tory. But masses cannot move without leaders; and in English Boroughs we are grievously deficient in Tory leaders.' For Hart Dyke's nonchalant response to Gorst's anxieties, see his letter printed in Hanham, p. 390. On the position in the boroughs at the end of 1875, see Gorst to Disraeli, 10 Nov. 1875: Disraeli Papers, B/XXI/G/253.

[2] Hardy (then Viscount Cranbrook) told Cairns in 1880: 'My impression however was strong that we held many Boroughs by accident . . .' (letter of 6 April 1880 (typescript copy): Cairns Papers, vol. ix).

[3] Callender to Corry, 29 April 1875: Disraeli Papers, B/XXI/C/17.

It was, indeed, 'hardly advantageous for the interests of the party' that it should so readily neglect to cultivate the great popular constituencies. But the outlook and interests of the shires and market towns still predominated in the Conservative ranks, and to many Tory members the urban masses remained as far removed as the Christians of Bulgaria.

In 1874–6 the Conservative party, even while it pursued through social legislation the Disraelian aim of elevating the condition of the people, made no substantial effort to realise in concrete form that alliance between Toryism and the working classes of which its leader had been, and still was, the prophet. The failure was one both of imagination and of will. Conservatives could not envisage any relationship between party and people other than that of guarded benevolence on the one side and grateful deference on the other, nor did they wish for anything different. They had neither the impulse nor the capacity to build a party capable of incorporating and expressing the interests and the aspirations of the working class. They wanted working-class votes, and were prepared to pay for them in the hard currency of social reform; further than that they did not care to go. The reforming years of Disraeli's second ministry saw no drawing together of party and people. The gulf remained, and across it no spark of intimate sympathy flashed.

VI
DECLINE AND FALL, 1877-80

THE legislation of 1874–6 had largely exhausted the social reforming energies of the government. As they made ready for the session of 1877, ministers had in mind few measures significantly affecting the condition of the working classes. The largest and most pressing questions had almost all been tackled: apart from the vexed problem of employers' liability for injuries to workmen, there seemed little of moment left. Cross was preparing his long-contemplated consolidation of the factory acts; the Board of Trade was ready to deal with the extension to merchant seamen of the labour laws of 1875; Sclater-Booth was considering some amendments of the sanitary law and a consolidation of the poor laws, but wanted above all 'breathing time for consolidating and developing the office routine and machinery, and for putting recent Statutes into operation'.[1] It did not make an impressive programme, and even this much, as it turned out, could not be achieved.

The appearance in September 1876 of Gladstone's pamphlet on the 'Bulgarian Horrors' heralded a period of public absorption in foreign affairs which lasted for two years, and was succeeded by an equally intense concentration on the empire, set off by the Afghan and Zulu Wars of 1878–9. The Eastern question, Afghanistan, and South Africa took up so much of the time both of government and of Parliament between the middle of 1876 and the general election of 1880 that little was left for major domestic legislation, and that little was curtailed by the outbreak of Irish obstruction and the necessity of paying increased attention to the problems from which it stemmed. The swing of emphasis to foreign and imperial questions was hardly unwelcome to a ministry which had, to some extent, shot its bolt in the sphere of domestic reform. Certainly it suited the Earl

[1] Printed memorandum by Sclater-Booth for the cabinet, 7 Nov. 1876: P.R.O. 30/6/72, pp. 167–83.

of Beaconsfield, as Disraeli had become in August 1876, when increasing ill-health forced him to abandon the Commons for the less strenuous arena of the Lords. Upon the elder statesman of seventy-two, the high issues of diplomacy and empire exercised a far greater fascination than the problem of the condition of the people, which had touched his imagination as a young man. As Salisbury later told the Queen:

> The honour of the Crown and the honour of the country were in his mind inseparable: and in comparison to them, questions of internal policy occupied a secondary rank.[1]

'Let us remember!', he had used to say, 'we are a Senate: not a Vestry!'[2] It was in the senatorial pursuits of international politics and imperial rule that he sought the satisfactions of his old age, not in the parochial business of social amelioration. The mild impetus towards social reform which he had given to his ministry since 1874 disappeared altogether after 1876.

Foreign and imperial commitments did not merely absorb the government's time and energy; they also made heavy calls on its finances, at a moment when economic depression was seriously affecting the revenue. The demands of the Eastern crisis, of Afghanistan, and of South Africa were responsible for a series of deficits—£2.6m. in the financial year 1877–8, £2.3m. in 1878–9, £3.35m. in 1879–80—and Liberal denunciations of Conservative extravagance grew in vehemence. For political reasons, the ministry was reluctant to meet its difficulties by heavy new taxation, especially indirect taxation which would hit the working classes. The income tax was raised from 3d to 5d in 1878, but in 1879 Northcote was stopped by the cabinet from increasing the tea duties to pay the bill for the Zulu War,[3] and had not only to resort to fresh borrowing but also to raid his cherished sinking fund. In these circumstances, it was imperative to keep expenditure to the minimum: the question of economy, as Cross said in cabinet in August 1878, 'was one of life & death to the Party & Government'.[4]

Not merely were new expenditures for social amelioration shunned, but existing ones were threatened. Northcote attempted to check the fast rising cost of education under the acts of 1870–6,[5] and set himself to curb the growth of loans to local authorities, most of which were for sanitary or educational purposes. His Public Works Loans Bill

[1] Salisbury to Queen Victoria, 25 April 1881, in *Letters of Queen Victoria*, 2nd series, iii. 216.

[2] Quoted in Sir W. Fraser, *Disraeli and His Day*, 2nd ed., p. 246.

[3] M. & B., vi. 447–9.

[4] Sandon's Cabinet Journal, 10 Aug. 1878: Harrowby Papers, vol. cdviii.

[5] See below, pp. 285–6.

of 1879 raised the interest rates for long-term loans, and placed a limit of £100,000 on advances to any one body in one year. But this measure ran into fierce criticism from Joseph Chamberlain, who castigated the government for burdening the local authorities with excessively stringent terms for loans raised to carry out the duties which it had itself imposed on them, and in particular alleged that the Chancellor was 'killing the Artizans' Dwellings Act'.[1] In the upshot, Northcote retreated: he made provision for short-term loans at 3½% for the erection of working men's dwellings, and accepted Chamberlain's amendment striking out the higher interest rates in the bill, but enabling the government to charge whatever rate might be necessary to prevent loss to the Exchequer.

While external preoccupations and financial stringencies combined to relegate social reform to the background, the opinion of the party continued to grow less rather than more favourable to the constructive activity of government and legislation in the sphere of social questions. 'Social questions are apt to be put too much out of sight at present', remarked E. W. Harcourt, Conservative member for Oxfordshire, in July 1879;[2] but many of his colleagues were not sorry that this was so, and some inclined to think that social questions had been altogether too vigorously pursued in late years. Many answering chords were struck on the Conservative benches when the right-wing Liberal Goschen lamented the increasing tendency of government and Parliament to give in wholesale to the demands of the newly-enfranchised classes, and asserted 'that political economy had been dethroned in that House, and that philanthropy had been allowed to take its place'. Goschen cited the Conservative ministry's social legislation by way of example, and maintained that members opposite, under 'democratic' influence, 'were no longer Conservatives in the old sense. They no longer performed the function which they used to perform—they had not the power of resistance'.[3] But, in fact, 'the power of resistance' was not extinct in the Conservative party, and voices were heard to ask whether the intervention of the state on behalf of the poorer classes had not gone far enough—or even too far. Douglas Straight told Brighton Conservatives in May 1877 that he was 'sick and tired of hearing of these proposals of exceptional legislation in the interests of the working man . . .',[4] and the archetypal Tory squire Barttelot declared in the Commons in March 1879:

> He was bound to say that since household suffrage had come into play many things had been done in the interests of the working classes which

[1] *3 Hansard*, ccxlix. 611–23, 752–8.

[2] *Ibid.*, ccxlviii. 1388.

[3] *Ibid.*, ccxxxv. 563–6; ccxxxviii. 232–5 (29 June 1877 and 22 Feb. 1878).

[4] Quoted in McKenzie, 2nd ed., p. 150.

> were not for their interests at all. There was the shortening of the hours of labour, for instance. They had been, he would almost say, pampering these men, and now they would not exert themselves to the degree that was necessary to maintain the enterprize of this country in competition with foreign nations.[1]

It was largely the economic depression overshadowing the close of the 'seventies that led Conservatives to question the wisdom of what had been done for the mass of the people since 1867. The troubles of industry and agriculture, it began to be suspected, might in part be attributable to the effects of social legislation, interfering with the conditions and supply of labour, and tending to undermine the spirit of endeavour and self-reliance among the working classes on which national prosperity depended.[2] The depression, too, damaged the cause of social improvement by intensifying the irritation of the agriculturalists at the burden of rates. The education rate, applied to deprive them of the cheap juvenile labour which would have helped to cut their losses in the years of bad harvests and low prices, was especially resented.[3] The poor rate, also, was felt more harshly, and the Central Poor Law Conference, under Pell's chairmanship, pressed the Local Government Board, in January 1877, to impose further very stringent restrictions on outdoor relief, though without obtaining great satisfaction.[4] Under the impact of economic recession, the attitude of the Conservative party towards social reform and social expenditures was taking on a note not merely of doubt but even, at moments, of reaction.

There could be no question in these circumstances of appealing to the mass electorate on a platform of further social improvement. Conservatives, indeed, were increasingly nervous of the mass electorate and resentful of its power, and much of their attention was devoted not to appeasing its demands but to circumscribing its action and resisting its enlargement. The government's refusal to assent (except in the case of London) to the Radical demands for an extension of polling hours in boroughs, where the existing hours made it difficult for many working-class electors to cast their votes, was symptomatic of the Conservative desire to limit the consequences and evade the implications of 1867. So was its opposition, abandoned only in 1880, to Mundella's bill to abolish the property qualification

1 *3 Hansard*, ccxliv. 205.

2 Cf. pp. 274–5 below.

3 See, for instance, *3 Hansard*, ccxliv. 1711, 1725–6, 1729, 1747–8; ccxlvii. 1435–6; ccli. 1247–8.

4 Sclater-Booth was ready to do a good deal to discourage outdoor relief, but the Conference's suggestions (which included making all relief recoverable) went too far. See S. and B. Webb, *English Poor Law Policy*, pp. 152–3, 155–7, 175–8, 207–10; and the papers in M.H. 25/28 (43934/77).

for membership of town councils and other local bodies. Still more significant was the party's resistance to Trevelyan's campaign for household suffrage in the counties, a demand endorsed from 1877 by the Liberal leadership. 'The distribution of political power in the community', Disraeli stated flatly in 1874, 'is an affair of convention, and not an affair of moral and abstract right';[1] and Conservative spokesmen, while admitting the force of Trevelyan's case, insisted that the change proposed was 'inopportune'.[2]

Some Conservatives, it is true, feeling that household suffrage in counties was inevitable, contemplated dealing with the question in order to forestall the Liberals and secure their own interests in the consequent redistribution of seats.[3] One or two even supported Trevelyan—Spinks, of Oldham, for instance, and Charley, who, from his experience of the Salford electorate, told the Commons that working-class voters were 'better able to rise to the contemplation and vindication of great principles than the class immediately above them'.[4] But in general the party was very hostile to the idea of working-class predominance in the county constituencies, where it had its traditional strongholds. There was no knowing how the rural labourer would vote, and considerable fear that he would try, under the influence of his union leaders, to exploit the franchise to secure higher wages and to agitate the land question.[5] Moreover, the county constituencies contained large numbers of industrial workers, also under union influence. It seemed to many Conservatives that household suffrage in counties would simply complete the transfer of political power to the working man which 1867 had begun, and that that power would necessarily be used for class advantage. The Gloucestershire member Plunkett voiced a common view when, in 1878, he warned that 'the agricultural labourer in this question was only the stalking-horse of the trade unionist', and that the result of the legislature's giving the working classes 'a sudden flood of political power' would be to send them on 'a worse wild-goose chase after high wages by Act of Parliament than they were ever led by trade unions'.[6] This time, at least, there was no danger that Conservative members would be sold down the river by their front bench. Beaconsfield had no inclination to repeat his performance of 1867, and

[1] *3 Hansard*, ccxix. 250.

[2] E.g. Salt, moving the rejection of Trevelyan's motion in 1875 (*ibid.*, ccxxv. 1061–9).

[3] See C. S. Read to Corry, 20 Dec. 1877: Disraeli Papers, B/XXI/R/56.

[4] *3 Hansard*, ccxxxviii. 201.

[5] Another fear was that household suffrage in counties might lead to the democratisation of *local* government, and consequently to excessive expenditure from the rates on such objects as free education and poor relief.

[6] *3 Hansard*, ccxxxviii. 191, 192. Cf. *ibid.*, ccxxxviii. 240 (Newdegate).

hazard the party's fortunes in a further gamble with 'democracy'. 'The measure will not be passed for ten years', his mouthpiece told C. S. Read, 'and when ten years are over it will be harmless.'[1]

The party's growing apprehension at the progress of 'democracy' intensified its habitual reluctance to seek a real *rapport* with the working-class voter, and accelerated the decay of the organisation which provided its main point of contact with him. Gorst, perhaps the most genuine apostle of 'Tory Democracy', grew tired of the thankless struggle against indifference and hostility, and in 1877 withdrew from the work of party organisation.[2] He told Beaconsfield some months later that he regarded the antipathy of the party managers towards him as

> the natural consequence of my steadfast adherence to those popular principles in politics, which you taught me, which won the boroughs in 1874, and which though for the time being in discredit must ultimately prevail.[3]

The National Union got no more backing from the party leadership than its mentor. At its 1877 conference, Gorst, deprecating 'the idea which he said had found support in some quarters that the Associations should be discouraged', asserted confidently that 'there was no danger to the Conservative Party from independence of political thought and that no man had less fear on this account than Lord Beaconsfield'.[4] But Lord Beaconsfield, whatever his views, did nothing to help the Union, and its condition at the end of the 'seventies was hardly flourishing.

Partly under Gorst's impulsion, the National Union showed some disposition in 1877–8 to seek greater independence and to make its council more closely representative of the local associations.[5] This to some degree reflected the desire of the middle-class leaders of urban provincial Conservatism to make their voice heard in the party organisation and to integrate themselves with the party's traditional ruling caste,[6] and it emphasised the growing importance within the party of the bourgeoisie. The shift in the social basis of Conservatism towards the urban middle classes was, of course, reflected only

[1] Corry to Read, 27 Dec. 1877, in M. & B., v. 310, n. 2.

[2] See Feuchtwanger, 'J. E. Gorst', pp. 201–2. Gorst was especially wounded by his failure to obtain office. He had been offered the Secretaryship to the Local Government Board in 1875, but had declined, because with his chief also in the Commons he would have had only a limited rôle.

[3] Gorst to Beaconsfield, 4 April 1878: Disraeli Papers, B/XXI/G/259 (printed by Feuchtwanger, p. 201).

[4] National Union Conference 1877, MS. minutes.

[5] National Union Conferences of 1877 and 1878, MS. minutes.

[6] See, for this point, Cornford, pp. 45–8.

to a very limited extent in the personnel and attitudes of the party's higher echelons at the end of the 'seventies. The Conservative party in 1880 was still being run by the aristocracy, the gentry, and the Earl of Beaconsfield. Yet the accession to the cabinet in 1877 of 'the bookstall man', W. H. Smith, who became First Lord of the Admiralty, was a sign of things to come. Smith was perhaps the first man directly engaged in trade to enter a Conservative cabinet, and he was the first borough member to sit in Beaconsfield's, though another was soon added when, in 1878, Sandon came in as President of the Board of Trade (Adderley having been relegated to the Lords as Baron Norton). Sandon and Smith renewed in the cabinet the alliance with Cross which had been cemented in the Parliament of 1868–74,[1] and the three of them formed a group largely representative of the quasi-Peelite Liberal-Conservatism of the professional and commercial middle classes, to which Cross and Smith belonged, and with which Sandon, as a Liverpool member, was in close contact. It was still not altogether easy for the party hierarchy to assimilate the new bourgeois Conservatives: Beaconsfield had winced in 1874 at Cross's middle-class solecisms,[2] and continued to express contempt by saying that someone had 'the mind of a Tradesman' or (the victim was Joseph Chamberlain) 'looked, and spoke, like a cheese-monger';[3] and the differences of style and tone between men like Cross and Smith on the one hand and the older type of Tory on the other led to occasional awkwardness and misunderstanding.[4] Yet the rôle of the new men was bound to increase as the classes for which they spoke formed an ever more important element in Conservative electoral strength.

The influx into the Conservative party of those members of the middle classes who saw in it the best agency of defence against Radicalism and 'democracy', or for whom identification with it was

[1] When Sandon arrived with Smith for his first cabinet, 'Cr.[oss] joined us, & said most cordially "here we are all 3 once more together" (alluding to our sitting & working together in opposition from 1868)—"we are the people in fact who brought the Govt. into power" ' (Sandon's Cabinet Journal: Harrowby Papers, vol. cdvii).

[2] See Disraeli to Lady Bradford, 18 April 1874, in *Letters of Disraeli to Lady Bradford*, i. 72.

[3] See Sandon's Cabinet Journal, 31 July 1878 (Harrowby Papers, vol. cdviii); M. & B., vi. 588.

[4] The point is well illustrated by an anecdote in Sir Henry Drummond Wolff's aptly titled *Rambling Recollections* (ii. 128–9). Wolff once went to the theatre with Sir William Hart Dyke, the whip, Admiral Sir William Edmondstone, and Cross and Smith. When an attendant asked the cheerful Edmondstone and Wolff to moderate their tones, Dyke burst out laughing, but Cross and Smith 'affected to ignore our existence, turning their backs upon us, morally as well as physically'.

a means of emphasising their distinctness from a working class with which, economically and socially, they had more in common than they relished, continued at the end of the 'seventies. Fear and dislike of the rising social and political power of the working class and its trade unions were accentuated by the depression, for which the concessions already made to working-class interests were held partly to blame, and which further concessions seemed bound to worsen. Apprehension at the advance of 'socialistic' ideas was increased by the growth of socialism on the Continent, especially in Germany, where in 1878 Bismarck introduced repressive legislation against the rising Socialist party. A certain slackening, after the struggles of the 'sixties and early 'seventies, in the tension between Church and Dissent perhaps lowered the barrier which nonconformity constituted to the movement of the bourgeoisie into the Conservative ranks.[1] The agitation for free trade in land contributed to enhance the sense of common interest in resisting interference with the rights of private property which was gradually drawing landowners and business men together[2]—a sense sufficiently developed by 1879 to cause Carnarvon to fear that Toryism would engross too much of the total of land and wealth.[3] The influx of the bourgeoisie was turning the Conservative party into the great party of property, and from the dissolution of the politics of 'interests' the division of politics on lines of 'class' was beginning to emerge.

The increasing importance of the middle-class element in the social base of the Conservative party inevitably militated against the adoption of policies designed to appeal to the material interests of the working classes. Most of the new urban (or, very often, suburban) Conservatives had entered the party expressly to resist the advance of organised labour, of 'democracy' and socialism, and their economic and social demands, and their influence necessarily ran counter to the development of the popular Toryism with which the name of the party's leader was associated. When Carnarvon grumbled in 1879 that the Conservatives had become 'Tory democrats, avowedly

[1] Telling Sandon of a local election success, a Liverpool Conservative leader wrote that although every nonconformist minister had opposed them, the result proved that in Liverpool at least the congregations did not follow their ministers, but largely voted Conservative. Incomplete letter in the hand of the Liverpool Conservative Whitley, to Sandon, [? 11] March 1878: Harrowby Papers, vol. l, ff. 240–1.

[2] See Thompson, pp. 284–5.

[3] Carnarvon to Derby, 13 Nov. 1879, in Hardinge, iii. 42–3. In the same year he wrote: 'Nothing could be more dangerous I believe than a shift of the whole political ballast of property towards the Conservative side' (*ibid.*, 43). Both Carnarvon and Derby had left the government in 1878 over the Eastern question.

appealing to a combination of the Crown and Populace',[1] he did not mean that the party had decided to seek a union with the people in the spirit of the Disraelian dream. The Disraelian dream was almost extinct, not least in the mind of its creator, and if the party appealed to the people it was not in the terms of *Sybil* that it did so. It might call upon their patriotic pride, but upon the theme of their social condition its own internal metamorphosis ensured that its words would be cautious and restrained. The shadow so long cast over Liberal social policies by vested industrial and commercial interests, and by the economic ideology of the business classes, was shifting to the other side, and positive social reform was receding further into the background of the Conservative mind.

The impact of adverse economic conditions on Conservative attitudes to social questions was naturally most direct in the sphere of the regulation of labour. By 1878 there was some tendency in the party to feel that the apparatus of labour regulation built up since the 'thirties was a main factor in rendering British industry vulnerable to foreign competition. When the consolidation of the factory acts was debated in that year, the Leeds industrialist Tennant, who had supported Cross's factory bill on his advent to Parliament in 1874, declared:

> I must, however, confess that my views as to the general policy of these Acts have been undergoing a great change, owing mainly to the severe competition we are suffering from our manufacturing rivals in other countries, whose freedom from all restrictions confers enormous advantages which it is almost impossible to contend against; and the time will come, and is not as far distant as many of us may imagine, when all these legislative restrictions on the freedom of labour, and all this Parliamentary interference with the right of contract between employer and employed will be swept from the Statute Book, and master and workman will be left unfettered to make their own arrangements in their own way.[2]

Knowles, the Wigan coal-owner and cotton-spinner, thought likewise that 'they had gone far enough in handicapping the trades of this country, seeing the deplorable condition they were now in';[3] and to show that misgivings were not confined to the new Conservatives of the industrial and commercial middle class, old Newdegate, one of the last surviving Protectionist supporters of the ten-hours bill, remarked:

> He was quite sure they were restraining the productive power of the country by their factory legislation; and although he was as sternly

[1] Hardinge, iii. 43.
[2] *3 Hansard*, ccxxxvii. 1465–6.
[3] *Ibid.*, ccxxxvii. 1468.

determined as in 1844 to protect the interests of the young, he still thought the Legislature might push the restrictions on labour too far.[1]

Such views were not universal in the party—Fielden, for instance, himself a cotton manufacturer, maintained against Tennant that the trade depression was in no way a result of factory legislation[2]—but they affected the thinking of many, and seriously discouraged further measures for the regulation of industry.

In agriculture, too, the effect of depression was to intensify Conservative reluctance to apply legislative action to the improvement of the labourer's condition. For a party so intimately involved with the established economic and social order of the countryside, it was difficult to view the claims of the rural working man in an objective spirit. The rise of the National Agricultural Labourers Union had alarmed Conservatives, and while there was a good deal of sympathy for the labourers' grievances, there was strong hostility to the influence of Arch and his 'agitators'. If the party had, on the whole, avoided identifying itself with the farmers' campaign against the union,[3] many of its members had nonetheless welcomed the farmers' victory, and were now glad to see the union further weakened by the falling demand for labour consequent upon the depression. What they really disliked about agricultural unionism was the threat it conveyed to the quasi-feudal autocracy of the rural upper classes and employers. As Read wrote in December 1877:

> Before the Agl. Labourers' Union, our men looked up to the farmers & trusted those above *us*. That is all changed, as every one in authority from the Queen to the Parish Constable, has been denounced by these Agitators; so everyone who has any power, money, or station, is now looked upon as the natural enemy of 'the down trodden labourer'. No doubt in time this nonsense will evaporate & they will put a different value upon their democratic leaders. The Agl. Labourer is honest & well disposed, but sadly *gullable* [*sic*]—& somewhat impulsive,—a quality I did not know he possessed, & one that is certainly not natural to him.[4]

[1] *Ibid.*, ccxxxviii. 598. [2] *Ibid.*, ccxxxvii. 1471.

[3] There were exceptions here and there. Fawcett and Trevelyan claimed that Rodwell, elected Conservative member for Cambridgeshire at a by-election in 1874, had been chosen by the farmers as one who had helped them to beat the labourers, to the exclusion of the candidate supported by Disraeli; though Rodwell himself denied this (*ibid.*, ccxxxv. 1084–5, 1086–7, 1104–5).

[4] Statement by Read on the county franchise: Disraeli Papers, B/XXI/R/56a. The *Quarterly Review*, in 1879 (cxlvii. 75), attacked the Agricultural Labourers' Union as the ally of 'aggressive nonconformity', and declared that for its leaders, 'the downfall of the Church is only a stepping-stone to the destruction of the landed gentry'. But sometimes Conservatives looked more kindly on union activities. Pell records (*Reminiscences*, p. 295) a village meeting of the union in 1877 for which the rector lent the school and took the chair: 'A temperate, mild affair', he says, 'with justice on the labourers' side.'

While withholding the vote from the agricultural labourer for fear of what, under union influence, he might try to do with it towards the betterment of his economic and social condition, the Conservative party made no effort to ameliorate that condition itself. Indeed, its members sometimes talked as though no amelioration was needed. The agricultural labourer had never been so well off, argued Read in a debate of 1879; his real wages had risen, and 'the only thing he thought the labourer should now be asked to do was to give a fair day's work for a fair day's pay'.[1] Sandon contended that the labourers had not shared in the hardships of the depression: wages were high, 'the work, in too many cases, clearly bad', and everything suggested that in a few years the agricultural labourer's position would be 'one of the most comfortable in the country'.[2] Men who suspected that the labourer was not only doing well but failing to give his employer value for money were not likely, in a moment of agricultural crisis, to employ the force of the state in his behalf. Of any serious attempt to attack the deficiencies of rural wages and housing there was no sign, and when Fawcett, in the debates on the consolidating Factory Act of 1878, tried to have children employed in agriculture brought under the more stringent regulations as to hours of labour and educational attendance which governed children's employment in industry, he met solid Conservative opposition: the provisions of the Education Act of 1876 were declared to be sufficient, and Onslow of Guildford expressed much back-bench feeling in his remark that it was already hard enough to get juvenile labour in the south, 'on account of the obstacles thrown in the way by education'.[3]

Given the climate of opinion which existed in the Conservative party at the end of the 'seventies, it is not surprising that the government should have been reluctant to contemplate further interference with the operations of productive industry. Its own quasi-Peelite economic liberalism inclined it to limit state action as much as possible. This came out very clearly with the railways, whose high accident rate, traceable largely to the overworking of their employees, caused a strong demand for greater governmental supervision. Beaconsfield himself resisted the application of the provisions of the factory acts to railway employees, pointing out that care had been

[1] *3 Hansard*, ccxliv. 1726. In 1880 Read told Beaconsfield that the labourers had made their employers pay 30% more for shorter hours, less work, and worse work (Read to Beaconsfield, 30 Aug. 1880: Disraeli Papers, B/XXI/R/61).

[2] *3 Hansard*, ccxliv. 1747, 1749.

[3] See *ibid.*, ccxxxviii. 63–85. Children employed in agriculture could go over to full-time work at age ten, if they had attained the Education Code's 4th standard, or made 250 school attendances in the previous year, whereas children employed under the factory acts had to continue part-time school attendance up to age thirteen or fourteen.

taken hitherto not to extend these provisions to adult males, and declaring: 'between men and their employers, the law to my mind, should not interfere';[1] while Sandon replied to the anxieties of the Queen on the subject simply by explaining his 'views against state interference with private enterprise'.[2] Such attitudes smacked more of classical political economy than of Tory paternalism, and emphasised how far ministers were wedded to the liberal concept of 'holding the ring'. Nevertheless, the government's activity in the field of labour questions could not and did not come to a complete halt. The pressure of concrete problems and the need to conciliate the power of organised labour[3] continued to push ministers along paths whose abstract desirability they might doubt. The closing years of Conservative rule saw Cross round off his reforming career with a consolidation of the factory acts, and witnessed serious, if unhappy, attempts to grapple with the important problems concerning the extension to seamen of the labour laws of 1875 and the revision of the law on employers' liability for injuries to workmen.

A man with a passion for tidiness, Cross had projected a consolidation of the factory acts from his first months in office,[4] and consolidation was one of the main recommendations of the Royal Commission on the working of the factory and workshops acts which he set up in 1875.[5] His bill to consolidate the existing law, and to carry out certain other proposals of the Royal Commission (notably to extend the application of the acts, and to abolish as far as possible the distinction between factories and workshops created in 1867), was first introduced in 1877, but had to be deferred until the following session. Despite some Conservative misgivings about the handicaps imposed upon industry in a period of depression by the factory acts,[6] and Fawcett's fierce opposition to restrictions on the labour of adult women, it passed triumphantly, seeming to set the coping-stone on the great edifice of factory legislation to which the Conservative party could claim to have contributed so much. Shaftesbury, welcoming the measure, made explicit one of the principal motives of that contribution when he said:

[1] *Ibid.*, ccxxxiv. 15–16 (April 1877).

[2] Sandon's Cabinet Journal, describing a visit to Osborne, 27 July 1878: Harrowby Papers, vol. cdviii. The handling of the railway question was, of course, complicated by the heavy representation of railway interests in Parliament.

[3] Though this power was much weakened by the fall in union membership consequent on the depression.

[4] See Cross to Cairns, 3 Aug. 1874 (typescript copy): Cairns Papers, vol. v.

[5] For the Commission's report (Feb. 1876), see *P.P.* 1876, xxix. 1; xxx. 1.

[6] See above, pp. 274–5.

A system of order and discipline had been established, which made revolutionary agitation as against the ruling Powers throughout the country very difficult.[1]

The Factory Act of 1878 was not perfectly devised, and contained loopholes.[2] But it was a necessary and useful measure, and enhanced Cross's reputation with the representatives of labour. After the labour laws of 1875 and the factory acts of 1874 and 1878, the Home Secretary could claim to have done as much for the working man as any previous holder of his office. His work, careful and conciliatory always of the interests of labour, not only in legislation but in administration, had gone as far as anything could to convince the urban workers that the Conservatives were their friends.

Seamen, however, had less cause than factory operatives to believe in Conservative benevolence. The legislation of 1875–6 had by no means solved the problem of ensuring their safety and equitable treatment, and merchant shipping questions continued to harass the ministry. Two main reforms remained to be tackled after the act of 1876: the limitation of marine insurance (which many thought the only means of checking losses at sea), and the extension to seamen of the labour laws of 1875, especially as regarded breach of contract. With the first, a complex subject which poor Adderley dreaded,[3] no progress was made: the Maritime Contracts Bill of 1876 was reintroduced in 1877, but was later withdrawn, and by the end of the year Northcote and Adderley were agreed that marine insurance would have to be left alone for the time being.[4] The government's attempt to deal with the extension of the labour laws was more serious and sustained, but it added nothing to their laurels.

By May 1877 Adderley had ready a Merchant Seamen's Bill dealing with breach of contract and seamen's discipline, but the press of business prevented its introduction that year, to the vocal annoyance of Gorst, who was carrying on the rôle of seaman's friend which he had assumed in 1875, and had lent his support to Thomas Burt's bill for the extension of the Employers and Workmen Act to seamen, which Burt had withdrawn to make way for the government measure.[5] In 1878, however, the bill was introduced. It brought seamen within the labour laws of 1875, but only until they joined their ships: after

[1] *3 Hansard*, ccxxxix. 948.

[2] The effective supervision of workshops was especially difficult, and many escaped the act altogether. Indeed, in certain respects, the act marked a slackening of control.

[3] See his autobiographical notes for 1877, in Childe-Pemberton, p. 232.

[4] Northcote to W. H. Smith, 13 Nov. 1877 (copy): Add. MS. 50053, f. 88.

[5] For Gorst's criticism of the government's default, see *3 Hansard*, ccxxxvi. 723.

that, Adderley maintained, they must necessarily be subject to special discipline, the law governing which the bill consolidated and revised. There were clauses also to ensure the prompter payment of seamen's wages, to permit survey of a ship to be demanded by a single seaman, and to check crimping.[1]

The bill met trouble from the outset. Gorst thought the labour laws should apply to seamen on board ship as well as on land,[2] while from an opposite viewpoint the shipowners were hostile to almost the whole of the measure.[3] Referred to a Select Committee, the bill had got into total confusion by April 1878, when at long last it became possible to move Adderley from the Presidency of the Board of Trade, and to replace him by Sandon, who, unlike his predecessor, was given a cabinet seat.[4] Sandon found the difficulties surrounding the bill too great to surmount in the session of 1878, and postponed it. A fresh measure was prepared for 1879, but despite Gorst's urging was not introduced, and the dissolution put paid to its chances in 1880. The bringing of seamen under the labour laws, and the reform of their system of wage payment, were left to Sandon's successor, Joseph Chamberlain.

To Chamberlain, too, was ultimately bequeathed another merchant shipping question which caused some stir at the end of the government's term. The carriage of grain cargoes in bulk, which permitted their shifting dangerously at sea, was regarded as a major cause of sinkings, and in 1880 Plimsoll, with Gorst among his backers, introduced a bill to stop the practice. After its experience in 1875, the last thing the ministry wanted was another stand-up fight with Plimsoll, and Northcote suggested to Sandon that if the bill was a good one they might even promise Plimsoll support for it, provided he did not make it impossible by his own violence.[5] Either Plimsoll's bill proved unpalatable or it was thought best to sidestep the issue, for what Sandon did was to move for that well-tried instrument of delay, a Select Committee. But he was unhappy that the government should again appear to be holding up a Plimsollian reform, and got Russell to ask a parliamentary question in reply to which it was made known that he had arranged for the Select Committee to report on Plimsoll's proposals soon enough to permit legislation, if necessary, that year. 'I concocted this plot', he told his wife, 'to upset his [Plimsoll's]

[1] Much of this had been in the abortive bill of 1875.

[2] *3 Hansard*, ccxxxvii. 309–10, 609.

[3] See the memorial of the Chamber of Shipping of the United Kingdom to the Board of Trade, 25 Feb. 1878: M.T. 9/151/M.3233/78.

[4] Adderley went to the Lords as Baron Norton. 1878 saw a change also in the Parliamentary Secretaryship at the Board of Trade, J. G. Talbot replacing Edward Stanhope.

[5] Northcote to Sandon, 17 Feb. 1880: Harrowby Papers, vol. liii, ff. 239–40.

position against us on this subject in the Elections.'[1] The elections, of course, upset Sandon's position, and put an end to six years of persistent but singularly inglorious efforts by the government to cope with the problems involved in the safety and welfare of the merchant seamen. The problems, it is true, were complex and intractable, the vested interests which they touched large and obstinate, the civil servants who alone, perhaps, had mastered their intricacies hidebound and unimaginative, but the ministry could have done much had it shown greater decision and will, had it been less limpet-like in its attachment to precepts of freedom and individualism which stultified action, and had it not suffered Adderley's hand to remain so long nerveless on the tiller.

To working men in general, much the most important labour question with which the government attempted to deal in its closing years was that of employers' liability for injuries to workmen. A major grievance was felt in the existing state of the law, whereby an employer, though liable to the public at large for injury caused by the negligence of his employees, was not liable to an employee for injury occasioned by the negligence of a fellow-employee. The application of the doctrine of 'common employment' (as lawyers termed it) was regarded as peculiarly unjust where the fellow-employee was, in fact, a manager or overseer, exercising delegated authority from the employer. Reform of the law had been in the programme of the Trade Union Congress since 1872, and several draft bills had been drawn by the Home Office between 1871 and 1874.[2] When the Conservatives took office, they were immediately confronted by the problem. Bills to remove the doctrine of common employment were introduced from the Liberal side by Watkin in 1874–5 and by Alexander Macdonald in 1876, and it became necessary for the government to decide upon its attitude.

Cross's principal adviser in this field, the Home Office counsel, Lushington, despite his sympathies with labour, was reluctant to contemplate the entire abolition of the doctrine of common employment. He agreed that the existing law was unjust, but pointed out that if masters were made liable for injury to a servant caused by the negligence of any other servant, this would have very serious consequences for large employers—shipowners, mineowners, railway companies—in whose businesses a single act of negligence might cost many lives. Lushington suggested that an obvious compromise was to make the master liable for the negligence only of those servants

[1] Sandon to Lady Mary Sandon, 8 March 1880: *ibid.*, vol. xlv, ff. 263–4. For the question and answer, both written by Sandon, see *3 Hansard*, ccli. 555–6.

[2] They are to be found in H.O. 45/9458/72731A/2.

(foremen and the like) who were *in loco magistri.*[1] It was this middle-of-the-road approach which ministers and Conservative backbenchers adopted when Macdonald's bill was debated in May 1876: the measure was stoutly opposed, but the need for some emendation of the law was readily admitted, and Macdonald was persuaded to accept Cross's offer of a Select Committee.[2] The Committee reported in June 1877:[3] it rejected the abolition of the doctrine of common employment, but felt that where employers could not personally discharge their duties as masters (as with corporate companies), the agents to whom management was delegated should be made liable in their place. At the same time, the Royal Commission appointed to inquire into railway accidents recommended that a railway company should be held liable for the acts of its chief officers.[4] These proposals were not enough to satisfy organised labour, and Macdonald brought in once more, in 1878, a bill to remove the doctrine of common employment, and forced the government again to declare its position.

Conservative feeling was much against Macdonald's view. Only Gorst, in his lonely rôle of sympathiser with labour, supported the bill of 1878 from the Conservative side.[5] His colleagues, while ready for legislation, were unwilling to go beyond the Select Committee report. The Attorney-General, Holker, made it clear that the government would take a cautious line. He found the grievance of the workmen 'to some extent, sentimental', spoke of 'ignorant clamour' on the subject, and would himself have liked, ideally, to relax rather than tighten the law, making the employer liable for his own negligence, the negligence of his partners, and negligent acts committed under his express authority, but no further. Still, he realised the impracticability of this course, and promised a government bill, hinting that it would make masters responsible for injuries caused by the neglect of servants to whom the duties of master were delegated.[6]

The promise was easier to make than to fulfil. Ministers immediately became bogged down in the complexities of the problem, and were hampered in extricating themselves by their keen fear of any alteration in the law which might have the effect of disrupting the operations of industry and commerce. The compromise approach

[1] See his memoranda on Watkin's and Macdonald's bills, 16 May 1874, 5 June 1875, May 1876, in H.O. 45/9458/72731A/1; also some unsigned notes on Macdonald's bill, dated 23 May 1876 (*ibid.*).

[2] See *3 Hansard*, ccxxix. 1154–81.

[3] Select Committee on Employers' Liability for Injuries to Their Servants, 2nd report; *P.P.* 1877, x. 551.

[4] Report of Royal Commission on Railway Accidents, p. 27 (*ibid.*, 1877, xlviii. 27).

[5] *3 Hansard*, ccxxxix. 1053–4.

[6] *Ibid.*, ccxxxix. 1067–71.

favoured by the Home Office and the government was embodied by Holker in a draft bill of June 1878, 'which', he told Cross, 'I have made as harmless as possible'.[1] This did away with the doctrine of 'common employment' where the employees concerned were in distinct branches of service, and made employers liable to their employees for the negligence of 'servants in authority'. But it quickly sank beneath a welter of memoranda pointing out the difficulties of its details, not least among which was the problem of deciding exactly who should be classified as a 'servant in authority'.[2] Sir Matthew White Ridley, who had just succeeded Selwin-Ibbetson as Under-Secretary at the Home Office, was inclined to think the bill would not solve the question at all, and asked Cross whether anything could be done by compulsory insurance, both of employer and employed,[3] a suggestion of some interest, but which does not seem to have attracted any support. It proved impossible to formulate a satisfactory measure in time to redeem the promise of a bill in the current session, and the whole issue had to be taken up afresh at the beginning of the session 1878–9.

Setting out the employers' liability question for the cabinet in November 1878, Holker stressed again that the existing law, making employers liable for the negligent acts of their employees, was just as wrong as the exception, excluding liability where the person injured by the negligence was a fellow-employee; and he reiterated his belief that much the best course would be to enact that employers should not be liable to anybody for the negligence of their employees.[4] But, as Holker himself knew, this was not a line that the government could follow in Parliament or the country, and in the draft bill which he produced at the beginning of 1879, he sought a middle term between his personal view and the claims of organised labour and the general public by making the employer liable to *any* person for the negligence of a 'servant in authority', but not liable for the negligence of a servant not 'in authority'.[5] Ministers, however, quickly saw that they could hardly oppose this measure to Macdonald's bill, which was again before the Commons, or to the bill brought in in February

[1] Holker to Cross, 8 June 1878, with draft of bill: H.O. 45/9458/72731A/1.

[2] See the MS. draft of the bill annotated by Lord Justice Bramwell, and memos. by Liddell (the permanent under-secretary), Lushington, and Sir M. W. Ridley, June–July 1878: *ibid.*

[3] Memo. for Cross by M. W. R.[idley], 22 July 1878: *ibid.* Ridley, however felt this would probably be impracticable, since the employers would have to pay all the insurance.

[4] Printed memorandum for the cabinet, initialled 'J.H.'[olker], 27 Nov. 1878: *ibid.*

[5] Draft bill for the use of the cabinet, annotated by Cairns, in H.O. 45/9458/72731A/2.

1879 by the Conservative Earl de la Warr in the Lords and by a group of Liberals in the Commons, which rendered employers liable to employees for the negligence of servants to whom superintendence was delegated, without removing their liability to the public at large for the negligence of any servant. Holker's draft was completely altered by Cairns: the employer's liability to the general public was left untouched, but he was made liable to his employees for the negligence of 'servants in authority'—the result being very much the same as de la Warr's measure.[1] This was the basis of the government bill which at last reached the Commons in March 1879.

Introducing the bill, Holker explained that to render employers liable to employees for the negligence of *any* fellow-employee would be to render them 'unable to compete in the race of life'—hence the compromise approach adopted by the government.[2] This was not good enough for Macdonald and his friends, and it was clear that the employers' liability question was far from nearing a solution. Ministers may not have been sorry that the pressure of external events stopped their bill from being proceeded with in the session of 1879, and they were diffident enough to have it referred to a Select Committee when they reintroduced it in 1880. There, of course, it expired with the dissolution. The problem reverted to the incoming Liberal ministry, which sought to tackle it on lines similar to those of the Conservative bill, and provided the occasion for one of the Fourth Party's most consummate harassments. The Liberals passed a bill, but did not settle the question, and only when a Conservative government, impelled by Chamberlain, and with Ridley as its Home Secretary, carried the Workmen's Compensation Act of 1897 was employers' liability placed on a more satisfactory footing.

In its struggle with employers' liability, as in its dealings with merchant shipping questions, the ministry had revealed both lack of grasp and deficiency of will. Its inglorious fumbling with labour problems in 1877–80 is in sharp contrast to the success story of 1874–5. True, it was hampered by external preoccupations, but the basic trouble lay deeper. The legislation of 1874–5 had been freely conceded in the belief that it would satisfy the legitimate claims of organised labour. After 1875 ministers were on the defensive, less apt to give concessions, more conscious (because of the depression) of the possible economic drawbacks of further interference with industry and commerce, increasingly mindful of the objections to working-class demands entertained by the entrepreneurial class

[1] See *ibid.*, and with it the printed draft bill of 5 March 1879.

[2] *3 Hansard*, ccxliv. 1135–9. Holker used an example concerning a greengrocer, which, as Macdonald (1139–40) pointed out, cast some doubt on his comprehension of the subject.

which was providing an ever-growing segment of their support. The calculated benevolence which had carried the labour laws was largely spent by 1880, and the Conservatives went into the general election looking and sounding much more like the party of the employers than had been the case on their last appearance at the polls.

'Properly, for some years to come, the Education Acts & the Codes ought to require very little handling.' Thus Sandon to W. H. Smith, on 9 December 1876.[1] The Vice-President and his chief, Richmond, were agreed in feeling that after the act of 1876 there should be a moratorium on further structural alterations to the educational system, and a note of complacency, even of lethargy, began to creep into their conduct of the Education Department. They had no significant plans for the future development of elementary education, and seemed imperfectly aware of the shortcomings of the existing order.

Sandon, in fact, was getting tired of education, and his translation to the Board of Trade in April 1878 came none too soon. Had he left the Council Office a year earlier, his successor might well have been W. H. Smith.[2] As it was, the choice fell upon Lord George Hamilton, who since 1874 had been Indian Under-Secretary. Hamilton's health, the Queen was told, 'could not stand the hard work' of the India Office,[3] and the Education Department was evidently considered at this period to be a convenient place for a convalescence. The new Vice-President regretted the change: 'after the big Indian questions', he wrote to Salisbury, 'the petty technical points of the Education Office are dull indeed.'[4] He was without special knowledge of or interest in educational matters. But he was not a man to tackle any job half-heartedly, and his forcefulness soon came into play, its first manifestation being when he ruffled Richmond by describing himself as 'Minister for Education', and, on that worthy's complaining, persuaded Beaconsfield to agree that he must have a large measure of independent initiative.[5] He very quickly saw the stultifying effects of 'the Manchester theory of testing everything by pecuniary results', which permeated elementary education, and too

[1] Harrowby Papers, vol. lxv, ff. 291–8.

[2] There was some talk of Smith's becoming Vice-President in the summer of 1877, when Sandon was considered for the Irish Secretaryship: see Cairns to Richmond, 3 June and 31 July 1877 (Goodwood Papers, box 31); Richmond to Cairns, 1 Aug. 1877 (typescript copy; Cairns Papers, vol. viii).

[3] Queen Victoria's Journal, 30 March 1878, in *Letters of Queen Victoria*, 2nd series, ii. 610.

[4] Hamilton to Salisbury, n.d., but endorsed 21 April 1878: Salisbury Papers, S.C. Cf. Hamilton's *Parliamentary Reminiscences and Reflections*, p. 156.

[5] *Ibid.*, pp. 151–2.

often meant that the children, under a 'pernicious system of forcing', were 'mere paying-machines', and he did his best to mitigate the rigours of payment by results.[1] The vigour which he brought to his office was timely, for after the lull of 1877–8 education was again entering a difficult and contentious period.

The basic trouble was the cost of the educational expansion initiated by the act of 1870. Hamilton's appointment coincided with the growth of a new hostility towards the rapid increase of educational expenditure, both on the part of the government, desperate to find means of financing its foreign and imperial policies, and on the part of the ratepayers and their parliamentary representatives, made more conscious of the burden of the education rate by the depression. The Vice-President had to attempt to reconcile the demands of national education with the anxious desire of his ministerial colleagues and backbenchers for the maximum of economy in a system under which the education estimates had risen from £1.55m. for 1875–6 to £2.15m. for 1878–9, and the average expenditure per child from 25s. in 1870 to 35s. in 1878.[2]

It was from the Treasury that the strongest pressure came. Hamilton had his first brush with that department's routine and unintelligent parsimony when his first estimates (which he had already pared to the bone) were cut by £10,000, for no better reason, apparently, than that the Treasury always cut the education estimates by £10,000.[3] Northcote, meanwhile, was embarking on a serious effort to hold down educational expenditure. He began early in 1878 with loans to local authorities for educational purposes, endeavouring to make arrangements between the Public Works Loan Commissioners and the Education Department which would restrict calls for loans unremunerative to the Exchequer.[4] The Public Works Loans Act of 1879[5] continued this line of policy. But more fundamental cuts were in the Chancellor's mind. 'I am going', he told Beaconsfield in January 1879, 'to make a push for a reduction of the Education grants.'[6]

It was a delicate business to reduce the grants. The government itself had removed the biggest check on the increase of grants in 1876,

[1] *Ibid.*, pp. 157–9, and cf. *3 Hansard*, ccliv. 2020–1. Lowe, who had started payment by results, now told Hamilton that he would second a motion for its abolition.

[2] For the latter figure, see *3 Hansard*, ccxlviii. 1678–9, where Hamilton also stated that between 1870 and 1878 the government grant per child in average attendance had risen from 9s. 9d. to 15s. 3d.

[3] Hamilton, pp. 304–5. After this, of course, Hamilton sent in his estimates unpared, 'and the result', he notes, 'was certainly not to the advantage of the Exchequer'.

[4] See *3 Hansard*, ccxxxix. 1170–1.

[5] For which, see above, pp. 276–8.

[6] Northcote to Beaconsfield, 9 Jan. 1879: Add. MS. 50018, ff. 129–33.

when, in order to help the voluntary schools, it had abolished the rule that a school's grant must not exceed its income from other sources. Was it to retrace its steps, at the expense largely of the voluntary system which it was sworn to uphold? Certainly this was what Northcote envisaged: the increase of grant, he felt, had to be stopped, and he asked the secretary of the Education Department, Sandford, whether grants to schools might not be limited to a maximum of, say, 15s. per head on the average attendance, admitting that this was to some extent 'reversing our policy of 1876'.[1] The real crisis for the education grants came in 1880. Hamilton and Sandford cut their estimates to the lowest point compatible with efficiency, but failed to satisfy a harassed Northcote, who, in conjunction with Richmond, took the drastic step of largely curtailing the grant for the three Rs. Knowing the damage this would do, not only to education but to the ministry's election prospects (for the change struck directly at the Church schools, which principally relied on this part of the grant), Hamilton appealed to the prime minister, who, in a characteristically bizarre stroke, convened the dormant and, indeed, almost purely notional Committee of Council on Education, and had it endorse the Vice-President's stand.[2] The government was thus restrained from concluding its life by financing out of money intended for investment in the nation's future the doubtful glories of Zululand and Afghanistan.

Pressure for the reduction of educational expenditure did not come only from Northcote and the Treasury. Conservative backbenchers, too, urged economy, especially those with rural constituencies, where the level of the education rate was counted among the factors aggravating agricultural depression. By 1879 the feelings of some Conservatives could no longer be contained, and there was harsh criticism both of the cost of elementary education and of what was considered to be its excessively high level and elaborate content—the ratepayers, it was alleged, were being mulcted by school boards for an education more suited to middle-class than working-class children.[3] It was, of course, the school boards in particular that were under fire; the attack on educational expenditure was largely an attempt to check their advance. The most savage onslaught on their misdeeds came in June 1879, when J. R. Yorke, Conservative member for East Gloucestershire, set about the expenditure of the London School Board, long a favourite target of the ratepayers' champions.

[1] Northcote to Sandford, 7 Jan. 1879 (copy): Add. MS. 50053, f. 147.

[2] Hamilton, pp. 152–4.

[3] See, for instance, *3 Hansard*, ccxliv. 1338 (Barne); ccxlviii. 619–20 (Jenkinson); *Quarterly Review*, cxlvii (1879), 155–82—'Our Schools and Schoolmasters'.

> The present system [said Yorke] was Communistic in its working. Elementary education, like physical existence, was guaranteed to everybody by the State from motives of public policy. This was very proper; but the moment they outstepped the limits of what was reasonably necessary they trenched upon Communism. . . . all had a right to be educated, but not to be educated luxuriously.

The Board's schools, he argued, were in fact providing advanced education for middle-class children at public expense. Properly, the compulsory teaching in board schools should not go beyond the three Rs, since that was 'all that the State owed to the children', and the education 'should have some practical reference to the object of the child's life—to the pursuit by which he was to gain his bread . . . the boy who was to become a groom should learn how to manage horses, and . . . the boy who was to become a gardener should learn to dig'. Yorke wanted the education rate to be limited, and thought payment by results should be less in rate-supported than in voluntary schools.[1] The tendency of even a mild pain in the pocket to bring out the old, virulent Tory dislike of any but the most basic and functional education for the people, and the old, virulent Tory determination to do down the school board system, was much in evidence as the Beaconsfield ministry neared its close.

Hamilton was not the man to give in to the cruder forms of back-bench atavism. He insisted, in reply to Yorke's assault on the London School Board, that nothing must be done to impair the efficiency of elementary education, and that no undue favour could be shown to voluntaryism.[2] But with a good deal of the back-bench disquiet he was inclined to sympathise. He was especially concerned about the increasing tendency of board schools to give advanced education, beyond the three Rs. He could not approve of costly instruction in special subjects for which most of the children, he felt, had neither time nor capacity. 'Of all forms of education', he later wrote, 'the worst for the children of the industrial class is an ambitious programme truncated by the necessity of the children going to work before they have mastered the extra subjects taught.'[3] At the same time, he believed in giving 'ample opportunities to those children who, either by their industry or their capacity, or by their aspirations, might wish to avail themselves of a more advanced or higher education'.[4] The solution which recommended itself to him was to grade

[1] *3 Hansard*, ccxlvi. 1604–17. Cf. Leighton (1618–24).

[2] *Ibid.*, ccxlvi. 1644. In opposition, in August 1880, he felt able to say 'it was absolutely essential that the children of this country should be properly educated, and if that could only be done at a very great cost, so much the worse for the taxpayers' (*ibid.*, ccliv. 2018).

[3] Hamilton, p. 186. Cf. his speech of July 1879, in *3 Hansard*, ccxlviii. 1682–3.

[4] *Ibid.*, ccxlviii. 1683–4.

elementary schools into two classes, the lower class providing basic instruction for the mass, the higher class (with higher fees) giving more advanced education—a system which, he hoped, would 'ensure for the ordinary child a grip of a few subjects, and for the cleverer children schools where the class and extra specific subjects now perfunctorily taught should be thoroughly taught'.[1] Moreover, when Hamilton outlined this scheme to the Commons, in July 1879, he made it clear that the higher-grade schools were to be a step in an educational ladder leading right up to the universities: citing the case of an elementary school boy who had won a university scholarship, he declared that that 'seemed to him rather to indicate the direction in which they ought to go'.[2] The Vice-President had secured his colleagues' approval for the setting-up of the higher-grade schools, and was preparing for the lower-grade schools 'a simpler and more compact curriculum', when the general election put an end to his authority.[3]

Grading of elementary schools was not the only major project which Hamilton was prevented from implementing by the election. He had intended also to introduce universal compulsion. By 1879 school accommodation and the supply of teachers were considered adequate for the national needs, but out of a population of about 23 million in England and Wales, seven million were still not subject to compulsory bye-laws.[4] Hamilton opposed universal compulsion in July 1879 on the ground that it would be very hard to enforce,[5] but he changed his mind during the ensuing nine months, and was preparing a measure for compulsion when the government left office.[6] Even after the election, he and Richmond wanted to introduce the

[1] Hamilton, p. 185. Some school boards had already established higher-grade schools: Wheelhouse had attacked them in August 1878 for making the ratepayers pay for advanced education for better-class children (*3 Hansard*, ccxlii. 1241–4).

[2] *Ibid.*, ccxlviii. 1684.

[3] Hamilton, p. 186. Just before the election, Hamilton issued a new Education Code which, *inter alia*, raised the standard required before children could take up special subjects. For his own commentary on the changes, see *3 Hansard*, ccliv. 2016–17. His Liberal successor, Mundella, took up his scheme, but, in Hamilton's eyes, perverted it by adding an extra standard and additional subjects instead of simplifying the curriculum in the lower-grade schools (Hamilton, p. 186). Norton, in June 1880, succeeded in carrying in the Lords a motion for the removal from the Education Code of a number of special subjects, the teaching of which in elementary schools, he argued, amounted to secondary education of the middle classes at the community's expense. He was supported by Beaconsfield, Richmond, Salisbury, Cranbrook, and Rowton (the title taken in 1880 by Montagu Corry) (*3 Hansard*, ccliii. 264–83).

[4] See Hamilton's statement, *ibid.*, ccxlviii. 1675–7.

[5] *Ibid.*, ccxlviii. 1678.

[6] Hamilton, p. 185.

bill,[1] but it was ultimately left to the Liberal Vice-President, Mundella, to pass the act which made elementary education compulsory throughout England and Wales.[2]

'Sanitas sanitatum' was little in evidence in the last years of the Beaconsfield ministry—the prime minister's taste in Latin tags running by this time more to 'imperium et libertas'. In what related to the health and sobriety of the people, the government had no substantial advances to offer after 1876. There was some tinkering with the housing problem, and much agitation around the opposite poles of beer and water, but small profit emerged, and the London water question, indeed, occasioned the government serious political damage.

That the Artizans Dwellings Act was too cumbersome and costly in operation to have a great effect on the problem of urban working-class housing had become evident by the late 'seventies. The cost of compensation under the act was the main trouble. Local authorities might well hesitate to implement the measure when the chairman of the Metropolitan Board of Works announced to the Commons, in July 1879, that the loss to the metropolitan ratepayers on fourteen sites cleared under the act would be £1,076,000.[3] The government was pressed for action, and Cross responded with an amending bill designed to reduce the cost of putting the act into effect. At the same time, he helped the Liberal Torrens to pass a bill extending the provisions of the latter's Artizans Dwellings Act of 1868. The bill, in fact, represented Torrens's original measure of 1868, before its mangling by the Lords: it restored the clauses permitting local authorities to acquire property and to provide for its rebuilding which the Lords had struck out, and for lack of which the act of 1868 had been virtually inoperative.[4] Neither of these two acts of 1879 had a pronounced effect. The limited impact of Cross's Artizans Dwellings Act, even in its amended form, can be gauged from the fact that in 1881 a Charity Organisation Society

[1] See Northcote to Salisbury, 22 May 1880 (Salisbury Papers, S.C.); Northcote to Cranbrook, 22 May 1880 (Cranbrook Papers, T501/271); Hamilton to Sandon, 23 May 1880 (Harrowby Papers, vol. liii, f. 56).

[2] Richmond said (*3 Hansard*, ccliii. 1620–1) that Mundella's measure was much the same as the one he would have introduced. But Mundella did not simply take up and pass the Conservative bill, and Sandon had to apologise to him for suggesting that he did. See Mundella to Sandon, 10 Aug. 1881, and a copy of the reply (same date), in Harrowby Papers, vol. liii, ff. 192–3, vol. lv, ff. 51–4.

[3] *3 Hansard*, ccxlviii. 302. Cf. *ibid.*, ccxlviii. 1157–67. For the difficulties experienced by the Metropolitan Board of Works in utilising the act, see the L.C.C.'s *The Housing Question in London*, pp. 36–9.

[4] See Torrens's speech, *ibid.*, ccxlv. 1936. At the government's instance, the bill was limited largely to London.

committee on working-class housing, with Cross among its members, found that of the 87 English and Welsh towns outside London to which the act applied, 77 had done nothing towards implementing it.[1] The attempt of Beaconsfield's ministry to cope with the housing problem, so bravely begun in 1875, ended, as perhaps it was bound to do, in comparative failure.

With the drink problem the ministry had never really tried to cope, and it was not minded to undertake any novel exertions in its closing years. The Conservative party at the end of the 'seventies had, as a whole, little inclination to embark on any further significant regulation of the licensed trade. Its attitude was not unfairly represented by a National Union pamphlet of 1877, which, referring to the Licensing Act of 1874, apologised not for its leniency to the trade, but for its failure to undo all the mischief of Bruce's act—a failure attributable to the influence over the House of Commons of

> the delusion now pretty well dissipated, that drunkenness prevails in proportion to the amount of public-house accommodation, and that consequently by limiting the number of public-houses and closing them earlier intemperance could be greatly diminished.

It was now generally felt, said the pamphlet, that trust must be placed in 'moral means' to repress the evils of drink.[2] Selwin-Ibbetson, in March 1877, ascribed increasing drunkenness to rising wages and greater leisure, rather than to the number of public houses, and left the Commons to draw the inference that it was not in licensing reform that the solution was to be found.[3]

And yet, despite its repugnance to legislative interference, the party could not remain wholly unaffected by the growing public feeling (not least in Church circles) that new efforts to check intemperance were essential. It was doubtless true that closing public houses earlier, or limiting their number, would not of itself stop drunkenness, and that the path of improvement lay largely in the direction of bettering the social conditions which drove men and women to drink, but it seemed undeniable also that legislative restrictions could afford some help. Cross felt bound to allow, in March 1877, that people *could* be made sober by act of Parliament,[4] though he showed no dis-

[1] *Dwellings of the Poor. Report of the Dwellings Committee of the Charity Organisation Society, presented to the Council August 2 1881* . . ., p. 17. The report discusses in detail the difficulties of implementing the act. See also the reports of the Select Committee on Artizans' and Labourers' Dwellings (*P.P.* 1881, vii. 395; 1882, vii. 249), and the first report of the Royal Commission on the Housing of the Working Classes, pp. 44–7 (*ibid.* 1884–5, xxx. 48–51).

[2] *Three Years of Conservative Government* (Publications of the National Union, no. XXX, March 1877), p. 5.

[3] *3 Hansard*, ccxxxii. 1876–7. [4] *Ibid.*, ccxxxii. 1955.

position to do anything about it, and Selwin-Ibbetson continued to press for at least one item of licensing reform—the further control of off-licences.[1] A few backbenchers were prepared to go further: there was some Conservative support in 1877 for a Scottish licensing bill which aimed not only to regulate grocers' licences but to restrict licences according to population,[2] and three Conservatives backed Chamberlain's scheme to empower town councils to buy up and manage their public houses.[3]

It was not, however, until 1879 that support for the further regulation of the licensed trade appeared in any strength on the Conservative benches. In March of that year the Liberal champion of temperance, Lawson, moved a resolution in favour of local option (the system whereby the inhabitants of a district could restrict the issue or renewal of licences) which he had taken from the work of a committee appointed by the Convocation of Canterbury, and which, he said, was supported by the Church of England Temperance Society. The debate made it clear that a number of Conservatives, impressed by the trend of public opinion, and anxious to avert the full-scale ratepayers' control of licensing which temperance militants demanded, were ready for new regulatory action. Birley seconded Lawson, Stewart supported him, and Earl Percy, Kennaway, and Rodwell all agreed on the desirability of giving the ratepayers some kind of voice in licensing.[4] Significantly, Wheelhouse's amendment aimed at preserving the *status quo* got no support from any quarter.

The line taken by the government was cautious. Lawson's reply to the objection that his motion was subversive of individual liberty had been simply:

> Of course—all acts of Parliament are. We sit here to subvert individual liberty, and to prevent anyone doing wrong to the public.[5]

To this Radical paternalism the good Liberal-Conservatives on the ministerial benches were fundamentally opposed. Sternly rejecting Lawson's local option, Ridley rejected also his contention that the main purpose of the licensing system was to protect 'public welfare'—it was, said the Under-Secretary, to protect public order—and declined to 'subordinate the privileges of the sober man to the refor-

[1] See his minute on a letter to Cross from the chairman of the Bury justices, 26 Sept. 1877: H.O. 45/9527/36620/545.

[2] For the second reading debate, see *3 Hansard*, ccxxxii. 1901–59.

[3] See *ibid.*, ccxxxii. 1861–98. Kennaway seconded Chamberlain's motion, and Benett-Stanford and Dalrymple voted for it.

[4] For the debate, see *ibid.*, ccxliv. 632–753.

[5] *Ibid.*, ccxliv. 650.

mation of the drunkard'.[1] But the speeches of both Ridley and his predecessor as Under-Secretary, Selwin-Ibbetson, pointed to an increase of magisterial control over licences, and the latter also took up Rodwell's idea that local demand should be certified before new licences were granted.[2] So, in effect, did Cross, who supported a Liberal proposal that in granting new licences the licensing authority should consider the district's population and the number of existing licences, and should find on sworn evidence that new licences were required for the public's convenience.[3]

The moment seemed ripe, after the debate on Lawson's resolution, for a moderate measure of licensing reform. It was made still riper by the appearance of the report of the Lords' Select Committee on Intemperance, appointed in 1877, the need to await which had for two years furnished the standard excuse for governmental inaction. The Committee, which included both archbishops and three bishops (one of them Magee), rejected such remedies for drunkenness as the Permissive Bill or ratepayers' control of licensing through elected boards, but recommended legislation to permit the adoption of Chamberlain's scheme of municipal purchase or of the Gothenburg system (whereby a municipality let its licences to a non-profit making company). It pressed also for a considerable increase in licence duties, and for a marked reduction in opening hours, especially on Sunday.[4] There was much moderate opinion behind the report's proposals, and it rendered even more favourable the chances of a well-considered measure in Parliament. But ten days after its production, Northcote told the Commons that the government did not intend to legislate upon it.[5]

The government, in fact, did not intend to legislate on the drink question at all.[6] It is hard to avoid the conclusion that ministers were afraid to annoy the trade interest. Certainly they were much embarrassed by the drink issue at this time, and unwilling to commit themselves in any direction. This came out in their attitude to the Sunday Closing Bill, when it was debated in July 1879. Though only Birley and Kennaway actually supported the bill, all the Conservative backbenchers who spoke favoured some restriction of Sunday drinking, the limiting of the Sunday trade to off-sales only being the leading suggestion.[7] Ridley, however, did his best to evade the whole issue:

[1] *Ibid.*, ccxliv. 666–7. Ridley declared: 'it appears to me the only ground for interfering with any trade would be that it possessed special characteristics affecting public order.' Cf. Selwin-Ibbetson, *ibid.*, ccxliv. 736.

[2] *Ibid.*, ccxliv. 672–3, 735–7. [3] *Ibid.*, ccxliv. 751–3.

[4] House of Lords Select Committee on Intemperance, final report: *P.P.* 1878–9, x. 469.

[5] *3 Hansard*, ccxliv. 1851. [6] As Cross said, in July 1879. *Ibid.*, ccxlviii. 309.

[7] For the debate, see *ibid.*, ccxlvii. 1970–2008.

he did not even discuss the off-sales only proposal, and while recognising the need for action on Sunday hours, said that the government had not had time to consider its course.[1] Eight months later, in March 1880, with a general election in the offing, the government was still apparently considering its course, and still apparently reluctant to move. Cairns was worried at the failure of his fellow peers in the cabinet to realise the importance of the question in the country, and felt obliged to state that he 'could not bear the responsibility of a declaration on the part of the Government against a change in the direction of a curtailment of the present Sunday hours'.[2]

The result of the ministry's timorousness was that the initiative in attempting licensing reform had to be assumed by backbenchers. Rodwell, with Mills, Stewart, and two Liberals, introduced a bill requiring magistrates, before granting a new licence, to be satisfied of the public demand and need for it—as Rodwell said, 'a qualified local option'.[3] Cross supported the bill, which was trivial enough, and was eventually dropped.[4] He supported also another minor bill which was passed in 1880 by Ritchie and Gorst, with the Liberals Mundella and Torrens: it gave magistrates discretion over the issue of retail licences for off-sales of beer.

The government, it seems clear, was anxious to retain for the coming election that trade allegiance from which it was generally supposed to have profited in 1874. Northcote's speech to the annual dinner of the Exeter licensed victuallers in December 1879,[5] in which the Chancellor dwelt fondly on his hosts' importance to society and declared himself opposed to drastic new legislation, set the tone for the ministry's relations with the drink interest in its final period. And in the party at large temperance feeling seemed to subside as the election drew nearer. It was less prominent in the debate on Lawson's local option motion in March 1880 than it had been in 1879, and more emphasis was given to the familiar and, indeed, cogent argument that it was from social improvement rather than the limitation of hours or licences that a lessening of intemperance was to be expected. Ritchie, having made his contribution to temperance with his Beer Licences Bill, now reminded the Commons:

> A great deal of drunkenness was the effect of a life of hard toil without sufficient recreation, and to close the public-houses would be only to deal with the effect, and not with the cause.

[1] *Ibid.*, ccxlvii. 2003–5. Selwin-Ibbetson, on the other hand, favoured off-sales only (*ibid.*, ccxlvii. 2000).

[2] Cairns to Sandon, 8 March 1880: Harrowby Papers, vol. lii, ff. 73–4.

[3] *3 Hansard*, ccxlv. 189.

[4] As was a similar bill for Scotland, brought in by Stewart.

[5] *The Times*, 31 Dec. 1879.

Rather quaintly he added:

> If they wished to lessen drunkenness, they must provide amusement and recreation for the great masses of the country, by means of music-halls, to which men could take their wives and families; by providing more open spaces, and by other means of that character.[1]

In music-halls fit for the family, then, and not in more rigorous legislation, the Conservative party placed its trust, and hoped that the licensed victuallers would repay it with theirs. To judge by the help they gave young Edward Clarke in his victorious Southwark by-election in February 1880, it seemed they might.[2]

Beer was not more in the government's mind than water at the beginning of 1880. The long-neglected question of the water supply of London had come to a head in peculiarly embarrassing fashion. For years the deficiencies of the metropolitan water had been canvassed, and the need proclaimed for a supply which should be purer, cheaper, and in all cases constant (the latter requirement being vital not only for health reasons but for fire-fighting purposes). Reporting in 1869, the Royal Commission under Richmond set up by Derby's ministry had recommended taking the London water supply out of the hands of the eight water companies and entrusting it to a public authority,[3] and in 1877 a Select Committee on the Metropolitan Fire Brigade, with Selwin-Ibbetson in the chair, reached the same conclusion.[4] Government action to dispossess the water companies had been attempted in 1871, and at the end of the 'seventies its renewal was widely expected.

The record of the Conservatives on the London water question was not an encouraging one. Derby's ministry of 1852 had weakly knuckled down to the companies in its Metropolis Water Act, and the attempt of the Liberal government in 1871 to provide for the compulsory purchase of the companies by the Metropolitan Board of Works had received scant Conservative support. The government of 1874 showed no inclination to grapple with the problem, or help others grapple with it. The efforts of Colonel Beresford and his fellow metro-

[1] *3 Hansard*, ccli. 493. Cf. Bulwer (*ibid.*, ccli. 490). Cross took the same line—changing public opinion, education, more comfortable homes, the provision of amusements and recreation would 'speedily settle the question' (*ibid.*, ccli. 523–4).

[2] For the Southwark contest, at which local option was a leading issue, see Clarke, pp. 154–63; and for the help given Clarke by the publicans, *3 Hansard*, ccli. 512.

[3] Report of the Royal Commission on Water Supply: *P.P.* 1868–9, xxxiii. 1.

[4] Report of Select Committee on the Metropolitan Fire Brigade, p. xxix (*P.P.* 1877, xiv. 65). The members of the Committee included the metropolitan Conservatives Forsyth and Ritchie, and the Conservative chairman of the Metropolitan Board of Works, Hogg.

politan Conservatives, Forsyth, Ritchie, and Russell, to make more effective provision for constant supply got little encouragement from Sclater-Booth,[1] and no help was given to the bill for the purchase of the companies by the Metropolitan Board of Works which the Board's Conservative chairman, Hogg, introduced in 1878.[2] But action was becoming increasingly difficult to evade. The raising of the companies' charges in 1878 sparked off a strong demand that the government should protect the interests of the ratepayers and consumers by consolidating them under public authority, and this was forcibly expressed in Parliament in the first half of 1879.[3] There was a considerable agitation in the capital, where the Bishop of London and Cardinal Manning took up the water question from the standpoint of the poorer classes. It was plain that the ministry would lose credit by refusing to act.

In August 1879, therefore, when Fawcett again brought the water question before the Commons, Cross indicated that the government would take it in hand. He was cautious about revealing his plans (if, indeed, he had any at that stage) because of the effect on the companies' shares, but he made an important statement: if the government did take over the companies, it would take their stocks at the price at which it found them 'on such a day as, say, the last day of the last half-year' (i.e. 30 June 1879), paying no attention to prospective additions to their value or to speculative changes.[4] The promise of action was generally welcomed. Probably ministers expected no great trouble in implementing it.

In dealing with the water question, Cross chose to use as his adviser and agent a surveyor named E. J. Smith.[5] It was quickly decided, on Smith's advice, that the water companies must be taken over. There seems to have been some suggestion that the state itself might assume

[1] Beresford urged the government to take up his Metropolis Water Supply and Fire Prevention Bill (in whose preparation Edwin Chadwick had been concerned), but Sclater-Booth advised Disraeli against any action. See the papers on the subject in the Disraeli Papers, especially: Beresford to Corry, 28 March 1874; memo. by Edwin Chadwick, with covering letter to Corry, 13 April 1874; memo. by Sclater-Booth for Disraeli, 11 Feb. 1876 (B/XXI/B/395, 397, 399, 400c).

[2] Hogg asked the government in the autumn of 1878 to help his Board carry a bill for the purchase of the companies, but met with a refusal. *3 Hansard*, ccxlix. 652–3.

[3] *Ibid.*, ccxlv. 760, 764–5; ccxlvi. 1113–28, 1813–32. The pressure for action came mainly from Liberals, but Shaftesbury and other Conservatives were also concerned.

[4] *The Times*, 14 Aug. 1879; *3 Hansard*, ccxlix. 941–7.

[5] For Smith's rôle, see his lengthy evidence before the Select Committee on London Water Supply, 1880 (printed in the Committee's report: *P.P.* 1880, x. 111).

control of the water supply, but this was deprecated by Northcote, who showed his habitual reluctance to extend the area of state responsibility. He told Cross, in October 1879:

> I own to much uneasiness on the subject, both as regards principles and as regards details. On the whole I am of opinion that the State ought not to undertake the business at all, any more than it should undertake the Railways. Clearly, we could not work it ourselves; we must find, or create, some independent body to do that, and make it pay the State a proper return for the capital expended on the purchase, reserving a fund for maintenance and extensions, and giving the public the benefit of any profits in the shape of reduced charges. But I fear there would be difficulty in working even such a system as this satisfactorily. It would involve us in more responsibility than I like, and would carry with it principles of larger and still more questionable application.[1]

Northcote's idea was to set up an elective board to purchase the companies on terms approved by the government—more or less the course that was in fact adopted. The difficulty lay in settling what the terms should be. The companies had for years been striving to maintain or even artificially inflate the value of their stock in order to ensure heavy compensation if they were taken over,[2] and they were determined to exact the highest possible price.

Smith, who conducted the negotiations with the companies, preferred purchasing them by agreement to acquiring them compulsorily,[3] and Cross, whom few Conservatives excelled in respect for the rights of property, concurred. But this necessarily gave the companies the upper hand in the bargaining, and meant that the government would have to accept the terms of the most recalcitrant. By January 1880 Smith had agreed with the companies the terms on which they would sell out, but the price was a high one, for he had abandoned the principle laid down by Cross in August, and had consented to take into account prospective additions to the value of the companies' stock.[4] This large concession was known (or

[1] Northcote to Cross, 25 Oct. 1879: Add. MS. 51265 (unfoliated).

[2] In 1876–7, the government auditor under the Metropolis Water Act, 1871, Stoneham, had caught two of the companies artificially sustaining dividends by charging to capital expenditure which should have fallen on revenue, in the expectation that they would be compensated on dividend values if bought out. See Stoneham to the Local Government Board, 26 Feb. 1877, and memo. by Stoneham for Lambert of the L.G.B., 6 March 1878: M.H. 29/3. And cf. Beckett-Denison's allegations (Aug. 1879) in *3 Hansard*, ccxlix. 650.

[3] He contended before the Select Committee of 1880 that compulsory purchase would have been more costly than the terms which he eventually agreed. Select Committee report, minutes of evidence, qs. 31, 39, 41.

[4] These prospective additions were large, the companies having laid mains through districts now rapidly becoming densely populated.

suspected) in the City,[1] and the companies' shares rocketed in the first weeks of 1880. The market, *The Times* reported on 19 January, thought there were large profits to be made: 'the buying has lately been very strong, and points to an attempt to force Parliament to take over the works at a speculative price'.

There were serious dangers for the government in these developments. Though the cabinet generally approved Cross's (or Smith's) plans on 17 January,[2] Northcote at least was unhappy, and on 20 January told Cross that if they accepted the terms negotiated by Smith, they would find themselves on 'uncomfortable ground' in Parliament. The Chancellor foresaw very clearly how the public would react. He wrote:

> Your announcement in August, as to our taking our stand on the price of that time, and not recognising any prospective advance in the value of the Stocks, seems to be rendered not only nugatory but even mischievous by the action which he [Smith] now recommends.
>
> Although it may not have been intended to do so, it certainly led many people to believe that we should take as our basis of calculation the prices of August or July last, adding perhaps some moderate percentage for compulsory purchase. But nobody supposed that we should take into account the prospective and speculative additions to be made, as Mr. Smith now proposes to make them, in respect of certain unexhausted powers to make back dividends up to ten per cent. This, however, having been proposed, and discussed, and admitted by the Government agent as a reasonable arrangement, up go the prices of the Stock to the tune of 30 per cent. Will it not be suggested that this rise was not quite accidental, and that some of those who knew the course which the negotiations were taking may have profited by their knowledge?
>
> Looking to the very large sum with which we intend to charge the water-rate-payers, I am sure these terms will be very severely criticised; and I do not think we ought to allow Mr. Smith to sign any agreements binding the Government until we have had an opportunity for discussing the matter more carefully.
>
> I did not quite like Mr. Smith's tone. He spoke too much as an advocate of the Companies; and he did not give very satisfactory replies to my questions as to the variance between the views expressed by himself in October and in January.[3]

Northcote's anxieties communicated themselves to Beaconsfield. The water question, the prime minister felt, was 'assuming a not very

[1] *The Times*, 12 Jan. 1880.

[2] Cranbrook's diary, 18 Jan. 1880: Cranbrook Papers, T501/297. There is a copy of a printed cabinet memorandum on London water supply, by E. J. Smith, 10 Jan. 1880, in the Disraeli Papers (box xxiii, packet 16, in old classification; not traced in new classification).

[3] Northcote to Cross, 20 Jan. 1880: Add. MS. 51265 (unfoliated). See also Northcote to Cross, 22 Jan.: *ibid.*

satisfactory aspect'.[1] Yet the cabinet allowed Cross to persevere with his scheme, accepting, perhaps, his belief that he had achieved the most favourable possible terms. On 2 March the Metropolis Waterworks Purchase Bill was presented to the Commons. Cross did his best to justify his course *vis-à-vis* the companies, especially the decision to take account of prospective increases in the value of their stocks. He explained that the water supply was to be taken over by a partly elective Water Trust, at a total ultimate cost of about £31m. (the companies taking their payment in the form of water stock issued by the Trust and backed by the rates). The bill was to go to a hybrid committee, which might accept or reject the terms agreed with the companies, but not alter them.[2] Then the storm broke.

A sizeable agitation was got up in the capital against what was widely thought to be the intolerable cost of the purchase, and there was sharp criticism of the government for giving way on prospective additions to stock values.[3] The wave of speculation roused suspicions that there had been shady dealing, and that the bill was a job. Sir Henry Drummond Wolff warned Salisbury and Northcote five days after the bill's introduction of its likely effects on the metropolitan elections: a Ratepayers' League was being organised to protest against being forced to pay £30m. for a bad supply of water.[4] There was little alternative to retreat: on 9 March, the day after the announcement of the forthcoming dissolution, Cross said that the bill would be dropped for that session.[5]

The handling of the London water question reinforces the impression derived from other spheres that the government was losing its grip. The basic error was Cross's decision, following Smith, to proceed by agreement with the companies. The Home Secretary should have been prepared to use compulsion (or the threat of it) to secure a fair price, and he should not, after his August statement, have allowed Smith to give way on prospective additions to stock values. Moreover, in January, when to Northcote at least impending trouble was obvious, the cabinet should have reconsidered the whole problem and insisted on a firmer line towards the companies. The agreement reached was not wholly bad: it would have brought the ratepayers the centralised and accountable control of London's water

[1] Beaconsfield to Cross, 23 Jan. 1880: *ibid.*

[2] *3 Hansard*, ccli. 222–38.

[3] The *Times* leader of 8 March 1880 is representative of public feeling. It alleged that the companies would receive for their properties 75% more than they had been valued at six months before. For E. J. Smith's reply to criticism of his agreement, see *ibid.*, 27 March.

[4] Wolff to Salisbury, 7 March 1880 (Salisbury Papers, S.C.); to Northcote, 7 March 1880 (Add. MS. 50040, ff. 217–18).

[5] *3 Hansard*, ccli. 688.

system which they wanted, and which eventually, in 1902, cost them not thirty-one but forty-six million pounds. It did not, perhaps, altogether deserve the condemnation it received from the Select Committee on London Water Supply appointed by the Liberals in 1880.[1] But the price it embodied was undoubtedly somewhat inflated, and the whole business, underlining the tenderness of the Conservative party towards vested interests which was so apparent in the licensing question, formed the worst possible prelude to the general election.

The government's record on social questions in its last three years was an inglorious one. The Disraelian drive for social reform, never very powerful or coherent, even in the good days of 1874–6, had slackened and disintegrated. Its protagonist had lost interest; his colleagues lacked enthusiasm and ideas. The ministry's outlook became noticeably more restricted towards the end of its term, as the impact of the depression on the one hand and the influx of the bourgeoisie on the other increasingly discouraged the expansion of state intervention on behalf of the working classes and intensified the deference of Conservatism towards vested economic interests. In the party at large there were even signs of reaction, on labour legislation and education. Absorbed in foreign and imperial imbroglios, and harassed by financial strains, the government handled social questions without plan, grasp, energy, or will. Almost everything it touched, it fumbled: the problems of the merchant service, employers' liability, the drink traffic, and London water were all weakly and unsuccessfully tackled. The only achievement, Cross's Factory Act, was primarily a consolidating measure; the only major schemes of advance, Hamilton's in education, were stillborn at the dissolution.

What came out most clearly was the ministry's total want of any considered social policy. Problems were dealt with piecemeal as they emerged into prominence, on the basis not of any agreed overall concepts but of empiricism qualified by preconception. The 'elevation of the condition of the people' meant simply a series of *ad hoc* remedies for what were seen as isolated cases of malfunctioning in an economic and social system whose basic structure was taken for granted. Such an approach was not disastrous, and not necessarily inadequate to win working-class support, so long as economic conditions remained

[1] For which see the Committee's report, pp. iii–v (*P.P.* 1880, x. 113–15). Hamilton contends (pp. 181–3) that the Committee was appointed to condemn the agreement. He, Cross, and Sclater-Booth were members, but Cross was too dazed by the election to vindicate himself. Hamilton thought Cross's bargain excellent, and its rejection a disaster for the ratepayers. Cf. on the Committee, A. G. Gardiner, *The Life of Sir William Harcourt*, i. 382–4.

favourable and the system appeared to work. But the end of the 'seventies saw a major economic recession, with sharp effects on the condition of the working classes, and the welfare of the people came to seem dependent less on piecemeal social amelioration than on the capacity of government to control and mitigate the fluctuations of the economy as a whole. Social improvement, it appeared, required an economic policy for its foundation. A party which professed among its ideals 'the elevation of the condition of the people' was guilty of issuing a false prospectus unless it had the economic means which alone could render such an aim capable of achievement. Disraeli had told his audience at the Crystal Palace in 1872 that the great problem was to have social improvement 'without violating those principles of economic truth upon which the prosperity of all States depends'.[1] By 1880 it seemed that upon the ability of his party if not to violate at least to reconsider the 'principles of economic truth' would depend its capacity to provide the social amelioration which it had promised, and so to forge the links with the working class towards which the reforms of the 'seventies had been in part directed.

The depression which the government encountered at the end of its term was a severe one. The ending of the world railway boom in 1873 had 'opened a new phase in the history of the British economy'.[2] Profits and prices fell sharply, and the rise of foreign competition, behind tariff walls, struck hard at British industry. From the end of 1877 to the middle of 1879 output declined, and unemployment rose fast. There was strong and often successful pressure by employers for the adjustment of wages to the reduced level of prices and profits. The winter of 1878–9 especially saw much hardship among the industrial working class. In agriculture, things were still worse. A run of bad harvests (1879 was the worst of the century) was accompanied not by the usual compensatory price rise but by a price fall, because of the advent of competition from the wheat lands of North America, and British farming entered into a period of extreme difficulty. By 1878–9 the sense of depression was general in the country, and the attitude towards the government of large sections of the working population began to hinge on their notion of its responsibility for, and capacity to alleviate, the economic situation.

The government's responsibility for the recession, whatever Liberal partisans might say about the effects of the heavy expenditures entailed by its foreign and imperial policies,[3] was virtually nil. But if it

[1] *Selected Speeches*, ii. 531.

[2] J. D. Chambers, *The Workshop of the World: British Economic History from 1820 to 1880*, p. 65.

[3] E.g. in the financial debate of 24 April 1879, *3 Hansard*, ccxlv. 987–1086. It was argued that the taxation required by these expenditures was hindering

could not do something towards reviving trade and maintaining employment and wages, its past protestations of concern for the working man would seem hollow irrelevancies. The moment called for measures to combat the depression and secure the economic base upon which social progress must depend. But to produce such measures was a task beyond the economic thinking of either Conservatives or Liberals in the 1870s.

Beaconsfield's government was, in fact, helpless in face of the general economic problem which the depression presented to it. Like most practical politicians, ministers depended for their tools of analysis and prescription on the orthodox political economy of their day—or, more often, since fundamental concepts are seldom revised after the age of forty, of their youth. This offered singularly little help when it came to the question of state action to aid an ailing economy, and, indeed, tended to suggest that action was better not attempted. The City, from which the government sometimes took economic advice, was hardly well-equipped to give it,[1] and the Conservative party had no economic brains-trust engaged in policy formulation.[2] The government was thus mentally imprisoned within the confines of a system of economic ideas which prevented it not only from trying to implement but even from contemplating general plans of action.

To most ministers, indeed, the depression seemed as much a natural phenomenon as lightning, and as little susceptible of human control. W. H. Smith adopted a cyclical view, and maintained that it was the inevitable consequence of the pre-1875 boom.[3] The government was relieved of the responsibility not merely of having started the trouble but also of trying to stop it. There is no evidence—or likelihood—that the cabinet ever considered measures of intervention to aid the economy, which it would certainly have felt to be doubtful in principle and of dubious efficacy in practice. It was accepted that government could, and probably should, do little.[4] There was no thought of

[1] S. G. Checkland, 'The Mind of the City 1870–1914', *Oxford Economic Papers*, new series, ix (1957), 261–78.

[2] Its lack of intellectuals hindered it in the economic as in other spheres. Conservatives, Derby had admitted to his leader in 1875, 'are weakest among the intellectual classes: as is natural' (Derby to Disraeli, 18 Aug. 1875: Disraeli Papers, B/XX/S/968).

[3] *3 Hansard*, ccxlv. 1013–14.

[4] Accepted, of course, by most Liberals as well as Conservatives. Granville, in February 1879, welcomed the fact that Beaconsfield's announcement of the session's business indicated no attempt to meet the 'unreasonable' wish for a 'panacea' for the depression. 'Any such measure', said Granville, 'would be in violation of those principles of political economy in which I am a sincere believer' (*ibid.*, ccxliii. 1048–9). Cf. Hartington, *ibid.*, ccxliii. 97.

trade, and also that commercial recovery was being impeded by the lack of confidence induced by the government's policies.

artificial stimulation of the economy and of employment—by public works, for example, though public works had been used to mitigate the effects of the Lancashire cotton famine, and Beaconsfield's government itself tried to alleviate Irish distress by providing money for useful works on easy terms.[1] The deliberate expansion of state spending was unthinkable in the eighteen-seventies, especially to a Chancellor of such rigorous Gladstonian orthodoxy as Northcote, whose God was the balanced budget (with a surplus for debt reduction thrown in). All that Northcote would do was to refrain as far as possible from increasing taxation—even when this meant, as in 1879–80, holding over the repayment of debt—on the ground that higher taxes diminished spending power and checked improvement.[2] This was something, but it was a negative rather than a positive measure, aimed less at improving the situation than at preventing it from getting worse. More active policies the government does not seem to have considered.

There was, of course, one policy which was in the tradition of the party, and which, by 1879, a tiny section of the party had come once more to support.[3] This was protection. The depression in both industry and agriculture stemmed largely from the rise of foreign competition and foreign tariffs, and the government might conceivably have sought to revive the home economy by erecting a shelter of protective duties. Protection might have been sold to the working men as the only means of stimulating trade and employment, and thus of providing the economic base without which social reform would be impossible of achievement; it might have been coupled, too, with imperial preference, and made to furnish an economic foundation for the Conservative vision of a united empire. The policy which Chamberlain was to embrace twenty-five years later might have come alive in the hands of Beaconsfield, linking in a coherent scheme the upholding of the empire and the elevation of the condition of the people, two of the objects which he had written into the credo of his party. But Beaconsfield had never grappled with the need to formulate an economic policy, and saw in protection primarily its political disadvantages.[4]

[1] See Northcote's statement, 6 Feb. 1880: *ibid.*, ccl. 170–2. Interest and repayment were even remitted in the first two years of the loan. Cf. M. & B., vi. 510.

[2] *3 Hansard*, ccxxxiii. 1710; ccxlii. 1336; ccxlv. 288–9; ccli. 1050. This policy was sharply criticised by the Liberal financial purists, including Gladstone. Beaconsfield concurred in it: see his letter to Queen Victoria, 5 Nov. 1879, in M. & B., vi. 494.

[3] See below, pp. 306–9.

[4] He had aired the idea of imperial preference in the late 'forties and early 'fifties (M. & B., iii. 24, 237, 333), and at the Crystal Palace in 1872 had advocated an imperial tariff (*Selected Speeches*, ii. 530), but nothing was heard of these notions in the late 'seventies.

The cabinet, despite pressure even from within the party, did not for a moment contemplate any form of protection. It did not believe in it. Manners was probably the sole convinced protectionist. His colleagues nearly all accepted the validity of free trade economics: several had been staunch free traders all their lives, like Cross and Northcote. The Chancellor, informed by a correspondent in January 1879 of urban working-class discontent at the government's failure to find means of alleviating the depression, expressed his anxiety lest people should be 'beguiled into the delusive remedy of a return to Protection'.

> Against that [he wrote], whatever may be the consequences to the party, I must resolutely protest; because I believe that it would be no remedy, but rather an aggravation of the evils complained of.
>
> Anything we can do to get foreigners to reduce their duties we will do: but this I think is the limit to which we ought to go.[1]

The doctrines of free trade, he told the Commons in July, he believed to be 'the doctrines of truth'.[2]

In any case, as well as being wrong, protection, in the eyes of the cabinet, was politically impossible. It would be difficult for the party of the landed interest to concede protection to industry without conceding it to agriculture as well, and agricultural protection meant the revival against the Conservatives of the cry of 'dear bread', whose effect on the mass electorate was expected to be potent. Ministers imagined the effect of a protectionist platform on so vital a Conservative stronghold as industrial Lancashire,[3] conjured up the spectre of a second Anti-Corn Law League, uniting the urban working and middle classes against the landed interest, calculated the electoral effects, and shrank away.[4] It meant abandoning British agriculture

[1] Northcote to Rev. T. N. Farthing, 17 Jan. 1879 (copy): Add. MS. 50053, f. 149. See also Northcote to A. J. Balfour, 3 May 1879 (copy; *ibid.*, ff. 164–5), arguing against countervailing duties on bounty-aided foreign sugar; Northcote to Sir E. Sullivan, 13 May 1879 (copy; *ibid.*, f. 167), asking how much protection would help British manufacturers in competing with foreign rivals in third markets.

[2] *3 Hansard*, ccxlvii. 1535.

[3] Protection made little headway in Lancashire, despite the difficulties of the cotton industry: see R. Smith, 'The Manchester Chamber of Commerce and the Increasing Foreign Competition to Lancashire Cotton Textiles, 1873–1896', *Bulletin of the John Rylands Library*, xxxviii (1955–6), 507–34.

[4] That they may well have been right to do so, the experience of the party in the general elections of 1906 and 1923 suggests. As Hicks Beach told a deputation of West Indian proprietors and merchants in 1878, 'We must remember that in this country the interest of the consumer is stronger than the interest of the producer' (quoted in W. L. Burn, 'English Conservatism', *Nineteenth Century and After*, cxlv (1949), 4).

to its fate, but that, perhaps, had already been settled by the nation, in 1846, and was past altering.

Unwilling to contemplate protection, and unable to think of anything else, the government was left to confront the depression and its social consequences without even the vestige of a remedial policy. In the winter of 1878–9, when severe distress among the working classes led to strong demands for some kind of action, it became impossible to avoid admitting the fact. Explaining the omission of any reference to the depression from the Queen's Speech, on 5 December 1878, Beaconsfield revealed his ministry's nakedness. He said:

> it is a questionable course to allude publicly to the distress of the country when it is not peculiar to the country itself; when you are not yourselves prepared with any remedial measures; and when, if you express your real opinions, you may give rise to hopes and miscalculations which afterwards may be disappointed and defeated, and which you must deplore. That is the reason that has governed us in this case. . . . Her Majesty's Government are not prepared—I do not suppose any Government would be prepared—with any measures which would attempt to alleviate the extensive distress which now prevails.

The prime minister had to take refuge in vague optimism and hopes of a cyclical upturn, seeing

> symptoms of amelioration and general amendment which must in time—and perhaps sooner than the country is prepared for—bring about those advantageous results which, after periods of suffering, we have before experienced.[1]

Ministers had little inclination even to try to mitigate the distress by special relief measures. At the end of 1878 they discussed a project of a national relief fund, but nothing came of it,[2] and when, in January 1879, the cabinet, apparently prodded by the Queen, considered the possibility of aid to specific areas, it could see only difficulties. There was some feeling that by strike action the workers had themselves contributed to their hardships, and Beaconsfield told Victoria:

[1] *3 Hansard*, ccxliii. 79–80.

[2] The idea originated with the editor of the *Pall Mall Gazette*, Greenwood. There is some correspondence on the subject in the Disraeli, Salisbury, Cairns, and Iddesleigh Papers. See also Beaconsfield to Lady Bradford, 27 Dec. 1878, in M. & B., vi. 403–4. The Home Office eventually found, by circularising mayors in the manufacturing districts, that local means were considered sufficient to cope with distress (for the circular and an abstract of replies, see H.O. 45/9471/79559/4 and H.O. 45/9471/79559/9). An interesting feature of the discussion on the fund is the light it throws on Beaconsfield's dependence on his colleagues in his last years. His letter of 27 Dec. 1878 to Lady Bradford, stating the case against action, is partly simple paraphrase of Northcote's letter to him of 23 Dec. (Add. MS. 50018, ff. 121–2).

It would be a terrible mistake if workmen acting so injudiciously, and so unworthily, should be encouraged in their conduct and sustained by the charity of other communities.[1]

The majority of the parliamentary party shared its leaders' conviction that there was little or nothing which the government could, or should, do to tackle the depression. Many Conservatives saw the crisis as a cyclical contraction which would automatically be succeeded by an upturn, and were able to cling to a Micawberish optimism. The Liverpool member, Torr, said in February 1877:

no one can see clearly when 'the good times will come again'. But that they will come, ere long, is just as certain as that the light of day follows the darkness of night. Prosperity and adversity move in cycles; and the one is simply the reflex of the other, and has nothing to do with politics.[2]

It was not the responsibility of the government to take action. 'The thing must right itself', said Lord Norton, opposing a Liberal motion for an inquiry into the causes of the depression, '... The people should be looking to their own exertions, and not to Parliament for a remedy.'[3] Moreover, state intervention to relieve the distress of the working classes did not commend itself to the many Conservatives who believed that those classes, pampered, perhaps, by recent social legislation, and intent on the pursuit of immediate material interests, had powerfully contributed to their own plight. Newdegate was not alone in feeling that the unions, 'threatening the security of capital', had aggravated commercial distress, and that wages would have to go down in order to make the country competitive.[4]

But there were Conservatives who thought that the government should do something to relieve the situation. Gorst wanted Northcote in 1878 to defer debt extinction in order to avoid having to increase the income tax and thus withdraw investment funds.[5] Lloyd in July 1879 called for a ministry for commerce and agriculture, with its head in the cabinet. 'The interests of commerce and agriculture', he maintained, 'were too great to be left alone', and 'there could never be a distinct and definite commercial policy in England until they had a Minister of Commerce to give them one'.[6] This outright request for more direct state intervention in economic affairs drew from Newde-

[1] Beaconsfield to Queen Victoria, 26 Jan. 1879: *Letters of Queen Victoria*, 2nd series, iii. 9–10.

[2] *3 Hansard*, ccxxxii. 71. Ritchie was another who took a cyclical view (*ibid.*, ccxlv. 1054–5). Liberals often said the same—e.g. Samuda: 'The inevitable result of bad times must be to produce good ones' (*ibid.*, ccxxxiii. 1705).

[3] *Ibid.*, ccxliv. 1975 (March 1879). The inquiry asked for was rejected by Beaconsfield (*ibid.*, ccxliv. 1976–86).

[4] *Ibid.*, ccxxxviii. 240; ccxliv. 1738.

[5] *Ibid.*, ccxxxix. 1239–42.

[6] *Ibid.*, ccxlvii. 1922, 1923.

gate the comment that *laisser-faire* 'had completely passed away', and from Northcote a homily on the benefits of private enterprise.[1] Lloyd supported also another cause, which by 1878–9 had gained the allegiance of a few Conservatives. It went under the names of 'Fair Trade', or 'Reciprocity', but to its opponents, and, indeed, to some of its friends, it was protection.

Protectionist (or reciprocitarian) sentiment was not very strong in the Conservative party at the end of the 'seventies. Most Conservatives, out of conviction, or habit, or sloth, continued, despite the questions raised by the depression, to believe in the doctrines of free trade. Birley, of Manchester, said in 1877:

> most thinking men now considered that it was the only policy which was worthy of a great commercial country. The question might, in fact, be taken as settled, so far as this country was concerned . . .[2]

Even the agriculturalists showed little inclination to press for protection. As Henry Chaplin said, moving in July 1879 for a Royal Commission on agricultural depression, free trade had always seemed an issue which 'whether for good or for evil, was settled during the last generation with the deliberate sanction and approval of the nation . . .'[3] Phipps, of Northampton, speaking of agricultural imports, declared:

> The British farmers expressed no desire that these importations should be restricted by law, for they knew that no Government could, or ought to, place any obstacles in the way of the consumers obtaining cheap food.[4]

Yet as the depression wore on, protectionist ideas gradually gained ground, until they had the services of a vocal group of Conservative supporters.

It was in April 1877 that MacIver said in the Commons:

> An impression was gaining ground that the practice of free trade had been pushed a little too far by Great Britain where there was no reciprocity. Not that he would advocate retaliation; but some part of the

[1] *Ibid.*, ccxlvii. 1930, 1936. Despite Northcote's opposition, Lloyd's motion carried.

[2] *Ibid.*, ccxxxv. 1086.

[3] *Ibid.*, ccxlvii. 1428. But Chaplin was moving towards protection.

[4] *Ibid.*, ccxliv. 1711. In this debate, of 25 March 1879, Phipps, Read, Chaplin, and Sandon all put bad seasons rather than imports first among the causes of depression. One reason for the failure of the agricultural interest to make a push for protection was no doubt that the largest landowners were deriving enough income from industrial and urban development to cushion them against falling agricultural receipts (Thompson, p. 268).

revenue for national purposes might be raised from the produce of those nations which did not receive our produce without taxation.[1]

This was one of the first statements of a new Conservative scepticism towards free trade, and it heralded a significant movement of opinion. A few months later, another Conservative, Lord Bateman, attacked free trade without reciprocity in a letter to *The Times*, and called for 'limited' protection.[2] From then on, there was a stream of protectionist propaganda in the press, and a steady growth of protectionist feeling in the country.[3] In the Conservative party, the neo-protectionists gained strength only slowly, and Bateman's Conservative Protectionist Association proved abortive.[4] But the continuation and deepening of the depression reinforced their arguments, and by 1879 they were a not insignificant group. In Parliament their chief spokesmen were Bateman and the old protectionist Duke of Rutland in the Lords, and MacIver in the Commons. Outside Westminster, other Conservatives were leaders in the movement, such as the worsted manufacturer Ecroyd, and the silk manufacturer Lister.[5] The neo-protectionists launched something of a parliamentary campaign in 1879–80, with frequent speeches, and motions by Bateman and Wheelhouse for reciprocity and inquiry into the effects of foreign tariffs and the state of the country's commercial relations.

The neo-protectionist case was simple, not to say crude. The hope of the early free traders that England's example would be universally followed had been disappointed, and what now obtained was 'one-sided' free trade, in which England put herself at an impossible disadvantage by pursuing free trade in a protectionist world. The result, with foreign goods coming in free and British manufactures running into hostile tariffs, was the wreck of home industry. What was needed was 'reciprocity'—treating other nations as they treated us, and if necessary applying import duties to their products. There was extreme anxiety to avoid the use of the word 'protection'. Reciprocity, Bateman said, was 'not necessarily Protection', and he and MacIver

[1] *3 Hansard*, ccxxxiii. 1480. He suggested a charge on Russian and American grain. Hermon, member for Preston, confirmed that 'the working men of the North of England did not like to have free trade on the one hand and protection on the other' (*ibid.*, ccxxxiii. 1483).

[2] The letter (12 Nov. 1877) was reprinted as a pamphlet, *Lord Bateman's Plea for Limited Protection or for Reciprocity in Free Trade.*

[3] On the rise of protectionist sentiment in 1877–80, see B. H. Brown, *The Tariff Reform Movement in Great Britain 1881–1895*, pp. 9–17; McDowell, p. 153.

[4] Brown, pp. 15–16.

[5] For whom, see *ibid.*, pp. 17–19. Ecroyd was a Conservative candidate in 1874 and 1880 (advocating tariffs each time), and was returned for Preston in 1881. Lister was a Conservative candidate in 1880.

argued that in fact reciprocity was the essential precondition of genuine free trade.[1] With reciprocity Bateman, MacIver, Rutland, Wheelhouse, and most of the other Conservative neo-protectionists combined an imperial *zollverein* and imperial preference.[2] But while linking the cause of empire to the cause of economic prosperity, they failed to stress also, as Conservative tariff reformers were to do after them, the cause of social reform.

They did, obviously, emphasise that their programme, by reviving industry and employment, was in the interest of the working man, for whom, said MacIver, so-called free trade meant 'hard work, long hours, and low wages'.[3] But they were not really deeply concerned about the working man, and they do not seem to have viewed reciprocity as providing the economic base for social reform. Most of them wanted reciprocity for the welfare of the employers rather than the employed. Many, like Ecroyd, Lister, and the member for Plymouth, S. S. Lloyd, were employers themselves. Several were anxious to secure protection for the industrial interests of their constituencies, like Wheelhouse of Leeds, or Ritchie, member for Tower Hamlets, who championed the cause of the home sugar industry,[4] or Eaton of Coventry, where the silk trade (in which Eaton was engaged) traced its ruin to the Cobden Treaty of 1860.[5]

Moreover, while it was easy to show how the working classes might gain from the protection of industry, it was more difficult to appeal to them with the protection of agriculture, which would involve an increase in the price of basic foodstuffs. The old-fashioned protectionists of the 'forties still surviving in the Conservative party, like Rutland, Newdegate, and G. W. P. Bentinck, had no reluctance to advocate agricultural protection, but the newer disciples of reciprocity often had. Bateman thought that taxing the food of the people was a mistake, though he was prepared for an import duty on foreign wheat for the purposes of imperial preference.[6] Clarke, in his South-

[1] *3 Hansard*, ccxlv. 404, 1366. MacIver described himself as 'no Protectionist, but rather a disappointed would-be Free Trader'.

[2] *Ibid.*, ccxlv. 1367–8, 1381; ccxlvii. 1465; ccl. 611.

[3] *Ibid.*, ccxlvii. 1463.

[4] Ritchie disclaimed association with protection or reciprocity, but favoured a countervailing duty on bounty-supported foreign sugar, arguing that it was merely the restoration of fair competition (*ibid.*, ccxlv. 865, 869–70, 912–14). Later in life, of course, as a Conservative Chancellor of the Exchequer, he was to support free trade against Chamberlain. Another Conservative who saw the case for a sugar duty was the young A. J. Balfour: he told Northcote so in a letter of 2 May 1879 (Add. MS. 50210, ff. 124–5), but added: 'Of course I know well enough that there are unanswerable reasons, administrative and political, which make the imposition of such a duty perfectly out of the question.' Northcote's reply is cited above, p. 303, n. 1.

[5] *3 Hansard*, ccl. 611–12.

[6] *Ibid.*, ccxlv. 1360–1, 1367–8. Cf. *Lord Bateman's Plea*, p. 8.

wark by-election of February 1880, while supporting reciprocity in regard to manufactures, opposed taxes on food.[1] But most of the neo-protectionists felt obliged to include agriculture in their cause, and tariffs on food as well as manufactures figured in the programme drawn up in November 1879 by MacIver, Lloyd, Ecroyd, Lister, and others.[2] This made much more delicate the task of putting the neo-protectionist case to the country. The familiar arguments of the 'forties were brought out of retirement to show that even with food taxes, the working classes would benefit by protection:

> The working man [said MacIver] required work and wages; but that was precisely what our so-called Free Trade system took from him. We offered him cheap bread instead, but left him no money to buy it; and then the Free Traders told him it was all for his good . . .[3]

Hermon, member for Preston, felt that 'until the majority of the consumers were ready to submit to a tax upon food, it would be useless to talk about Reciprocity or anything else'. He was hopeful, believing that 'ultimately they would consent to that, if they found the price of their labour enhanced in consequence'.[4]

The neo-protectionists had a programme which might have been made to serve as the essential economic basis of a coherent Conservative social policy. But they showed little sign of developing it in that direction. Nor did they show any sign of gaining the party, still less the government.[5] In a thin House, in February 1880, a motion by Wheelhouse for a Select Committee on England's commercial relations and the effects of 'one-sided so-called Free Trade' was crushed by seventy-five votes to six, and the government spokesman, Bourke, the Under-Secretary for Foreign Affairs, declared flatly that 'one-sided Free Trade was better than no Free Trade at all'.[6] On this note the party went into the general election, without a notion of that economic policy which alone could provide the foundation for the betterment of the condition of the people.

In March 1880 Lord Beaconsfield went to the country. His government was showing signs of exhaustion, and it faced mounting diffi-

[1] Clarke, p. 157.
[2] Brown, pp. 22–3.
[3] *3 Hansard*, ccxlvii. 1470. Cf. *ibid.*, ccxlv. 1380 (Rutland); ccxlvii. 1477 (Bentinck).
[4] *Ibid.*, ccxlv. 908.
[5] Beaconsfield had, of course, supported reciprocity in the 'forties and 'fifties (see above, p. 16, n. 5, and his *Lord George Bentinck: a Political Biography* (1852), c. xiii), but he now dismissed it as impracticable, because Britain had little left in her tariff to bargain with and was bound by commercial treaties (see, e.g., *3 Hansard*, ccxlvi. 817–18; ccli. 1250–1).
[6] *Ibid.*, ccl. 622.

culties if it remained in office. Irish obstruction was perhaps the largest, but there were a number of others, including several social questions. Reciprocity, employers' liability, London water, local option and Sunday closing, Plimsoll's grain cargoes bill, all figured in ministers' minds as hazards ahead.[1] Beaconsfield was especially anxious to forestall a movement which he expected among the farmers, disaffected by the experience of depression,[2] and he was encouraged to think the moment ripe for dissolution by striking by-election victories in Liverpool and Southwark. On 8 March, then, the impending dissolution was announced.

The prime minister tried to focus the attention of the electorate on the Irish problem, but inevitably the main election issue was the government's foreign and imperial policy, which Gladstone made the theme of his Midlothian campaigns, and whose defence was greatly hampered by the convention which, barring peers from the electoral battle, deprived the Conservative party of its three best speakers, Beaconsfield himself, Salisbury, and Cranbrook. Social issues played a secondary rôle. Some attempt was made by the Liberals, including Gladstone,[3] to represent themselves as the party of the nation and the people, and the Conservatives as the representatives of rank, wealth, and sectional interests, and a note of class antagonism crept into the campaign.[4] But the Conservatives made little serious effort to counteract this attack by appealing to the working men on a platform of social improvement. As usual, they appealed to them less in terms of their special interests as working men than in terms of their common interest with other classes as Englishmen. A party which professed to aim at removing, not emphasising, class antipathies, could logically do no other; and the need to retain and expand its bourgeois support, not to mention its increasingly bourgeois composition and outlook, obviously restrained it from large concessions to working-class interests and demands.

Of course, Conservative speakers and journalists stressed the government's record of social legislation in the interests of the working man.[5] Yet Cross, who had had more to do with that legislation than

[1] Paper in Sandon's hand, endorsed 'Mentioned at Cabinet' and 'Difficulties before us as a Government if we remain in office this year & do not dissolve at once. March 1880': Harrowby Papers, vol. lv, f. 191.

[2] See Queen Victoria's Journal, 5 March 1880, in *Letters of Queen Victoria*, 2nd series, iii. 71–2; Beaconsfield to Salisbury, 2 April 1880 (Salisbury Papers. S.C.).

[3] E.g. speech quoted in Morley, ii. 610–11.

[4] 'The election riots show us', declared the *Globe* (6 April 1880), 'that the mob almost invariably attacks the Conservatives, looking upon them as the antagonists of their class.'

[5] E.g. *Globe*, 20 March 1880—'The Government and the Working Classes'.

anyone, made merely a passing reference to it in his election manifesto, and as for future plans, offered no suggestions at all.[1] Conservatives clearly did not regard the social reforms of 1874–9 as the foundation of any Disraelian union with the people, or as signposts to Conservative policy. They appeared as the champions of prestige abroad, of imperial destiny, of the constitution and the social order, but not of social reform. 'Imperium et libertas' was thrusting into the background 'sanitas sanitatum', with which it might have been linked. The Conservatives were showing, too, all their customary dislike of 'democracy' and the mass electorate, and resentment at having to come to terms with it. Their appeal to it was often sluggish and inept. The efforts made to reach working-class voters in 1880 were patently inadequate. As usual, the lack of cheap Conservative newspapers for working men was a major handicap, and the National Union recognised after the election that the party had heavily lost the propaganda battle.[2] With the rise of the 'caucus', Conservative organisation was no longer, as in 1874, better than Liberal, and its deficiencies were not to be atoned for by employing shady characters like Peters and Kelly to agitate the working men.[3] The result was that in many areas the Conservative party failed to get its case across effectively to the working-class voter, and to persuade him that it had his interests at heart.

In those social questions which did play a part in the campaign, the Conservative party was generally on the defensive, trying to explain its errors and omissions, or justify the *status quo*, rather than offer prospects of reform. The general economic and social problem of the depression overshadowed everything else, and the Conservatives were copiously and unscrupulously blamed by their opponents for the 'bad times' and the consequent distress, to which their costly and rumbustious foreign and imperial policies were held to have contributed much. Many working men undoubtedly felt, in an obscure way, that the government bore some responsibility for the depression,

[1] Address to the electors of S.W. Lancs., 12 March 1880 (copy in Add. MS. 51273, unfoliated). The address concentrates on foreign policy.

[2] National Union Conference, 23 July 1880, MS. minutes.

[3] Peters and Kelly were a pair of rascals on the fringes of the labour movement, who had helped form in 1878 the Workmen's National Association for the Abolition of Foreign Sugar Bounties, and in the 'eighties were to be associated with Conservative politicians and businessmen in the fair trade agitation, besides organising opposition to London municipal reform, and strike-breaking (Brown, pp. 31ff., 47; J. Saville, 'Trade Unions and Free Labour: the Background to the Taff Vale Decision', in *Essays in Labour History*, ed. A. Briggs and J. Saville, pp. 331ff.). For their employment in 1880, see E. Stanhope to Salisbury, 14 April 1882 (Salisbury Papers, S.C.). Salisbury evidently wanted them employed again, but Stanhope was reluctant.

and that a change might mend matters,[1] and Conservative candidates could not promise any remedial measures.[2] More specific points which interested labour, and appeared in the T.U.C. Parliamentary Committee's list of questions for candidates, included employers' liability, the extension of the labour laws to seamen, and an increase in the factory inspectorate.[3] Here again, the government had failed to give satisfaction, and candidates were embarrassed. In the Metropolis, the water question damaged the ministry, though the Liberal jibe that the Conservatives had 'come in on beer and gone out on water' was a gross exaggeration at both ends.

Beer, as in 1874, played a substantial part in the election, in the minds as well as the stomachs of voters. The campaign of the temperance militants for local option was fiercely resisted by the licensed trade, who again threw much of their weight on to the Conservative side. The Conservative party had not identified itself with their cause, and of late, largely under the influence of the temperance movement in the Church, had perhaps been growing less favourable to it; but the government of Lord Beaconsfield had passed the Licensing Act of 1874, and had steadily blocked temperance assaults on the trade, while it was the Liberal party which provided the temperance movement with the great bulk of its parliamentary support. As the *Morning Advertiser* put it, calling on the licensed victuallers to unite against the temperance faction:

> its allies are, in ninety-nine cases out of a hundred, Liberals. It is Liberalism which has made a political issue out of the licensing question. It is to the action of the Ministerialists that the real defeat of the fifty or more measures of the past few years, some of them ruinous, all of them hostile, to the Trade, has been due.[4]

The *Morning Advertiser* was openly for the Conservatives in the election. The other trade organ, the *Licensed Victuallers' Guardian*, discouraged identification with either party, and pointed out that in many places leading brewers and victuallers were on the Liberal side, but it was generally friendly to the Conservatives, and printed as a leading article a letter by the general secretary of the Licensed

[1] A Lancashire Liberal told Henry Cecil that the operatives had long been saying: 'We shall never have good luck under a Jew.' Cecil to Salisbury, 21 May 1880: *ibid.*

[2] The neo-protectionists had remedies to offer, but they made little impact. Brown, p. 23.

[3] B. C. Roberts, *The Trades Union Congress 1868–1921*, p. 100, n. 4. The Parliamentary Committee also wanted household suffrage in counties, and re-distribution. The railwaymen's union exerted pressure in constituencies with a large railway vote for a bill giving railwaymen compensation for accidents (Hanham, p. 86, n. 1).

[4] 31 March 1880.

Victuallers' National Defence League, showing how much more favourable than the Liberals they had been to the trade.[1] Undoubtedly, the Conservative party got a good deal of help from the publicans. The *Morning Post* asserted that it was generally admitted the Conservatives might reckon on the support of the licensed victuallers in almost every constituency, and, expressing its feeling that legislative interference with the licensed interest had gone far enough, it remarked that the licensed victuallers 'know that they are perfectly safe with the Conservatives . . .[2] Of twenty candidates in ten London constituencies endorsed by the local licensed victuallers' organisations, seventeen were Conservatives,[3] and Conservative placards were all over the public houses.[4] The *Pall Mall Gazette* elevated the partnership between the party and the licensed trade to the plane of the highest principle, and declared:

> In fighting the battle of the licensed victuallers the Conservatives are fighting the battle of individual liberty against the encroachments of philanthropic despotism . . .[5]

Beaconsfield himself seemed to have set the seal on the association between Conservatism and drink when, among his last creations of peers, he included a barony for the brewer Guinness—'the first direct entry of beer into the Lords'.[6]

It is doubtful, however, how much benefit the Conservatives derived from trade support in 1880. It alienated some people, and may have helped to account for the loss of clerical votes which they seem to have suffered.[7] Moreover, it was probably not as strong as in 1874. So the *Licensed Victuallers' Guardian* thought,[8] and the president of the Licensed Victuallers' National Defence League said:

> The publicans were not and are not ungrateful to the Conservative Government for services rendered, and no doubt if the ballot box were

[1] 27 and 31 March 1880. [2] 18 and 23 March 1880.

[3] Advertisement by the London licensed victuallers' organisations in *Morning Advertiser*, 26 March 1880. This called on the publicans to vote and to canvass customers, friends, and neighbours, and take them to the poll. 'Commence at Eight to catch working men's votes, and do not relax your efforts until the Poll is Closed . . .' Some 300 committees formed to assist the return of the selected candidates were listed—most of them meeting in public houses.

[4] *Saturday Review*, 27 March 1880. [5] 23 March 1880.

[6] Thompson, p. 293. Salisbury, in his first ministry, was to follow suit by ennobling the Conservative brewer Allsopp.

[7] See Salisbury to Lady John Manners, 18 April 1880 (typescript copy; Salisbury Papers, 'Manners', p. 111); Lady John Manners to Salisbury, 'Wednesday' [endorsed April 1880] (Salisbury Papers, S.C.). Lady Manners said that 'many excellent people believe most Tories are Topers', because of their position on local option.

[8] 17 April 1880.

to reveal its secrets that fact would be seen; but at the same time they did not give them a solid vote, as in 1874.[1]

The Conservative failure to impress their case effectively on the working man was, in any event, past remedying by the efforts of the publicans. Depression, and the virulent Liberal criticism of the government's foreign and imperial ventures, had a greater impact on the working-class voter than the terrors of local option. Nor could they be adequately offset by a record of social reforms most of which were now four or five years in the past, and beyond the limit of electoral memory—or at any rate of electoral interest. Disraelian Conservatism, it seemed, had failed to root the party's power in the support of the masses. True, the Conservatives retained a substantial body of working-class adherents in 1880, and their Conservatism was perhaps more open and demonstrative than ever before. A correspondent of Salisbury noted 'the popular enthusiasm' for Conservative candidates—'marked enough to be almost a new feature of the occasion'—and had found in Lancashire 'artizans openly parading our favours who, within my own remembrance, dare scarcely have done it for their lives'.[2] But all this did not prevent disaster at the polls, and a net Conservative loss of over a hundred seats, which brought them back only 237 strong, to face 353 Liberals and 62 Irish.[3]

The Conservatives took their worst beating in the boroughs, where they not only lost the ground gained in 1874, but did worse than in 1868. In the great centres of population and industry, where the working-class vote was largest, they suffered major setbacks. Of the 114 seats in towns with a population (at 1871) of over 50,000, they had only 24, compared with 44 in 1874, and 25 in 1868.[4] The percentage of the poll won by Conservatives in large English boroughs in 1880 appears to have been less than in 1868, as well as 1874, and less than the average for constituencies as a whole.[5] In the great

[1] *Licensed Victuallers' Guardian*, 1 May 1880. The president thought one reason for this was the Church's having taken up temperance.

[2] Henry Cecil to Salisbury, 24 May 1880: Salisbury Papers, S.C.

[3] Following *The Times*, 29 April 1880.

[4] Figures from Hanham, p. 92, n. 2.

[5] *Ibid.*, p. 193, table VII (figures for a sample of 52 constituencies, including 14 large English boroughs). But in the *very largest* constituencies as a whole, including counties, it seems that the Conservatives, while losing more of their proportion of the vote than elsewhere in 1880, still increased their total vote and did much better than in 1868. Basing his figures on an approximate calculation of *voters* on each side, a contemporary statistician estimated that in the 29 English and Welsh constituencies with an electorate (in 1880) of over 17,500, and contested by both parties in 1868 and 1880, the Conservative percentage of voters rose from 37.5 in 1868 to 44.3 in 1880. Solely because of these constituencies, the Conservative percentage of voters in all English and Welsh constituencies contested by both sides at each election also rose, from 44.3 in 1868

London boroughs, the Conservatives relinquished their gains of 1874 in Chelsea and Marylebone, and lost both seats in Southwark. There was a string of Liberal gains in the towns of the industrial north and midlands: Ashton, Bolton, Bradford, Leeds, Newcastle, Nottingham (2), Oldham, Salford (2), Stalybridge, Stoke, Wakefield, Warrington—fourteen Liberal gains, in seats which had provided nine Conservative gains in 1874. The only Conservative gains in 1880 in large urban constituencies were at Greenwich and Sheffield—cold comfort, though Beaconsfield made what he could of them, combining them with the Conservative successes in the City and Westminster to prove that 'the enlightened masses are with us'.[1]

Its decline in the larger boroughs weakened the party's links with the great centres of population, industry, and the working-class vote, and rendered it as dependent as it had been in 1868 on its traditional sources of support in the counties and small, bucolic towns. While boroughs of over 50,000 inhabitants now furnished only 10.1% of Conservative members, compared with 12.5% in 1874, the English and Welsh counties and the English boroughs of up to 20,000 inhabitants (in 1871) furnished 67.9%, compared with 60.1% in 1874, and 66% in 1868.[2] But though thrown back to some degree upon its rural roots, the party did not fail to show the marks of the increased bourgeois element in its support. It did conspicuously well in the City, where the three Conservative seats were held with much enlarged majorities, and in the constituencies around London, where the suburban middle-class vote was heavy. When the result of the election became clear, Sandon was told by his brother: 'In London in the upper & business classes the consternation is great, & no sympathy is felt in the change'.[3] The composition and economic interests of the parliamentary party reflected to some extent the growth of bourgeois Conservatism. The percentage of landholders dropped slightly from the 1874 figure of 73 to 71.3, and by comparison with 1874 proportionately many more financial and industrial interests were represented

[1] Beaconsfield to Lady Bradford, 2 April 1880, in *Letters of Disraeli to Lady Bradford*, ii. 266. Cf. Beaconsfield to Salisbury, and to Queen Victoria, 2 April 1880 (Salisbury Papers, S.C.; M. & B., vi. 526).

[2] The percentages for the counties and small boroughs are based on the figures in *Pall Mall Gazette*, 17 April 1880, and Hanham, p. 39, n. 2. The English and Welsh counties actually provided more than half the Conservative members (120 out of 237).

[3] Henry Ryder to Sandon, 21 March 1880: Harrowby Papers, vol. xliv, pt. 1, ff. 253–6.

---

to 45.9 in 1880 (A. Frisby, 'Has Conservatism Increased in England Since the Last Reform Bill?', *Fortnightly Review*, xxx new series (1881), 727–9). Cf. Dunbabin, 'Parliamentary Elections', p. 88; Vincent, p. xxiii.

on the Conservative benches.[1] The outcome of the election thus helped to emphasise that what was emerging from the 'seventies was not a 'Disraelian' party, based largely on working-class support, but a 'Peelite' party, resting principally on an alliance between the old landed property and the newer industrial and commercial wealth, and drawing an increasing amount of its strength from the urban middle classes.

The Conservatives were dumbfounded at the extent of their defeat. There was a bewildered groping after the causes of the crash, and much nervous speculation about its implications. Beaconsfield fixed first on 'Hard Times', and 'that sympathy for change which is inherent in man', to explain the disaster, adding later the 'new foreign political organisation' of the Liberals.[2] There was general agreement on these factors. But there was also a strong tendency to lay the principal blame upon 'the fickleness of the multitude',[3] and to see in the election result a proof of the untrustworthiness and ingratitude of the working men, who had gone against the Conservatives, 'although almost the whole domestic legislation of the past six years has concerned itself in improving their conditions and lightening their burdens'.[4]

Beaconsfield did his best to defend the conduct of the voters he had created, and to mask, from himself as well as others, the apparent failure of the popular Conservatism for which he had stood. At a party meeting:

> He argued that the great and sudden change was not due, as some would have it, to the fickleness of the newly enfranchised classes. . . . he analysed our losses, so as to show that they had been most marked in the counties where the suffrage is more restricted.[5]

But many of his followers, especially on the right of the party, felt that their rout was all too clearly due to the newly enfranchised classes. Here at last were the real fruits of the second Reform Act. 'Alas! how right we were in 1867!' wrote Lord Eustace Cecil to Salisbury. Lord Eustace concluded that 'we have been in the full tide of democracy consequent on the 1867 Bill, for many years, without

[1] Thomas, pp. 15, 16. Perhaps significantly, however, the number of brewers and distillers fell sharply, from 14 in 1874 to 7 in 1880. The Liberals continued to have a greater proportionate representation of financial and industrial interests than the Conservatives.

[2] Letters of 2 April 1880 to Queen Victoria, Salisbury, and Lady Bradford, cited above, p. 315, n. 1; speech at a party meeting, 19 May 1880, reported to the Queen by Lord Rowton (M. & B., vi. 576).

[3] The phrase is from A. J. Balfour to Salisbury, 7 April 1880: Salisbury Papers, S.C.

[4] *Globe*, 3 April 1880.

[5] Northcote's diary, 19 May 1880 (typescript copy): Add. MS. 50063A, ff. 335–6.

knowing it'.[1] Salisbury himself, ruminating on the 'hurricane' that had swept the party away, wondered whether it was 'the beginning of a serious war of classes'.[2] To a large section of the Conservative party the defeat of 1880 marked the self-assertion of that Radical democracy which they had so long feared, and heralded a new political era of conflict and peril, in which Conservatism would stand at bay.

As in 1868, so in 1880 defeat at the polls tended to discredit the idea of a 'Tory Democracy', and to turn the Conservative party back into the paths of stolid resistance to change. Any notion of a positive appeal to the people was at a discount; the party considered rather how it could defend its world against them. The strategy of waiting for the violence of the Radicals to reinforce Conservatism by driving over the moderate elements of the other side was re-adopted in default of a positive Conservative policy, and perhaps as a means of avoiding having to formulate one. Even as the election results came in, Selwin-Ibbetson wrote to Cross:

> Our only hope, that the Radical demands may before long create a fusion which for a moment may stem the democratic flood.[3]

A few weeks later, Northcote was speculating on the chances of a Conservative 'cave' on the Liberal side, and concluding that the party should manage its opponents 'discreetly', so as to encourage their conversion[4]—a line of thought which explains the moderation in opposition that so infuriated the Fourth Party. Chamberlainite Radicalism was to save the Conservative party in the 'eighties, as Gladstonian energy had saved it in the 'seventies.

Even Beaconsfield acquiesced in this attitude, as indeed he had to, for he could offer nothing better. To his followers he counselled 'moderation, and the maintenance of a dignified attitude, supporting the moderate and Whig sections of the Government against their Radical colleagues and friends, so that the Conservative party might be recognised as a real power in the country'.[5] Significantly, in stating

[1] Cecil to Salisbury, 12 and 19 April [1880]: Salisbury Papers, S.C.

[2] Salisbury to Balfour, 10 April 1880, in *Chapters of Autobiography*, pp. 127–8.

[3] Selwin-Ibbetson to Cross, 'Thursday' [evidently April 1880]: Cross Papers (seen at the India Office Library; not traced in British Museum Add. MSS.).

[4] Northcote's diary, 26 April 1880, in Lang, ii. 150. Northcote thought that the 'cave' might centre on Goschen, and that some of the Liberals might ultimately be got into a Conservative cabinet. In this he was prophetic.

[5] Northcote's diary, 19 May 1880, recording Beaconsfield's speech at a party meeting (typescript copy; Add. MS. 50063, ff. 335–6). Cf. Rowton's report of the meeting, in M. & B., vi. 576, and Manners to Northcote, 16 Nov. 1880 (Add. MS. 50041, ff. 43–4), where Manners says Beaconsfield 'is impressed with the wisdom of making much of the moderate Whigs at the expence [*sic*] of Gladstone and the Radicals'.

Conservative policy, he reduced the three points of 1872 to two: 'The policy of the Conservative party is to maintain the *Empire* and preserve the *Constitution.*'[1] On these two essentially conservative objects the party could unanimously agree; the more positive, and therefore more divisive, aim of the elevation of the condition of the people was quietly pushed into the background, and with it the popular, reformist Conservatism associated with Beaconsfield's name. The Conservative leader had not abandoned his faith in the conservative potential of the people. In the letter of November 1880 in which he gloomily told Manners that 'Old England seems to me to be tumbling to pieces', he wrote (principally in reference to the Irish question):

> The only portion of the Constituencies, in my opinion, who may be depended on when affairs are riper, are the English working-classes . . .[2]

But the time for appealing to the working classes was not now, and Lord Beaconsfield was tired. He still retained, at seventy-six, enough interest in the social question to listen patiently for three hours to the socialistic ideas expounded to him by one of his admirers, H. M. Hyndman, but there was weariness in his reply:

> It is a very difficult country to move, Mr. Hyndman, a very difficult country indeed, and one in which there is more disappointment to be looked for than success.[3]

For him the difficulty and the disappointment quickly ceased, on 19 April 1881.

[1] Speech at party meeting, 19 May 1880, as reported by Rowton (M. & B., vi. 576). The Earl of Midleton says (*Records & Reactions 1856–1939*, p. 298) that Beaconsfield gave his audience the watchword, 'Ireland, and the defence of the Land'.

[2] Beaconsfield to Manners, 24 Dec. 1880, in Whibley, ii. 203–4. Replying, Manners wrote: 'The working Classes in the large towns require very little further provocation to resist whatever or whomsoever finds favour with the Irish, and I agree with you in looking forward hopefully to their cooperation when the time comes' (letter of 27 Dec. 1880; Disraeli Papers, B/XX/M/283. Partly printed in Whibley, ii. 204).

[3] H. M. Hyndman, *The Record of an Adventurous Life*, pp. 244–5

CONCLUSION

THE study of the Conservative party's attitude to the major social problems bearing on the condition of the working classes between 1866 and 1880, and of the influences which affected it, provides some assistance in the important task of analysing the character of the adjustment which the party was making in these years to economic and social change, and in particular to the advance of urban and industrial civilisation and the growing power of the urban bourgeoisie and workers. The examination of the place of social reform in Conservative strategy and tactics helps to emphasise that despite the emergence of the mass electorate and the increasingly central rôle of social issues in politics, the main element in this adjustment was not any effort to create a party on 'Disraelian' lines, closely linked to the people by the bonds of social paternalism, and preaching the tenets of 'Tory Democracy'; it was the gradual coming to fruit of the course which Peel had pursued in the 'thirties and early 'forties, and Derby and Disraeli had tried to resume in the 'fifties, a course which aimed to draw the satisfied and defensive sections of the bourgeoisie into alliance with the land, in a party combining the defence of the constitution and the social order with the pursuit of cautious progress.

Paradoxically, it was the second Reform Act of 1867, at first sight the coup by which Disraeli committed his party to the pursuit of 'Tory Democracy', that in the long run did most to establish the conditions necessary for the assimilation of the bourgeoisie. While it gave the urban working men a substantial instalment of political power, and made the consideration of working-class interests vital to politicians, it intensified the pressures and fears which tended to drive elements of the middle classes into the Conservative party, as the only reliable agency of resistance to the advance of Radicalism and labour. The gradual polarisation of politics after the Palmerstonian truce, and the re-emergence of the social tensions on which Conservatism had fed in the 'thirties and 'forties, and whose anaesthesia through prosperity had done much to account for its weakness in the 'fifties and early 'sixties, acted increasingly towards giving the Conservative party what Palmerston had denied it, and what was essential for its electoral success, a near-monopoly of the conservative forces in the country, and hastened the coalescence of industrial and commercial with landed property in the 'Peelite' alliance.

The result was that in the years after 1867, just when the enlargement of the franchise had made it vital for the Conservatives to build up working-class support and show their capacity and will to deal with the social questions which must in future be a major political theme, they were inhibited in their approach to the masses by the counter-attraction of a growing middle-class support, largely dependent on their potential as a bulwark against popular demands. It was impossible for them (even had they been willing) to adopt a very 'popular' platform or to go very far in appealing to the working men in terms of their special interests as a class. Their main emphasis, as Disraeli saw clearly, had to be on the idea of the 'national' party, demonstrating the community of class interests in the maintenance of existing institutions. This prevented them from seriously trying to fill the vacuum left by the inability of official Liberalism to give complete satisfaction to working-class claims and aspirations, and in particular meant that there could be no question of their exploiting social issues in the spirit of the paternalist and radical Toryism of the 'thirties and 'forties, with which their leader's name was associated. Conservative social reform, in the Disraelian era, had to be cautious and restrained.

The party's tactical necessities corresponded, of course, to its natural inclinations. Very few Conservatives had any taste for appealing to the people at large, and genuine 'Tory Democrats', like Gorst, were rare and unappreciated. For most, the essential problem was not how to take the newly-enfranchised working men into partnership, but how best to reconcile the acknowledgement of their novel political influence with the maintenance of their economic and social subordination. As representatives of property, Conservatives were necessarily opposed to working-class claims which trenched upon what they held to be its rights, and to schemes of social improvement which did likewise. Most of the property, still, was landed, and it was very largely in relation to rural society that social questions were viewed, with generally narrowing effects. This was especially true of such vital matters as education, health, and poor relief, which had a direct impact upon the rural ratepayers, local autonomy, and the stability of the rural social order. If its bucolic (and predominantly southern) roots made it a little easier for the party to support, say, factory legislation, which hardly touched rural and agricultural interests, they rendered it in general difficult for it adequately to understand and come to grips with the social wants of the working classes in the great centres of industry and population in the midlands and north.

There was never any distinctive Conservative approach to social questions, though it would perhaps be true to say that the party was slightly more influenced by paternalism and slightly less by economic orthodoxy than the Liberals. On the general problem of the rôle of government and legislation in dealing with social matters, the Conservative attitude was always ill-defined, but with an engrained bias against the extension of central intervention and control unless a very good case could be shown for it. This bias tended to become deeper after 1867 had made real the prospect that ultimately the power and authority of government would be applied at the behest of the working classes, to give effect to their own interpretation of their own interests; and it was reinforced by the influx into the party of the conservative bourgeoisie, anxious to restrict the employment of the force of the state to satisfy the claims of the labouring population. Such paternalism as the Conservative party possessed could not be transposed into support for the collectivism which seemed to threaten as a consequence of the widened suffrage, and Conservative pronouncements on social problems became increasingly marked by adherence to the tenets of freedom and individualism commonly regarded as characteristic of classical liberalism. All this militated against any attempt to formulate a positive and coherent Conservative social policy. Such a policy, in any case, would have required an economic policy as its base: the Conservatives did not have an economic policy, or the intellectual resources and taste for schematic thought required to produce one.

In these circumstances, there was no possibility of the party's going far along the 'Disraelian' road of popular appeal and social reform. Nor did Disraeli make very strenuous efforts to lead it in that direction. The popular Toryism of his youth had been in part a romantic extravaganza, in part a gesture against Peel, without much practical content, and after 1846 it was pushed into the background as he saw that the resumption of Peel's policy was the only viable course for the party. His coup of 1867 was not an attempt to re-establish the party's fortunes on the support of the masses, but a manoeuvre designed to break the Whig monopoly of the cause of constitutional progress, which the tactical situation forced him to carry further than he would have chosen. After Reform, he was conscious as much of the necessary limits on the party's cultivation of working-class votes as of its importance. Not until 1872 did he seriously attempt to make political capital out of support for the improvement of the social condition of the people. Then, indeed, he elevated social reform into one of the principal objects of his party. But he followed this with no concrete initiative or plan, and the imperialism which he proclaimed at the same time was in the end to be a more potent influence. In power, in 1874, he had no specific projects of social advance, though the weight of his general approval of the measures which his colleagues devised was vital to the development of the ministry's reforming effort. It was not that Disraeli lacked a genuine predilection for social improvement, or a keen appreciation of its political uses, but he understood the need for caution to reconcile its pursuit with the interests and prejudices of his existing and potential followers of the propertied classes, and knew that the emphasis of the Conservative platform must lie rather on the furtherance of the common cause of all classes than on the special promotion of the welfare of one. Living in uneasy symbiosis with a party to which he was in many ways alien, at once its leader and its prisoner, he could not transform its character or reshape its thinking; he could only influence and modify its outlook and course. He did not found modern Conservatism; indeed, in destroying Peel, he had retarded its main line of development, the absorption of the bourgeoisie, by some twenty years. What he did was to assist its gestation, and facilitate its achievement of some kind of *modus vivendi* with the working classes.

Given the built-in hindrances to Conservative social reform, it seems remarkable that the party contributed as much as it did in the social field in 1866–80. Even in the short minority ministry of 1866–8 something was done for factory reform, the sick poor, and the merchant seamen, and the government of 1874–80 was responsible for one of the most notable instalments of social reform of the century, conspicuously shaming its Liberal predecessors. To some extent, these achievements were the product of a deliberate intention to use social improvement as a means of gaining working-class favour. But very largely they were semi-enforced responses to problems which ministers could not ignore, shaped principally by the results of formal inquiry, the pressure of public opinion, and the promptings of the civil service. They implemented no programme and embodied no philosophy. Nearly all were cautious and limited, and some were weak and ineffectual in working. Only the labour laws of 1875 went substantially beyond what the immediate situation demanded, presumably—we have little evidence on the genesis of these two measures —because Disraeli thought that a generous settlement would definitively establish his party as the real friends of the working man. Taken as a whole, the measures of 1866–8 and 1874–80 form an impressive corpus of work by contemporary standards, but what they symbolise is less Conservative zeal for social reform than Conservative empiricism in the face of concrete problems.

How much good they did the party is open to argument. Coupled with the second Reform Act, they enabled it to claim that it had the true interests of the labouring classes at heart. It is inconceivable that this had no electoral effect, but doubtful whether it had a great deal. The Conservatives could always rely, after 1867, on a certain amount of working-class support from 'deference' voters and from men who simply were, on general grounds, Conservative; there appears to be little evidence that this was markedly increased (though it was doubtless consolidated) by social reform. The appeal to national solidarity and patriotic pride, which Disraeli made a Conservative stock-in-trade, was probably more powerful than the promise of social improvement. Neither, in any case, succeeded in detaching the bulk of the working-class electors and the organised labour movement from Liberalism. A main reason for this (which in the end was to damage Liberalism also) was the failure to offer the working men enhanced social status. True, the Conservative party had given many of them the franchise, but it showed small inclination to follow out the implications of this step by paying genuine deference to their feelings and aspirations and giving them a significant rôle in its organisation and councils. The National Union exemplified the party's deficiencies in this respect: its existence was a recognition of the need to build up working-class Conservatism, but the indifference and even hostility of much of the party to its work showed in what a grudging spirit that need was approached. The gulf between the 'two nations' was not bridged; too firm a sense resided in one of its qualitative difference from the other.

After the defeat of 1880 and the death of Disraeli, the themes of popular appeal and social reform were more at a discount than ever. The bulk of the Conservative party was content to rely for future revival on the alienation of the moderate middle-class voter by its opponents. There was, of course, Lord Randolph Churchill, with his Tory Democracy, pursuing the supposedly 'Disraelian' tradition. But Churchillian Tory Democracy was a collection of postures and slogans, rather than a policy, whose main purpose was to serve as a vehicle for its author. To some extent, it was the gesture of a young cavalier aristocrat against the respectable, middle-aged, bourgeois Conservatism represented by men like 'Marshall and Snelgrove', as Lord Randolph called Cross and W. H. Smith. 'Marshall and Snelgrove' and their like, however, were coming increasingly to form the basis of the Conservative party, and Churchill's approach stood no chance against them.

Perhaps the only important effect of Lord Randolph's reassertion of 'Disraelian' ideals was to retard a little his party's true course of development by alarming the moderate opinion that was moving to the Conservative side in recoil from Chamberlainite Radicalism.[1] The bourgeoisie continued, however, to flow into the party in force, and their importance to it went on increasing. They brought it badly-needed resources, at a moment when agricultural depression was weakening the strength of its traditional mainstay, the landed interest; and after the redistribution of 1885, with its recognition of the primacy of the urban and industrial areas and its single-member constituencies, they were in a position to bring it a larger number of seats.[2] The Liberal split over Home Rule gave a considerable impetus to the middle-class movement towards Conservatism, but it only intensified a process that had been perceptible for at least twenty years and was already showing significant results.[3]

Coming over Ireland, the Liberal schism gave the Conservatives Chamberlain, but such strength as he brought to the popular and reforming side of the party was more than counterbalanced by the accession of the Whigs and 'Commercial Liberals', with their deep distaste for the expansion of state intervention for the welfare of the working classes.[4] As politics crystallised increasingly along class lines, the Conservatives became more and more a union of propertied interests, embattled against organised labour and socialism, and largely wedded to the classical liberal tenets of individualism and free enterprise. The type of party Peel had tried to construct in the 'forties finally materialised in the 'eighties and 'nineties. It did not (electorally it could not) lose sight of the working man or of social reform, but the 'Disraelian' themes were very subdued under Salisbury, Balfour, and Bonar Law.[5] By the beginning of the twentieth century, there was a feeling among those who found inspiration still in Disraelian ideas that the soul of the party had been corrupted. In 1907 Gorst, soon to be a Liberal candidate, lamented the decline of Tory Democ-

1 Cf. Southgate, p. 392.

2 See Cornford, especially pp. 58, 66.

3 Except, perhaps, in Scotland, where the Home Rule issue does seem to have been decisive in the Conservative breakthrough to substantial middle-class support. See D. W. Urwin, 'The Development of the Conservative Party Organisation in Scotland until 1912', *Scottish Historical Review*, xliv (1965), 94–6.

4 Cf. Southgate, p. 420, who contends that in the absence of effective competition from the Liberals in the field of social policy, the Conservatives 'tended to become "Goschenised" '.

5 Cf. Beer, pp. 271–6.

racy, and complained that the Conservative leaders had abandoned Disraeli's principles for the pursuit of class interest, and had become 'the champions of vested interests and the protectors of monopoly and privilege'.[1]

The strain of Conservative social consciousness, however, did not die out, and it was stimulated by reflection on the causes of the disaster of 1906. There continued to be those who saw the necessity of grappling with social problems, if the party was to operate successfully in the age of the mass electorate; even those who carried on the tradition of Tory paternalism and favoured the social action of the state, agreeing with Lord Hugh Cecil that there was 'no antithesis between Conservatism and Socialism'.[2] If no Conservative social policy emerged, and no economic policy on which one could be based (though the association of tariff reform with the cause of social improvement might have provided both), the activities of elements like the pre-1914 Social Reform Committee and the 'Group' of 1918 kept open a vital channel through which Conservatism could attempt to reach the mass of the people. Even in the locust years between the wars the vein of social responsibility occasionally touched the surface: but for Hitler, it is for his efforts at social reform that we should remember Neville Chamberlain.

Modern Conservatism is essentially 'Peelite' in its structure and outlook, and it became so partly under Disraeli's auspices. But its striking electoral success since 1867 would have been impossible without its capacity to command a significant working-class vote, and here it owes something to Disraeli's sense of the necessity of accepting the enlargement of the political nation and making the social condition of the people one of the prime objects of the party's concern. Disraeli could not create, and did not really try to create, a 'Disraelian' party, but he was able to introduce into the personality of Conservatism an element that assisted it in coming to terms with the rise of democracy and labour. He could not marry the party to the people, or fuse the 'two nations', but he did much to ensure that between them there should be no complete and fatal divide.

[1] Letter to *The Times*, 6 Feb. 1907 (written, not inappropriately, 'at sea, off Australia'). Cf. J. M. Kennedy, *Tory Democracy* (1911), and Lord Henry Bentinck, *Tory Democracy* (1918).

[2] Lord Hugh Cecil, *Conservatism* (1912), p. 195.

SELECT BIBLIOGRAPHY

The bibliography is arranged on the following plan (works of reference are not included):

(A) MANUSCRIPT SOURCES

(1) Private Papers
(2) Records of Government Departments
(3) Records of the National Union of Conservative and Constitutional Associations

(B) PRINTED SOURCES

(1) Primary Sources
- (i) Diaries and Letters
- (ii) Books, Pamphlets, Reports, Speeches, etc.
- (iii) Newspapers, Periodicals, and Transactions
- (iv) Parliamentary Debates
- (v) Parliamentary Papers

(2) Secondary Sources
- (i) General Works and Articles
- (ii) Books and Articles on the Conservative Party and Conservatism
- (iii) Biographical and Autobiographical Works and Articles
- (iv) Books and Articles on Social Questions
  - (a) General
  - (b) Drink Traffic
  - (c) Education
  - (d) Friendly Societies
  - (e) Public Health
  - (f) Housing
  - (g) Labour Questions
  - (h) Poor Relief

(A) MANUSCRIPT SOURCES

(1) PRIVATE PAPERS
(listed in approximate order of usefulness)

Disraeli Papers
Papers of Benjamin Disraeli, Earl of Beaconsfield, at Hughenden.
Carnarvon Papers
Papers of the 4th Earl of Carnarvon, in the Public Record Office (P.R.O. 30/6).
Iddesleigh Papers
Papers of Stafford Northcote, 1st Earl of Iddesleigh, in the British Museum (Add. MSS. 50013–50064, 50209–50210).
Harrowby Papers
Papers of the 2nd and 3rd Earls of Harrowby, at Sandon Hall, Stafford.
Salisbury Papers
Papers of the 3rd Marquis of Salisbury, at Christ Church, Oxford.
Cranbrook Papers
Papers of Gathorne Hardy, 1st Earl of Cranbrook, in the Ipswich and East Suffolk Record Office (HA 43).
Cross Papers
Papers of R. A. Cross, 1st Viscount Cross, first seen at the India Office Library, now in the British Museum (Add. MSS. 51263–51289).
Cairns Papers
Papers of the 1st Earl Cairns (typescript copies of correspondence), at Clopton Hall, Suffolk.
Goodwood Papers
Papers of the 6th Duke of Richmond, in the Goodwood MSS., in the West Sussex County Record Office, Chichester.
Marlborough Papers
Papers of the 6th Duke of Marlborough, at Blenheim.
Hambleden Papers
Papers of W. H. Smith, seen at the National Register of Archives, now at Strand House, Portugal Street, London, W.C.2.

(2) RECORDS OF GOVERNMENT DEPARTMENTS
(All in the P.R.O.)

Home Office Papers
H.O. 34—entry books of out-letters to government offices.
H.O. 45—registered papers.
H.O. 87—entry books of out-letters on factories.
H.O. 95—entry books of out-letters on mines.
Ministry of Education Papers
Ed. 10—general education: general files.
Ed. 23—establishment files.
Ed. 24—private office papers.

Ministry of Health Papers

M.H. 25—miscellaneous correspondence and papers.

M.H. 29—correspondence on water works.

Ministry of Transport Papers

M.T. 9—records of the Mercantile Marine Department of the Board of Trade.

(3) RECORDS OF THE NATIONAL UNION OF CONSERVATIVE AND CONSTITUTIONAL ASSOCIATIONS

MS. minutes of the annual conferences of the National Union, 1867–1882, at the Conservative and Unionist Central Office.

(B) PRINTED SOURCES

(the place of publication is London, unless otherwise stated)

(1) PRIMARY SOURCES

(i) *Diaries and Letters*

BUCKLE, G. E. (ed.), *The Letters of Queen Victoria*, 2nd series, 3 vols., 1926–8.

BURGHCLERE, LADY (ed.), *A Great Lady's Friendships: Letters to Mary, Marchioness of Salisbury, Countess of Derby, 1862–1890*, 1933.

CARTWRIGHT, JULIA (ed.), *The Journals of Lady Knightley of Fawsley*, 1915.

DISRAELI, R. (ed.), *Lord Beaconsfield's Letters, 1830–1852*, new ed., 1887.

KENNEDY, A. L. (ed.), *'My Dear Duchess': Social and Political Letters to the Duchess of Manchester 1858–1869*, 1956.

KINGSLEY, MRS. (ed.), *Charles Kingsley: His Letters and Memories of His Life*, 4 vols., 1901–2 (vols. I–IV of *The Life and Works of Charles Kingsley*).

LONDONDERRY, MARCHIONESS OF (ed.), *Letters from Benjamin Disraeli to Frances Anne Marchioness of Londonderry, 1837–1861*, 1938.

RAMM, A. (ed.), *The Political Correspondence of Mr. Gladstone and Lord Granville 1868–1876*, 2 vols., 1952 (Camden 3rd series, vols. lxxxi–lxxxii).
The Political Correspondence of Mr. Gladstone and Lord Granville 1876–1886, 2 vols., Oxford, 1962.

WALLING, R. A. J., (ed.), *The Diaries of John Bright*, 1930.

ZETLAND, MARQUIS OF (ed.), *The Letters of Disraeli to Lady Bradford and Lady Chesterfield*, 2 vols., 1929.

(*ii*) *Books, Pamphlets, Reports, Speeches, etc.*

ADDERLEY, C. B., *A Few Thoughts on National Education and Punishments*, 1874.
Punishment is Not Education, 1856.

BARRINGTON, MRS RUSSELL (ed.), *The Works and Life of Walter Bagehot*, 10 vols., 1915.

BARRY, P., *The Workman's Wrongs and the Workman's Rights*, 1871.

BATEMAN, LORD, *Lord Bateman's Plea for Limited Protection or for Reciprocity in Free Trade*, 1877.

SELECT BIBLIOGRAPHY

BENTINCK, LORD HENRY, *Tory Democracy*, 1918.

CECIL, LORD HUGH, *Conservatism*, 1912.

[CHARLEY, W. T.], *Conservative Legislation for the Working Classes: no. I—Mines and Factories*, 1868; rev. ed., 1877 (Publications of the National Union, no. VI).

Conservative Legislation and the Working Classes. No. II—The Truck Acts, 1868; rev. ed., 1877 (Publications of the National Union, no. X).

Conscience Clause in 1866. Speeches delivered in the Chapter-House of York Minster, on the 13th of October, 1866, by John Gellibrand Hubbard, M.P., and the Rev. George Trevor, Canon of York, 1866.

DERBY, 15th EARL OF, *Speeches and Addresses of Edward Henry XVth Earl of Derby K.G.*, ed. Sir T. H. Sanderson and E. S. Roscoe, with a prefatory memoir by W. E. H. Lecky, 2 vols., 1894.

The Conservative Working-Man. Speech of the Earl of Derby at Edinburgh. December 17th, 1875, 1875 (Publications of the National Union, no. XXVII).

DISRAELI, B., *General Preface to the Novels*, in the collected edition of 1870, vol. I.

Novels, especially *Coningsby* (1844) and *Sybil* (1845).

Selected Speeches of the Late Right Honourable the Earl of Beaconsfield, ed. T. E. Kebbel, 2 vols., 1882.

The Chancellor of the Exchequer in Scotland, being two speeches delivered by him in the city of Edinburgh on 29th and 30th October 1867, Edinburgh and London, 1867.

Vindication of the English Constitution in a Letter to a Noble and Learned Lord, 1835.

Whigs and Whiggism. Political Writings, ed. W. Hutcheon, 1913.

Dwellings of the Poor: Report of the Dwellings Committee of the Charity Organisation Society, presented to the Council November 3, 1873, 1873.

Dwellings of the Poor. Report of the Dwellings Committee of the Charity Organisation Society, presented to the Council August 2, 1881, 1881.

Essays on Reform, 1867.

FERRAND, W. B., *The Speech of Mr. Ferrand, President of the Bradford Working Men's Conservative Association, at the Inaugural Banquet, on the 20th November, 1866, in St. George's Hall*, Bingley, n.d.

[FORSYTH, W.], *An Appeal to the Moderate Liberals*, 1874.

HAILSHAM, VISCOUNT, *The Conservative Case*, Harmondsworth, 1959.

KEBBEL, T. E., *The Agricultural Labourer: a Short Summary of His Position*, 1870.

KENNEDY, J. M., *Tory Democracy*, 1911.

LINDSAY, LORD, *Conservatism: its Principle, Policy, and Practice. A Reply to Mr. Gladstone's Speech at Wigan, 23rd October, 1868*, 1868.

MANNERS, LORD JOHN, *A Plea for National Holy Days*, 2nd ed., 1843.

PAKINGTON, SIR J., *National Education. Address delivered by the Right Honourable Sir John Pakington, Bart., M.P., to the members of the Manchester Athenaeum, November 18th, 1856*, London and Droitwich, n.d. [1856].

PELL, A., *Out-Relief: a Paper Read by Mr. Albert Pell*, n.d. [1890].

Political Future of the Working Classes; or, Who are the Real Friends of the People? by 'E. B.', 1868; rev. ed. 1873 (Publications of the National Union, no. VII).

Practical Suggestions to the Loyal Working Men of Great Britain on Points of Policy and Duty at the Present Crisis, by 'E. A.', 1868 (Publications of the National Union, no. V).

Questions for a Reformed Parliament, 1867.

READ, C. S., *The Education and Wages of the Agricultural Labourer. An Address to the Prize Takers of the Tunstead and Happing Labourers' Association at North Walsham*, Norwich, n.d. [1867].

Reports of Proceedings at the annual conferences of the National Union, 1872–5 (Publications of the National Union, nos. XV, XXI, XXV, XXVI).

RUTLAND, DUCHESS OF, *The Collected Writings of Janetta Duchess of Rutland*, 2 vols., Edinburgh and London, 1901.

SHAFTESBURY, 7th EARL OF, *Speeches of the Earl of Shaftesbury, K.G., Upon Subjects Having Relation Chiefly to the Claims and Interests of the Labouring Class*, 1868.

The National Education Union and the Denominational System. Speech delivered by the Rt. Hon. the Earl of Shaftesbury at the Demonstration of the National Education Union, in St. James' Hall, London, on Friday evening, April 8th, 1870, 2nd ed., London and Sheffield, n.d. [1870].

Three Years of Conservative Government, 1877 (Publications of the National Union, no. XXX).

(*iii*) *Newspapers, Periodicals, and Transactions*

Bee-Hive

British Conservative (published June–July 1875, by those responsible for the *Finsbury Conservative*).

British Lion (published as 'The Organ of the Conservative and Constitutional Associations in the United Kingdom'; nos. 46–55 only, May–July 1868, held by the British Museum).

Cambridge Independent Press

Capital and Labour

Conservative (nos. 36–62 only, June–Dec. 1873, held by the British Museum).

Daily Courier [Liverpool].

Daily Telegraph

Economist

Finsbury Conservative (published Oct. 1874–June 1875, as the organ of the Conservative party in Finsbury).

Fortnightly Review

Globe

Hour (Conservative daily, published March 1873–Aug. 1876).

Imperial Review (published Jan. 1867–Dec. 1868).

Licensed Victuallers' Guardian

Manchester Guardian

Morning Advertiser

Morning Herald

Morning Post
Pall Mall Gazette
Press and St. James's Chronicle
Quarterly Review
Saturday Review
School Guardian
Sheffield Daily Telegraph
Spectator
Staffordshire Advertiser
Standard
Sun
Times
Transactions of the National Association for the Promotion of Social Science.

(*iv*) *Parliamentary Debates*
Hansard's Parliamentary Debates, 3rd series.

(*v*) *Parliamentary Papers*
(arranged by subject; R.C. = Royal Commission, S.C. = Select Committee)
Adulteration of Food Act (1872), S.C. report; 1874 (262), vi, 243.
Artizans' and Labourers' Dwellings Improvement, S.C. reports; 1881 (358), vii, 395; 1882 (235), vii, 249.
Children's Employment Commission, reports; 2nd, 1864 Cmd. 3414, xxii, 1; 3rd, 1864 Cmd. 3414—I, xxii, 319; 4th, 1865 Cmd. 3548, xx, 103; 5th, 1866 Cmd. 3678, xxiv, 1; 6th, 1867 Cmd. 3796, xvi, 67.
East London Water Bills & the Operation of the Metropolis Water Act 1852, S.C. report; 1867 (399), ix, 1.
Education, annual reports of the Committee of Privy Council on.
Education, S.C. reports; 1865 (403), vi, 1; 1866 (392), vii, 115.
Electoral Statistics: Return of the Proportion of Working-Class Electors in Boroughs; 1866 (170), lvii, 47.
Employers Liability for Injuries to their Servants, S.C. reports; 1876 (372), ix, 669; 1877 (285), x, 551.
Factories, annual reports of the Inspectors of.
Factory Acts Extension and Hours of Labour Regulation Bills, S.C. report; 1867 (429), ix, 575.
Friendly and Benefit Building Societies, R.C. reports; 1st, 1871 Cmd. 452, xxv, 1; 2nd, 1872 Cmd. 514, xxvi, 1; 3rd, 1873 Cmd. 842, xxii, 291; 4th, 1874 Cmd. 961, xxiii, 1.
Housing of the Working Classes, R.C. 1st report; 1884–5 Cmd. 4402, xxx, 1.
Infirmary Wards of the Metropolitan Workhouses, report of H. B. Farnall to the Poor Law Board on; 1866 (387), lxi, 389.
Intemperance, House of Lords S.C. reports; 1st, 1877 (171), xi, 1; 2nd, 1877 (271), xi, 357; 3rd, 1877 (418), xi, 759; 4th, 1878 (338), xiv, 1; last, 1878–9 (113), x, 469.
Licensing Act, 1872, Reports from Borough Authorities in England and Wales relating to the; 1874 (160), liv, 243.
Local Government and Local Taxation of the Metropolis, S.C. reports; 1866 (186), xiii, 171; 1866 (452), xiii, 317.

Local Government Board, annual reports of the.
London Water Supply, S.C. report; 1880 (329), x, 111.
Master and Servant, S.C. report; 1866 (449), xiii, 1.
Merchant Seamen Bill, S.C. report; 1878 (205), xvi, 77.
Metropolitan Fire Brigade, S.C. reports; 1876 (371), xi, 53; 1877 (342), xiv, 37.
Metropolitan Workhouse Infirmaries and Sick Wards, report of Dr Edward Smith to the Poor Law Board on; 1866 (372), lxi, 171.
Mines, annual reports of the Inspectors of.
Mines Not Coming Under the Provisions of 23 & 24 Vict., c. 151, R.C. report; 1864 Cmd. 3389, xxiv, pt. I, 371.
Poor Law Board, annual reports of the.
Poor Relief, S.C. report; 1864 (349), ix, 187.
Prevention of Rivers Pollution, R.C. reports; 1st, 1866 Cmd. 3634, xxxiii, 1; 2nd, 1867 Cmd. 3835, xxxiii, 1; 3rd, 1867 Cmd. 3850, xxxiii, 231.
New Commission (1868) reports; 1st, 1870, Cmd. 37, xl, 1; 2nd, 1870, Cmd. 180, xl, 499; 3rd, 1871 Cmd. 347, xxv. 689; 4th, 1872 Cmd. 603, xxxiv, 1; 5th, 1874 Cmd. 951, xxxiii, 1; 6th, 1874 Cmd. 1112, xxxiii, 311.
Proposed Changes in Hours and Ages of Employment in Textile Factories, report to the Local Government Board on, by J. H. Bridges and T. Holmes; 1873 Cmd. 754, lv, 803.
Railway Accidents, R.C. report; 1877 Cmd. 1637, xlviii, 1.
Sanitary Commission, reports; 1st, 1868–9 Cmd. 4218, xxxii, 301; 2nd, 1871 Cmd. 281, xxxv, 1; 2nd, vol. iii, pt. II, 1874 Cmd. 1109, xxxi, 603.
Scottish Education Commission, 2nd report; 1867 Cmd. 3845, xxv, 1.
State of Popular Education in England, R.C. report, vol. i; 1861 Cmd. 2794—I, xxi, pt. I, 1.
Trades Unions, R.C. reports; 1st, 1867 Cmd. 3873, xxxii, 1; 2nd 1867 Cmd. 3893, xxxii, 167; 3rd, 1867 Cmd. 3910, xxxii, 197; 4th, 1867 Cmd. 3952, xxxii, 289; 5th–10th, 1867–8, Cmd. 3980—I–VI, xxxix, 1; 11th, 1868–9 Cmd. 4123, xxxi, 235.
Unseaworthy Ships, R.C. reports; preliminary, 1873 Cmd. 853, xxxvi, 315; final, 1874 Cmd. 1027, xxxiv, 1.
Water Supply, R.C. report; 1868–9 Cmd. 4169, xxxiii, 1.
Working of the Factory and Workshops Acts, R.C. report; 1876 Cmd. 1443, xxix, 1, and xxx, 1.
Working of the Master and Servant Act, 1867, and the Criminal Law Amendment Act, 34 & 35 Vict. Cap. 32, etc., R.C. reports; 1st, 1874 Cmd. 1094, xxiv, 391; 2nd, 1875 Cmd. 1157, xxx, 1.

(2) SECONDARY SOURCES

(*i*) *General Works and Articles*

ASHWORTH, W., *An Economic History of England 1870–1939*, London & New York, 1960.
AYDELOTTE, W. O., 'The House of Commons in the 1840's', *History*, n.s., xxxix (1954), 249–62.
'Voting Patterns in the British House of Commons in the 1840s', *Comparative Studies in Society and History*, v (1962–3), 134–63.

SELECT BIBLIOGRAPHY

BARRY, E. E., *Nationalisation in British Politics*, 1965.

BEER, S. H., *Modern British Politics*, 1965.

BRAND, C. F., 'The Conversion of the British Trade-Unions to Political Action', *American Historical Review*, xxx (1924–5), 251–70.

BREBNER, J. B., 'Laissez Faire and State Intervention in Nineteenth-Century Britain', *Journal of Economic History*, supplement viii (1948), 59–73.

BRIGGS, A., *The Age of Improvement*, 1959.
Victorian Cities, 1963.
Victorian People, 1954.
and SAVILLE, J. (eds.), *Essays in Labour History*, 1960.

BRINTON, C., *English Political Thought in the Nineteenth Century*, 1933.

BROWN, B. H., *The Tariff Reform Movement in Great Britain 1881–1895*, New York, 1943.

BURN, W. L., *The Age of Equipoise*, 1964.
'The Age of Equipoise: England, 1848–1868', *Nineteenth Century and After*, cxlvi (1949), 207–24.

CAZAMIAN, L., *Le Roman Social en Angleterre (1830–1850)*, Paris, 1903.

CHAMBERS, J. D., *The Workshop of the World: British Economic History from 1820 to 1880*, 1961.

CHECKLAND, S. G., 'Economic Opinion in England as Jevons Found It', *Manchester School of Economic and Social Studies*, xix (1951), 143–69.
'The Mind of the City 1870–1914', *Oxford Economic Papers*, new series, ix (1957), 261–78.

CHEYNEY, E. P., *Modern English Reform. From Individualism to Socialism*, Philadelphia, 1931.

CHILSTON, VISCOUNT, 'The 1880 Election: a Historical Landmark', *Parliamentary Affairs*, xiv (1961), 477–92.

CLAPHAM, J. H., *An Economic History of Modern Britain*, 3 vols., Cambridge, 1950–2.

CLARK, G. KITSON, *The Making of Victorian England*, 1962.
' "Statesmen in Disguise": Reflexions on the History of the Neutrality of the Civil Service', *Historical Journal*, ii (1959), 19–39.

CLAYDEN, P. W., *England Under Lord Beaconsfield*, 1880.

COLE, G. D. H., *British Working Class Politics 1832–1914*, 1941.
A Short History of the British Working-Class Movement 1789–1947, new ed., 1948.

COLLINS, H., and ABRAMSKY, C., *Karl Marx and the British Labour Movement: Years of the First International*, 1965.

COWLING, M., 'Disraeli, Derby and Fusion, October 1865 to July 1866', *Historical Journal*, viii (1965), 31–71.

COX, H., *A History of the Reform Bills of 1866 and 1867*, 1868.

DICEY, A. V., *Lectures on the Relation Between Law and Public Opinion in England during the Nineteenth Century*, 2nd ed., 1962.

DUNBABIN, J. P. D., 'Parliamentary Elections in Great Britain, 1868–1900: a Psephological Note', *English Historical Review*, lxxxi (1966), 82–99.

DYOS, H. J., *Victorian Suburb: a Study of the Growth of Camberwell*, Leicester, 1961.

EDWARDS, M., *Methodism and England: a Study of Methodism in its Social and Political Aspects during the Period 1850–1932*, 1943.

EMDEN, C. S., *The People and the Constitution*, 2nd ed., Oxford, 1956.

ENSOR, R. C. K., *England 1870–1914*, Oxford, 1936.

'Some Political and Economic Interactions in Later Victorian England', *Transactions of the Royal Historical Society*, 4th series, xxxi (1949), 17–28.

GASH, N., *Politics in the Age of Peel*, 1953.

Reaction and Reconstruction in English Politics 1832–1852, Oxford, 1965.

GILL, C., and BRIGGS, A., *History of Birmingham*, 2 vols., Oxford, 1952.

GILLESPIE, F. E., *Labor and Politics in England 1850–1867*, Durham, North Carolina, 1927.

GLASER, J. F., 'English Nonconformity and the Decline of Liberalism', *American Historical Review*, lxiii (1957–8), 352–63.

GUTTSMAN, W. L., *The British Political Élite*, 1963.

GWYN, W. B., *Democracy and the Cost of Politics in Britain*, 1962.

HALEVY, E., *A History of the English People in the Nineteenth Century*, 2nd ed., 6 vols., 1949–52.

HANHAM, H. J., 'British Party Finance, 1868–1880', *Bulletin of the Institute of Historical Research*, xxvii (1954), 69–90.

Elections and Party Management. Politics in the Time of Disraeli and Gladstone, 1959.

HARRISON, J. F. C., 'The Victorian Gospel of Success', *Victorian Studies*, i (1957–8), 155–64.

HARRISON, R., *Before the Socialists: Studies in Labour and Politics 1861–1881*, London and Toronto, 1965.

'The British Working Class and the General Election of 1868', *International Review of Social History*, v (1960), 424–55; vi (1961), 74–109.

'E. S. Beesly and Karl Marx', *International Review of Social History*, iv (1959), 22–58, 208–38.

'The 10th April of Spencer Walpole: the Problem of Revolution in Relation to Reform, 1865–1867', *International Review of Social History*, vii (1962), 351–99.

HENNOCK, E. P., 'Finance and Politics in Urban Local Government in England, 1835–1900', *Historical Journal*, vi (1963), 212–25.

HERRICK, F. H., 'The Reform Bill of 1867 and the British Party System', *Pacific Historical Review*, iii (1934), 216–33.

'The Second Reform Movement in Britain 1850–1865', *Journal of the History of Ideas*, ix (1948), 174–92.

INGLIS, K. S., *Churches and the Working Classes in Victorian England*, London and Toronto, 1963.

'Churches and Working Classes in Nineteenth Century England', *Historical Studies, Australia and New Zealand*, viii (1957), 44-53.

JENNINGS, SIR I., *Party Politics*, 3 vols., Cambridge, 1960–2.

JOHNSON, L. G., *The Social Evolution of Industrial Britain*, Liverpool, 1959.

JONES, I. G., 'The Election of 1868 in Merthyr Tydfil: a Study in the Politics of an Industrial Borough in the Mid-Nineteenth Century', *Journal of Modern History*, xxxiii (1961), 270–86.

KEMP, B., 'The General Election of 1841', *History*, n.s., xxxvii (1952), 146–57.

LOWELL, A. L., *The Government of England*, 2 vols., New York, 1908.

LUCY, H. W., *A Diary of Two Parliaments: the Disraeli Parliament 1874–1880*, 1885.

Memories of Eight Parliaments, 1908.

Men and Manner in Parliament, new ed., 1919.

MCCALLUM, R. B., *The Liberal Party from Earl Grey to Asquith*, 1963.

MACCOBY, S., *English Radicalism 1832–1852*, 1935.

English Radicalism 1853–1886, 1938.

MCCREADY, H. W., 'The British Election of 1874: Frederic Harrison and the Liberal-Labour Dilemma', *Canadian Journal of Economics and Political Science*, xx (1954), 166–75.

MACDONAGH, O., 'The Nineteenth-Century Revolution in Government: a Reappraisal', *Historical Journal*, i (1958), 52–67.

MCKENZIE, R. T., *British Political Parties*, 2nd ed., 1963.

MAEHL, W. H., 'Gladstone, the Liberals, and the Election of 1874', *Bulletin of the Institute of Historical Research*, xxxvi (1963), 53–69.

MATTHEWS, A. H. H., *Fifty Years of Agricultural Politics, being the History of the Central Chamber of Agriculture, 1865–1915*, 1915.

MOSSE, G. L., 'The Anti-League; 1844–1846', *Economic History Review*, xvii (1947), 134–42.

O'LEARY, C., *The Elimination of Corrupt Practices in British Elections 1868–1911*, Oxford, 1962.

OSTROGORSKI, M., *Democracy and the Organization of Political Parties*, 2 vols., 1902.

PARK, J. H., *The English Reform Bill of 1867*, New York, 1920.

PARRIS, H., 'The Nineteenth-Century Revolution in Government: a Reappraisal Reappraised', *Historical Journal*, iii (1960), 17–37.

PELLING, H., *The Origins of the Labour Party, 1880–1900*, 1954.

PUMPHREY, R. E., 'The Introduction of Industrialists into the British Peerage: a Study in Adaptation of a Social Institution', *American Historical Review*, lxv (1959–60), 1–16.

READ, D., *The English Provinces c. 1760–1960: a Study in Influence*, 1964.

RECKITT, M. B., *Maurice to Temple: a Century of the Social Movement in the Church of England*, 1947.

ROACH, J., 'Liberalism and the Victorian Intelligentsia', *Cambridge Historical Journal*, xiii (1957), 58–81.

ROBERTS, D., *Victorian Origins of the British Welfare State*, New Haven, 1960.

ROSTOW, W. W., *British Economy of the Nineteenth Century*, Oxford, 1948.

SAVILLE, J. (ed.), *Democracy and the Labour Movement*, 1954.

SEYMOUR, C., *Electoral Reform in England and Wales*, New Haven, 1915.

SMELLIE, K. B., *A History of Local Government*, 3rd ed., 1957.

SMITH, F. B., ' "Democracy" in the Second Reform Debates', *Historical Studies, Australia and New Zealand*, xi (1964), 306–23.

SMITH, R., 'The Manchester Chamber of Commerce and the Increasing

Foreign Competition to Lancashire Cotton Textiles, 1873–1896', *Bulletin of the John Rylands Library*, xxxviii (1955–6), 507–34.

SOUTHGATE, D., *The Passing of the Whigs 1832–1886*, 1962.

SPRING, D., 'The English Landed Estate in the Age of Coal and Iron: 1830–1880', *Journal of Economic History*, xi (1951), 3–24.

THOLFSEN, T. R., 'The Transition to Democracy in Victorian England', *International Review of Social History*, vi (1961), 226–48.

THOMAS, J. A., *The House of Commons, 1832–1901: a Study of its Economic and Functional Character*, Cardiff, 1939.

'The System of Registration and the Development of Party Organisation, 1832–1870', *History*, n.s., xxxv (1950), 81–98.

THOMPSON, A. F., 'Gladstone's Whips and the General Election of 1868', *English Historical Review*, lxiii (1948), 189–200.

THOMPSON, F. M. L., *English Landed Society in the Nineteenth Century*, London and Toronto, 1963.

'Land and Politics in England in the Nineteenth Century', *Transactions of the Royal Historical Society*, 5th series, xv (1965), 23–44.

THOMPSON, G. C., *Public Opinion and Lord Beaconsfield 1875–1880*, 2 vols., 1886.

THOMPSON, P., 'Liberals, Radicals and Labour in London 1880–1900', *Past and Present*, no. 27 (April 1964), 73–101.

VINCENT, J. R., 'The Electoral Sociology of Rochdale', *Economic History Review*, 2nd series, xvi (1963–4), 76–90.

The Formation of the Liberal Party 1857–1868, 1966.

WALPOLE, SIR S., *The History of Twenty-Five Years*, 4 vols., 1904–8.

WHITE, W., *The Inner Life of the House of Commons*, ed. J. McCarthy, 2 vols., 1897.

WILLSON, F. M. G., 'The Routes of Entry of New Members of the British Cabinet, 1868–1958', *Political Studies*, vii (1959), 222–32.

WINTER, J., 'The Cave of Adullam and Parliamentary Reform', *English Historical Review*, lxxxi (1966), 38–55.

WOODWARD, SIR L., *The Age of Reform 1815–1870*, 2nd ed., Oxford, 1962.

YOUNG, G. M., *Victorian England: Portrait of an Age*, Oxford, 1936.

(*ii*) *Books and Articles on the Conservative Party and Conservatism*

BELLAIRS, C. E., *Conservative Social and Industrial Reform 1800–1945* (Conservative Political Centre), 1947.

BIRCH, N., *The Conservative Party*, 1949.

BURN, W. L., 'English Conservatism', *Nineteenth Century and After*, cxlv (1949), 1–11, 67–76.

CORNFORD, J., 'The Transformation of Conservatism in the Late Nineteenth Century', *Victorian Studies*, vii (1963–4), 35–66.

CRAPSTER, B. L., 'Scotland and the Conservative Party in 1876', *Journal of Modern History*, xxix (1957), 355–60.

FEUCHTWANGER, E. J., 'The Conservative Party Under the Impact of the Second Reform Act', *Victorian Studies*, ii (1958–9), 289–304.

'J. E. Gorst and the Central Organisation of the Conservative Party, 1870–1882', *Bulletin of the Institute of Historical Research*, xxxii (1959), 192–208.

GLICKMAN, H., 'The Toryness of English Conservatism', *Journal of British Studies*, i (1961–2), 111–43.

GORST, H. E., *The Fourth Party*, 1906.

HEARNSHAW, F. J. C., *Conservatism in England: an Analytical, Historical, and Political Survey*, 1933.

HILL, R. L., *Toryism and the People 1832–1846*, 1929.

KEBBEL, T. E., *A History of Toryism*, 1886.

KIRK, R., *The Conservative Mind*, 1954.

MCDOWELL, R. B., *British Conservatism, 1832–1914*, 1959.

Political Quarterly, xxiv, no. 2 (1953), and xxxii, no. 3 (1961): special numbers on the Conservative party.

RIGGS, R. E., 'Peel and Disraeli: Architects of a New Conservative Party', *Western Humanities Review*, xi (1957), 183–7.

ROBERTS, D., 'Tory Paternalism and Social Reform in Early Victorian England', *American Historical Review*, lxiii (1958), 323–37.

URWIN, D. W., 'The Development of the Conservative Party Organisation in Scotland until 1912', *Scottish Historical Review*, xliv (1965), 89–111.

WHITE, R. J. (ed.), *The Conservative Tradition*, 2nd ed., 1964.

WILKINSON, W. J., *Tory Democracy*, New York, 1925.

WOODS, M., *A History of the Tory Party in the Seventeenth and Eighteenth Centuries, with a Sketch of its Development in the Nineteenth Century*, 1924.

(iii) *Biographical and Autobiographical Works and Articles*

AGG-GARDNER, SIR J., *Some Parliamentary Recollections*, n.d. [1927].

ARCH, J., *Joseph Arch: the Story of His Life, told by Himself*, ed. the Countess of Warwick, 1898.

ARMYTAGE, W. H. G., *A. J. Mundella 1825–1897: the Liberal Background to the Labour Movement*, 1951.

ASTLEY, SIR J. D., *Fifty Years of My Life*, 2 vols., 1894.

AWDRY, F., *A Country Gentleman of the Nineteenth Century: Being a Short Memoir of the Right Honourable Sir William Heathcote, Bart., of Hursley, 1801–1881*, Winchester and London, 1906.

BALFOUR, A. J., *Chapters of Autobiography*, ed. Mrs Edgar Dugdale, 1930.

BEST, G. F. A., *Shaftesbury*, 1964.

BLAKE, R., 'The Rise of Disraeli', in *Essays in British History presented to Sir Keith Feiling*, ed. H. R. Trevor-Roper, 1964.

BREADY, J. W., *Lord Shaftesbury and Social-Industrial Progress*, 1926.

CECIL, LADY G., *Biographical Studies of the Life and Political Character of Robert Third Marquis of Salisbury*, n.d. (printed for private circulation).
Life of Robert Marquis of Salisbury, 4 vols., 1921–32.

CHILDE-PEMBERTON, W. S., *Life of Lord Norton*, 1909.

CHILSTON, VISCOUNT, 'W. H. Smith (1825–1891): the Reluctant Statesman', *Parliamentary Affairs*, xiii (1959–60), 198–212.
W. H. Smith, London and Toronto, 1965.

CHURCHILL, W. S., *Lord Randolph Churchill*, new ed., n.d. [1951].

CLARK, G. KITSON, *Peel and the Conservative Party*, 1929.

CLARKE, SIR E., *The Story of My Life*, 1918.

COOK, SIR E., *The Life of Florence Nightingale*, 2 vols., 1913.

CROSS, VISCOUNT, *A Political History*, privately printed, 1903.

DENISON, G. A., *Notes of My Life, 1805–1878*, Oxford and London, 1878.

DISRAELI, B., *Lord George Bentinck: a Political Biography*, 1852.

DRIVER, C., *Tory Radical: the Life of Richard Oastler*, New York, 1946.

DUGDALE, B. E. C., *Arthur James Balfour, First Earl of Balfour*, 2 vols., 1936.

DWYER, F. J., 'The Rise of Richard Assheton Cross and his Work at the Home Office, 1868–1880' (Oxford Univ. B.Litt. thesis 1954).

ELLIOT, HON. A. D., *The Life of George Joachim Goschen, First Viscount Goschen, 1831–1907*, 2 vols., 1911.

FABER, R., *Beaconsfield and Bolingbroke*, 1961.

FINER, S. E., *The Life and Times of Sir Edwin Chadwick*, 1952.

FLYNN, J. S., *Sir Robert N. Fowler, Bart., M.P.: a Memoir*, 1893.

DE FONBLANQUE, E. B., *Lives of the Lords Strangford*, n.d. [?1877] (for George Smythe).

FORWOOD, SIR W. B., *Recollections of a Busy Life, being the Reminiscences of a Liverpool Merchant 1840–1910*, Liverpool, 1910.

FRASER, SIR W., *Disraeli and His Day*, 2nd ed., 1891.

GARDINER, A. G., *The Life of Sir William Harcourt*, 2 vols., 1923.

GARVIN, J. L. and AMERY, J., *The Life of Joseph Chamberlain*, 4 vols. to date, 1935–51.

GASH, N., 'Ashley and the Conservative Party in 1842', *English Historical Review*, liii (1938), 679–81.

Mr. Secretary Peel: the Life of Sir Robert Peel to 1830, 1961.

'Peel and the Party System 1830–50', *Transactions of the Royal Historical Society*, 5th series, i (1951), 47–69.

GILL, J. C., *The Ten Hours Parson*, 1959 [George Bull].

GORST, H. E., *The Earl of Beaconsfield*, 1900.

GRAUBARD, S. R., *Burke, Disraeli, and Churchill: the Politics of Perseverance*, Cambridge, Mass., 1961.

GREENWOOD, F., article on 'Beaconsfield', *Encyclopaedia Britannica*, 11th ed., vol. iii, Cambridge, 1910.

GREGORY, SIR W., *An Autobiography*, ed. Lady Gregory, 1894.

HAMILTON, LORD G., *Parliamentary Reminiscences and Reflections 1868 to 1885*, 1916.

HARDINGE, SIR A., *The Life of Henry Howard Molyneux Herbert Fourth Earl of Carnarvon 1831–1890*, ed. Elisabeth Countess of Carnarvon, 3 vols., Oxford, 1925.

HARDY, A. E. GATHORNE, *Gathorne Hardy First Earl of Cranbrook: a Memoir*, 2 vols., 1910.

HENDERSON, G. B., 'Ralph Anstruther Earle', *English Historical Review*, lviii (1943), 172–89.

HICKS BEACH, LADY VICTORIA, *Life of Sir Michael Hicks Beach* (*Earl St. Aldwyn*), 2 vols., 1932.

HILL, W. T., *Octavia Hill*, 1956.

HINTON, R. J., *English Radical Leaders*, New York, 1875.

HIRST, F. W., *Early Life & Letters of John Morley*, 2 vols., 1927.

HODDER, E., *The Life and Work of the Seventh Earl of Shaftesbury, K.G.*, 3 vols., 1888.

HOLYOAKE, G. J., *Bygones Worth Remembering*, 2 vols., 1905.
Sixty Years of an Agitator's Life, 3rd ed., 2 vols., 1893.

HUMPHREY, A. W., *Robert Applegarth: Trade Unionist, Educationist, Reformer*, Manchester and London, n.d.

HYNDMAN, H. M., *The Record of an Adventurous Life*, 1911.

JAMES, R. RHODES, *Lord Randolph Churchill*, 1959.

JERMAN, B. R., *The Young Disraeli*, Princeton: London, 1960.

JONES, W. D., *Lord Derby and Victorian Conservatism*, Oxford (Blackwell), 1956.

KEBBEL, T. E., *Life of the Earl of Derby, K.G.*, 1890.
Lord Beaconsfield and Other Tory Memories, 1907.

LAMINGTON, LORD (A. Baillie-Cochrane), *In the Days of the Dandies*, Edinburgh and London, 1890.

LANG, A., *Life, Letters, and Diaries of Sir Stafford Northcote First Earl of Iddesleigh*, 2 vols., Edinburgh and London, 1890.

LAW, H. W. and I., *The Book of the Beresford Hopes*, 1925.

LEWIS, C. J., 'Theory and Expediency in the Policy of Disraeli', *Victorian Studies*, iv (1960–1), 237–58.

LEWIS, R. A., *Edwin Chadwick and the Public Health Movement 1832–1854*, 1952.

LONDONDERRY, MARCHIONESS OF, *Henry Chaplin: a Memoir*, 1926.

MacDONNELL, J. C., *The Life and Correspondence of William Connor Magee, Archbishop of York, Bishop of Peterborough*, 2 vols., 1896.

MALMESBURY, EARL OF, *Memoirs of an Ex-Minister*, 2 vols., 1884.

MAXWELL, SIR H., *Life and Times of the Right Honourable William Henry Smith, M.P.*, 2 vols., Edinburgh and London, 1893.

MIDLETON, EARL OF, *Records & Reactions 1856–1939*, 1939.

MONYPENNY, W. F. and BUCKLE, G. E., *The Life of Benjamin Disraeli, Earl of Beaconsfield*, 6 vols., 1910–20.

MORLEY, J., *The Life of William Ewart Gladstone*, 3 vols., 1903.

MOWBRAY, E. M. (ed.), *Seventy Years at Westminster, with Other Letters and Notes of the Late Right Honble. Sir John Mowbray, Bart., M.P.*, Edinburgh and London, 1900.

PELL, A., *The Reminiscences of Albert Pell Sometime M.P. for South Leicestershire*, ed. T. Mackay, 1908.

PETRIE, SIR C., *The Powers Behind the Prime Ministers*, 1958 (chapter on Montagu Corry).

PRESTON-THOMAS, H., *The Work and Play of a Government Inspector*, Edinburgh and London, 1909.

RAIKES, H. ST. JOHN, *The Life and Letters of Henry Cecil Raikes, late Her Majesty's Postmaster-General*, 1898.

REID, T. WEMYSS, *Life of the Right Honourable William Edward Forster*, 4th ed., 2 vols., 1888.

ROGERS, J., *Reminiscences of a Workhouse Medical Officer*, ed. J. E. Thorold Rogers, 1889.

SAINTSBURY, G., *The Earl of Derby*, 1906.

SOUTTER, F. W., *Recollections of a Labour Pioneer*, 1923.

SPRING, D., 'Ralph Sneyd: Tory Country Gentleman', *Bulletin of the John Rylands Library*, xxxviii (1955–6), 535–55.

TAYLOR, A. J., 'The Third Marquis of Londonderry and the North-Eastern Coal Trade', *Durham University Journal*, xlviii (1955–6), 21–7.

TAYLOR, A. J. P., *Englishmen and Others*, 1956.

TUCKER, A., 'Disraeli and the Natural Aristocracy', *Canadian Journal of Economics and Political Science*, xxviii (1962), 1–15.

WALKER-SMITH, D., and CLARKE, E., *The Life of Sir Edward Clarke*, 1939.

WARD, J. T., 'Revolutionary Tory: the Life of Joseph Rayner Stephens of Ashton-under-Lyne (1805–1879)', *Transactions of the Lancashire and Cheshire Antiquarian Society*, lxviii (1958), 93–116.

WHIBLEY, C., *Lord John Manners and His Friends*, 2 vols., Edinburgh and London, 1925.

WOLFF, SIR H. DRUMMOND, *Rambling Recollections*, 2 vols., 1908.

YOUNG, K., *Arthur James Balfour*, 1963.

(*iv*) *Books and Articles on Social Questions*

(*a*) *General*

BACKSTROM, P. N., JR., 'The Practical Side of Christian Socialism in Victorian England', *Victorian Studies*, vi (1962–3), 305–24.

BRIGGS, A., 'The Welfare State in Historical Perspective', *Archives Européennes de Sociologie*, ii (1961), 221–58.

BRUCE, M., *The Coming of the Welfare State*, 2nd ed., 1965.

CAMPBELL, R. H., 'The Church and Social Reform', *Scottish Journal of Political Economy*, viii (1961), 137–47.

FERGUSON, T., *Scottish Social Welfare, 1864–1914*, Edinburgh and London, 1958.

GUTCHEN, R. M., 'Local Improvements and Centralization in Nineteenth-century England', *Historical Journal*, iv (1961), 85–96.

HART, J., 'Nineteenth-Century Social Reform: a Tory Interpretation of History', *Past and Present*, no. 31 (1965), 39–61.

HENDERSON, W. O., 'The Public Works Act, 1863', *Economic History*, ii (1930–3), 312–21.

INGLIS, K. S., 'English Nonconformity and Social Reform, 1880–1900', *Past and Present*, no. 13 (1958), 73–88.

MCGREGOR, O. R., 'Social Research and Social Policy in the Nineteenth Century', *British Journal of Sociology*, viii (1957), 146–57.

MECHIE, S., *The Church and Scottish Social Development 1780–1870*, 1960.

MOWAT, C. L., *The Charity Organisation Society 1869–1913*, 1961.

O'NEILL, J. E., 'The Authorship of the 1872 "Memorial on Government Insurance" ', *Notes and Queries*, n.s., x (1963), 458–9.

OWEN, D., *English Philanthropy 1660–1960*, Cambridge, Mass.: London, 1965.

RODGERS, B., 'The Social Science Association 1857-1886', *Manchester School of Economic and Social Studies*, xx (1952), 283–310.

WAGNER, D. O., *The Church of England and Social Reform since 1854*, New York, 1930.

(*b*) *Drink Traffic*

MATHIAS, P., 'The Brewing Industry, Temperance and Politics', *Historical Journal*, i (1958), 97–114.

SHADWELL, A., *Drink, Temperance and Legislation*, 1902.

WILSON, G. B., *Alcohol and the Nation*, 1940.

(*c*) *Education*

ADAMSON, J. W., *English Education 1789–1902*, Cambridge, 1930.

ARMYTAGE, W. H. G., 'Francis Richard John Sandford, First Baron Sandford, 1824–1894', *Bulletin of the John Rylands Library*, xxxi (1948), 110–19.

'Patric Cumin, 1823–1890', *Bulletin of the John Rylands Library*, xxx (1946–7), 271–7.

BEST, G. F. A., 'The Religious Difficulties of National Education in England, 1800–70', *Cambridge Historical Journal*, xii (1956), 155–73.

BROWN, C. K. F., *The Church's Part in Education 1833–1941*, 1942.

BURGESS, H. J., *Enterprise in Education*, 1958.

CRUICKSHANK, M., *Church and State in English Education: 1870 to the Present Day*, 1963.

GREGORY, R., *Elementary Education: Some Account of its Rise and Progress in England*, 1895.

HUGHES, K. M., 'A Political Party and Education: Reflections on the Liberal Party's Educational Policy, 1867–1902', *British Journal of Educational Studies*, viii (1959–60), 111–26.

KNOX, H. M., *Two Hundred and Fifty Years of Scottish Education 1696–1946*, Edinburgh and London, 1953.

MALTBY, S. E., *Manchester and the Movement for National Elementary Education 1800–1870*, Manchester, 1918.

SIMON, B., *Studies in the History of Education 1780–1870*, 1960.

SMITH, F., *A History of English Elementary Education 1760–1902*, 1931.

SPALDING, T. A., *The Work of the London School Board*, 1900.

WEST, E. G., *Education and the State*, 1965.

(*d*) *Friendly Societies*

GOSDEN, P. H. J. H., *The Friendly Societies in England, 1815–1875*, Manchester, 1961.

(*e*) *Public Health*

ABEL-SMITH, B., *The Hospitals 1800–1948*, 1964.

DYOS, H. J., 'Some Social Costs of Railway Building in London', *Journal of Transport History*, iii (1957), 23–30.

FRAZER, W. M., *A History of English Public Health 1834–1939*, 1950.

KEITH-LUCAS, B., 'Some Influences Affecting the Development of Sanitary Legislation in England', *Economic History Review*, 2nd series, vi (1953–4), 290–6.

LAMBERT, R., 'Central and Local Relations in Mid-Victorian England: the Local Government Act Office, 1858–71', *Victorian Studies*, vi (1962–3), 121–50.

Sir John Simon 1816–1904 and English Social Administration, 1963.

'A Victorian National Health Service: State Vaccination 1855–71', *Historical Journal*, v (1962), 1–18.

O'NEILL, J. E., 'Finding a Policy for the Sick Poor', *Victorian Studies*, vii (1963–4), 265–84.

SIMON, SIR J., *English Sanitary Institutions*, 2nd ed., 1897.

(*f*) *Housing*

CLARKE, J. J., *The Housing Problem: its History, Growth, Legislation and Procedure*, 1920.

DYOS, H. J., 'Railways and Housing in Victorian London', *Journal of Transport History*, ii (1955–6), 11–21, 90–100.

LONDON COUNTY COUNCIL, *The Housing Question in London*, n.d. [1900].

(*g*) *Labour Questions*

BLAUG, M., 'The Classical Economists and the Factory Acts—a Re-examination' *Quarterly Journal of Economics*, lxxiii (1958), 211–26.

CLAYDEN, A., *The Revolt of the Field*, 1874.

CLEMENTS, R. V., 'British Trade Unions and Popular Political Economy 1850–1875', *Economic History Review*, 2nd series, xiv (1961–2), 93–104.

'Trade Unions and Emigration, 1840–80', *Population Studies*, ix (1955–6), 167–80.

DUNBABIN, J. P. D., 'The "Revolt of the Field": the Agricultural Labourers' Movement in the 1870s', *Past and Present*, no. 26 (Nov. 1963), 68–97. See also *ibid.*, no. 27 (April 1964), 109–13.

ERICKSON, C., 'The Encouragement of Emigration by British Trade Unions, 1850–1900', *Population Studies*, iii (1949–50), 248–73.

GARBATI, I. 'British Trade Unionism in the Mid-Victorian Era', *University of Toronto Quarterly*, xx (1950–1), 69–84.

GREEN, F. E., *A History of the English Agricultural Labourer, 1870–1920*, 1920.

HEDGES, R. Y. and WINTERBOTTOM, A., *The Legal History of Trade Unionism*, 1930.

HOWELL, G., *Labour Legislation, Labour Movements and Labour Leaders*, 1902.

HUTCHINS, B. L. and HARRISON, A., *A History of Factory Legislation*, 3rd ed., 1926.

JONES, E. L., 'The Agricultural Labour Market in England, 1793–1872', *Economic History Review*, 2nd series, xvii (1964–5), 322–38.

MCCREADY, H. W., 'British Labour and the Royal Commission on Trade Unions, 1867–9', *University of Toronto Quarterly*, xxiv (1954–5), 390–409.

'British Labour's Lobby, 1867–75', *Canadian Journal of Economics and Political Science*, xxii (1956), 141–60.

MASTERS, D., *The Plimsoll Mark*, 1955.

PELLING, H., *A History of British Trade Unionism*, 1963.

ROBERTS, B. C., *The Trades Union Congress, 1868–1921*, 1958.

ROBSON, A. H., *The Education of Children Engaged in Industry in England 1833–1876*, 1931.

SORENSON, L. R., 'Some Classical Economists, Laissez Faire, and the Factory Acts', *Journal of Economic History*, xii (1952), 247–62.

THOMAS, M. W., *The Early Factory Legislation*, Leigh-on-Sea, 1948.

WALKER, K. O., 'The Classical Economists and the Factory Acts', *Journal of Economic History*, i (1941), 168–77.

WARD, J. T., *The Factory Movement 1830–1855*, 1962.

'The Factory Reform Movement in Scotland', *Scottish Historical Review*, xli (1962), 100–23.

WEBB, S. and B., *The History of Trade Unionism*, 2nd ed., 1920.

(*h*) *Poor Relief*

MACKAY, T., *A History of the English Poor Law*, vol. iii, 1899.

DE SCHWEINITZ, K., *England's Road to Social Security*, Philadelphia, 1943.

WEBB, S. and B., *English Poor Law Policy*, 1910.

English Poor Law History, pt. II, 'The Last Hundred Years', 2 vols., 1929.

INDEX

(cr. = created; kn. = knighted)

www.ingramcontent.com/pod-product-compliance
Lightning Source LLC
LaVergne TN
LVHW040756070826
844660LV00025B/1162